Banking and Finance

Edited by Razali Haron,
Maizaitulaidawati Md Husin and Michael Murg

Published in London, United Kingdom

IntechOpen

Supporting open minds since 2005

Banking and Finance
http://dx.doi.org/10.5772/intechopen.87329
Edited by Razali Haron, Maizaitulaidawati Md Husin and Michael Murg

Scientific Contributors: Ubaldo Comite and Oguzhan Ozcelebi

Contributors
Mariantonietta Intonti, Rosa Adamo, Antonella Notte, Domenica Federico, Simona Mele, Ellis Kofi Akwaa-Sekyi, Teimuraz Tsabadze, Wojciech Grabowski, Djieufack Roland, Dimas Wiranatakusuma, Naji Mansour Nomran, Razali Haron, Mehmet Selman Colak, Yavuz Selim Hacıhasanoğlu, İbrahim Ethem Güney, Maya Puspa Rahman, Naima Andleeb, Shahab Aziz, Md Fauzi Ahmad, James Akinbode Olalekan, Wooi Keong Yong, Wooi Meng Yong, Taslima Julia, Salina Kassim, Hongwei Wang, Shiqin Chen, Aysa Siddika, Oluwaseun James Oguntuase, Imamuddin Yuliadi, Ikhwan Victhori

First published in London, United Kingdom, 2021 by IntechOpen
IntechOpen is the global imprint of INTECHOPEN LIMITED, registered in England and Wales, registration number: 11086078, 5 Princes Gate Court, London, SW7 2QJ, United Kingdom
Printed in Croatia

British Library Cataloguing-in-Publication Data
A catalogue record for this book is available from the British Library

Additional hard and PDF copies can be obtained from orders@intechopen.com

Banking and Finance
Edited by Razali Haron, Maizaitulaidawati Md Husin and Michael Murg
p. cm.
Print ISBN 978-1-78984-682-9
Online ISBN 978-1-78984-683-6
eBook (PDF) ISBN 978-1-78985-563-0

For EU product safety concerns:
IN TECH d.o.o., Prolaz Marije Krucifikse Kozulić 3, 51000 Rijeka, Croatia, info@intechopen.com or visit our website at intechopen.com.

Meet the editors

Dr. Razali Haron holds a DBA and MBA and is currently an associate professor at the Institute of Islamic Banking and Finance. He joined the university in 2003 and served as the deputy dean (Research) of the Institute and head of the program of the Graduate School of Management. He has more than ten years of extensive experience in the corporate sector covering fund management and capital markets. His research interests are banking, corporate finance, and governance, and he published works with international publishers like Emerald, SAGE, Elsevier, Inderscience, Palgrave Macmillan, and IGI Global. His recently edited books include *Islamic Wealth and Fund Management* and *Islamic Social Finance and Economic Recovery after a Global Health Crisis.*

Maizaitulaidawati Md Husin PhD, IFP, is an experienced academician with strong enthusiasm and passion for Islamic banking and finance. She has more than twelve years of experience in teaching and supervision. Dr. Husin holds a PhD in Islamic Economics from the University of Malaya, Kuala Lumpur, Malaysia. She is also a certified Islamic financial planner. She has led and participated in no less than twenty consultancy and research projects with a total value of more than RM7 million. She has also authored and co-authored more than sixty research papers, book chapters and conference papers. She served on the faculty of Azman Hashim International Business School (AHIBS) as a research manager in 2017 and held several other managerial positions there as well.

Dr. Michael Murg is chair of the Institute of Banking and Insurance Industry at FH Joanneum University of Applied Sciences, Austria. He has more than ten years' experience as a financial advisor for private wealth management and corporate finance and spent several years in the financial industry. Dr. Murg's scientific career began at the Department of Finance, University of Graz, Austria, where he was a quantitative research scientist and lecturer for finance. He is a licensed exchange trader for spot and derivative markets (XETRA) and was co-founder and the head of Portfolio and Risk Management for a FinTech company before returning to academia. Dr. Murg's current research focuses on the digitization of business models in finance, banking and insurance industries, innovation management in insurance companies and banks, digitization of business processes, and data analytics.

Contents

Preface

The banking and finance industry plays a significant role in the economy of a nation. As such, it demands continuous research and up-to-date feeds for it to stay competitive and resilient. Due to its revolving and dynamic nature as well as its significance and interlinkages with other industries, a well-functioning banking and finance system is vital in safeguarding the interest of all stakeholders. The hard lessons and experiences learned from the financial crises of 1997/1998 and 2008/2009, as well as the recent COVID-19 pandemic, have instigated extensive postmortems and re-evaluations of the banking and financial system among related players in the field to improve and perhaps share and adopt best practices of every aspect in the industry.

Realizing the significant impacts of this industry, this book, Banking and Finance, highlights major issues related to banking and finance and puts forth recent empirical evidence, scientific research, best practices, and recommendations. This book discusses all major areas of banking and finance. With the wide range of topics highlighted and discussed, together with recent scientific research and findings using advanced econometrical approaches, this book not only enriches the literature but also offers policy implications that will benefit all players including academicians and practitioners in the field of banking and finance.

The book contains sixteen chapters by thirty-one authors divided into two sections. The first section discusses banking while the second covers finance.

In the banking section, Aysa Siddika and Razali Haron provide a concise overview of capital adequacy regulation and the importance and evolution of regulation. They further explain how several banking crises and banks' defaults motivated the Basel Committee on Banking Supervision (BCBS) to provide a comprehensive guideline in managing bank capital.

Ellis Kofi Akwaa-Sekyi explores a qualitative self-regulation approach to address a major risk facing banks using the BCBS framework of internal controls. The chapter specifically examines the effect of the qualitative principles of the BCBS internal control framework on credit risk covering banks from selected EU countries. The author provides evidence on the significant relationship between board functions and activities, board structure and board monitoring, and credit risk and concludes that investment in high-risk assets, bank profitability, and the board chair being a former CEO increases credit risk in European banking.

Naji Mansour Nomran and Razali Haron examine the impact of governance mechanisms on the performance of Islamic banks (IBs) in eighteen countries during the financial crisis of 2008. The study provides justifications on Shariah Supervisory Board effectiveness in improving IBs' performance even during the crisis periods. They conclude on the importance of IBs to adopt appropriate governance structures to sustain future performance.

Dimas Bagus Wiranatakusuma, Imamuddin Yuliadi, and Ikhwan Victhori analyze the risk of IBs in Indonesia and identify the most dominant risk that could trigger other risks. Their study suggests that financing risk is the most dominant risk triggering vulnerability in Indonesian IBs.

Oluwaseun James Oguntuase examines climate change and the associated uncertainties, acknowledging it as one of the greatest global challenges to the governance of the global socioeconomic and financial system. The author demonstrates the triangular relationship between the three notions of climate-related risks, credit risk, and financial stability by enumerating the channels through which climate risks can cause credit risk and affect the stability of the financial system.

Taslima Julia and Salina Kassim study green banking and the impact it has on sustainable development goals (SDGs) and its relationship with the objective of Islamic law. The authors argue that banks can contribute enormously to restore environmental balance and to preserve a livable condition for future generations through green banking. They further establish that green banking, SDGs, and the objective of Islamic law are complementary to each other.

Wooi Keong Yong and Wooi Meng Yong discuss the impact of recent local political development Brexit and the trade war between the United States and China on the banking sector of Malaysia. The chapter concludes that the global economic events of Brexit and the US–China trade war in the last few years along with the unanticipated COVID-19 pandemic coupled with the political uncertainty domestically poses great credit risk to Malaysian banks.

Naima Andleeb, Md Fauzi Ahmad, and Shahab Aziz explore the importance of knowledge sharing in banking management along with the organizational culture. The chapter proposes a framework in which knowledge sharing is expected to be influenced by the organizational culture of banks. The authors explain that organizational culture itself is comprised of uncertainty avoidance, performance orientation, and gender egalitarianism.

Akinbode James Olalekan discusses the progress of bank service delivery in Nigeria. The country has recorded significant efficiency in bank service delivery via the effective use of an electronic banking system. Despite progress, some improvement is still required in employees' knowledge gaps, technology, legal framework, labor, and attitude. The improvement in these critical aspects is imperative for further improvement of banking service delivery in the country.

Moving on to the finance section, Wojciech Grabowski analyzes the interlinkages between stock markets in the Central European countries (Czech Republic, Poland, Slovakia, and Hungary; CEE4) and stock markets of Germany and the United States. The chapter divides the study period according to a few important events and identifies three significant breakpoints in variance. Stock markets in the CEE-4 countries turned out to be informationally efficient in three of the four sub-periods. Stock markets in Poland and Hungary were more sensitive to changes in rates of return on the German market.

Maya Puspa Rahman reports that based on past research, a yield curve contains information for future growth and, to a certain extent, was accurate in predicting recessions through the signal of yield curve inversion. In line with this argument, the chapter provides new evidence on the long- and short-run relationship between economic growth and yield spread in Malaysia, based on a twenty-year span of data divided according to sample periods. The study finds strong evidence of co-integration between the yield spread and growth, concurring on the long-run and short-run dynamics between them.

Mehmet Selman Çolak, İbrahim Ethem Güney, and Yavuz Selim Hacıhasanoğlu study the relationship between economic uncertainty and balance sheet strength of non-financial firms quoted in Borsa İstanbul. To measure the balance sheet strength, the authors make use of a multivariate indicator (MFA score), which is a composite index to gauge the credit risk of the firms. MFA scores are then compared with some uncertainty indicators for the study period. The chapter concludes that when the uncertainties in global or Turkish economy are high, a significant causal relationship is observed from uncertainty indicators to firms' balance sheet strength. More specifically, economic uncertainties negatively affect firms' balance sheet performance in such an environment.

Teimuraz Tsabadze proposes a new approach for the assessment of credit risk. The chapter first discusses the existing models of credit risk assessment and justifies the need for a new approach. Fuzzy mathematics is employed since the new approach is created for conditions of uncertainty. The proposed approach is based on group decision-making, where experts' opinions are expressed by trapezoidal fuzzy numbers. The theoretical basis of the proposed approach is laid out in the metric space of trapezoidal fuzzy numbers, and two realization algorithms are given.

Hongwei Wang and Shiqin Chen highlight the common problem of sparse data for crowdfunding recommendations. They argue collaborative filtering (CF) performs poorly in the case of sparse data like Kickstarter. Considering this limitation, they propose a method of enabling indirect crowdfunding campaign recommendations based on a bipartite graph. Experimental results show that the bipartite graph-based CF achieves better performance in the recommendation for the extremely sparse data from crowdfunding campaigns.

Rosa Adamo, Domenica Federico, Mariantonietta Intonti, Simona Mele, and Antonella Notte analyze the characteristics of a crowdfunding platform operating on the Italian market (Produzioni dal Basso), highlighting its characteristics, strengths, and weaknesses. Italy is unique as crowdfunding was introduced for the first time in Europe. The study also carries out a simulation for the realization of a crowdfunding project by an Italian foundation operating in the social sector of child and adolescent distress, implemented through the use of the same platform.

The book ends with a legal discourse on sales and conformity of goods and its importance to economic development. Djieufack Roland adopts an in-depth analysis on the matter and embraces that conformity of goods can conveniently be addressed from a number of different angles: contract law, consumer patterns, local and international standards, and the principles of caveat venditor and caveat emptor. The author explains that the concept of conformity is dynamic and amorphous as it is recognized as an impetus to economic development and plays a major role in matters of sales of goods within an economy.

It was indeed a great experience editing this book, which is filled with knowledge from various perspectives. It is truly an eye opener to what is happening in the field of banking and finance all over the world regardless of the economic landscapes.

This book would not have been possible without the chapter authors as well as two scientific contributors, Ubaldo Comite and Oguzhan Ozcelebi. We appreciate and acknowledge all who contributed to the success of this book. We also extend thanks to Anja Filipovic and Mateo Pulko of IntechOpen who guided us through the process of compiling and editing this book to its completion.

Razali Haron
Associate Professor,
IIUM Institute of Islamic Banking and Finance,
Malaysia

Maizaitulaidawati Md Husin
Azman Hashim International Business School,
Universiti Teknologi Malaysia,
Malaysia

Michael Murg
Universities of Applied Sciences Joanneum,
Austria

Section 1

Banking

Chapter 1

Capital Adequacy Regulation

Aysa Siddika and Razali Haron

Abstract

This chapter aims to provide a concise overview of the capital adequacy regulation, importance of the regulation, and evolution of the capital adequacy regulation. Bank capital executes the significant role of preventing the bank from failure and acts as a buffer against possible losses. Capital adequacy is the least amount of capital a bank has to preserve to execute the business, take advantage of profitable growth opportunities, absorb losses, and sustain the customers' confidence on it. Several bank crises and bank defaults motivate the Basel Committee on Banking Supervision to provide a comprehensive guideline in managing bank capital. The capital adequacy regulation is an international standard to safeguard the banks through setting a risk-sensitive minimum capital requirement. The regulatory authority sets the regulatory capital, and the operating banks are required to maintain the adequate level of capital.

Keywords: capital adequacy regulation, Basel Accord, Basel Committee, regulatory capital, risk-weighted asset

1. Introduction

History of several bank failures evidences how the excessive risk taking can affect the whole economy as well as the global financial scenario. Since bank deals with different kinds of risks, the regulators strive to minimize this risk exposure through different regulations. The key regulations aiming to minimize the risk and bank failure is the capital adequacy regulation. The principle of the capital adequacy regulation is based on the fact that the minimum capital should be high enough to absorb the potential losses. While capital acts as a buffer for the bank, in the distressed period, the higher the buffer, the lower the risk of default. Therefore, the importance of maintenance of adequate level of capital is never overestimated. This chapter will present a brief history of capital adequacy regulation and the evolution of the regulation over time.

2. Basel Committee on Banking Supervision

Bank for International Settlement (BIS), the oldest international financial organization, was founded in 1930. Its members are central banks or the regulatory authorities of 60 countries. The committee aims to serve as a regulatory authority for monetary and financial stability and foster international cooperation.

West Germany's Herstatt Bank closed its operation on June 26, 1974, due to excessive foreign exchange risk that posed counterparty risk in international settlement with the banks in New York. Subsequently, at the end of 1974 due to this cross-jurisdiction implication, BIS formed "Committee on Banking Regulations and Supervisory Practices" also known as Basel Committee on Banking Supervision (BCBS) headquartered in Basel. Since the inception, the committee has established a series of banking standards to promote monetary and financial stability. Though at the beginning, the group's members were the governor of Central banks of G10 countries, at present, it has 45 institutions from 28 jurisdictions.

BCBS provides assistance to the central banks through regular cooperation to improve the quality of supervision in the banking industry. The committee sets regulations for the central banks. In addition, it acts consistently to enhance the financial stability and level playing field to avoid competitiveness conflicts globally. The member countries implement its prudential regulations and report to the committee periodically. BCBS decisions are expected to be followed by the member countries toward sound practice and standard guidelines in the financial industry [1].

The Committee's members are Argentina, Australia, Belgium, Brazil, Canada, China, European Union, France, Germany, Hong Kong SAR, India, Indonesia, Italy, Japan, Korea, Luxembourg, Mexico, the Netherlands, Russia, Saudi Arabia, Singapore, South Africa, Spain, Sweden, Switzerland, Turkey, the United Kingdom, and the United States. BCBS performs as a forum for regular cooperation on banking standard, regulation, and supervision issues between the member countries. It provides comprehensive guidelines for managing bank capital to safeguard against operational and financial risk in an international standard. Toward this standardization in banking operation and supervision, the committee has published a number of landmark guidelines on capital adequacy known as Basel I, Basel II, and Basel III.

This guideline advises holding a minimum amount of capital on the risk-weighted assets of the bank. This regulation is called the capital adequacy regulation (CAR) or minimum capital requirement (MCR).

2.1 Regulatory capital and economic capital

Banks as public confidence institution are strictly guided by regulations and supervision by the regulatory authority. Since risk is an integral part of any financial institution, in the process of providing different services to the economy banks come across different types of risk in their operation. As a result, risk is the subject of all regulation bases [2]. Regulators and risk managers define risk as an uncertainty that has adverse effect on the positive outcome of the bank like banks return, asset, or goodwill. Hence, the regulations intend to enhance the resilience of the bank in the stressed situations to protect the interest of the depositors and other associated counterparts of the bank.

In discussion of bank capital, the most widely used terms that come together are regulatory capital and economic capital. Regulatory capital as its name implies is the minimum level of capital required by the regulatory authority. Principally, the regulatory capital should be derived from the maximization of the social welfare function that takes into account the cost and benefit of the capital regulation [3]. Economic capital is the level of capital chosen by the shareholder of the bank. It relates with a desired rating required to safeguard the bank's losses at a certain confidence level. So, if the bank's loss during a period is higher than the initial level of capital, it will be in default. Therefore, the shareholder trades off between the costs of raise or increase of the equity against the benefit of reducing the banks probability of default. Mainly, cost of capital determines the relative position of the economic and regulatory capital. When the cost of capital is low, the economic capital is higher than the level of regulatory capital [3].

While discussing the economic capital and regulatory capital levels, the actual level of capital or actual capital arises. Actual capital is higher than the regulatory level chosen by the shareholder taking into consideration different regulatory requirements. Threat of closing the undercapitalized bank or avoidance of penalty insists the bank management and shareholders to keep the actual capital level above the minimum requirement.

In this chapter, we will discuss the regulatory capital or the minimum capital requirement (MCR) of the bank.

2.2 Basel I

In 1998, when the world economy faced the economic recession, the Latin American countries could not sustain their debts due to higher interest rates of loans and shorten repayment period [1]. These sovereign defaults possess critical situation for the international banks by eroding the capital buffer and global financial stability. The concern for global financial stability encouraged the BCBS committee to set up an international standard for risk measurement. The committee released a capital measurement system referred to as the "Basel Capital Accord" in July 1988 [4]. The principal of this measurement was to weigh the on-balance sheet and off-balance sheet asset according to the risk they possess. The accord required banks to hold at least 8% of risk-weighted assets (RWA) as capital; 50% of which must be Tier 1 or core capital.

Initially Basel Accord I focused to the credit risk of the bank measured by the Cookie ratio. However, being criticized for exaggerating on the credit risk in 1996, an amendment was issued through incorporating the market risk to address banks' exposure in foreign exchange risk, securities trade, equities, commodities, and options [4]. This amendment permitted the bank to use internal model to measure the market risk and associated capital against this risk.

The first Basel Accord, i.e., Basel I was introduced among the member countries of G-10 which includes Belgium, Canada, France, Germany, Italy, Japan, the Netherlands, Sweden, Switzerland, the United Kingdom, and the United States. The accord was designed to implement among all of the internationally active banks across countries to make a level playing field, i.e., to avoid competitiveness conflicts globally. For large and complex institutions, the regulation becomes less significant. Finally, a more risk-sensitive and comprehensive capital structure guideline—Basel II—was developed.

2.3 Basel II

As a response to Enron scandal and innovation of financial derivatives after the execution of Basel Accord I, a new regulatory framework was imperative to introduce.

A more sensitive new capital requirement known as Basel II was initiated shortly in 2004 to accommodate the highly complex on- and off-balance sheet items, promote more risk sensitive capital requirement through banks own assessment, and provide greater transparency. The purpose of the Basel II accord was to address the risk areas that were not covered by Basel I, to measure the capital requirement above the minimum level.

The Basel II accord released in 2004 was developed on three pillars, which are as follows:

i. Pillar I or minimum capital requirement (MCR)

ii. Pillar II or supervisory review process (SRP)

iii. Pillar III or market discipline (MD)

2.3.1 Pillar I or minimum capital requirement (MCR)

Pillar I or MCR states that banks are required to maintain regulatory capital that is 8% of risk-weighted assets (RWA). The RWA refer to the total assets of the bank that are risk-adjusted or weighted against credit risk, market risk, and operational risk according to the risk grade. Bank assets consist of cash, investment in securities, loans to governments, and businesses individuals that bear different risk characteristics. Therefore, risk weight is assigned to this asset group to indicate the level of riskiness in each asset group. To calculate the capital requirement, it takes into account both the on-balance sheet and off-balance sheet items of the bank.

Eligible regulatory capital is constituent of core capital or **Tier 1 capital** and supplementary capital or **Tier 2 capital**. Pillar I states the maintenance of regulatory capital on these two types. Core capital is the equity capital of the bank, retained earnings, and other reserves. For supervisory purposes, the committee determined to present the capital of the bank in two groups Tier 1 and Tier 2 where Tier 1 or the core capital should not be less than 50% of the total capital base of the bank that consists of common equity and approved reserves from the retained earnings. Other elements of the capital will have to be grouped in Tier 2 that is limited to 100% of the core capital or Tier 1 capital. Tier 2 includes the following:

- Undisclosed reserve or unpublished reserves
- Revaluation reserve of certain assets
- General provision/general loan-loss reserves
- Hybrid debt capital instrument
- Subordinated term debt

Short-term subordinated debt covering market risk or **Tier 3 capital**. Even though the eligible regulatory capital consists of core capital and supplementary capital, to cover the market risk, bank at its discretion can build Tier 3 capital that consists of short-term subordinated debt. This Tier 3 capital base can be built to support solely the market risk and cannot be higher than 250% of the core capital or Tier 1 capital.

The items to be deducted from the capital base are goodwill (deduction from Tier 1 capital), increase in equity due to securitization exposure, and investment in subsidiaries performing in the banking and financial sector that is not included in the national system.

Minimum capital requirement (MCR) is calculated for credit risk, market risk, and operational risk. BCBS advises that the minimum capital requirement under Basel II must be 8%, which will be calculated as follows:

$$\text{CAR} = \frac{Tier\ 1 + Tier\ 2 - Deductions + Tier3}{Cr\ risk\ RWA + Oper\ risk\ RWA + Mkt\ risk\ RWA} \geq 8\% \qquad (1)$$

where CAR is the capital adequacy ratio, Tier 1 is the Tier 1 capital, Tier 2 is the Tier 2 capital, Tier 3 is the Tier 3 capital, Cr risk RWA is the risk-weighted asset for credit risk, Oper risk RWA is the risk-weighted asset for operational risk, and Mkt risk RWA is the risk-weighted asset for market risk.

The following sections present a brief discussion on calculation of capital requirements for these risk areas, i.e., credit risk, operational risk, and market risk.

2.3.1.1 Credit risk

Risk-weighted asset for credit risk is calculated for credit RWA for exposure in banking book except the counterparty credit risk arising from equity investment, securitization exposure, and trading book instruments. Bank can choose either standardized approach (SA) or internal ratings-based approach (IRBA) to calculate their capital requirement against credit risk. In standard approach the risk is measured by the support of external rating or credit assessments whereas internal rating based approach is conducted by banks internal rating system and subject to the approval of the supervisors [5].

In case of standardized approach, claims against different counterparties are risk weighted against their rating. This credit rating is assessed by external credit rating institutions. In case of absence of any credit rating, the banks are advised to follow the instruction by the regulatory authorities. National regulatory or supervisory authorities permit the eligibility of the external credit assessment institution upon fulfillment of certain conditions. The credit rating agency must fulfill six criteria: objectivity, independence, international access/transparency, disclosure, resource, and credibility.

BCBS advises risk weight for claims on sovereigns, non-central government public sector entities, multilateral development banks, banks, securities firms, corporates, included in the regulatory retail portfolios, secured by residential property, commercial real estate, past due loans, and off-balance sheet items. A higher credit score signifies lower risk weight in calculating the risk-weighted asset of the bank. In standardized approach, bank calculates the total risk-weighted asset of the bank taking into consideration the whole credit portfolio. Along with the regular claims, the unsecured loans that are past due for more than 90 days are also risk weighted. This unsecured portion of the loan is risk weighted after the net of specific provision.

In standardized approach, the off-balance sheet items are converted into credit exposure equivalents through the use of credit conversion factors (CCF). The original maturity time determines the CCF of different commitments in the off-balance sheet items.

Internal ratings-based approach (IRB) as its name implies relies on own estimates of risk measurement in determining the capital requirement against credit risk, which are subject to fulfillment of certain conditions as well as disclosure requirements by the regulatory authorities. In IRB, the risk management team identifies the probability of default (PD), loss given default (LGD), the exposure at default (EAD), and effective maturity (M). Through these risk components, banks measure the unexpected loss (UL) and expected loss (EL). The capital requirements are calculated on the basis of unexpected loss. Expected losses are treated separately [5].

2.3.1.2 Operational risk

BCBS defines operational risk as "the risk of loss resulting from inadequate or failed internal processes, people, and systems or from external events." It includes the legal risk and excludes strategic and reputational risk. The committee advises three measurement approaches to calculate the capital charge against the operational risk of the bank. The approaches are (i) the basic indicator approach (BIA), (ii) standardized approach (SA), and (iii) advanced measurement approach (AMA).

Banks are encouraged to follow the sequential order of the measurement approaches. The level of sophisticated risk measurement system and practice would decide to follow the later approaches, i.e., standardized approach and advanced measurement approach. Internationally active banks with significant risk exposure in the operational areas are permitted to follow the standardized or advanced measurement approach.

In basic indicator approach, the capital charge for operational risk is equal to the 15% of average positive annual gross income of the bank. Gross income is the total of net interest income and net non-interest income. It does not include any realized profit or loss from the sale of securities and any income derived from insurance. The calculation of capital charge in basic indicator approach is as follows:

$$K_{BIA} = [\Sigma(GI_{1...n} \times \alpha)]/n \quad (2)$$

Here K_{BIA} is the capital charge in basic indicator approach; GI is the gross income, which was positive, over the previous 3 years; n is the number of previous 3 years for which gross income is positive; and α is 15% required capital level against the operational risk.

In standardized approach, a bank's activities are divided into eight sectors: corporate finance, trading and sales, retail banking, commercial banking, payment and settlement, agency services, asset management, and retail brokerage. In standardized approach, for every sector separate gross income is calculated separately. To measure the capital charge, this sectoral gross income is multiplied by denoted beta (a factor). Beta is a proxy variable that denotes relationship between the operational risk (of loss) for the particular business sector and aggregate level of gross income for that business sector [5]. Unlike basic indicator approach, standardized approach measures capital charge for each business line separately.

In SA, capital charge is calculated by taking the 3 years average of simple summation of the regulatory capital charge for each of the business sectors. Any negative capital charge due to negative gross income for any business sector may offset the positive capital charge in other business sector without limit. If the aggregate capital charge across all business lines in a certain time period is negative, then the numerator will be considered as zero. BCBS expressed the equation as follows:

$$K_{SA} = \{\Sigma_{\text{Years } 1\text{–}3} \max [\Sigma(GI_{1\text{–}8} \text{ X } \beta_{1\text{–}8}), 0]\}/3 \quad (3)$$

where K_{SA} is the capital charge under the standardized approach; $GI_{1\text{–}8}$ is the annual gross income in a given year, for each of the eight business sectors; and $\beta_{1\text{–}8}$ is a fixed percentage, set by the BCBS, the level of required capital to the level of the gross income for each of the eight business sectors.

Table 1 presents the value of β for each business sector as prescribed by BCBS [5] as follows.

Sl. no.	Business sector	Value of β (%)
1	Corporate finance	18
2	Trading and sales	18
3	Retail banking	12
4	Commercial banking	15
5	Payment and settlement	18
6	Agency services	15
7	Asset management	12
8	Retail brokerage	12

Table 1.
Value of β for different business sectors.

In advanced measurement approach, banks use some qualitative and quantitative criteria to calculate the risk exposure and capital charge by their own. This approach requires complex modeling and is subject to the approval of the supervisory authority.

2.3.1.3 Market risk

BCBC defines market risk as "the risk of losses in on- and off-balance sheet positions arising from movements in market prices." Sources of market risk are interest rate risk, foreign exchange risk, and commodities risk [5]. Interest risk arises from the loss due to movement of interest rate. Foreign exchange risk arises from changes in banks' assets and liability due to the fluctuation of foreign exchange rate. In the case of cross-border investments, when banks invest in different currencies risk arises due to adverse changes in the exchange rate. Similarly, commodity risk arises from the uncertain future market price changes in commodity prices.

Market risk is measured using the standardized measurement method and value at risk (VaR) or internal model approach. The choice of method is subject to the permission of the regulatory authorities. In standardized measurement method, four risks are addressed which are interest rate, equity position, foreign exchange, and commodities risk. The practice of internal model approach is subject to compliance of certain conditions and approval of the supervisory authorities.

Therefore, bank's total minimum capital requirement will be the summation of the capital requirement against the credit risk, capital charge for operational risk, and capital charge for market risk of the bank.

2.3.2 Pillar II or supervisory review process (SRP)

Pillar II or supervisory review process intends to assure that the bank has sufficient capital to support different risks arising in the business operation as well as encourage developing and practicing better risk management technique. SRP concedes the bank management to set capital target through developing an Internal Capital Assessment Process (ICAAP) that commensurate with banks own risk profile [5]. It also ensures that the bank management bears the responsibility to maintain the adequate level of capital beyond the minimum level to support its risk. The committee identifies the appropriate relationship between the risk and amount of capital and the effectiveness of bank's internal control and risk management process. The role of supervisory authority is to evaluate how the operating banks are assessing their risk and capital requirement and intervene if necessary. SRP intends to intervene the bank regulators to prevent capital shortfall from the minimum level in the early stage and to take rapid corrective action [5]. The SRP takes into account other risk factors that are not considered in Pillar I (i.e., liquidity risk and interest risk). The regulatory authority evaluates the bank's assessment of capital, ability to monitor, and be compliant with the capital regulations.

2.3.3 Pillar III or market discipline

Pillar III promotes market discipline through a set of qualitative and quantitative disclosure requirements that allow the market participants to understand the scope of application, capital position, risk exposure, and assessment of the banks. It is complement to Pillars I and II. Therefore, the disclosure allows a bank to present its risk position that is based on a common and consistent framework to the regulatory authority as well as public for comparison and credibility.

Bank supervisors having their power to disclose requirements to the operating banks contribute to safe and sound banking practices. Banks will have a formal disclosure policy approved by the board of directors, which exhibits the items to be disclosed, frequency, and internal control over the process. These capital and risk disclosure requirements do not conflict with and minimize the scope of the accounting requirements.

2.4 Basel III

Global economy suffers severe financial distress during 2007–2008. Excess liquidity in the banking sector resulting in too much weak credit or loans to subprime borrowers is at the top of the list behind the crisis of 2007–2008. Other reasons that triggered the global crisis are excessive risk taken by the financial firms, excess leverage, lack of adequate quality capital, inadequate liquidity buffer, and excess dependence on the credit rating agency [6]. The crisis revealed the lapses in the regulatory framework, market transparency, and supervision quality [7]. The crisis of 2007–2008 exposed the shortcomings of Basel II in managing the systematic risk and revealed the moral hazard problem linked with the systematically important banks.

In response to the crisis, BCBS addressing the weaknesses proposed revised capital framework that enforces raising higher quality of capital. It suggests building more common equity to improve loss absorption capacity and maintaining two liquidity standards and leverage ratio. The purpose of the regulation is to increase the level and quality of capital, enhance risk capture, constrain bank leverage, improve bank liquidity, and limit pro-cyclicality. In 2017, the committee reforms Basel III 2010 that seeks the credibility in risk calculation and improvement in comparison on the capital position of the bank [8].

The minimum amount of common equity to be maintained is increased from 2 to 4.5% and capital conservation buffer of 2.5% of the risk-weighted assets of the bank. In addition, the regulatory authority can enforce additional capital buffer during the period of excess credit growth. For systemically important banks, additional loss absorbency capacity can be introduced [7]. In 2017 reform, the committee has brought some changes in calculating credit risk through detailed risk weighing rather than flat risk weight for loans against residential and commercial real estate. In addition, banks are advised to perform due diligence in case of relying on external credit ratings.

To make the banking industry more stable, building capital alone is not sufficient. Therefore, to protect against buildup of excessive balance sheet leverage, Basel III introduced non-risk-based leverage ratio. This non-risk-based leverage ratio is Tier 1 capital to average total restated balance sheet assets over the quarter. The leverage ratio should be minimum 3%.

Moreover, for better resilience, (a) liquidity coverage ratio (LCR) for short-term disruption and (b) net stable funding ratio (NSFR) for long-term liquidity mismatch in the balance sheet are introduced. LCR is a standard for a minimum level of liquidity where the institution can generate enough cash outflow from the high-quality liquid assets in any short-term distress situation. The LCR standard is measured by the ratio of stock of high liquid assets to total net cash outflows over the next 30 calendar days. However, NSFR measures the sustainable funding ratio relating to the assets and off-balance sheet activities [9]. NSFR is the ratio of the available amount of stable funding to the required amount of stable funding, which should be greater than 100%. It suggests the banks to rely on long-term liabilities over short-term liabilities and small and retail liabilities over wholesome liabilities in case of short-term maturity (less than 1 year) for better resilience.

Particulars	Minimum % of RWA
Common equity	4.5
Capital conservation buffer	2.5
Tier 1 capital	6
Total capital	8
Liquidity coverage ratio	≥100
Net stable funding ratio	≥100

Table 2.
Minimum capital requirement ratio.

The crisis also revealed that the existing regulation has not appropriately covered major on- and off-balance sheet items, trading book, and derivative-related risk exposure. BCBS advises a revised framework to address the trading book exposure under Basel III that increases the capital charges around three to four times of previous level. Basel III upholds the counterparty credit risk management and collateral risk management and addresses the pro-cyclicality effect and credit valuation adjustment risk to reduce the reliance on external credit rating agencies. **Table 2** presents the present capital ratio and liquidity ratio advised by the committee [10].

2.4.1 Capital conservation buffer and countercyclical buffer

The case of Lehman Brothers and AIG call attention to how a single firm can boost up shock in the financial market as well as in the global economy. The financial crisis of 2007–2008 has revealed that microprudential guideline alone is not sufficient to address the systematic risk. Macroprudential regulation that takes into account the risk arising from interconnectedness of the financial institutions is important to respond to the systematic risk and financial stability in the economy.

Therefore, the macroprudential guidelines impose additional capital requirement for systematically important banks to reduce their default probability. BCBS advises building common equity of 2.5% of risk-weighted asset as capital conservation buffer so that in times of distress, this buffer can be scaled down to absorb losses. BCBS also advises the regulatory authorities to raise an additional countercyclical capital buffer of 2.5% to respond with excessive credit growth that may induce systematic risk in the financial sector. Banks incur a huge loss during downturn followed by a long excessive aggregate credit growth. After the asset price bubbles loans go unpaid, prices go down, banks loan decrease, and level of defaults even increases more [11]. To prevent this systematic risk, banks are advised to build additional capital up to 2.5% during the credit growth time that ensures the sufficient level of capital during the distress periods. It ensures that during the downturn, the banking institution has enough cushions to absorb the additional loss and provisioning. It also intends to support the financial stability by building countercyclical capital buffer during boom period through increasing to the cost of credit which reduces the demand for it [12].

3. Islamic banking and capital regulation

BCBS provides capital standard for conventional banks but Islamic banks are also under the same jurisdiction toward a safe and sound banking system. Islamic banks differ from the conventional banks in their operation due to unique items in the liability side of the balance sheet, risk sharing with the depositor and investor, absence of interest, and so on. Moreover, Islamic banks cannot access some credit derivatives to mitigate risk like conventional banks because of governing by the Shariah Principle. Wide range of financing mode also poses Islamic banking to face different kinds of risk. Since the operation of Islamic banking differs from the conventional banking, the determination of capital requirements also differs [13]. Studies find BCBS capital regulation does not address the risk of Islamic bank and lacks the goal to minimize the level of risk faced by the Islamic banks. Furthermore, it contributes to increase the risk of Islamic banks [14].

The Islamic Financial Services Board (IFSB) is an international organization that provides prudential guidelines and standards for the Islamic banks, insurance (takaful), and capital markets to enhance the stability of the Islamic financial industry. IFSB provides the standards aligning with the global regulatory standards in calculating capital requirements, thereby making disclosure toward transparency and market discipline [12]. However, because of asset-based financing, profit-loss sharing, profit bearing, or loss sharing principle, the capital determination is different from the conventional banking institution. Like the BCBS, IFSB also advises countercyclical capital buffer to the Islamic banks to reduce the systematic risk during the period of excessive credit growth.

4. Empirical studies on capital regulation and bank risk

The relationship between bank capital level and risk management is the most studied issue after the capital regulation regime. The empirical evidence provides useful insights about the factors affecting the risk undertaking of the banks. However, the studies focusing on the relationship between capital, risk management, and performance found contrasting results. Several studies found, in effect, that capital regulation stimulates the banks to take excessive risk through allowing the banks to increase riskier investment with the increase of bank capital [6]. Regulatory restriction, lower rate of return, riskier portfolio, and deposit insurance are the major causes identified behind the positive association between risk and capital regulations [15, 16]. Building capital raises cost of capital, decreases expected profit and rate of return, and induces the bank to invest in riskier sector that is more riskier in the long run [16]. Conversely, strict regulation, income diversity, and bank size are the factors identified behind the negative relationship between capital regulation and bank risk [17–20]. However, studies also find that capital regulation has different impact on conventional and Islamic banks.

5. Conclusion

Bank regulations and supervisions are to make the financial system more resilient that facilitate the stakeholders, creditors, depositors, and different counterparties. It prevents banks to take excessive risk. Therefore, to increase the financial stability around the world, BCBS a committee of BIS provides prudential guidelines for the banks and other financial institutions. The committee has advised three capital accords: Basel I, Basel II, and Basel III. Basel III is addressed to mitigate the regulatory lapses and systematic risk faced by the banks during recent financial crisis of 2007–2008.

Author details

Aysa Siddika[1]* and Razali Haron[2]

1 Institute of Business Administration (IBA-JU), Jahangirnagar University, Dhaka, Bangladesh

2 IIUM Institute of Islamic Banking and Finance (IIiBF), International Islamic University, Malaysia

*Address all correspondence to: aysasiddika25@gmail.com

References

[1] Akkizidis I, Kalyvas L. Final Basel III Modelling: Implementation, Impact and Implications. Switzerland: Springer; 2018

[2] Bessis J. Risk Management in Banking. New Jersey, United States: John Wiley & Sons; 2011

[3] Elizalde A, Repullo R. Economic and regulatory capital in banking: What is the difference? International Journal of Central Banking. 2007;**3**(3):87-117

[4] Basel Committee on Banking Supervision. History of the Basel Committee: Bank for international settlements. Available from: http://www.bis.org/bcbs/history.htm [Accessed: 19 September 2017]

[5] Basel Committee on Banking Supervision. International convergence of capital measurement and capital standards: A revised framework: Bank for international settlements. 2006. Available from: https://www.bis.org/publ/bcbs128.htm [Accessed: 29 December 2019]

[6] Siddika A, Haron R. Capital regulation and ownership structure on bank risk. Journal of Financial Regulation and Compliance. 2019;**28**(1):39-56

[7] Basel Committee on Banking Supervision. The Basel Committee's response to the financial crisis: report to the G20: Bank for international settlements. 2010. Available from: https://www.bis.org/publ/bcbs179.htm [Accessed: 19 December 2019]

[8] Basel Committee on Banking Supervision. Finalising Basel III in brief: Bank for international settlements. 2017

[9] Basel Committee on Banking Supervision. Basel III: The net stable funding ratio: Bank for international settlements. 2014

[10] Basel Committee on Banking Supervision. RBC 20 calculation of minimum risk based capital requirements: Bank for international settlements. 2020

[11] King P, Tarbert H. Basel III - An overview. Banking & Financial Services Policy Report. 2011;**30**(5):1-18

[12] IFSB. Core Principles for Islamic Finance Regulation (IFSB 21). Islamic Financial Services Board. 2018. Available from: https://www.ifsb.org/published.php [Accessed: 11 February 2020]

[13] Hassan MK, Chowdhury A. Islamic banking regulations in light of Basel II. The American Journal of Islamic Social Sciences. 2004;**27**:1-28

[14] Zins A, Weill L. Islamic banking and risk—The impact of Basel II. Economic Modelling. 2017;**64**:626-637

[15] Lundtofte F, Nielsen CY. The effect of stricter capital regulation on banks' risk-taking: Theory and evidence. 2018. DOI: 10.2139/ssrn.2674236. Available from: [Accessed: 25 November 2019]

[16] Diamond DW, Rajan RG. A theory of bank capital. The Journal of Finance. 2000;**55**(6):2431-2465

[17] Maji SG, Kumar DU. Regulatory capital and risk of Indian banks—A simultaneous equation approach. Journal of Financial Economic Policy. 2015;7(2):140-156

[18] Ghosh S. Risk capital and financial crisis—Evidence for GCC banks. Borsa Istanbul Review. 2014;**14**(3):145-157

[19] Hsieh MF, Chen PF, Lee CC, Yang SJ. How does diversification

impact bank stability? The role of globalization, regulations, and governance environments. Asia-Pacific Journal of Financial Studies. 2013;**42**(5):813-844

[20] Agoraki ME, Delis MD, Pasiouras F. Regulation, competition and bank risk taking in transition countries. Journal of Financial Stability. 2011;**5**:38-48

Chapter 2

Internal Controls and Credit Risk in European Banking: The Basel Committee on Banking Supervision Framework Approach

Ellis Kofi Akwaa-Sekyi

Abstract

Poor corporate governance practices have been cited as contributory to the 2007 global financial crisis. The chapter explores a qualitative self-regulation approach to address a major risk facing banks using the Basel Committee on Banking Supervision (BCBS) framework of internal controls. The study examines the effect of the qualitative principles of the BCBS internal control framework on credit risk. Corporate institutions use internal control frameworks to address the most operational risks, but the current study hypothesizes a possible relation with the credit risk. This research covers banks from selected EU countries covering some period before and after the 2007 financial crisis using a fixed-effect model. We report a significant relationship between board functions and activities, board structure and board monitoring, and credit risk. The results indicate that investment in high-risk assets, bank profitability and board chair being ex-CEO increases credit risk in European banking. The chapter extends the scope of a previous work that used the elements of the COSO internal control framework on a single country. This quantitative measure of qualitative constructs of the framework complements existing research that uses algorithms and simulations to study credit risk.

Keywords: Basel Committee on Banking Supervision Framework, Board of Directors, credit risk, European banking, internal controls

1. Introduction

The aftermath of the 2007 global financial crisis led to the tightening of corporate governance practices among financial institutions. As the apex of the internal governance system, board of directors have a duty in ensuring adherence and compliance with sound banking practices. The internal control framework of the Basel Committee on Banking Supervision (BCBS) reiterates the role of board of directors and senior management in ensuring that there is efficiency, compliance and standard reporting of banking activities. Prior to the 2007 global financial crisis, the BCBS had reported the importance of bank internal controls. The breakdown of internal control systems is attributable to weak management oversight, accountability and control culture, inadequate risk assessment of banking activities, failure of control structures and activities, ineffective share and flow of internal information and ineffective internal audit and monitoring activities [1].

Some researchers argue that poor risk management practices and weak corporate governance systems partially or significantly account for the 2007 global financial crisis [2, 3]. The crisis led to high rates of non-performing loans which affected several economies in the US and Europe. In a briefing to the European Parliament, the authors lament the rate of non-performing loans leading to credit risk among EU countries during and after the global financial crisis [4]. Prior research identifies factors such as low profitability, bank size and high concentration of banks in lending as key determinants of credit risk in the banking industry [5]. This study explores qualitative self-regulation approach using the BCBS internal control framework to investigate how internal controls affect credit risk in European banking. This chapter extends prior research about the banking industry in Spain where the authors find significant relation between the elements of internal controls using the COSO framework [6]. The study differs from existing ones in several ways. Whilst previous study focuses on a single country, the current chapter covers several countries within the EU thus making it broader and wider. The work of Akwaa-Sekyi and Moreno [6] uses single variables to measure the elements of internal controls but the current study uses several variables which cover the principles of internal controls. Unlike the previous study which uses the COSO framework, this chapter uses bank-related framework suggested by the BCBS. To the best of our knowledge, this is the first chapter to use the BCBS internal control framework to study its relationship with credit risk within the European banking.

This chapter derives motivations from three sources. The first motivation for this study comes from Cho and Chung [7]. They find that banks with weak internal control weakness report high provision for loan losses and loan loss reserves which exacerbates credit risk. Anytime banks intensify efforts to strengthen internal control weaknesses, there were reductions in provisions and loan loss reserves [7]. Based on their findings, we propose the use of the BCBS internal control framework to minimize bank credit risk. Second, prior research by Uhde et al. [8] motivates this chapter. In reviewing existing literature Uhde et al. [8] underscore the relevance of a framework that combines board structure and composition to ensure effective board monitoring. We concur with this integrated framework approach and therefore propose the joint effect of board functions and activities, board structure and board monitoring to minimize bank credit risk. Finally, the work of Karkowska and Acedański [9] motivates this chapter. The authors conclude that there is no much change in the corporate governance and bank stability nexus after the financial crisis and therefore suggest the need to strengthen corporate governance practices. This implies there is still room for banks to improve upon their corporate governance practices to deepen and sustain investor confidence in the banking system. For this reason, we suggest an internal control framework that is quite exhaustive in addressing the menace of investor losses such as credit risk. Failures to detect breakdowns in internal controls lead to massive fraud which puts shareholder investment in jeopardy and lack of confidence in the banking sector. The chapter seeks to fill these research gaps by analyzing how internal governance of the BCBS framework of internal controls affects credit risk.

The contributions of this chapter are not far-fetched. First, this chapter extends the literature on the relationship between board functions and activities and bank credit risk. The findings suggest that effective board functions and activities minimize bank credit risk. Second, this study proffers evidence to support the agency and institutional theories to monitor managerial behavior likely to result in investment losses through credit risk. The result complements existing research that independent board structure minimizes credit risk. Another contribution of this chapter to the agency theory is how board chair being ex-CEO increases bank risks. Prior research [10–12] uses CEO duality which is defined as situations where existing CEOs double as board chair. Our study uses current chair being ex-CEO to determine the effect of previous position (ex-CEO) in influencing board functions. We find that board chair being ex-CEO increases bank credit risk which is contrary to the views of John et al. [12] that CEO duality increases corporate governance. One other strength of this chapter is its complementarity to existing and widely used quantitative approaches to managing credit risk. The chapter encourages the use of internal governance mechanisms to address a major problem in banking. The rest of the sections cover hypotheses development, methodology, results and discussion, and conclusion.

1.1 Basel Committee of Banking Supervision framework for internal control systems

Following significant losses in banking organizations, the concerns to minimize such occurrences triggered the coming together of experts from various countries to develop a framework that will guide the conduct of banking business. The motivation behind the development of the framework for internal control systems is to address and enhance supervisory issues that encourage sound risk management practices [1]. The confidence in an effective and functioning control system is its ability to prevent and enable earlier detection of catastrophic but avoidable potential losses. Thus the framework is meant for member countries worldwide to use in evaluating internal control systems among banks albeit the situational circumstances pertaining to different countries. The Basel Committee on Banking Supervision which is a subcommittee of the risk management committee of the Bank for International Settlements outline 13 principles for assessing internal control systems captioned under five main areas or elements. The broad areas include management oversight and the control culture, risk recognition and assessment, control activities and segregation of duties, information and communication and monitoring activities.

1.2 Thirteen principles of the BCBS internal control framework

- The role of board of directors includes reviewing policies, have understanding and ability to manage risks and ensure that senior management complies. The board has a duty to ensure the establishment and maintenance of internal control systems.

- Senior management has a duty to ensure the implementation of board developed policies, develop processes for identifying, measuring, monitoring and controlling risks and internal control systems through delegation and segregation of duties.

- Board of directors and senior management must exemplify a culture of ethical behavior and integrity and respect for internal controls by full engagement

- Regular, effective and continuous assessment of all material risk exposures of the bank

- Appropriate control structure at all business levels, ensuring enforcement of compliance and approval limits, reconciliation and verification systems, physical controls

- Ensure segregation of duties and elimination of potential conflict of interest in the conduct of business
- Detailed and comprehensive internal financial, operational and compliance data, external market information (events and conditions) which is reliable, timely and easily accessible in a consistent and user-friendly format
- Reliable and secured information systems independently monitored and supported by adequate contingency arrangements
- Effective flow and share of information across personnel in functional areas and departments and units
- Periodic ongoing and daily monitoring of key risks by internal audit and business lines
- Independent and competent internal audit ensuring adherence to internal control systems and reporting to senior management and board of directors
- Reporting material internal control weakness to senior management and board
- Supervisors should ensure that all banks irrespective of size have effective internal controls that are consistent with the complexity and risks of business

The reasons behind the enforcement of these principles are to ensure that internal control systems achieve performance, information and compliance objectives [1]. The Basel framework is a risk-based approach which grants some independence to banks to manage their own risks and to ensure safe and sound bank practices through effective balancing of supervisory and principle-based regulatory approaches [13]. Well-functioning internal controls serve as bedrock for capital adequacy under prudential risk management regulation.

To ensure sound governance and protection shareholder and other stakeholder interests, board of directors exercise oversight responsibilities over senior management. Board of directors owe it a duty to ensure a culture of control, adherence to principles and statutes exist to put management in check. This function has been given alternative names such as "tone at the top" by researchers. The International Federation of Accountants [14] emphasizes the tone at the top and culture and ethical framework as vital to the implementation of internal controls. The federation attributes serious accounting scandals to a situation of poor tone on the part of top management. Hansen et al. [15] and Hermanson et al. [16] report that the tone at the top should be assessed and reported periodically to ensure that management and upper management continuously conform to systems put in place. They admit the importance of the tone at the top and culture of control as very key to ensuring effective internal controls among public and non-public organizations. The board must be seen to be doing more than just enough to ensure good tone and corporate culture that minimizes risk [17]. Financial organizations must pursue a risk culture that seeks to improve oversight structures and risk metrics and good compliance [18]. Effective implementation of board policies sustains and fuels management oversight and control culture. Schwartz [19] identifies board policies among other dimensions of effective corporate culture. Management oversight and control culture covers the roles and responsibilities of board of directors, executive management and the maintenance of high honesty and ethical culture.

Risk recognition and assessment involves the determination, identification and evaluation of risks or unfavorable events likely to impede the achievement of organizational objectives. Under risk management, companies should specify suitable objectives, identify and analyze risks, assess fraud risk and identify and analyze significant change. The expertise and experience of management and board members and their ability to identify, measure, monitor and evaluate risks goes a long way to reduce the consequences of bank risks. These functions means ensuring acceptable rates of risk weighted asset density [20], diversification and enforcement of internal controls to address operational risks.

The BCBS framework emphasizes the use of relevant information and communication to internal (functional areas and employees) and external users (stakeholders) through various reports (Abbas and Iqbal [21]). Banks earn reputational capital by providing reliable timely information to internal and external stakeholders [22]. Information flow, information sharing and representation on various committees within banks improves upon the risk culture [18] and transparency. Board meetings and committee functions helps information production. The control activities comprise selecting and developing control activities in general and over technology and deploying policies and procedures. It concerns taking precautionary measures and determining acceptable risk tolerance levels through policies, checks, and balances [21]. Bank control activities were found to significantly minimize credit risk [6]. Monitoring is about conducting on-going and/or separate evaluations and evaluating and communicating deficiencies [23]. The use of internal and external audit units, enforcement of internal control policies and adherence to regulatory measures improve bank monitoring. The agency problem can be linked to major banking activities which increases the probability risk exposure. Bank complexity and opacity (especially in the credit creation function) have the tendency to exacerbate the agency problem [24]. Bank managers in their effort to originate, fund, service and monitor credit supply may engage in certain actions or inactions that will impair the loan portfolio leading to the loss of assets. It is to avert such occurrences that effective internal control systems that minimizes such losses should be in place and effectively enforced.

1.3 Credit risk

Credit risk is crucial for bank management because of its relationship with other risks such as operational, market, and liquidity risks. Players in the financial services industry especially large-sized institutions use unproven and untested credit risk models and this could be cited as one of the causes of the 2007 financial crisis [3]. A publication on the role of credit risk in bank management and corporate governance, Lang and Jagtiani [3] argue that over-reliance on advanced quantitative credit risk models did not prove successful during the mortgage crisis. Thus, a multi-approach that adopts qualitative approaches to complement prudential quantitative models will enhance bank risk management. The chapter proposes this multi-approach by employing the BCBS framework for internal controls to address bank credit risk. Credit risk is a destination point for loan default and non-performing loans. Series of loan defaults transform into non-performing portfolio before it gets to the stage of credit risk. **Figure 1** shows the credit risk trajectory.

In this trajectory (**Figure 1**), unpaid loans transform into default, then prolonged default graduates into non-performing loans which leads to credit risk and eventually the effect on related market participants could lead to financial crisis. The final destination of this trajectory is financial crisis, which affects the wider industry players because of the interconnectedness of the banking model. In the event of increasing default, there is increase in portfolio credit risk [25]. Bank

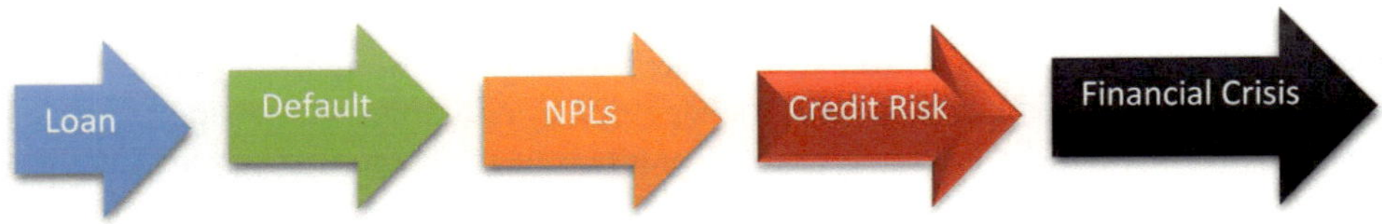

Figure 1.
The credit risk trajectory. Source: Author's construct.

credit risk management strategies should therefore be comprehensive to address issues of default and prevent increasing non-performing loans. Most literature on credit risk uses ratios such as non-performing loans to total loans, provision for loan losses and loan loss reserves [5, 6, 26] to measure credit risk.

2. Hypotheses development

In spite of the distinctive nature of the principles of internal controls according to the BCBS framework, they overlap and reinforce each other. For this reason, the author proposes three broad thematic areas which comprise board activities and functions, board structure and board monitoring.

2.1 Board functions and activities

The functions and activities of board of directors affect their supervisory and fiduciary role in protecting the interest of shareholders. The activities and functions of the board of directors affect managerial behavior. From the institutional theory, Zucker [27] explains that it is a complex view of the organization and how it responds to normative pressures from the internal and external environment that compels the organization to take legitimate stance to respond to such pressures. Institutional theories emphasize standard systems and procedures for the conduct of business to ensure survival of the organization. Scott [28] outlined three factors of institutionalization which comprises cognitive elements (systems and cultural foundations of society), normative elements (expectation from acceptable behavior) and enforcement processes (assessment, surveillance and sanctioning). Relating this theory to the BCBS internal controls framework, it implies drafting, implementing and improving policies that lead to acceptable behavior. It connotes a policy of creating, exemplifying and sustaining a culture of ethical behavior and compliance. The BCBS framework emphasizes enforcing sound internal control measures and this is a function of the expertise of the audit committee. The expertise of the board provides assurance for quality and efficiency in discharging board functions [29]. Board of directors carry out their activities by attending meetings and participating in committee tasks. The activities of board members are also about the number of meetings held within the financial year. We expect audit committee expertise, board policy functions and number of board meetings to significantly reduce credit risk. We therefore hypothesize that:

H1: Board functions and activities minimize credit risk.

2.2 Board structure

The structure of a board determines their effectiveness and efficiency with which they carry out their activities. Different studies use different variables to measure board structure. For example, Farag and Mallin [30] models board structure in terms of unitary and dual boards and CEO duality and report no significant relation with bank fragility. Studying the UK financial sector, Akbar et al. [10] use board size, board independence and combined role of CEO and board chair as variables for board structure. The results from the UK study show that there is little evidence of CEO duality. The regression results confirm low risk taking behavior. Other authors use board size, board independence and board member affiliations as proxy for board structure [9]. The authors report that independent board structure reduces bank risks. The inconclusiveness in the findings stimulates further investigation into board structure. The structure of board of directors should ensure minimizing the agency problem through segregation of duties (as enshrined in the BCBS internal control framework). The structure, composition and characteristics of board of directors could be relevant in their oversight and control functions [31]. Board characteristics such as board composition, independence, size, and gender diversity are efficient in monitoring and control of management [32]. The authors explain that these board characteristics motivate board members in the quest to control and maintain a risk culture and sound bank management to the satisfaction of stakeholders. The current study measures board structure by non-executive board members, board diversity, and board chair being ex-CEO. We expect that boards with non-executive members, few cases of board chair being ex-CEO and boards with adequate female representation can demonstrate higher degree of independence. This leads to the hypothesis that:

H2: Independent board structure reduces credit risk whilst boards with weak independence increase credit risk.

2.3 Board monitoring and control

Board monitoring has undergone several evolutions in corporate governance research [33]. The authors emphasize the role of the internal audit in responding to the agency problem through effective monitoring. The agency theory provides strong theoretical foundation to internal control research. The theory (traceable to the late 20th century and attributable to Jensen and Meckling) provides an underlying explanation of internal controls with the assumption that institutional behavior emanates from individual pursuit of self-interest and that there should be separation of ownership from control in order to minimize possible conflict of interest between the agent and the principal. The theory emphasizes separation of ownership from control, protection of minority interests, reducing conflict of interest and minimization of information asymmetry [34]. Jensen and Meckling [34] explain that the firm is a nexus of contracts among individual factors of production with conflicting objectives. Thus the best way of unifying these conflicts of interest is the use of contracts that minimizes the agency costs and enhances performance to maximize the value of the firm. A managerial tool put in place to check management and employee misbehavior through auditing, budgeting, compensation and other forms of control have proven successful in minimizing the agency costs [33, 35, 36]. Some high level of transparency and reporting is mandatory in order to effectively deal with information asymmetry. Internal control frameworks through the internal audit unit ensure the reporting and compliance objectives. Board audit committees reinforce the monitoring functions by ensuring compliance and adherence to internal controls [37]. Upadhyay et al. [37] conclude that board monitoring committees mitigate costs. We measure board monitoring by audit committee independence. Firms prefer using control-based approaches through audit committees with emphasis on high risk areas [38]. We propose the use of risk assessment and control by ensuring appropriate risk-weighted assets to total assets ratio to check possible insolvency. The use of risk weighted density (ratio or risk weighted assets to total assets) has a positive relation with bank credit risk [20]. From the discussions above, two hypotheses emerge:

H3: Higher risk weighted density increases bank credit risk.

H4: Effective board monitoring reduces bank credit risk.

2.4 Control variables

Bank management practices such as profitability motives affect the level of credit risk. Mixed findings exist in the relationship between credit risk and bank profitability. Studying the drivers of credit risk in the Indian banking industry, the authors find negative relation between ROA and credit risk [5]. The authors explain that banks engage in more prudent lending practices with improved borrower monitoring mechanisms to minimize the level of credit risk. Their findings confirm the work of Ghosh [39]. Others use credit risk as explanatory variable and conclude that there is a relation between credit risk and bank profitability in the US and Asia [26]. We argue that, the pursuit of profitability motives in the presence of weak internal control systems exacerbate bank credit risk exposure. In the model, we use return on assets (ROA) as proxy for profitability motives. The size of banks determines the volume of activities including loan portfolio which can determine credit risk. The BCBS internal control framework emphasizes coordinated effort between internal and external controls such as the regulator. Central banks use regulatory tools such as capital adequacy ratio and bank reserves to minimize bank risks.

3. Data and methodology

The initial sample comprises listed banks of countries within the European Union from Datastream and Worldscope databases. The websites of individuals and central banks of respective banks and countries provide further information about the banks under study. The period under study spans from 2004 to 2016. The chapter seeks to cover some period prior to the crisis, during and after the crisis. Based on data availability author analyzed the time period around the financial crisis, therefore some years before and some years after the crisis were taken into account. The databases compile bank-level data on corporate governance and financial performance variables. The analyses exclude banks with less than 5 years of data on the variables of interest. This makes the panel data unbalanced. Even though the data shows an initial 586 bank-year observations in the descriptive statistics, the regressions use 368 observations for the analyses.

3.1 Internal controls variables

The study classifies the 13 principles of the BCBS internal controls framework under three headings namely board activities and functions, board structure and board monitoring. The model is found below:

$$CR_{i,t} = \alpha + \beta \sum_{J=1}^{3} BodFtns_{i,t} + \theta \sum_{J=1}^{3} BodFtns_{i,t} + \delta \sum_{J=1}^{2} BodMonit_{i,t} + \gamma Contr + \varepsilon_{i,t} \quad (1)$$

Where *CR* represents credit risk, $i = 1 \ldots \ldots 56$ banks, $t = 2004 \ldots 2016$ α is the constant, β, θ, δ, γ are coefficients to be estimated and ε is the error term. *BodFtns* represents the set of variables on board activities and functions which affect credit risk, *BodStruc* represent the set of variables on board structure, *BodMonit* represent the set of variables on board monitoring activities and *Contr* represent the set of control variables.

$$BodFtns = f(Audit\ Committee\ expertise, Board\ policy\ function, Number\ of\ board\ meetings) \tag{2}$$

$$BodStruc = f(Board\ diversity, Non-executive\ members, Chairman\ is\ ex-CEO \tag{3}$$

$$BodMonit = f(Audit\ committee\ independence, Risk\ Weighted\ Assets\ to\ Total\ Assets) \tag{4}$$

$$Contr = f(Capital\ adequacy\ ratio - Tier\ 1, Bank\ profitability, Bank\ size) \tag{5}$$

An extended model which comprises all the variables (including control variables) follows:

$$\begin{aligned} CR_{i,t} = {} & \alpha + \beta_1 Audit\ Committee\ expertise_{i,t} + \beta_2 Board\ policy\ functions_{i,t} \\ & + \beta_3 Number\ of\ board\ meetings_{i,t} + \theta_1 Board\ diversity_{i,t} + \theta_2 Non \\ & - executive\ member_{i,t} + \theta_3 Chairman\ is\ ex - CEO_{i,t} \\ & + \delta_1 Audit\ committeee\ independence_{i,t} + \delta_2 Risk\ weighted\ assets\ to\ total\ assets_{i,t} \\ & + \gamma_1 Capital\ adequacy\ ratio - Tier\ 1_{i,t} + \gamma_2 BankSize_{i,t} + \gamma_3 Bank\ profitability_{i,t} \\ & + \varepsilon_{i,t} \end{aligned} \tag{6}$$

The chapter uses the OLS, fixed effect and random effect estimation techniques. Sometimes, the assumptions of OLS may lead to biases and misleading standard errors hence the use of fixed and random effect models. The fixed effect model assumes that certain individual characteristics within may bias the model [40]. Torres-Reyna [40] explains this as the rationale behind the correlation between the error term and predictor variables. The fixed effect model removes the effect of time-invariant characteristics thereby perfectly estimating the true effect of the explanatory variables. In addition to addressing possible endogeneity issues associated with panel data, we include control variables at bank and country levels to suppress the possible effect of such characteristics. Random effect models have superiority in higher-level estimations. In order to select whether fixed or random effect models is suitable for estimation, we perform the Hausman test.

4. Results and discussion

The results comprise descriptive statistics, correlation matrix and regression results for OLS, fixed effect, random effect and Hausman specification test.

Table 1 shows the descriptive statistics (number of observations, means, standard deviation, minimum and maximum values) for the variables. The result shows high credit risk (mean = 0.948). Variables on board functions such as audit committee expertise (mean = 0.516) and board policy function (mean = 0.610) are average or just above average. This is a good sign for effective internal controls. The structure of the board shows good representation of females, more than average non-executive members and some banks having board chair who were former CEOs. Thus the banks have a balanced board which enables effective board activities. There is evidence of board monitoring and control as can be seen from audit committee independence and control activities. The mean risk-weighted assets

Variable	Obs	Mean	Std.Dev.	Min	Max
Net loans total loans	586	0.948	0.147	0	1.892
Audit committee independence	503	75.827	28.665	0	100
Audit committee expertise	586	51.62	30.667	3.46	89.04
Board policy functions	586	61.041	23.166	0.4	77.78
Board diversity	563	60.202	28.377	11.81	100
Non-executive members	532	66.63	19.392	3.99	100
Capital adequacy ratio-Tier 1	555	10.725	3.458	−7.3	26.9
Chairman is ex-CEO	586	0.169	0.375	0	1
Number of board meetings	486	13.403	7.603	0	68
RWA to total assets	586	0.483	0.395	0	4.932
ROA	539	0.836	1.245	−12.42	4.99
Bank size	586	19.44	1.479	16.624	22.579

Table 1.
Descriptive statistics.

(RWA) to total assets is almost 50%. This is an indication of high risk and it is therefore not surprising that credit risk is high among the banks sampled for the study.

Table 2 shows the correlation matrix for the variables. High correlation coefficients (for example, 0.8 and above) are indications of high collinearity and this may cause problems in econometric estimations. The coefficients of the independent variables show that the variables are not highly correlated among themselves. This is an indication that the variables do not suffer multicollinearity problems.

We estimate the first model using OLS technique. Among board function variables, a number of board meetings show very significant relation with credit risk. Non-executive board members and chairman being ex-CEO are board structure variables that show significant relations with credit risk. Board activities (number of board meetings) shows significant positive relation with credit risk in the OLS model but the sign changes in the panel data analysis. Overall explanatory power of the OLS model is 26% which is far higher than those of fixed and random effects. Perhaps, this account for some of the biases of using OLS models instead of fixed and random effect models because OLS assumes that all the observations in the dataset are conditionally independent. This brings about bias and misleading standard errors. The study addresses bank heterogeneity using fixed and random effect models in a model that encompasses individual and time-specific effects. Based on the assumption that individual bank error term correlates with the predictor variables, we employ fixed effects model to cater for time-invariant omitted variables.

The difficulty in choosing fixed or random effect models is addressed by performing Hausman specification test. The significant variables for both fixed and random effect models are almost the same and consistent. The directions of association of the significant variables are the same. The use of Hausman specification test faces some criticisms. For example, when the between effect R^2 is larger than the within effect R^2, it is not appropriate to employ the fixed effect estimation technique even when Hausman test recommend the fixed effect model. The current study does not suffer such complications. In spite of the criticisms against the Hausman test, it is still widely used and accepted in research. The result from the Hausman test found in **Table 3** recommend the use of fixed effect model because

DOI: http://dx.doi.org/10.5772/intechopen.92889

Variables	Net loans to total loans	Board policy function	Number of board meetings	RWA to total assets	Audit comm indep	Audit comm expertis	Non-exec. Board	Board diversity	Chairman is ex-CEO	CAR-Tier 1	ROA	Bank size
Net loans to total loans	1.000											
Board policy function	0.054	1.000										
Numb of board meetings	0.159***	−0.034	1.000									
RWA/Total Assets	0.176***	−0.203***	0.054	1.000								
Audit com independence	0.208***	0.223***	0.086	0.175***	1.000							
Audit com expertise	0.041	0.133***	0.039	−0.089**	0.090**	1.000						
Non-exec board	−0.128***	−0.043	−0.037	−0.003	−0.061	0.036	1.000					
Board diversity	0.039	0.198***	−0.058	−0.217***	0.158***	0.185***	0.106**	1.000				
Chairman is ex-CEO	0.064	0.060	−0.062	−0.042	0.036	0.042	0.021	0.095**	1.000			
Capital adequacy ratio 1	0.003	0.032	0.033	−0.187***	−0.169***	0.239***	0.010	0.250***	−0.179***	1.000		
ROA	0.161***	−0.160***	−0.190***	0.081*	0.083*	−0.041	0.064	−0.048	−0.039	0.132***	1.000	
Bank size	0.052	0.214***	−0.175***	−0.319***	0.252***	0.221***	0.054	0.567***	0.157***	0.184***	0.027	1.000

$^{*}p < 0.1.$
$^{**}p < 0.05.$
$^{***}p < 0.01.$

Table 2.
Correlation matrix.

Variables	b	B	(b-B)	sqrt (diag(V_b-V_B))
	Fixed	Random	Difference	SE
Audit committee expertise	0.0000728	0.0000751	−2.25e-06	—
Board policy function	−0.0004016	−0.0003986	−2.93e-06	—
Number of board meetings	−0.0018262	−0.0017807	−0.0000454	—
Non-executive board members	−0.0002097	−0.0002187	9.04e-06	—
Audit committee independence	−4.89e-06	5.24e-06	−0.0000101	—
RWA/Total assets	0.0478272	0.0536965	−0.0058693	—
Chairman is ex-CEO	0.0074286	0.0072844	0.0001442	—
Board diversity	−0.0000737	−0.0000732	−5.15e-07	—
Capital adequacy ratio-Tier 1	−0.000748	−0.0006744	−0.0000736	—
ROA	0.00425	0.0041675	0.0000825	—
Bank size	0.0120867	0.0122416	−0.0001548	0.0013089

b = consistent under Ho and Ha; obtained from xtreg.
B = inconsistent under Ha, efficient under Ho; obtained from xtreg.
Test: Ho: difference in coefficients not systematic.
$chi^2(11) = (b - B)'[(V\_b - V\_B)\wedge(-1)](b - B) = 7316.20$
$Prob>chi^2 = 0.0000$
(V_b − V_B is not positive definite)

Table 3.
Results for Hausman specification test.

the probability Chi^2 value is significant ($p < 0.05$). **Table 3** shows the results for Hausman test to choose whether fixed effects or random effects model is appropriate for estimation. When the p-value is significant (95% confidence interval), we reject the null hypothesis that random effect model is preferable. The result for the test shows high significance at 99% confidence interval. This implies the use of the fixed effect model for econometric estimation.

Apart from audit committee independence and board diversity, all the variables in model show some level of significance within 90–99% confidence interval. From **Table 4,** all the variables for board function show significant relation for the fixed and random effect models. This is unlike the OLS model which show significance for only number of board meetings. The fixed effect model caters for individual bank level biases that may influence credit risk. Even though all the countries are found within the European Union and may have some standardizations, there are still bank and country-specific factors which account for differences. This is why we assume that bank error terms do not correlate with the constant [40] thereby justifying the choice of fixed effects. The R^2 results for within the entities are 41% for the fixed effect model. This indicates higher within entity variations. It is interesting to find that the R^2 values for the fixed and random effect models are not different.

The expertise of the audit committee is within average which is a sign for good board function. However, this is unable to translate into credit risk mitigation. Contrary to the expectations that the expertise of the audit committee would minimize credit, the results indicate positive relation. The existence of quality audit committee does not guarantee effective risk reduction. Sun and Liu [41] caution that when members of the audit committee are too busy, the level of total and idiosyncratic risks is higher. Perhaps, members of the audit committee have a lot on their hands to deal with thereby making them less efficient in their functioning.

	OLS (1)	Fixed effects (2)	Random effects (3)
	Net loans to total loans	Net loans to total loans	Net loans to total loans
Audit committee expertise	0.000	0.000*	0.000*
	(0.000)	(0.000)	(0.000)
Board policy function	0.000	−0.000***	−0.000***
	(0.000)	(0.000)	(0.000)
Number of board meetings	0.003***	−0.002***	−0.002***
	(0.001)	(0.000)	(0.000)
Non-executive board members	−0.001***	−0.000**	−0.000***
	(0.000)	(0.000)	(0.000)
Audit committee independence	0.000	−0.000	0.000
	(0.000)	(0.000)	(0.000)
Risk weighted assets to total assets	0.418***	0.048***	0.054***
	(0.052)	(0.017)	(0.017)
Chairman is ex-CEO	0.039**	0.007**	0.007**
	(0.017)	(0.003)	(0.003)
Board diversity	0.000	−0.000	−0.000
	(0.000)	(0.000)	(0.000)
Capital adequacy ratio-Tier 1	0.005**	−0.001**	−0.001*
	(0.002)	(0.000)	(0.000)
ROA	0.004	0.004***	0.004***
	(0.006)	(0.001)	(0.001)
Bank size	0.031***	0.012***	0.012***
	(0.007)	(0.005)	(0.004)
Obs.	368	368	368
R^2 within		0.408	0.408
R^2 between		0.015	0.021
R^2 overall	0.258	0.025	0.032

Standard errors are in parenthesis.
**p < 0.1.*
***p < 0.05.*
****p < 0.01.*

Table 4.
Results for OLS, fixed and random effect models.

Board policy functions cover the development and implementation of internal controls, a culture of ethical behavior and compliance. The result shows high significant negative relation with credit risk. These conditions create a favorable environment for management oversight. Formulation and implementation of board policies ensure compliance with sound ethical behavior and enforcement of internal controls creates favorable environment to mitigate bank risks. The number of board meetings significantly reduces credit risk. It is not enough for board members to organize meetings but when members regularly attend and participate in board activities. Regular board meetings improve the information and communication prowess of institutions which earns reputational capital [21, 22]. The result amplifies the institutional theory that normative elements and implementation of policies of acceptable behavior through compliance make institutions better governed. The development and implementation of board policies and engagement in board activities among sampled banks help reduce credit risk. Policies which ensure active participation of board activities, practicing a culture of ethical behavior and enforcement of internal control systems helps minimize bank losses. In this chapter, we find that board policies and board meetings have significant inverse relation with credit risk. Since two of the three variables adequately meet the expectation of the chapter, we maintain the acceptance of the hypothesis that board activities and functions minimize bank credit risk.

The results sustain the hypothesis that independent board structure reduces credit risk, whereas boards with weak independence increase credit risk. The variables for board structure for example non-executive board members show significant negative relation with credit risk. Non-executive board members have greater independence which makes them effective in their monitoring role. The inverse relation between non-executive board members and credit risk indicates effective control and prevention of actions that can trigger high credit risk. The result confirms the agency theory that non-executive board members help minimize the conflict of interest likely to exist. The positive relation between chair being ex-CEO and credit risk is not unexpected. Usually, such board members are influential and might exert superior powers which might increase bank credit risk. There is the tendency for over-confidence and unnecessarily entrenched leading to high credit risk. The result is consistent with Fernando et al. [25] who hold the opinion that dual board chair and CEO undermines board effectiveness in dealing with risks and monitoring managerialism. The BCBS internal control framework advocates for segregation of duties to ensure efficiency. It is not surprising the result shows positive relation between board chair being ex-CEO and credit risk. Board diversity (the proportion of female board members) shows negative but insignificant relation with credit risk. Even though not significant, board diversity is inversely related to credit risk. Having females on the board helps reduce credit risk. A board structure that compromises on its independence may have difficulty in effectively protecting and safeguarding the assets of shareholders. This assertion confirms earlier research by Karkowska and Acedański [9] that independent board structure decreases bank risks.

The chapter supports the hypothesis that higher risk weighted density increases bank credit risk. Board monitoring reduces credit risk of sampled banks. On the use of risk control mechanisms, risk-weighted assets to total assets shows significant positive relation with credit risk and therefore confirmatory to literature [20]. The mean RWA to total assets is almost 50% which is an indication of management investing in high risk investments. It is therefore not surprising that banks experienced high credit risk during the period under study. Relating the result to the control variable on bank profitability, the risk-return theory is confirmed. Banks engage in risky assets and this could explain why profitability (ROA) shows significant positive relation with credit risk. The European Union has experienced high non-performing loans (NPLs) during and after the global financial crisis, a situation which worsens banks credit portfolio performance. Bank control activities need to be intensified to check managerial recklessness in generating NPLs and subsequent credit risk which might lead to financial crisis.

The result for board monitoring shows that, audit committee independence reduces credit risk but not significantly. The hypothesis that board monitoring reduces bank credit risk is accepted in spite of the fact that in the case of the sampled banks, the result is not significant. Even though there is 75% score of audit committee independence among sampled banks, there is no evidence of significant relation with credit risk. It is good if variables show significant relation with outcome variables but when the direction of association is consistent with researcher's expectation, it is still worth reporting. The result cast doubts on the monitoring functions of the board and need to be given much attention than previously. The audit committee has consistently shown ineptitude in significantly minimizing credit risk among the sampled banks. From earlier result, the expertise of the audit committee could not significantly minimize credit risk and same has been reported on audit committee independence.

The results of the control variables meet the expectations of the authors. Bank profitability shows significant positive relation with credit risk. This means that the ambitious pursuit of profitability may lead to high credit risk and this is contradictory to earlier studies [5, 39]. The positive relation of bank profitability with credit is not surprising because of presence of board chair being ex-CEOs. There is the tendency for over-confidence and heavy reliance of experience to the neglect of strictly enforcing internal control mechanisms. The results from **Table 4** show that bank size significantly increases credit risk. Contrary to [5] who find no significant relation between bank size and credit risk, our study report significant positive relation with credit risk. For the purpose of catering for country-wide controls from external bodies such as regulators, the model introduces capital adequacy ratio-tier 1 into the equation. The results show significant negative relation with credit risk, thus confirming the effectiveness of regulatory controls to ensure bank compliance and discipline. Perhaps, banks have learnt lessons from the financial crisis. The result reinforces the institutional and agency theories used as the theoretical underpinnings of this study.

Beside the Basel II framework which uses the Supervisory Review and Evaluation Process (SREP) to enforce capital requirements as risk management tool, banks are encouraged to develop and monitor other risk management techniques [42]. The use of the BCBS internal control framework through the governance systems complements the capital requirement models of bank risk management. The framework addresses issues of compliance, reporting and efficiency. The inclusion of capital adequacy ratio (also as a compliance mechanism) as proxy for regulatory control makes the chapter's conceptual model efficient in addressing credit risk in European banking. The results show that sampled banks invest in risky assets, have desire for profitability and therefore the board needs to intensify internal control measures in order to minimize credit losses.

5. Conclusion

The study sought to analyses how board functions and activities, board structure and monitoring affect credit risk in European banking. Based on the BCBS internal control framework, we model the 13 principles of the BCBS framework under three headings namely board functions and activities, board structure and board monitoring. The results show that integrated internal control frameworks are complementary and proven to effectively mitigate bank credit risks. The study concludes that developing and implementing board policies on supervision, risk control culture, compliance and enforcement of internal controls minimizes credit risk in European banking. A board structure that ensures independence, diverse and board chair not being ex-CEO may reduce bank losses through credit risk. Board monitoring is effective when regulatory controls are used to complement existing internal control mechanisms. From the results, board policies, board activities, non-executive boards and external regulations significantly reduce credit risk. Whilst audit committee independence and board diversity reduce credit risk but not significantly, audit committee expertise, board chair being ex-CEO, investments in risky assets, profitability and bank size significantly increase credit risk. The model for the chapter shows that the principles of the BCBS framework combines with regulatory compliance requirements to ensure credit risk reduction. The chapter supports the agency and institutional theories. The BCBS internal control framework provides reliable mechanism for controlling credit risk.

The study has implications for bank practice. Credit risk continues to be a thorny issue in the banking industry especially within the EU. Our study provides a diversified approach to addressing this market failure. The chapter shows that complementing regulatory controls with self-governing practices like internal controls reduce bank risks. This research is not devoid of limitations. But for the availability of data, the study could have substantially covered three periods (before, during and after the crisis). Despite these limitations, the methodology is consistent with existing research and all assumptions and diagnostic tests were statistically confirmed. These limitations cast no doubts about the findings of our study. The chapter suggests future research to consider internal control practices in the periods before, during and after the 2007 global financial crisis. It is further suggested that, various internal control frameworks could be compared to analyze their effects on other risks such as market, liquidity and operational risks. Future research could also consider using dynamic models such as system GMM to study corporate governance and bank risks.

Acknowledgements

I would like to appreciate Fauna Atta Frimpong, PhD candidate of University of Lleida, Lleida-Spain for reading through the chapter. I am also indebted to my sons Ellis Jnr and Quobby for helping with the data mining.

Author details

Ellis Kofi Akwaa-Sekyi
Catholic University College of Ghana, Sunyani, Ghana

*Address all correspondence to: el7teen@yahoo.com

References

[1] Basel Committee on Banking Supervision. Framework for Internal Control Systems in Banking Organizations. Basel, Switzerland: Bank for International Settlements; 1998

[2] Kirkpatrick G. The corporate governance lessons from the financial crisis. OECD Journal: Financial Market Trends. 2009;**2009**(1):61–87. Available from: http://www.oecd-ilibrary.org/finance-and-investment/the-corporate-governance-lessons-from-the-financial-crisis_fmt-v2009-art3-en

[3] Lang WW, Jagtiani JA. The mortgage and financial crises: The role of credit risk management and corporate governance. Atlantic Economic Journal. 2010;**38**(3):295–316. DOI: 10.1007/s11293-010-9240-4

[4] Mesnard B, Margerit A, Power C, Magnus M. Non-performing loans in the Banking Union: Stocktaking and challenges. In: European Parliament, Economic Governance and Support Unit. 2016. Available from: http://www.europarl.europa.eu/RegData/etudes/BRIE/2016/574400/IPOL_BRI(2016)574400_EN.pdf

[5] Gulati R, Goswami A, Kumar S. What drives credit risk in the Indian banking industry? An empirical investigation. Economic Systems. 2019; **43**(1):42–62. DOI: 10.1016/j.ecosys.2018.08.004

[6] Akwaa-Sekyi EK, Moreno JG. Effect of internal controls on credit risk among listed Spanish banks. Intangible Capital. 2016;**12**(1):357–389. DOI: 10.3926/ic.703

[7] Cho M, Chung K-H. The effect of commercial banks' internal control weaknesses on loan loss reserves and provisions. Journal of Contemporary Accounting and Economics. 2016;**12**(1): 61–72. DOI: 10.1016/j.jcae.2016.02.004

[8] Uhde DA, Klarner P, Tuschke A. Board monitoring of the chief financial officer: A review and research agenda. Corporate Governance: An International Review. 2017;**25**(2):116–133. DOI: 10.1111/corg.12188

[9] Karkowska R, Acedański J. The effect of corporate board attributes on bank stability. Portuguese Economic Journal. 2019;**19**:99–137. DOI: 10.1007/s10258-019.00162-3

[10] Akbar S, Kharabsheh B, Poletti-Hughes J, Shah SZA. Board structure and corporate risk taking in the UK financial sector. International Review of Financial Analysis. 2017;**50**:101–110. DOI: 10.1016/j.irfa.2017.02.001

[11] Pathan S. Strong boards, CEO power and bank risk-taking. Journal of Bank ing and Finance. 2009;**33**(7):1340–1350. DOI: 10.1016/jbankfin.2009.02.001

[12] John K, De Masi S, Paci A. Corporate governance in banks. Corporate Governance: An International Review. 2016;**24**(3):303–321. DOI: 10.1111/corg.12161

[13] Gualandri E. Basel 3, pillar 2: The role of banks' internal governance and control function. SSRN Electronic Journal. 2011:1–12. DOI: 10.2139/ssrn.1908641

[14] International Federation of Accountants. Internal Controls—A Review of Current Developments. 2006 (August). New York. pp.1-19. Available from: http://www.ifac.org/sites/default/files/publications/files/internal-controls-a-revie.pdf

[15] Hansen J, Stephens NM, Wood DA. Entity-level controls: The internal auditor's assessment of management tone at the top. Current Issues in Auditing. 2009;**3**(1):1–13. DOI: 10.2308/ciia.2009.3.1.A1

[16] Hermanson DR, Smith JL, Stephens NM. How effective are organizations' internal controls? Insights into specific internal control elements. Current Issues in Auditing. 2012;**6**(1): 31–50. DOI: 10.2308/ciia-50146

[17] Roboff G. The tone at the top: Assessing the board's effectiveness. ISACA Journal. 2016;**6**:1–8

[18] Power M, Simon A, Palermo T. Risk culture in financial organisations: A research report. In: Centre for Analysis of Risk and Regulation. 2012. Available from: http://www.lse.ac.uk/CARR

[19] Schwartz MS. Developing and sustaining an ethical corporate culture: The core elements. Business Horizons. 2013;**56**(1):39–50. DOI: 10.1016/j.bushor.2012.09.002

[20] Arroyo JM, Colomer I, Garcia-Baena R, González-Mosquera L. Comparing risk-weighted assets: The importance of supervisory validation processes. Estabilidad Financiera. 2012;**22**:9–29

[21] Abbas Q, Iqbal J. Internal control system: Analyzing theoretical perspective and practices. Middle-East Journal of Scientific Research. 2012; **12**(4):530–538. DOI: 10.5829/idosi/mejsr.2012.12.4.1793

[22] Zhang Y, Zhou J, Zhou N. Audit committee quality, auditor independence, and internal control weaknesses. Journal of Accounting and Public Policy. 2007;**26**(3):300–327. DOI: 10.1016/j.jaccpubpol.2007.03.001

[23] McNally SJ. COSO McNallyTransition Article-Final COSO Version Proof_5-31-13.pdf. Strategic Finance. 8. 2013. Available from: http://www.coso.org/documents/COSO McNallyTransition Article-Final COSO Version Proof_5-31-13.pdf

[24] Morgan DP. Rating banks: Risk and uncertainty in an opaque industry. The American Economic Review. 2002; **92**(4):874–888. DOI: 10.1257/00028280260344506

[25] Fernando JMR, Li L, Hou YG. Corporate governance and correlation in corporate defaults. Corporate Governance: An International Review. 2019;**28**(13):187–203. DOI: 10.1111/CORG.12306

[26] Abbas F, Iqbal S, Aziz B, Yang Z. The impact of bank capital , bank liquidity and credit risk on profitability in postcrisis period: A comparative study of US and Asia. Cogent Economics and Finance. 2019;**7**(1):1–18. DOI: 10.1080/23322039.2019.1605683

[27] Zucker LG. Institutional theories of organization. Annual Review of Sociology. 1987;**13**(1):443–464

[28] Scott WR. Institutions and Organizations. Ideas, Interests and Identities. Thousand Oaks: SAGE; 1995. pp. xi–xxiii

[29] Wang T, Hsu C. Board composition and operational risk events of financial institutions. Journal of Banking & Finance. 2013;**37**(2013):2042–2051. DOI: 10.1016/j.jbankfin.2013.01.02

[30] Farag H, Mallin C. Board diversity and financial fragility: Evidence from European banks. International Review of Financial Analysis. 2017;**49**:98–112. DOI: 10.1016/j.irfa.2016.12.002

[31] García Sánchez IM, Martínez-Ferrero J, García-Meca E. Board of Directors and CSR in banking: The moderating role of Bank regulation and investor protection strength. Australian Accounting Review. 2017;**28**(3):428–445. DOI: 10.1111/auar.12199

[32] de Andres P, Vallelado E. Corporate governance in banking: The role of the board of directors. Journal of Banking & Finance. 2008;**32**(12):2570–2580. DOI: 10.1016/j.jbankfin.2008.05.008

[33] Sarens G, Abdolmohammadi MJ. Monitoring effects of the internal audit function: Agency theory versus other explanatory variables. International Journal of Auditing. 2011;**15**(1):1–20. DOI: 10.1111/j.1099-1123.2010.00419.x

[34] Jensen C, Meckling H. Theory of the firm: Managerial behavior, agency costs and ownership structure. Journal of Financial Economics. 1976;**3**:305–360. DOI: 10.1016/0304-405X(76)90026-X

[35] Baran L, Forst A. Disproportionate insider control and board of director characteristics. Journal of Corporate Finance. 2015;**35**:62–80. DOI: 10.1016/j.jcorpfin.2015.08.006

[36] Otten J, Wempe B. Corporate governance and the Politics of Agency Theory. Rotterdam: RSM Erasmus University; 2009. DOI: 10.1016/j.jcorpfin.2006.03.001

[37] Upadhyay AD, Bhargava R, Faircloth SD. Board structure and role of monitoring committees. Journal of Business Research. 2014;**67**(7):1486–1492. DOI: 10.1016/j.jbusres.2013.07.017

[38] Coetzee P, Lubbe D. Improving the efficiency and effectiveness of risk-based internal audit engagements. International Journal of Auditing. 2014;**18**(2):115–125. DOI: 10.1111/ijau.12016

[39] Ghosh A. Banking-industry specific and regional economic determinants of non-performing loans: Evidence from US states. Journal of Financial Stability. 2015;**20**:93–104. DOI: 10.1016/j.jfs.2015.08.004

[40] Torres-Reyna O. Panel data analysis fixed and random effects using Stata. Data and Statistical Services. 2010;**3**(December):1–40

[41] Sun J, Liu G. Audit committees' oversight of bank risk-taking. Journal of Banking & Finance. 2014;**40**(1):376–387. DOI: 10.1016/j.jbankfin.2013.12.015

[42] Dietz T. The role of the risk control function under the Basel II framework. Virtus Nterpress. 2011;**1**(3):40–49

Chapter 3

Relevance of *Shari'ah* Governance in Driving Performance of Islamic Banks during the Financial Crisis: International Evidence

Naji Mansour Nomran and Razali Haron

Abstract

This study aims to examine the impact of *Shari'ah* governance mechanism on the performance of Islamic banks (IBs) during the financial crisis of 2008. Data were collected from 66 IBs over 18 countries covering the period of 2007–2015 and analyzed using the System-GMM estimator. The findings indicate that an increase in SSB effectiveness increases IBs' performance even during the crisis periods. A possible justification for this positive effect is related to the SG structure of IBs that allows them to undertake higher risks to achieve a high efficiency level. For this, the IBs, policymakers and practitioners should consider these findings when aiming to improve SG practices in the Islamic banking industry, which in turn may help in protecting IBs during crisis and non-crisis periods. More specifically, they should give due importance to SSB (size, cross-membership, educational qualification, reputation and expertise) in enhancing the performance of IBs during the crisis and non-crisis periods. This study provides additional evidence on how IBs can sustain their performance during either crisis or non-crisis periods through adopting appropriate SG structure. However, the study only focuses on a small sample of 66 IBs due to lack of the data.

Keywords: *Shari'ah* governance, Islamic banking, performance, global financial crisis of 2008

1. Introduction

In the current practice, Islamic banks (IBs) are subject to two internal mechanisms of CG: The Board of Directors (BoD) and the *Shari'ah* supervisory boards (SSBs). This extra layer of governance in the IBs, as represented by SSB, modifies their governance structure from a "single-layer" as in the conventional banks (CBs) into a "multi-layer" governance [1, 2]. Abdelsalam et al. [3] argue that this dual board structure strengthens both moral and legal accountabilities of IB management, and then, it may reduce these banks' risk. Therefore, the establishment of an SSB for IBs is essential [4]. For the IBs, in order to enhance their customers' trust, they must guarantee that all their products and operations are in compliance with the *Shari'ah* rules [5]. *Shari'ah* noncompliance can be a reason for reputational risk that can make the Islamic finance sector susceptible to instability and can trigger bank failure as most of the customers prefer the IBs for religious reasons [6]. These risks also include higher costs, financial losses, liquidity problems, bank runs, bank failure, industry smearing and financial instability [6, 7].

Providing an efficient *Shari'ah* supervision is crucial to the IBs for failing to do so may give negative impact on the Islamic finance industry as a whole; hence, the SSB has high responsibility and accountability in its role with regard to *Shari'ah* supervision. If IBs fail to ensure compliance with the *Shari'ah* rules, their position in the market will be negatively affected due to lack of customers' confidence [8, 9]. It is argued that one of the duties of SSB is to approve any new products before they go for full scale development, which in turn would decrease the risks of *Shari'ah* compatibility before developing the product [6]. New products will not be introduced to the customers before they are approved by the SSB [10]. Risks can arise when the product fails to meet market and customers' needs. Given the importance of SSBs for IBs, [11] claim that although some may compare SSB to BoD or to an investment committee, SSBs have more powers and rights. Thus, the roles and duties of SSB have no true equivalent in the West [11]. As such, [10] considers the SSBs as the substitute for the conventional BoD. Furthermore, the SSB is expected to advise the board, the management including the bank's subsidiaries and provide input to the bank on *Shari'ah* matters in order for the bank to comply with *Shari'ah* principles at all times [12].

The SSB plays an important role in determining the performance of IBs [4] and is responsible and accountable for all *Shari'ah* decisions, opinions and views provided by them to the IBs [12]. Given that SSB supervises bank investment, banks cannot invest beyond the SSB-approved investments even if they can earn a higher rate of returns [13]. The duties of the SSB include ensuring that the operations of the banks do not involve any dealings in prohibited industries [14]. Furthermore, the SSB has super authority to prevent the BoDs from charging interest (*riba*) payments and avoiding doubtful (*gharar*) investments in their products [15]. According to [6], the use of products that breach the *Shari'ah* principles is costly to the IBs in both the short run and the long run. In the short run, any revenue from the transactions that are not *Shari'ah* compliant is excluded from the income of the bank and donated to some charitable causes. Thus, *Shari'ah* noncompliance can affect the income and profitability of IBs adversely. In the long run, the dilution of *Shari'ah* principles can negatively affect the perception of stakeholders on the Islamic financial practice causing a serious loss of trust and credibility [6]. The nature of the SSBs' decision may influence the acceptance of one product over another; hence, the SSB approval could increase or decrease the volume of banking business [4], which may affect the bank's profitability [16]. The decision-making of the management in the IBs is indeed constrained by an SSB that rejects any proposals in light of *Shari'ah* principles [10].

The chapter is organized into four sections. The first section deals with the related literature and the hypotheses development. The second presents the data and methodology, while the third discusses the empirical result. The last section concludes the whole study.

1.1 Internal corporate governance mechanisms and financial crisis of 2008

In the current practices, CBs are not operating alone in the market as IBs have become their most competitive rival [17]. Many observers and industry players have shifted their interests toward the Islamic financial system as a viable alternative to the conventional one after the series of failures of several conventional financial institutions due to the crisis of 2008 [18]. Parallel with that attention, the importance of CG implementations has increased in the business environment especially after the financial crises, the Asian financial crisis of 1997 and the global financial crisis of 2008. According to [18], as the financial transactions in the Islamic system are trade and asset based, it is assumed that this system will be more resilient to the financial shocks. Despite this, there are many examples of Islamic financial institutions (IFIs) that suffer from poor CG especially during crisis periods. The fall of Ihlas Finance House of Turkey in 2001, South Africa's IB in 1997 and the Dubai Islamic IB's losses between 2004 and 2007 are the clearest evidences of the IFI's poor governance [9, 19]. Many scholars argue that poor CG of financial institutions is one of the main causes of the financial crisis of 2008 [20]. It is now widely acknowledged that shortcomings in bank CG may have had a central role in the development of the crisis [21].

The CG weaknesses and strengths are determined by many factors especially the CG mechanisms. Therefore, companies that have strong CG mechanisms tend to be more successful as compared to those companies having weak corporate mechanisms [22]. Accordingly, companies that have effective corporate boards during crisis periods are more likely to introduce turnaround plans [23]. As Abatecola et al. [24] assert, most of the empirical studies confirm that corporate board characteristics increase the survival probabilities of companies during crisis periods. Kowalewski [23] provides empirical evidence on how CG mechanisms operate differently in crisis and non-crisis periods. Adding to that, Srivastava [25] finds that BoD affects the company's performance, particularly during the period of financial crisis.

Being considered that IBs are subject to two internal mechanisms of CG, the BoD and the SSB, it is paramount to provide insights on how SSB influences the IBs' performance during crisis periods. In general, most of the empirical studies in the literature have given attention to the BoD, while there is a lack of studies in the SSB context. As Nomran and Haron [26] argue, there is a need for more empirical studies to examine whether the effect of SSB on IB's performance differs during crisis periods, especially the financial crisis of 2008. They add that this would help IBs in developing their strategies to adopt an appropriate SSB structure that will sustain their performance.

Few studies, however, have so far been focused on CG structure of IBs and link it to their performance during crisis such as the study of [15]. In this study, Mollah et al. [15] investigate whether the CG structure of IBs can help them in reducing the impact of the crisis of 2008. To do so, they examined the impact of the CG[1] on performance of the IBs vs. CBs and found that the SSB size influences the IBs' performance positively during the crisis period. They argue that the SG diminishes the negative impact of excessive risk taking and then improves the IBs' performance [15]. However, Nomran and Haron [27] claim that the study of [15] suffers from some limitations such as it used the SSB size as a single proxy of SSB governance and neglected many important SSB characteristics that may affect the board performances. Thus, Nomran and Haron [27] overcome this limitation by using an SSB score that takes into consideration the impact of other important SSB characteristics. Similarly, the current study also uses this SSB score to measure SSB supervision as it will be shown in the methodology.

Basically, IBs have unique framework against the backdrop of *Shari'ah* ruling that plays an important role in their resilience. The CG structure of IBs, which includes the SG, helps them undertake higher risks and decrease the effect of the crisis on their profitability [15]. Alman [28] asserts that taking the crisis period into

---

[1] BoD structure (board size and independence), CEO power (chair duality and internally recruited) and SSB size.

account while studying the impact of SSB is important. Thus, there is an open empirical research question as to whether the SSB supervision, as measured by an SSB score that takes into consideration the impact of the important SSB characteristics[2], contributes to better performance of IBs during crisis periods.

2. Hypotheses development

Literature reveals that comparing the impact of the SSB on IBs' performance during crisis periods has not been fully investigated in previous studies. Responding to what has been discussed above, this chapter aims to extend the investigation of [15] by examining the impact of SSB supervision on IBs' performance during crisis periods by focusing on the financial crisis of 2008.

2.1 *Shari'ah* supervision and bank performance

The SSB has a supra authority to prevent the BoDs from charging interest (*riba*) payments and to avoid doubtful (*gharar*) investments in their products [15]. Although economic calculation and the profit concerns of the IBs are allocated to the BoD, the appreciation of the licit character of this profit is allocated to the SSB [10]. Thus, SSBs play an important role in mitigating agency problems by acting as an additional monitoring mechanism [3, 33, 34]. SSBs offer an extra possible reduction in agency costs for IBs through organizational moral accountability constraints and shaping managerial behavior [3, 34]. As Mohammed and Muhammed [4] state, SSB is one of the four key stakeholders affecting the financial performance of IBs, besides the management, the ownership and the external auditor.

As mentioned above, SSB characteristics, for example, SSB size, cross-membership, doctoral qualification, reputation and expertise, may determine how effective the SSB is in performing its task [19, 32, 35]. Basically, SSBs' total effect should be measured using an SSB measurement that can reflect the total effect of SSB based on the most important characteristics that affect SSBs' performance [26]. Based on that, many studies used SSB score that captures the total impact of these SSB characteristics to measure SSB supervision, for examples [19, 27]. Recently, Nomran and Haron [27] find that SSBs positively affect Southeast Asia IBs' performance. That is to say that, SSB score provides the basis for the following hypotheses:

H_1: Effective SSB, as represented by the SSB score, will be positively associated with IBs' performance.

H_2: Effective SSB, as represented by the SSB score, will be positively associated with IBs' performance even for the period during the financial crisis of 2008.

3. Data and methodology

3.1 Sample

This chapter uses an unbalanced panel data of 66 IBs over 18 countries over the period 2007–2015 after eliminating banks with insufficient data on *Shari'ah* governance and performance. We choose the sample's starting period of 2007 in order to

[2] Several variables relating to the SSB characteristics may determine how effective the SSB is in conducting its task, namely, SSB size, doctoral qualification, reputation, cross-membership and expertise [19, 29–32].

capture the effect of the financial crisis of 2008; therefore, the study covers the period from 2007 to 2015, including crisis period (2007–2009) following the previous studies such as [36]. The data are merged from BankScope and World Bank country-level macroeconomic data with hand-collected data on SSB characteristics from annual reports of IBs for the sample period. The sample distribution is presented in **Table 1**.

3.2 Measures of variables

In this study, the dependent variable, which is the performance of IBs, is measured by ROA and ROE following the previous studies [15, 32].

The explanatory variables used are measured as the following. *Shari'ah* supervision is measured using SSB score [27]. The bank characteristics (size and age) and country-specific variables (GDP and inflation rate) that may affect performance are employed as control variables following previous research [15, 27]. **Table 2** provides a summary of the measurements of the dependent, control and explanatory variables used in this study.

3.3 Estimation method and model

This chapter employs the two-step system generalized method of moments (GMM). Studies on the relationships between CG and performance should control

Country	No of Islamic banks
Algeria	1
Bahrain	9
Bangladesh	6
Bosnia	1
Brunei Darussalam	1
Indonesia	2
Jordan	3
Kuwait	2
Malaysia	11
Maldives	1
Oman	4
Pakistan	9
Qatar	3
Sudan	6
Syria	2
Thailand	1
United Kingdom	3
Yemen	1
Total	66

Three of the four IBs in Oman are windows, but they have separate financial statements (Sohar Islamic, Muzn Islamic & Meethaq Islamic).

Table 1.
Sample of the study.

Variables	Definitions and coding	Measurement
Dependent variables (bank performance)		
ROA	Return on assets	Net income divided by average total assets
ROE	Return on equity	Net income divided by average total equity
Explanatory and control variables		
SSB-SCORE	*Shari'ah* supervision score	SSB-SIZE+SSB-CRM + SSB-DQ + SSB-REP+ SSB-EXPER*
SSB-SCORE × CRISIS	Interaction term between SSB score and financial crisis	SSB score multiplied by dummy variable: "1" for the period 2007–2009, "0" otherwise
BSIZE	Bank size	Log of total assets
BAGE	Bank age	Log of years since the bank was established
GDP	Gross domestic product	Log of GDP per capita
INFLATION	Inflation	Inflation rate
CRISIS	Financial crisis	A dummy variable: "1" for the period 2007–2009, "0" otherwise

**The SSB score sums the value of the dichotomous characteristics of the SSB, which takes a score bounded by 0–1, namely (SSB size: "1" for banks with 5 or more members & "0" otherwise), (SSB cross-membership: "1" if at least one SSB scholar with cross-membership & "0" otherwise), (SSB educational qualification: "1" if at least one SSB scholar with PhD & "0" otherwise), (SSB reputation: "1" if at least one SSB scholar sits on the SSB of AAOIFI and at least two* Shari'ah *board memberships & "0" otherwise) and (SSB expertise: "1" if at least one SSB scholar with experience and knowledge in the field of accounting/economic/finance & "0" otherwise).*
SSB-SIZE = SSB size; SSB-CRM = SSB cross-membership; SSB-DQ = SSB educational qualification; SSB-REP = SSB reputation; SSB-EXPER = SSB expertise.

Table 2.
Measurement of variables.

for endogeneity, and thereby GMM can be used to control for this issue [37, 38]. To test the hypotheses, the following regression model is employed:

$$PERFORM_{it} = \beta_0 PERFORM_{it(-1)} + \beta_1 SSB\text{-}SCORE_{it} + \beta_2 BSIZE_{it} + \beta_3 BAGE_{it} + \beta_4 GDP_{it} + \beta_5 INFLATION_{it} + \varepsilon_{it} \quad (1)$$

$$PERFORM_{it} = \beta_0 PERFORM_{it(-1)} + \beta_1 SSB\text{-}SCORE_{it} + \beta_2 SSB\text{-}SCORE \times CRISIS_{it} + \beta_3 BSIZE_{it} + \beta_4 BAGE_{it} + \beta_5 GDP_{it} + \beta_6 INFLATION_{it} + \beta_7 CRISIS_{it} + \varepsilon_{it} \quad (2)$$

where i indicates the IBs (i = 1, … .,66) and t indicates the annual time period (t = 2007, … .,2015), PERFORM = performance of IBs, SSB-SCORE = *Shari'ah* supervision score, SSB-SCORE × CRISIS = interaction term between SSB score and financial crisis[3], BSIZE = bank size, BAGE = bank age, GDP = gross domestic product, INFLATION = inflation rate, CRISIS = a dummy variable: "1" for the period 2007–2009, "0" otherwise[4] and ε = error term.

[3] Dummy interaction is employed following literature [39].

[4] To capture the crisis impact, dummy interaction is employed following literature, in which: "1" for the period 2007–2009, otherwise "0" [31].

4. Analysis and findings

4.1 Descriptive statistics

The results of descriptive statistics for the variables are presented in **Table 3**. **Table 3** shows that the mean of dependent variables (ROA and ROE) are 0.358 and 8.776, respectively. **Table 3** depicts that the mean of the SSB-SCORE is 3.399, ranges from 0 to 5. This is in line with the findings of [27] who report that the mean value of SSB-SCORE for GCC and Southeast Asia IBs is 3.500. Turning to the bank and country variables (bank size, bank age, GDP and inflation rate), **Table 3** shows that the mean of these variables are 5.977, 0.983, 4.062 and 5.591, respectively.

4.2 Correlation

Table 4 denotes the Pearson correlation coefficients between the explanatory variables. Based on **Table 4**, the highest correlation is found between INFLATION and SSB-SCORE (r = 0.39). **Table 4** also presents that all the correlation coefficients are less than 0.95; hence, the collinearity between the variables is not a concern, as suggested by [40]. According to **Table 4**, SSB-SCORE shows a significant correlation with BAGE and INFLATION (p = 0.01). Further, INFLATION has a significant

Variables	Mean	Std. dev.	Min	Max
Performance variables				
ROA	0.358	6.372	−45.311	31.953
ROE	8.776	21.819	−73.311	276.738
Explanatory and control variables				
SSB-SCORE	3.399	1.020	0.000	5.000
BSIZE	5.977	0.668	3.335	7.591
BAGE	0.983	0.422	−0.301	1.869
GDP	4.062	2.744	−7.080	12.670
INFLATION	5.591	4.996	−4.900	30.030

Number of IBs = 66; Number of observations = 381. ROA = return on asset; ROE = return on equity; SSB-SCORE = Shari'ah *supervision score, BSIZE = bank size, BAGE = bank age, GDP = gross domestic product, INFLATION = inflation rate.*

Table 3.
Descriptive statistics.

Variables	SSB-SCORE	BSIZE	BAGE	GDP	INFLATION
SSB-SCORE	1				
BSIZE	0.016	1			
BAGE	−0.144***	0.062	1		
GDP	0.051	0.056	0.029	1	
INFLATION	−0.395***	−0.178***	0.187***	−0.041	1

****Correlation is significant at 1%.*

Table 4.
Pearson correlations.

correlation with BSIZE and BAGE ($p = 0.01$). Nomran and Haron [27] found similar correlations for SSB-SCORE with the BAGE and INFLATION and for INFLATION with the BSIZE and BAGE.

4.3 Diagnostic test

To check the existence of the multicollinearity issue, variance inflation factor (VIF), as an indicator of multicollinearity, is used. Multicollinearity test in the data set is performed and no multicollinearity problem is found in the data, as the VIF of variables is less than 10 (refer **Table 5**). Based on this, there is no concern of multicollinearity among the set of explanatory variables.

4.4 Hypotheses test

Table 5 presents the regression results examining the study hypotheses based on the two-step system-GMM. Based on **Table 5**, the diagnostic tests show that the two models (1 & 2) are well fitted as AR(1) and AR(2) satisfy the conditions that there is first-order autocorrelation but no second-order, as suggested by the literature [32]. **Table 5** also depicts that the models (1 & 2) are well fitted with statistically significant test statistics for the Wald test, indicating that the instruments are valid in the GMM estimation for the measurements (ROA, ROE) (Model 1: $p = 0.00$, 0.00; Model 2: $p = 0.00$, 0.00).

Additionally, the Hansen *J*-statistic test does not reject the null hypothesis at any conventional level of significance for the two measurements (ROA, ROE) (Model 1: $p = 0.59$, 0.59; Model 2: $p = 0.70$, 0.35), indicating that all the models have valid instrumentation. Finally, in line with the rule of thumb [41], the number of instruments does not outnumber the number of groups in all the models.

As expected in the first hypothesis (H_1), SSB score is reported to relate positively to performance as measured by ROA and ROE (Model 1: at $p = 0.05$, 0.01); thus, the first hypothesis is supported. This result is in support of literature such as Nomran and Haron [27] who found a positive impact for the SSB score on the performance of Southeast Asia IBs.

For the second hypothesis (H_2), a positive relationship is found between the SSB score and performance in the presence of the financial crisis for all the measurements (ROA, ROE) (all at $p = 0.05$); the second hypothesis is, thus, supported but not at 1% level of significance. This result is consistent with the findings of [15], who found a positive and significant impact for SSB supervision on the IBs' performance during the financial crisis. The results indicate that SSBs slightly enhance IBs' performance during the financial crisis period. According to Mollah et al. [15], a possible justification for this positive effect is related to the SG structure of IBs that helps them undertake higher risks and decrease the effect of the crisis on their profitability. Ben Zeineb and Mensi [42] also found that the governance structure of IBs allows them to take higher risks to achieve a high efficiency level. Abedifar et al. [43] believe that components of IBs' governance systems may protect them from the problems faced by CBs.

The findings, therefore, suggest that an increase in SSB effectiveness increases IBs' performance even during the crisis periods. For this, the IBs, policymakers and practitioners should consider these findings when aiming to improve SG practices in the Islamic banking industry, which in turn may help in protecting IBs during crisis and non-crisis periods. They should give due importance to SSB characteristics (size, cross-membership, educational qualification, reputation and expertise) in

Model	(1)		(2)	
Variables	**ROA**	**ROE**	**ROA**	**ROE**
Constant	−10.256*** [0.000]	−67.202*** [0.000]	−5.346 [0.191]	−36.405** [0.014]
ROA (−1)	0.343*** [0.000]	—	0.404*** [0.000]	—
ROE (−1)	—	0.384*** [0.000]	—	0.396** [0.017]
SSB-SCORE	1.156** [0.025]	6.947*** [0.003]	0.875** [0.026]	4.420* [0.072]
SSB-SCORE × CRISIS	—	—	5.070** [0.049]	30.528** [0.031]
BSIZE	0.927*** [0.000]	6.738*** [0.000]	0.432 [0.423]	3.157 [0.282]
BAGE	0.465 [0.117]	1.331 [0.537]	0.160 [0.798]	2.085 [0.656]
GDP	−0.114 [0.223]	−0.213 [0.654]	−0.128 [0.281]	−0.267 [0.775]
INFLATION	0.160*** [0.001]	1.268*** [0.000]	0.081 [0.226]	1.010*** [0.004]
CRISIS	—	—	−19.974* [0.060]	−105.700** [0.044]
Wald test (*p*-value) $\chi 2$ statistic	781.260*** (0.000)	155.370*** (0.000)	259.690*** (0.000)	119.410*** (0.000)
Hansen test (*p*-value)	15.000 (0.595)	16.020 (0.591)	14.420 (0.701)	8.910 (0.350)
AR(1) (*p*-value)	−1.760* (0.079)	−1.750* (0.079)	−1.770* (0.078)	−1.720* (0.086)
AR(2) (*p*-value)	1.050 (0.292)	1.520 (0.128)	1.110 (0.266)	1.510 (0.130)
No. of instruments	24	25	27	17
No. of groups	62	62	62	62
No. of observations	263	278	264	277
VIF	VIF	VIF	VIF	VIF
SSB-SCORE	1.21	1.20	1.43	1.44
BSIZE	1.06	1.05	1.07	1.06
BAGE	1.08	1.07	1.10	1.10
GDP	1.03	1.02	1.04	1.02
INFLATION	1.25	1.25	1.27	1.26

The GMM model includes one lag of the dependent variables. Standard coefficients are presented (p-values in *parentheses).*
****, ** and * are the* p-values *significant at 1, 5, and 10%, respectively.*
ROA = return on assets; ROE = return on equity; SSB-SCORE = Shari'ah *supervision score, BSIZE = bank size, BAGE = bank age, GDP = gross domestic product, INFLATION = inflation rate. Model (1): Shows Eq. (1); Model (2): Shows Eq. (2). Stata software was used for analyzing hypothesis test based on System-GMM.*

Table 5.
SSB and IBs' performance in the presence of the financial crisis: two-step system-GMM estimation.

enhancing the performance of IBs. Regarding the appropriate SG structure, some empirical studies have been conducted in this context. Nomran and Haron [2] suggested that SSB size of IBs should neither be lesser than three nor greater than six. Further, Nomran and Haron [27] confirmed that IBs should balance the number of SSB scholars with experience in *Shari'ah*, as well as in law, accounting and finance. They also indicated that scholars with PhD in *Shari'ah* and law are more associated to enhance IBs' performance. Finally, they indicated that IBs should restrict the scholars' memberships across SSBs.

5. Conclusion

The importance of CG implementations has increased in the business environment especially after the financial crises: The Asian financial crisis of 1997 and the global financial crisis of 2008. Poor CG of financial institutions is considered to be one of the main causes of the financial crisis of 2008, and this CG weakness was not limited to the CBs, but IBs also suffered from this problem because their implementation of CG practices is still weak. Indeed, CG structure of IBs differs from its conventional counterparts as it follows *Shari'ah*-compliant characteristics and is closely guided by the SSBs. This extra layer of governance in the IBs modifies their governance structure from "single-layer" as in the conventional ones into "multi-layer" governance. This makes the establishment of an SSB essential for the IBs. Providing an efficient *Shari'ah* supervision is crucial to the IBs as failing to do so may give negative impact on the Islamic finance industry as a whole.

However, studies investigating the impact of the financial crisis of 2008 in the SSB context are very little, and hence, this chapter aims to examine SSBs' supervision effect on IBs' performance during the financial crisis of 2008. Based on the GMM estimation, the findings indicate that IBs with strong SSB supervision are likely to improve IBs' performance during the crisis and non-crisis periods.

It is expected that providing empirical evidence on this issue would help the IBs in developing their strategies to adopt appropriate SG structure that can enhance their performance during crisis and non-crisis periods. Therefore, the IBs, policymakers and practitioners should consider the strong SSB supervision when aiming to improve SG practices in the Islamic banking industry. More specifically, the IBs, policymakers and practitioners should give due importance to SSB (size, cross-membership, educational qualification, reputation and expertise) in enhancing the performance of IBs during the crisis and non-crisis periods. However, the main limitation of the study is that it only focuses on a sample of 66 IBs over 18 countries due to lack of data.

Author details

Naji Mansour Nomran[1*] and Razali Haron[2]

1 Department of Finance and Banking, Faculty of Administrative Sciences, Thamar University, Yemen

2 IIUM Institute of Islamic Banking and Finance (IIiBF), International Islamic University, Malaysia

*Address all correspondence to: naji_nomran@yahoo.com

References

[1] Safiullah M, Shamsuddin A. Risk in Islamic banking and corporate governance. Pacific-Basin Finance Journal. 2018;**47**(1):129-149

[2] Nomran NM, Haron R. Shari'ah supervisory board's size impact on performance in the Islamic banking industry. Journal of Islamic Accounting and Business Research. 2020a;**11**(1): 110-129

[3] Abdelsalam O, Dimitropoulos P, Elnahass M, Leventis S. Earnings management behaviors under different monitoring mechanisms: The case of Islamic and conventional banks. Journal of Economic Behavior & Organization. 2016;**132**(1):155-173

[4] Mohammed NSAS, Muhammed J. The relationship between agency theory, stakeholder theory and Shariah supervisory board in Islamic banking: An attempt towards discussion. Humanomics. 2017;**33**(1):75-83

[5] Grais W, Pellegrini M. Corporate governance and Shari'ah compliance in institutions offering Islamic financial services. World Bank Policy Research Working Paper. 2006. p. 4054

[6] Ahmed H. Islamic banking and Shari'ah compliance: A product development perspective. Journal of Islamic Finance. 2014;**3**(2):15-29

[7] Ginena K. Shari'ah risk and corporate governance of Islamic banks. Corporate Governance. 2014;**14**(1):86-103

[8] Hamza H. Sharia governance in Islamic banks: Effectiveness and supervision model. International Journal of Islamic and Middle Eastern Finance and Management. 2013;**6**(3):226-237

[9] Grassa R. Shari'ah supervisory systems in Islamic finance institutions across the OIC member countries: An investigation of regulatory frameworks. Journal of Financial Regulation and Compliance. 2015;**23**(2):135-160

[10] Ghayad R. Corporate governance and the global performance of Islamic banks. Humanomics. 2008;**24**(3): 207-216

[11] Ahmed Abdel Karim R. The independence of religious and external auditors: The case of Islamic banks. Accounting, Auditing & Accountability Journal. 1990;**3**(3):34-44

[12] Islamic Financial Services Act. 2013. Available from: www.bnm.gov.my/documents/act/en_ifsa.pdf

[13] Ullah MH, Khanam R. Whether Shariah compliance efficiency a matter for the financial performance: The case of Islami Bank Bangladesh Limited. Journal of Islamic Accounting and Business Research. 2018;**9**(2):183-200

[14] Kamla R, Rammal HG. Social reporting by Islamic banks: Does social justice matter? Accounting, Auditing & Accountability Journal. 2013;**26**(6): 911-945

[15] Mollah S, Zaman M. Shari'ah supervision, corporate governance and performance: Conventional vs. Islamic banks. Journal of Banking and Finance. 2015;**58**(1):418-435

[16] Bakar MD. Shariah Minds in Islamic Finance. Kuala Lumpur: Amanie Media; 2016

[17] Nomran NM, Haron R. Shari'ah governance for islamic banking: Evidence from diverse regulatory environments. In: Rafay A, editor. Growth and Emerging Prospects of International Islamic Banking. Pennsylvania, US: IGI Global; 2020 Available from: https://www.igi-global.

com/book/growth-emerging-prospects-international islamic/233690

[18] Kassim SH, Majid SA. Impact of financial shocks on Islamic banks: Malaysian evidence during 1997 and 2007 financial crises. International Journal of Islamic and Middle Eastern Finance and Management. 2010;**3**(4): 291-305

[19] Rahman AA, Bukair AA. The influence of the Shariah supervision board on corporate social responsibility disclosure by Islamic banks of Gulf Co-operation Council countries. Asian Journal of Business and Accounting. 2013;**6**(2):65-106

[20] Minton BA, Taillard J, Williamson R. Do independence and financial expertise of the board matter for risk taking and performance? Working paper. Ohio State University; 2010

[21] Peni E, Vähämaa S. Did good corporate governance improve bank performance during the financial crisis? Journal of Financial Services Research. 2012;**41**(1):19-35

[22] Aljifri K, Moustafa M. The impact of corporate governance mechanisms on the performance of UAE firms: An empirical analysis. Journal of Economic and Administrative Sciences. 2007; **23**(2):71-93

[23] Kowalewski O. Corporate governance and corporate performance: Financial crisis (2008). Management Research Review. 2016;**39**(11): 1494-1515

[24] Abatecola G, Farina V, Gordini N. Board effectiveness in corporate crises: Lessons from the evolving empirical research. Corporate Governance. 2014; **14**(4):531-542

[25] Srivastava NK. Does governance structure have any effect on firm performance during the financial crisis: Evidence from selected Indian companies. Journal of Strategy and Management. 2015;**8**(4):368-383

[26] Nomran NM, Haron R. A systematic literature review on Shari'ah governance mechanism and firm performance in Islamic banking. Islamic Economic Studies. 2020;**28**(1). Available from: https://www.emerald.com/insight/content/doi/10.1108/IES-06-2019-0013/full/html

[27] Nomran NM, Haron R. Dual board governance structure and multi-bank performance: A comparative analysis between Islamic banks in Southeast Asia and GCC countries. Corporate Governance: The International Journal of Business in Society. 2019;**19**(6): 1377-1402

[28] Alman M. Shari'ah supervisory board composition effects on Islamic banks' risktaking behaviour. Journal of Banking Regulation. 2012;**14**(1):134-163

[29] Farook S, Hassan K, Lanis R. Determinants of corporate social responsibility disclosure: The case of Islamic banks. Journal of Islamic Accounting and Business Research. 2011;**2**(2):114-141

[30] Nomran NM, Haron R, Hassan R. Bank performance and *Shari'ah* supervisory board attributes by Islamic banks: Does bank size matter? Journal of Islamic Finance. 2017;(Special Issue): 173-186

[31] Hakimi A, Rachdi H, Ben Selma Mokni R, Hssini H. Do board characteristics affect bank performance? Evidence from the Bahrain Islamic banks. Journal of Islamic Accounting and Business Research. 2018;**9**(2): 251-272

[32] Nomran MN, Haron R, Hassan R. Shari'ah supervisory board characteristics effects on Islamic banks'

performance: Evidence from Malaysia. International Journal of Bank Marketing. 2018;**36**(2):290-304

[33] Shibani O, de Fuentes C. Differences and similaritites between corporate governance principles in Islamic banks and conventional banks. Research in International Business and Finance. 2017;**42**(1):1005-1010

[34] Quttainah MA, Almutairi AR. Corporate ethics: Evidence from Islamic banks. Journal of Management and Governance. 2017;**21**(4):815-840

[35] Rahman AS, Haron R. The effect of corporate governance on Islamic banking performance: A Maqasid Shari'ah index approach on Indonesian Islamic banks. Journal of Islamic Finance. 2019;**8**:1-18

[36] Ozcan KS, Papaioannou E, Perri F. Global banks and crisis transmission. Journal of International Economics. 2013;**89**(2):495-510

[37] Haron R. Do Indonesian firms practice target capital structure? A dynamic approach. Journal of Asia Business Studies. 2016;**10**(3):318-334

[38] Haron R. Firm level, ownership concentration and industry level determinants of capital structure in an emerging market: Indonesia evidence. Asian Academy of Management Journal of Accounting and Finance (AAMJAF). 2018;**14**(1):1-23

[39] Afrifa GA, Adesina OO. How does directors' remuneration affect SMEs' performance? Review of Accounting and Finance. 2018;**17**(2):238-258

[40] Gujarati D, Porter D. Basic Econometrics. New York, NY: McGraw-Hill; 2009

[41] Roodman D. A note on the theme of too many instruments. Oxford Bulletin of Economics and Statistics. 2009;**71**(1): 135-158

[42] Ben Zeineb G, Mensi S. Corporate governance, risk and efficiency: Evidence from GCC Islamic banks. Managerial Finance. 2018;**44**(5):551-569

[43] Abedifar P, Molyneux P, Tarazi A. Risk in Islamic banking. Review of Finance. 2013;**17**(6):2035-2096

Chapter 4

Risk Analyses on Islamic Banks in Indonesia

Dimas Bagus Wiranatakusuma, Imamuddin Yuliadi and Ikhwan Victhori

Abstract

This study aims to analyze the risks on Islamic banks in Indonesia by identifying which risk is significantly dominant in triggering other risks to happen. For that purpose, the study uses time series data on a monthly basis from 2010:M1 to 2018: M8. The data are obtained from the Financial Services Authority (OJK) Indonesia and analyzed using vector autoregression (VAR). Some variables are employed to proxy risk vulnerability including financing-to-deposit ratio (FDR) as a proxy of liquidity risk, nonperforming financing (NPF) as a proxy of financing risk, and cost-to-income ratio (BOPO) as a proxy of operational risk. The findings suggest that financing risk is the most dominant risk triggering vulnerability on Islamic banks in Indonesia.

Keywords: liquidity risk, financing risk, operational risk, Islamic banks, Indonesia

1. Introduction

In 1997, the financial crisis began in Thailand and had destroyed economies of Asian countries, especially countries that had similar economic typologies. This crisis was triggered by speculators who launched a barrage of "attacks" on the Thai currency. Its currency became more deteriorated as the economic structure of Thai currency was not accompanied by strengthening in the real sector [1].

Given such important aspect on exchange rate stability, Bello et al. [2] argue that the efficiency of risk management practices on currency volatility can be sought as the main reason for a banking collapse. The banking collapse is mainly due to mismatch problem in its balance sheet. The balance sheet becomes imbalance as the growth of its assets linked to foreign currency is not as equal as the growth of its liabilities linked to foreign currency. Consequently, risks such as liquidity risk, credit risk, and operational risk are appeared. These risks will impair gradually the bank's balance sheet; hence, this condition would need a special treatment and force a bank into a critical level until it receives bailout funds. Subsequently, when the risks were not mitigated properly, it might transmit into financial system and economic at large.

One example of the impact on banking failure into financial crisis was in August 2007. A financial crisis started when one of the largest French banks announced a freeze of some securities in the United States concerning high-risk housing loans (subprime mortgage). This incident triggered a decline in the level of public confidence in the banking sector and led to bank failures around the world.

Liquidity crisis causes declining in the household and corporate sectors' confidence toward economic conditions. The long-term pressure on banking sector had flowed to currency depreciation, strong inflationary pressures, and rising interest rates [3].

Looking at the severe impact of banking failure, it can be traced out from to what extent the risk is systematically related among systems. According to Bank Indonesia [4], the systemic risk is the main reason on severe impact from the banking failure as it causes instability as a result of contagion in some or all financial systems. The systemic risk happens due to dynamic interaction components within a financial system referring to theirs size, complexity, interconnectedness of institutions and financial markets, and excessive behavioral tendencies from actors or financial institutions to follow the economic cycle (*procyclicality*).

Given such dynamic circumstances, it can trigger banking sector vulnerability and jeopardize economic growth through uncontrolled banking risks. Some common and influential risks in banking sector include the following: *First*, liquidity risk refers to banks that cannot meet the needs of customers due to mismatch balance sheets. According to the Banker Association for Risk Management, liquidity risk is influenced by several factors, including accuracy of cash flow planning, accuracy in managing funds, availability of assets that are ready to be converted into cash, and the ability to create access to the interbank market. Financing-to-deposit ratio (FDR) is used to proxy the liquidity risk given that it represents the potential of liquidity shortage.

Second, credit risk is the risk of loss due to the failure of the counterparties to fulfill their obligations. Credit risk arises from a variety of functional bank activities, such as credit (financing in Islamic banks), treasury activities (placement of funds between banks, buying corporate bonds), and activities related to investment and trade financings. Nonperforming financing (NPF) is used as a proxy to measure credit risk due to greater NPF, which indicates bank vulnerability as it can erode bank's capital through a gradual decrease in profitability.

Third, operational risk is the risk caused by inadequate or non-functioning internal processes, due to human error or technological system failure and external events that affect the bank's operational performance. According to Aldasoro et al. operational risk represents a significant portion of the total bank risks in the banking sector. In this regard, it needs to be measured by considering operational losses compared to operational income, which is proxied by a cost-to-income ratio (BOPO) variable.

The potential risk arising in the banking sector is based on basic banking operational framework. In the case of Islamic bank, **Figure 1** shows the sequential processes which embed risks in every step involved. Bank as a financial intermediary has the main function in connecting left-hand side (funding side) and right-hand side (financing side). The connection implies a build-up risk given that a balance sheet mismatch occurs. Referring to **Figure 1**, number 1 is connected to numbers 2, 3, and 4, which indicates funds deposited are subsequently utilized for financing purposes. Mismatches can be due to dominant proportion between right-hand and left-hand sides. The higher proportion on the left-hand side implies excessive

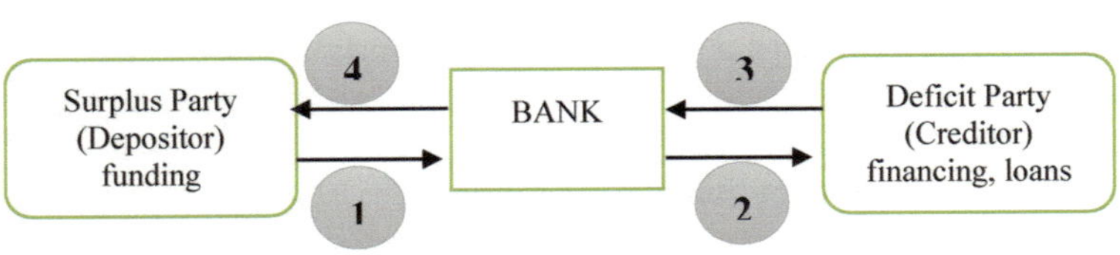

Figure 1.
Islamic banking as a financial intermediary. Sources: Bank Indonesia [5]. 1. Money deposited; 2. Money withdrawal; 3. Financing contract; 4. Profit loss sharing.

unutilized funds, which will burden the bank's balance sheet as profit diminishes, while the greater proportion on the left-hand side implies excessive utilized funds than deposited funds. Therefore, the imbalance, which potentially occurs as continuous banking operation, will always create risks, in the form of financing risk, liquidity risk, or operational risk.

Although Islamic banking cannot avoid from risk promulgation, there is no adequate evidence on what the source of risk which can lead to balance sheet's vulnerability. The existing literature however mainly focuses on factors that lead to build-up risk in Islamic banking. For example, studies by Abdullah [6], Abedifar et al. [7], Adrian and Hyun (2013), Alessi and Detken [8], and Ardiansyah et al. [9] specifically merely elaborate the determinants of risks and their relationship with a particular risk, such as credit, liquidity, and operational risks. In addition, other studies by Avdjiev et al. [10], Aysan et al. [11], and Borio [12] focus on the relationship of bank's risks with its stakeholders without taking peculiar attention to which risks frequently arise. Therefore, this study will close the gap by empirically examining what is the dominant risk in the Islamic banking given the dynamic and interrelated sides—funding and financing sides—on its operation. For that purpose, three main risks are observed—credit, liquidity, and operational—given that those risks are financially connected to Islamic banking operation. Finally, this paper contributes to the literature on risk management by investigating empirically what is the dominant risks, which are quite lacking, particularly looking at Indonesia's case. Hopefully, findings of the paper share benefits to bankers, depositors, investors, and regulators when taking decisions related to the Islamic banking industry.

2. Literature review

Risk arises when there is an unknown or unclear outcome and usually disrupts a particular system. According to Misman [13], risk is the volatility of unexpected results or variability. Risk can be divided into two types, systematic risk and unsystematic risk where numerically it can be measured by standard deviation of historical results. The main risks in the banking system, including Islamic banking, are credit and liquidity risks. The credit cycle, a mismatch of balance sheets [12], and funding constraints [14] are some of the triggering factors for risk exposures. These factors could deteriorate the banking system as a result of an inability to diversify their portfolios [15] and loan syndication [16]. Therefore, to manage risks in the banking system, credit risk and liquidity risk should be linked with the rate of growth of a bank's aggregate balance sheets that remain surplus (high liquidity borrowers and short-term debt) [17–20].

According to Wiranatakusuma and Duasa [21], there are two important risks that are embedded in Islamic bank, which include liquidity risk and credit risk. Credit risk issues are related to banking operations amidst high-nonperforming loans. Banks as financial intermediaries have to meet short-term obligations. When a bank fails to settle its obligations, that means the bank is at risk of bankruptcy. When there is long failure of insolvency situation, the capital will be affected due to the emergency need in maintaining operations and the systematic risk mitigation. Therefore, credit risk is followed by operational risk as capital is gradually eroded. Subsequently, insolvency in financing disbursement would affect the left-hand side (bank-depositor relationship) as the bank is unable to settle its deposited funds' return. It was the signal that the bank is facing liquidity problem due to balance sheet's mismatch.

Therefore, to further clarify the credit, liquidity, and operational risks, some studies explain as follows:

2.1 Liquidity risk

The definition of liquidity risk can be broadly defined as the ability to meet cash at an appropriate cost. Liquidity is important for banks to carry out their business transactions, address urgent needs, satisfy customer demands for loans, and provide flexibility in achieving attractive and profitable investment opportunities. For that purpose, Islamic bank needs to implement liquidity management practices in order to mitigate the potential risk occurrence. According to Sholikhah [22], banking liquidity management is about how banks can fulfill both current liabilities and future liabilities in the event of an asset liability withdrawal or repayment. In other words, the liquidity risk appears in accordance with the agreement which has not been agreed (unexpected) previously. Therefore, bank liquidity management is required to liability management through which banks can convince the depositors concerning their fund withdrawal at any time or at maturity. Hence, looking at the potential mismatch between assets and liabilities, the banking sector needs to monitor the potential liquidity risk through its financing-to-deposit ratio or FDR variable.

2.2 Credit risk

Credit risk is a major source of financial systems. According to the Indonesia Banks Association [23], credit risk is the risk of losses due to failure of counterparties to fulfill their obligations. Usually this risk comes from several banking functional activities such as credit or financing. Nowadays, the productive assets of banks are dominated by loans, while the most important sources of bank funds are from third-party funds or DPK so that if there is a significant increase in credit risk to banks, the influence on bank performance will be severe as the pressure from deposited funds. Hence, due to connected sources between deposited and disbursed funds, the potential loss due to financing activities must be controlled by monitoring nonperforming financing or NPF variable.

2.3 Operational risk

Operational risk affects basically the ability of banking sector to generate profits and its capacity to adjust revenues and expenses. Operational risks are triggered from banking sector activities in the midst of diversity and connectivity. Given that more diverse and competitive banking sectors exist, the banking sector tends to excessively generate assets as profit maximization motive. However, the lack of system and human capacity necessitates more investment or additional cost; otherwise, there will be less competitive and market penetration. Hence, the banking sector needs to properly monitor the ratio between its cost and revenue to ensure its sustainability and continuous profitability. The BOPO is variable to identify the potential operation risk in Islamic banking.

3. Data and methodology

3.1 Research objective and data type

The object in this study is Islamic banking in Indonesia. Its risks are analyzed by time series data published by Bank Indonesia and the Financial Services Authority Indonesia. The data spanned from January 2010 to August 2018 due to the new phase of the new normal of global economy where the global economy starts to increase after the global financial crises indicated by the growth of East Asian country and China economy, including in Indonesia. The new normal refers to the business cycle (expansion, peak, recession, trough, and recovery phase).

3.2 Data collecting techniques

According to the embedded risks in the banking sector, this study employs three main variables that are the proxies of the three main risks, including financing, liquidity, and operational risks. The FDR, NPF, and BOPO are used to proxy the observed risks.

3.3 Operational definition of observed variables

The operational definition of these variables is as follows:

3.3.1 FDR

FDR is a ratio that shows banking intermediaries and proxies to the liquidity of Islamic banks. The FDR is computed by dividing the total amount of financing with the total third-party funds. The FDR in Islamic bank is used to measure the capabilities of Islamic banking to meet the repayment of deposits upon maturity or without any delays. If the FDR is more than 1, it means that the total financing provided by the bank exceeds the funds collected from depositors. This situation has the potential risk to cause liquidity risk for Islamic banks. The FDR is formulated as follows:

$$FDR = \frac{Total\ Financing}{Total\ Third\ Party\ Funds\ collected} \times 100\% \tag{1}$$

3.3.2 NPF

NPF is the amount of unclaimed credit and represents the low quality of banks' assets. This variable is the ratio between the total nonperforming financing and the total financing provided by Islamic banks. The NPF is a nonperforming financing consisting of financing classified due to the lack of transparency and doubt in repayment. Usually the NPF value is the result of the failure of the debtors to fulfill their obligations. Bank Indonesia stipulated a 5% limit for Islamic banks concerning the NPF value. Technically, the NPF is formulated as follows:

$$NPF = \frac{Non\ Performing\ Financing}{Total\ Financing} \times 100\% \tag{2}$$

3.3.3 The BOPO

The BOPO measures the efficiency and ability of the bank to generate profits from its business activities. A smaller BOPO represents the fact that banks can cover their expenses by using their operational revenues. The BOPO is formulated as follows:

$$CIR = \frac{Total\ Operating\ Expenses}{Total\ Operating\ Revenue} \times 100\% \tag{3}$$

3.4 Research estimation method

Research problems will be analyzed by using vector autoregression (VAR), which is based on the risk of Islamic banks. Technically, if the data is found stationary at the first difference, the VAR model will be then combined with the error correction model becoming the vector error correction model (VECM). This study refers to the previous study, such as by Ascarya which mathematically develops a general model as:

Risk on Islamic bank, which is formulated as follows:

$$FDR_t = \Phi_0 + \Phi_1 NPF_t + \Phi_2 BOPO_t \tag{4}$$

$$NPF_t = \Phi_0 + \Phi_1 BOPO_t + \Phi_2 FDR_t \tag{5}$$

$$BOPO_t = \Phi_0 + \Phi_1 FDR_t + \Phi_2 NPF_t \tag{6}$$

where FDR_t is the financing-to-deposit ratio; NPF_t is the nonperforming financing; and $BOPO_t$ is the cost-to-income ratio.

3.5 Research model and analysis method

The data analysis technique involves a technique that analyzes data and tests its validity [24]. This study uses parametric inferential statistical techniques, specifically the vector error correction model (VECM) method. It is used to determine the relationship either in the short- or in the long-term relationship among variables. In terms of the research design, the steps for data analysis technique are as follows:

3.5.1 Testing stationary data

The first step that must be done in the VECM estimation is to test stationary data. The data can be declared stationary if the time series data have a tendency to move toward the average. According to Kuncoro [25], those data are stationary when they are drawn against time. It will often pass through the horizontal axis, and autocorrelation will decrease regularly for a considerable lag. Subsequently, the data are considered as stationary if it meets the following two conditions:

a. The average covariance is constant over time.

b. Covariance between two data sequences depends on lags between the two periods.

According to Basuki [26], to test the data stationarity, the augmented Dick-Fuller (ADF) test is used. If the t-ADF value is smaller than the MacKinnon critical value, it can be concluded that the data used are stationary or do not contain unit roots. The testing of the roots of this unit is carried out at the level up to the first difference. If the data level is not statistically achieved, a first difference test is necessary.

3.5.2 Selecting lag length criteria

Time (lag) in economics is used to explain the dependence of one variable on another variable. The determination of lag length is done to determine the parameter estimates in VECM. In the VECM estimation, the causality relationship is strongly influenced by lag length. In addition, Basuki and Yuliadi [27] also explained that if the lag entered is too short, it is feared that the resulted estimation is inaccurate. Conversely, if the lag entered is too long, it will produce inefficient estimation results. The determination of optimum lag length is then important and can be computed by using EViews software.

3.5.3 Testing the stability of VAR models

Before testing VAR estimation, a stability test must first be carried out. According to Basuki and Yuliadi [27], the stability of the model needs to be tested because it will affect the results of impulse response function (IRF) and variance decomposition (VDC). If stability is not tested, the results of the IRF and VDC analysis are invalid. A VAR system can be said to be stable or fulfill a stability test if the value of the entire root or root has a modulus smaller than one. In this study, it is known that the modulus value is less than one, which means that the result from IRF and VDC analyses is valid.

3.5.4 Testing cointegration test

A cointegration test is the test intended to see whether there is a long-term relationship between a particular variable and another variable. In the VECM estimation, a cointegration test is very necessary to determine whether each variable has a relationship in the long-term or just short-term relationship. Technically, if the observed variables do not have a cointegration relationship, then the VECM estimation does not apply. If, the opposite, data had a relationship in the long term (cointegration), then VECM is applied.

According to Basuki and Yuliadi [27] as stated by Engle-Granger, the existence of non-stationary variables causes the possibility of a long-term relationship between variables in the system. The cointegration test is performed to determine the existence of the relationship between variables, especially in the long term. If there were cointegration on the variables used in the model, it can be ascertained that there is a long-term relationship between the variables. The *Johansen cointegration* method can be then used to test the existence of this cointegration.

3.5.5 Applying VECM

The VECM is a derivative model of VAR. The difference between VAR and VECM is the VECM estimations, particularly in measuring cointegration condition. If there is a cointegration relationship between variables, it indicates a long-term relationship [27]. VECM is often referred for non-stationary series that has a cointegration relationship. The VECM specification limits the relationship of endogenous variables in the long run to remain convergent in cointegration relationships, but still considers the existence of short-term relationships. The process for deciding on the VECM method can be seen in **Figure 2**.

3.5.6 Applying IRF

The IRF analysis was conducted to check the shock response of each variable. Therefore, the effect of shock from one variable can be explained clearly against other variables. The IRF results prove how long it takes from one variable to respond to the other variable.

3.5.7 Applying VDC

VDC analysis aims to measure the size of the contribution or composition of the influence of each variable to other variable. VDC analysis will provide information

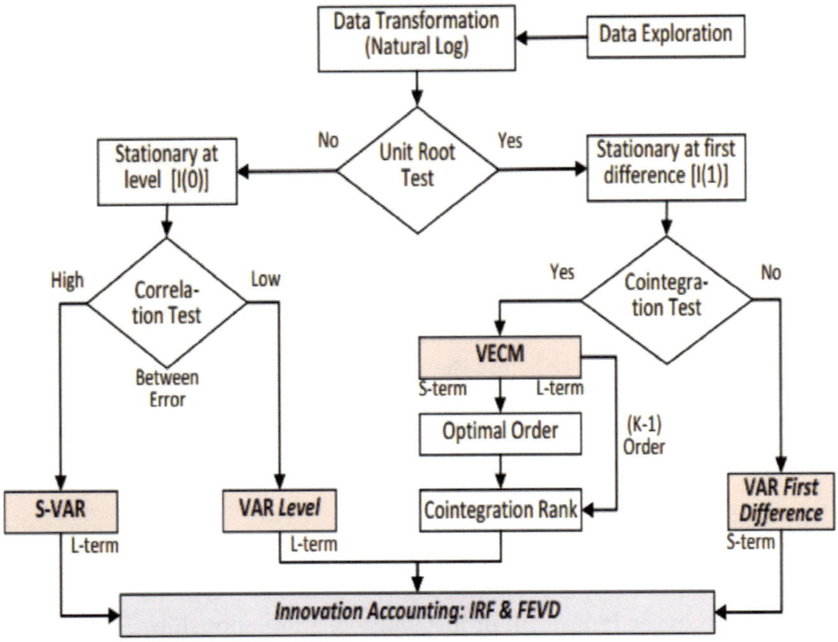

Figure 2.
Vector error correction model. Source: Gujarati [28].

about the magnitude and duration of the shock proportion of a variable to the variable itself and to other variables. According to Basuki [26], variance decomposition aims to measure the magnitude of the contribution or composition of the influence of each independent variable on the dependent variable.

3.5.8 Testing Granger causality

According to Basuki [26], the Granger causality test is used to see whether two variables have a reciprocal relationship or not. The variable can have a causal relationship with other variables significantly. It implies each variable has the opportunity to become an endogenous or exogenous variable.

4. Result and analysis

4.1 Causality test and data instruments

4.1.1 Unit root test

The VECM estimation is started by testing the data stationarity of each variable as the initial process. To detect the stationarity of each variable, the ADF test is used with the intercept model. Data sets are declared stationary if the average values and variants of the time series data do not change systematically over time or the averages and their variants are constant [29]. The ADF stationary test for each variable can be indicated as follows.

According to **Table 1**, at the level, there is no single variable that meets stationary requirements, either from FDR, NPF, or BOPO. It is indicated by the value of t-ADF which is greater than the Mackinnon critical value, so it is necessary to test at the first difference level shown in **Table 2**.

Based on **Table 2**, it can be concluded that all variables are stationary at the *first difference* with a predetermined critical value (α = 5%), as follows:

a. The FDR variable in the *first difference* level test shows that the ADF t-statistic value is smaller than the *MacKinnon critical value* 5%, which is −11.55782 < −2.890037, which means H_0 is rejected and H_1 is accepted or the FDR variable data is stationary.

b. The NPF variable in the *first difference* level test shows that the ADF t-statistic value is smaller than the *MacKinnon critical value* 5%, which is −4.724193 < −2.890623, which means H_0 is rejected and H_1 is accepted or the NPF variable data is stationary.

c. The BOPO variable at the first difference level test shows that the ADF t-statistic value is smaller than the MacKinnon critical value 5%, which is −11.03276 < −2.890037, which means H_0 is rejected and H_1 is accepted or the BOPO variable data are stationary.

From the above tests, all variables have met data stationary. The ADF t-statistics are smaller than the McKinnon critical value 5% at the first difference level. Therefore, the next step is to estimate the data by VECM by selecting its lag length criteria.

4.1.2 Lag length criteria

The lag length is used to determine the effect of the time taken from each variable on the past variable. The selected lag candidates are the length of lag according to the *likelihood ratio* (LR) criterion, *final prediction error* (PPE), *Akaike information criterion* (AIC), *Schwarz information criterion* (SIC), and *Hannan-Quinn criterion* (HQC). The determination of the optimal lag length in this study is based

Variable	t-Statistic	The Mackinnon critical value			Prob	Conclusion
		1%	5%	10%		
FDR	−1.011989	−3.495021	−2.889753	−2.581890	0.7440	Non-stationary
NPF	−1.55662	−3.497029	2.890623	−2.582353	0.5009	Non-stationary
BOPO	−1.786319	−3.495021	−2.889753	−2.58189	0.3854	Non-stationary

Sources: Author's calculation.

Table 1.
Unit root test-augmented Dickey-Fuller (level).

Variable	t-Statistic	The Mackinnon critical value			Prob	Conclusion
		1%	5%	10%		
FDR	−11.55782	−3.495677	2.890037	−2.582041	0.0000	Stationary
NPF	−4.724193	3.497029	2.890623	2.582353	0.0002	Stationary
BOPO	−11.03276	−3.495677	2.890037	−2.582041	0.0000	Stationary

Sources: Author's calculation.

Table 2.
Unit root test-augmented Dickey-Fuller (first difference).

on the sequential modified LR test statistical criteria. The lag length that was included in this study is from 0 to 3.

Based on **Table 3**, the optimal lag on all variables from FDR, NPF, and BOPO is in lag 3, that is, with the sequential modified LR test statistic 24.77971, PPE 4.037246, and AIC 9.907182. Therefore, the optimal lag has been statistically determined and the VAR stability test is carried out.

4.1.3 Stability VAR model test

The stability test of the VAR model was used to test IRF and VDC. The stability test for VAR estimation can be seen in **Table 4**.

Based on **Table 4**, it can be explained that the model used is stable in lags of 0–3. This can be seen from the range of modules with an average value of less than one. Therefore, the results of the IRF and VDC analyses are valid, so that the cointegration test can be done.

4.1.4 Cointegration test

The fourth stage that must be passed in the VECM estimation is the cointegration test. Cointegration tests are conducted to determine whether there is a long-term relationship on each variable. If there is no cointegration relationship, the VECM estimation cannot be used. This study uses the Johansen cointegration test method available in EViews 7.2 software with a critical value of 0.05. The cointegration test results are shown in **Table 5** as follows.

Based on **Table 5**, at the 5% test level, there are three ranks of cointegration variables. This can be proven from the values of trace statistic, which are 80.84738,

Lag	LogL	LR	FPE	AIC
0	−502.5902	NA	4.943996	10.11180
1	−491.1235	22.01603	4.706602	10.06247
2	−479.1256	22.31603	4.435183	10.00251
3	−465.3591	24.77971*	4.037246*	9.907182*

Sources: Author's calculation.
**5% level of significance.*

Table 3.
Lag length criteria.

Root	Modules
0.165181–0.446285i	0.475873
0.165181 + 0.446285i	0.475873
−0.239743–0.404530i	0.470235
−0.239743 + 0.404530i	0.470235
−0.239164–0.036076i	0.241869
−0.239164 + 0.036076i	0.241869

Sources: Author's calculation.

Table 4.
Test of VAR stability.

Hypothesized no. of CE(s)	Trace static	Prob	Critical value	Variable
None *	80.84738	0.0000	29.79707	FDR
At most 1 *	36.79544	0.0000	15.49471	NPF
At most 2 *	12.11161	0.0005	3.841466	BOPO

Sources: Author's calculation.
**5% level of significance.*

Table 5.
Cointegration test.

36.79544, and 12.11161 and which are greater than the critical value of 0.05, namely, 29.79707, 15.49471, and 3.841466, respectively. In this regard, H_0 is rejected and H_1 is accepted. It implies that all variables have influence in the long term or are cointegrated with each other. Therefore, the next step is to carry out analysis with the VECM estimation.

4.1.5 VECM estimation

Having tested the existence of VECM, the analysis is to estimate on how short-term and long-term relationships affect each other. The variables of FDR, NPF, and BOPO show the significant effect on lag 3 in monthly data.

Table 6 shows the influence of each variable to other variables, particularly the relationship between FDR with NPF and FDR with BOPO. The short-term estimation results show that the FDR variable is influenced by the NPF variable in lag 1, which has a positive effect of 1.36%. In lag 2, the relationship of the NPF negatively affects FDR for −0.37%. Furthermore, in lag 3, the NPF has a positive effect to FDR with a value of 0.34%. Then, the FDR variable is influenced negatively by the BOPO in the first lag until the third.

Table 6 shows the influence of BOPO and FDR to NPF. Results show that the NPF variable is influenced by the BOPO in the first lag which has a negative effect of −0.01% and the second lag also shows a negative effect of 0.02%. Then, the NPF variable is influenced by the BOPO in the third lag which has a positive effect that is 0.005%. Then, the NPF variable influenced by the FDR variable negatively affects the first lag until lag 3.

Furthermore, **Table 6** shows the relationship between BOPO with FDR and NPF. Empirically, BOPO is influenced positively by the FDR variable in the first and second lags for 0.12 and 0.11%, respectively, but in the third lag, the variables have a negative effect of −0.22%. On the contrary, the BOPO is influenced by the NPF, which has a negative effect on the first lag and third lag, which is −0.95 and − 0.60%, respectively, but in the third lag, it shows a positive effect on the BOPO, namely, 1%.

Table 7 shows the summary of direction among variables. Results generally indicate that NPF has positive effects toward FDR and BOPO. It implies that NPF that is a proxy variable for financing risk could trigger other risk occurrence, namely, liquidity and operational risks, in the short run.

Based on **Table 8**, VECM estimation analyzes the influence of variables in the long term. The FDR variable is influenced by NPF and BOPO variables. In the first lag, the FDR variable was influenced negatively by −72.58%. However, in contrast to the first lag, the FDR variable was influenced positively by BOPO for 9.02%. The NPF variable is influenced by the BOPO variable and the FDR variable. In the first lag, both variables negatively affect the values of 0.12 and 0.01%. The BOPO variables are influenced by FDR and NPF variables. In the first lag, the BOPO variable is

	Variable	Coefficient	t-Statistic partial
FDR	CointEq1	0.001081	[0.17523]
	D(FDR(−1))	−0.255421	[−2.50543]
	D(FDR(−2))	0.038103	[0.37947]
	D(FDR(−3))	0.271292	[2.86236]
	D(NPF(−1))	1.360963	[2.11235]
	D(NPF(−2))	−0.37662	[−0.59751]
	D(NPF(−3))	0.344605	[0.55659]
	D(BOPO(−1))	−0.207859	[−2.93623]
	D(BOPO(−2))	−0.223429	[−3.27360]
	D(BOPO(−3))	−0.01964	[−0.28727]
	C	−0.112072	[−0.60029]
NPF	CointEq1	−0.197484	[−2.69286]
	D(NPF(−1))	−0.081274	[−0.77003]
	D(NPF(−2))	−0.015491	[−0.15002]
	D(NPF(−3))	0.404753	[3.99059]
	D(BOPO(−1))	−0.015403	[−1.32823]
	D(BOPO(−2))	−0.023770	[−2.12593]
	D(BOPO(−3))	0.005957	[0.53189]
	D(FDR(−1))	−0.010509	[−0.62922]
	D(FDR(−2))	−0.015999	[−0.97261]
	D(FDR(−3))	−0.005072	[−0.32666]
	C	−0.008109	[−0.26512]
BOPO	CointEq1	−0.282793	[−3.19815]
	D(BOPO(−1))	0.042771	[0.38050]
	D(BOPO(−2))	0.034201	[0.31558]
	D(BOPO(−3))	0.052325	[0.48200]
	D(FDR(−1))	0.122321	[0.75564]
	D(FDR(−2))	0.119351	[0.74857]
	D(FDR(−3))	−0.224285	[−1.49029]
	D(NPF(−1))	−0.953621	[−0.93213]
	D(NPF(−2))	−0.600455	[−0.59994]
	D(NPF(−3))	1.006292	[1.02358]
	C	0.101554	[0.34256]

Sources: Author's calculation.

Table 6.
VECM in short term.

influenced by the FDR variable which has a positive effect of 0.01%. Then, in the first lag, the BOPO variable is influenced by the NPF variable, which has a negative effect of −8.03%. Therefore, in the long run, only operational risk—proxied by BOPO—affects positively the liquidity risk, proxied by FDR.

Dependent variables	Independent variables		
	NPF	FDR	BOPO
NPF	Positive (lag-3)	Not significant	Negative (lag-2)
FDR	Positive (lag-1)	Negative (lag-2)	Negative (lags-1 and − 2)
BOPO	Positive (lag −3)	Negative (lag-3)	Not significant

Source: Author's calculation.

Table 7.
Summary of direction of influence among variables.

	Variable	Coefficient	t-Static partial
FDR	NPF(−1)	−72.5889	[−4.47911]
	BOPO(−1)	9.029681	[4.64308]
NPF	BOPO	−0.1244	[−7.14765]
	FDR	−0.01378	[−0.67799]
BOPO	FDR	0.110746	[0.75713]
	NPF	−8.038916	[−7.70009]

Sources: Author's calculation.

Table 8.
Vector error correction model (VECM) in long term.

4.1.6 Impulse response function (IRF)

The IRF analysis explains the effects of shocks (shock) on one variable from the other variables, both in the short term and in the long term. The IRF also analyzes on how long the shocks take place. The horizontal axis shows the period of the year, while the vertical axis shows the response value in percentage, as the following details:

4.1.6.1 Impulse response FDR to NPF

The first IRF analysis will explain the response received by the FDR to the *shock* of NPF. According to **Figure 3**, the response of the FDR if there was a shock from NPF is positive (+), where it shows an increase trend from periods 1 to 3. But, then in the 3rd to 10th period, the response of the FDR variable to NPF shock decreased. These results are consistent with findings from VECM estimation either in the short or long run where FDR will be fluctuating in short period and tends to be less volatile in the long run due to shocks from NPF. This condition indicates that liquidity risk in Islamic banks is only influenced by financing risk in the short run and decreases toward equilibrium in the long run.

4.1.6.2 Impulse response FDR to BOPO

Figure 4 shows the response of FDR due to shocks coming from BOPO. Its responses are negative in the first three periods but tend to positive afterward. These conditions are consistent with VECM estimation where in the short run its relationship is negative, but positive in the long run. It indicates that liquidity risk is sensitive in both short and long runs due to shocks originated from operational risk.

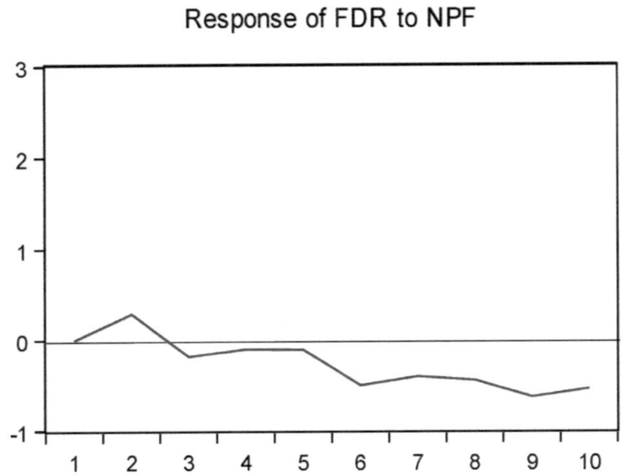

Figure 3.
Impulse response FDR to NPF. Source: Author's calculation.

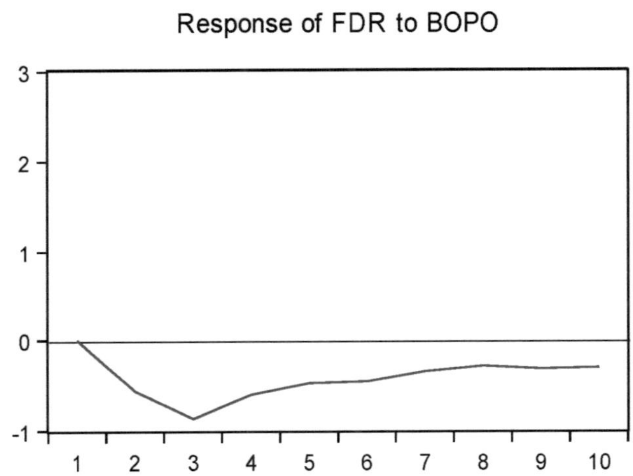

Figure 4.
Impulse response FDR to BOPO. Source: Author's calculation.

4.1.6.3 Impulse response variable NPF to variable FDR

Figure 5 shows the response of NPF due to shocks from FDR. Results indicate that NPF responds negatively but only for less than two periods, and then it is stable toward its long-term movements. These findings are in line with VECM estimation where NPF is significantly affected by FDR in the short run, but not significant in the long run. It implies that financing risk exists and sensitive only in the short run due to liquidity risk, but not in the long run.

4.1.6.4 Impulse response variable NPF to variable BOPO

Figure 6 shows the response of NPF due to shock from BOPO. Results suggest that in the first three periods, NPF responds positively and continues to increase in the long run. These findings are not linear with VECM estimation where NPF is suggested to be negatively influenced by BOPO, either short or long run. Furthermore, the findings suggest that financing risk is quite sensitive toward operational risk.

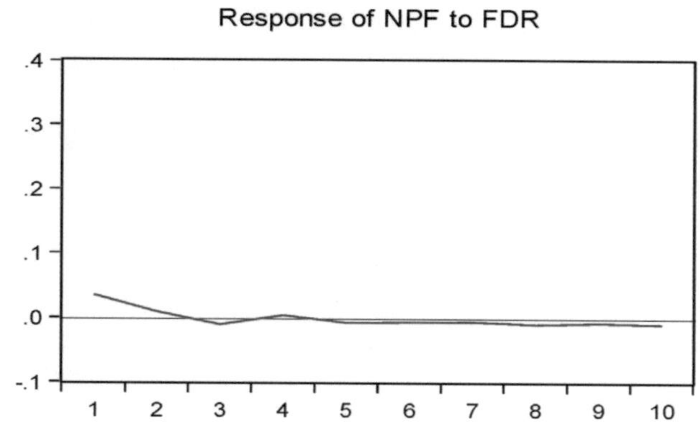

Figure 5.
Impulse response NPF to FDR. Source: Author's calculation.

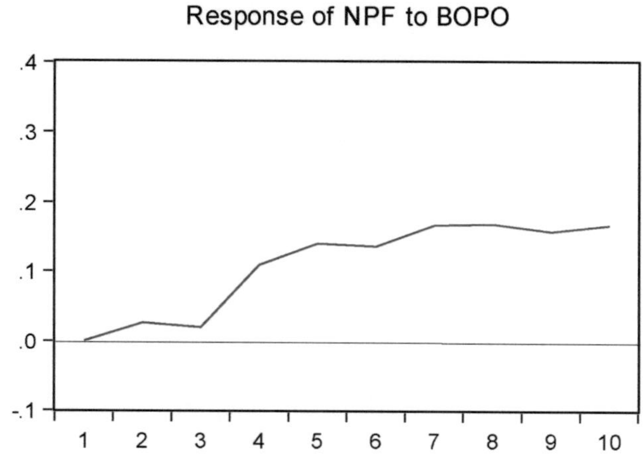

Figure 6.
Impulse response NPF to BOPO. Source: Author's calculation.

4.1.6.5 Impulse response variable BOPO to variable FDR

Figure 7 shows the response of BOPO due to shocks from FDR. The findings suggest initially it responds positively until the first three periods. However, the trend is negative in the long run. These conditions are consistent with VECM estimation where both variables have a negative relationship in the short run, but no relationship in the long run. It indicates that operational risk is only affected in the short run, not in the long run.

4.1.6.6 Impulse response variable BOPO to variable NPF

Figure 8 shows the response of BOPO due to shocks from NPF. The findings suggest that BOPO responds positively in the first four periods due to shocks from NPF, but tend to decline in the long run. In this regard, these findings are consistent with VECM estimation where BOPO is sensitive due to the change of NPF. These conditions also indicate that operational risk is sensitive toward financing risk in Islamic bank.

Table 9 shows the summary of risk sensitivity based on originated shocks into Islamic banks. The findings suggest that the risks in Islamic banks are interrelated to each other, in either the short or long run. Specifically, **Table 9** suggests as follows:

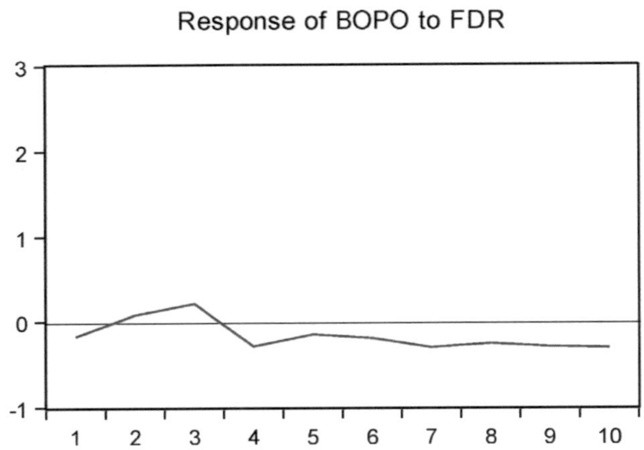

Figure 7.
Impulse response BOPO to FDR. Source: Author's calculation.

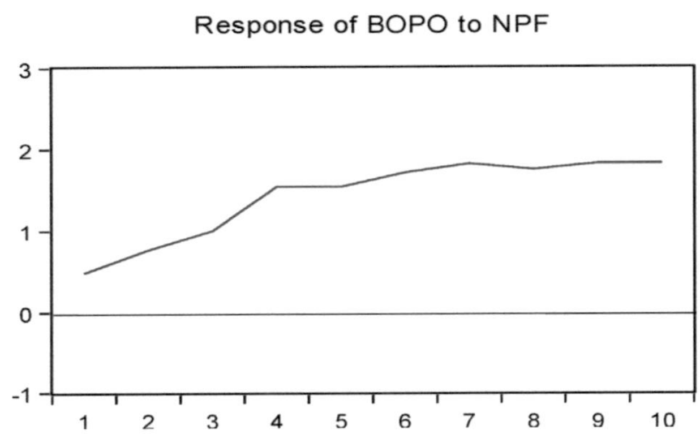

Figure 8.
Impulse response BOPO to NPF. Source: Author's calculation.

a. NPF which is the proxy of financing risk negatively responds shocks from FDR, but positively from BOPO. The former indicates that Islamic banks have conducted sound risk management practices, especially concerning with financing risk in the mid of higher financial intermediaries, while the latter indicates that Islamic banks have high sensitivity of financing risk due to failure in managing operational risk, such us human error, information system, and standard operational procedure.

Sensitivity of risk	Shock originator		
	NPF	FDR	BOPO
NPF—financing risk		Negative (short run)	Positive (short and long runs)
FDR—liquidity risk	Negative (short and long runs)		Negative (short run) and positive (long run)
BOPO—operational risk	Positive (short and long runs)	Positive (short run) and negative (long run)	

Source: Author's calculation.

Table 9.
Summary of impulse response results.

b. FDR which is the proxy of liquidity risk negatively responds originated shocks from both NPF and BOPO. These conditions imply that although the values of NPF and BOPO are high, Islamic banks are able to manage the liquidity risk, shown by negative responses of FDR variable.

c. BOPO which is the proxy of operational risk positively responds positively originated shocks from NPF and FDR. These conditions imply that operational risk in Islamic banks sensitively occurred and risk management procedure needs to be improved. The positive sign indirectly indicates that financing and liquidity risk would easily trigger the operational risk in Islamic banks, which means Islamic banks should take more serious efforts to settle the operational aspects.

4.1.7 Variance decomposition

This analysis aims to measure the composition or contribution of the influence of each variable to other variables. This study focuses on looking at the influence of variables, including FDR, NPF, and BOPO. The findings of VDC are shown as follows.

Table 10 shows the contribution of FDR, NPF, and BOPO toward FDR fluctuations. The findings suggest that FDR fluctuations are mainly influenced by FDR itself, even until the 10th period. Numerically, the shares of other variables are less than 10%. However, although the shares originated from NPF and BOPO are not dominant, any fluctuations of FDR are contributed by other variables. In other words, the liquidity risk existed in Islamic banks is insignificantly contributed by other risks, and it then implies Islamic banks frequently face liquidity problems in their balance sheets. In addition, these findings corroborate the previous findings suggested by impulse response that liquidity risk is negatively affected by financing and operational risks, which means it is mainly caused by liquidity itself (banks' balance sheet mismatch).

Table 11 shows the variance decomposition of NPF due to the fluctuations from NPF itself, FDR, and BOPO. Empirically, the fluctuations of NPF initially are influenced by NPF itself. However, its composition gradually declines as other

Period	SE	FDR	NPF	BOPO
1	1.843409	100.0000	0.000000	0.000000
2	2.433074	93.07333	1.419375	5.507292
3	3.025591	86.88472	1.272146	11.84314
4	3.645556	88.13094	0.948149	10.92091
5	4.108004	89.21504	0.809155	9.975805
6	4.599803	89.21948	1.820409	8.960113
7	5.051028	89.96607	2.130988	7.902945
8	5.459352	90.48151	2.479191	7.039295
9	5.876766	90.34842	3.281494	6.370083
10	6.257649	90.52347	3.623686	5.852848
Total average	4.2300232	90.784298	1.7784593	7.4372431

Sources: Author's calculation.

Table 10.
Variance decomposition of FDR.

Period	SE	FDR	NPF	BOPO
1	0.301986	1.284774	98.71523	0.000000
2	0.375125	0.886743	98.61763	0.495627
3	0.416529	0.785144	98.59483	0.620030
4	0.517248	0.513238	94.73262	4.754143
5	0.579325	0.428273	90.02078	9.550951
6	0.624881	0.380940	86.74632	12.87274
7	0.691786	0.319991	83.37349	16.30652
8	0.742180	0.297634	80.39042	19.31195
9	0.784787	0.277975	78.41862	21.30341
10	0.834778	0.269536	76.93120	22.80826
Total average	0.5868625	0.5444248	88.654114	10.8023631

Sources: Author's calculation.

Table 11.
Variance decomposition of NPF.

variables' shares gradually increase. On the 10th period, the share of NPF stands for 76.93, FDR remains small, but BOPO shares a majority portion around 22.8. These findings imply that financing risk frequently occurs in Islamic banks, and this risk is quite large contributed by the operational risk. In addition, the results strengthen the previous findings obtained through impulse response that financing risk is empirically triggered by operational risk.

Table 12 shows the variance decomposition of BOPO. Empirically, the results suggest that initially the fluctuation on BOPO is contributed by BOPO itself, but gradually other variables influence it. Until the 10th period, BOPO fluctuations are dominantly attributed by NPF for around 46.42%, but with a negligible portion of FDR. It implies that operational risk in Islamic banks is mainly contributed by financing risk and a small portion from liquidity risk.

Period	SE	FDR	NPF	BOPO
1	2.927100	0.357969	2.680542	96.96149
2	3.735015	0.265543	5.788679	93.94578
3	4.198097	0.466521	10.22600	89.30747
4	4.645547	0.781165	19.34129	79.87754
5	5.026835	0.754420	25.87602	73.36956
6	5.431698	0.777258	32.08065	67.14209
7	6.226521	0.940389	37.36899	61.69062
8	6.226521	1.003506	40.89494	58.10156
9	6.612534	1.089031	43.87340	55.03757
10	6.985251	1.172802	46.13966	52.68754
Total average	5.2015119	0.7608604	26.4270171	72.812122

Sources: Author's calculation.

Table 12.
Variance decomposition of BOPO.

Dependent variables	Independent variables		
	NPF	FDR	BOPO
NPF	76.93120	0.269536	22.80826
FDR	3.623686	90.52347	5.852848
BOPO	46.13966	1.172802	52.68754

Source: Author's calculation.

Table 13.
The summary of variance of decomposition at the 10th period (%).

Table 13 shows the summary of variance decomposition function at the 10th period. The findings suggest that the main risk that triggers Islamic bank is liquidity risk, while other risks that show the highest contribution toward risk vulnerability are financing risk and operational risk. Therefore, Islamic banks will always face these risks, and they are categorized as the core or main risk in Islamic banks, particularly in Indonesia.

4.1.8 The Granger causality test

The Granger causality test is used to determine the causal relationship of each variable with other variables. The test level used in the Granger causality test is the level of confidence ($\alpha = 0.05$) with lag length 2, according to the optimal lag length that has been done previously. Results of the Granger causality test are as follows.

Table 14 shows the causality between variables with various probability values. The findings suggest that the variables have one-directional relationship, namely:

a. There is one-directional relationship between NPF and FDR. It means that the vulnerability in Islamic banks due to liquidity risk is empirically caused by financing risk. This finding strengthens the previous findings obtained through VECM estimation and IRF that financing risk affects the liquidity risk though its relationship is negative and small.

b. There is one-directional relationship between BOPO and FDR. It means that the vulnerability in Islamic banks due to liquidity risk is empirically caused by operational risk. This finding corroborates the previous findings that liquidity

H0	Lag 2	
	f-Statistic	Prob
NPF does not Granger cause FDR	**5.44792**	**0.0057**
FDR does not Granger cause NPF	1.67488	0.1927
BOPO does not Granger cause FDR	**7.97421**	**0.0006**
FDR does not Granger cause BOPO	0.16992	0.8440
BOPO does not Granger cause NPF	2.40254	0.0959
NPF does not Granger cause BOPO	**4.91669**	**0.0092**

Source: Author's calculation.
1% level of significance

Table 14.
The Granger causality test.

risk exists if Islamic banks fail to settle operational problems, especially in the long run.

c. There is one-directional relationship between NPF and BOPO. It means that the vulnerability in Islamic banks due to operational risk is empirically caused by financing risk. This finding strengthens the previous results that operational risk is positively affected by financing risk, either short or long term, with a quite high degree of contribution.

In short, empirically the risks in Islamic banks are mainly caused by financing risk. The one-directional relationship implies that bank's vulnerability exists due to the inability of the bank to manage nonperforming financing. Bank's balance sheet is vulnerable toward any disruptions on financing problems. It is rational in the midst that Islamic banks have limited funds than conventional banks and offer various Islamic contracts. These conditions enable Islamic banks to face systemic risks when a problem occurs on the asset side as both sides are connected according to the bank's balance sheet flow process.

4.2 Analysis

Table 15 summarizes some empirical findings concerning embedded risks in Islamic banks with various assessment methods. In general, there is an interrelated risk in Islamic banks. However, based on several assessment methods, the findings suggest that only financing and operational risks have causal relationship with liquidity and operational risks. The details concerning these relationships are as follows:

4.2.1 Financing risk

According to **Table 15**, the financing risk will affect liquidity risk. The Granger causality test suggests that the one-directional relationship from financing risk to liquidity risk exists. It implies that this causal relationship is triggered by financing side which will affect the liquidity positively in the short run only. This situation is supported by IRF results where any shocks coming from financing side will be negatively responded by liquidity risk. The variance decomposition also informs

Risks	Financing risk → liquidity risk	Operational → liquidity risk	Financing risk → operational risk
Assessment methods			
VECM estimation—short term	Positive, significant (lag-1)	Negative, significant (lag-1 and lag-2)	Positive (lag-3)
VECM estimation—long term	Negative, significant (lag-1)	Positive, not significant (lag-1)	Negative, significant (lag-1)
IRF	Negative (short and long runs)	Negative (short run) and positive (long run)	Positive (short and long runs)
VDC	3.623686	5.852848	46.13966
Granger causality test	Significant	Significant	Significant

Source: Author's calculation.

Table 15.
Summary of empirical findings from various assessments.

that there is a small contribution of risk variation from financing risk to liquidity risk. Therefore, overall findings suggest that Islamic banks are resilient in absorbing shocks when financing side is vulnerable. In other words, Islamic banks are not sensitive to risk originated from financing side as its liquidity is sound. In addition, the findings elaborate that the liquidity management on Islamic banking in Indonesia is strong and resilient against financing risk.

4.2.2 Liquidity risk

Table 15 demonstrates the relationship of liquidity risk with other risks. The Granger causality test suggests that liquidity risk has a directional relationship with financing and operational risks. Given that liquidity risk is affected by other risks, generally it was affected negatively in the short run and positively in the long run, but did not show a significant sign according to VECM estimation. The IRF further explains that even though the liquidity risk gets shocks originated from financing and operational risks, Islamic banks remain resilient. The VDC results also strengthen the findings that the variation on liquidity risk is negligibly contributed by financing and operational risks. In other words, financing and operational risks do not matter for Islamic banks, especially related to liquidity side.

4.2.3 Operational risk

Table 15 shows the general performance of operational risk on Islamic banks in Indonesia. According to the Granger causality test, operational risk exists in Islamic banks where it was influenced by financing risk and liquidity risk. The former indicates that Islamic banks are sensitive toward operational risk particularly due to failure in repayment counterparty obligations. This condition is supported by some empirical evidences including the following: (1) VECM estimation suggests that there is a positive relationship between financing and operational risks only in the short run, but not in the long run. This implies that Islamic banks have adjustment capacity to settle their operational problems when financing problems exist; (2) IRF result explains that operational risk is quite sensitive in Islamic banks as the variation in operational risk is highly contributed by financing risk according to VDC estimations. In short, operational risk in Islamic banks is connected with the ability of Islamic banks to manage their financing allocations. In other words, financing risk matters for Islamic banks.

The latter shows that liquidity risk has a directional causal relationship with liquidity risk. However, some empirical evidences suggest operational problems in Islamic bank are not closely affected by liquidity risk. For example, VECM estimation found no positive and significant influence in either short or long run and small portion variation of liquidity due to operational problems. It implies that liquidity management in Islamic banks is strong and sound in absorbing any shocks from operational risk. In other words, operational risk does not matter for Islamic banks, particularly related to liquidity side.

5. Conclusion, research limitation, and further research

Islamic banking in Indonesia is a new institutional approach in promoting economic development. Although its shares are small, it has been growing rapidly and now becomes a new national policy in spreading growth and prosperity. Islamic banks, technically, have two sides, funding and financing, which are operationally connected and integrated. Given this condition, the potential risks are quite large to occur and might become systematic risk if not well managed. By using the VECM approach, this study investigates what is the main source of risk and how embedded risks in Islamic banks interacted with each other. After conducting sequential steps of analysis for financing, liquidity, and operational risks on Islamic banks in Indonesia since 2010–2018, the findings suggest that (1) liquidity risk is manageable and sound given that Islamic banks can absorb transmitted risk, particularly originated from financing and operational problems, indicated by no liquidity problems exist; (2) financing risk is considered as the strong source triggering operational risk in Islamic banks, and (3) operational risk matters for Islamic banks as it is quite sensitive with the problems from financing side.

Based on the findings, there are some research limitations concerning as follows: (1) the research does not analyze the policy rule concerning the tolerated level of risks, specific to Islamic banks in order to implement intervention for risk mitigation; (2) the research does not investigate the tolerated level of shocks, particularly from macroeconomic indicators in order to mitigate potential systemic risk due to adverse exogenous shocks; and (3) the research does not develop a comprehensive heat map as a surveillance tool to monitor the growing risks given the dynamic and interrelated aspects in Islamic banking operations.

Given the above findings and limitations, the research suggests some further potential and important investigation related to risk analyses in Islamic banks, including (1) developing a surveillance tool through a credible composite index to monitor regularly and intensively the growing risks in Islamic banks; (2) building the optimal thresholds of risks and shocks in order to ensure the vulnerability is manageable and resilience is maintained; and (3) building an early-warning system for risk mitigation as a risk management technique specific for Islamic banks.

Author details

Dimas Bagus Wiranatakusuma*, Imamuddin Yuliadi and Ikhwan Victhori
International Program for Islamic Economics and Finance, Faculty of Economics and Business, Department of Economics, Universitas Muhammadiyah Yogyakarta, Yogyakarta, Indonesia

*Address all correspondence to: dimas_kusuma@umy.ac.id

References

[1] Sach RS. The East Asia Financial Crisis: Diagnosis, Remedies, Prospects. Brookings Papers on Economic Activity. 1998;**1**:1-74

[2] Bello N, Hasan A, Buerhan S. The mitigation of liquidity risk in Islamic banking operation. Banks and Bank Systems; 2017

[3] Haryanti S. Pertumbuhan Kredit Perbankan di Indonesia: Intermediasi dan Pengaruh Variable Makro Ekonomi. Jurnal Keuangan dan Perbankan. 2009;**299**

[4] Bank Indonesia. Kajian Stabilitas Keuangan. Mitigasi Risiko Sistemik dan Penguatan Intermedasi Dalam Upaya Menjaga Stabilitas Sistem Keuangan; 2016

[5] Bank Indonesia. Bank Indonesia Bank Sentral Republik Indonesia. Sosialisasi Kebanksentralan Kepada Mahasiswa UNIKU. BOPOebon: Bank Indonesia; 2011

[6] Abdullah DV. Liquidity management in institutions offering Islamic financial services. In: Second Islamic Financial Stability Forum Jeddah. Jeddah: Kingdom of Saudi Arabia; 2010

[7] Abedifar P, Molyneux P, Tarazi A. Risk in Islamic banking. Review of Finance. 2013;**17**(6):1-62

[8] Alessi L, Detken C. Identifying Excessive Credit Growth and Leverage (August No. 1723). Frankfurt; 2014. Available from: https://www.ecb.europa.eu/pub/pdf/scpwps/ecbwp1723.pdf (European Central Bank)

[9] Ardiansyah M, Munandar A, Fauzi AS, Na'iman U. Default risk on Islamic banking in Indonesia. Global Review of Islamic Economics and Business. 2014;**2**(2):110-126

[10] Avdjiev S, Mccauley R, Mcguire P. Rapid credit growth and international credit: Challenges for Asia (No. 377). In: BIS Working Paper. Basel; 2012. Available from: https://www.bis.org/publ/work377.htm (Bank for International Settlements – BIS)

[11] Aysan AF, Disli M, Ozturk H, Turhan IM. Are Islamic banks subject to depositor discipline? (No. 871). In: Working Paper. Ghent; 2015

[12] Borio C. Ten propositions about liquidity Crises (No. 293). In: BIS Working Papers. Basel; 2010

[13] Misman FN. Risk exposure in Islamic banks: A case study of Bank Islam Malaysia Berhad (BIMB). School of Economics and Finance. 2010;**6**:24

[14] Borio C. Market distress and vanishing liquidity: Anatomy and policy options (No. 158). In: BIS Working Papers. Basel; 2004

[15] Stever R. Bank size, credit and the sources of bank market risk (No. 238). In: BIS Working Papers. Basel; 2007

[16] Nirei M, Caballero JA, Sushko V. Bank capital shock propagation via syndicated interconnectedness (No. 484). In: BIS Working Papers. Basel; 2014

[17] Adrian T, Shin HS. Liquidity and financial cycles (No. 256). In: BIS Working Papers. Basel; 2003. Available from: https://www.bis.org/publ/work256.htm (Bank for International Settlements – BIS)

[18] Cecchetti SG, Fender I, McGuire P. Toward a global risk map (No. 309). In: BIS Working Papers. Basel; 2010

[19] Drehmann M, Nikolaou K. Funding liquidity risk: Definition and measurement (No. 316). In: BIS Working Papers. Basel; 2013.

Available from: https://www.bis.org/publ/work316.pdf (Bank for International Settlements – BIS)

[20] Tirole J. Illiquidity and all its friends (No. 303). In: BIS Working Papers. Basel; 2011

[21] Wiranatakusuma DB, Duasa J. Building an early warning towards the resilience of Islamic banking in Indonesia. Journal of Islamics Economics. 2017

[22] Ush Sholikhah N. Analisis Likuiditas Pada Bank Syariah di Indonesia. Skripsi; 2018

[23] Ikatan Bankir Indonesia (IBI). dengan Banker Association for Risk Management (BARa). Manajemen Resiko 2. Jakarta: Gramedia; 2015

[24] Febianda B. Influence of Macroeconomic Variable's Toward Islamic Banking Depositor Funds in Indonesia. Universitas Muhammadiyah Yogyakarta; 2016

[25] Kuncoro M. Metode Kuantitatif: Teori dan Aplikasi untuk Bisnis dan Ekonomi. Yogyakarta: UPP AMP UKPN; 2004

[26] Basuki AT. Ekonometrika dan Aplikasi dalam Ekonomi (Dilengkapi aplikasi EVIEWS 7). Yogyakarta: Danisa Media; 2017

[27] Basuki AT, Yuliadi I. Ekonometrika Teori dan Aplikasi. 1st ed. Yogyakarta: Mitra Aksara Mulia; 2015

[28] Gujarati D. Dasar-dasar Ekonometrika. Jakarta: Erlangga; 2011

[29] Rosadi D. Ekonometrika dan analisis runtun waktu terapan dengan Eviews. Yogyakarta: CV Andi Offset; 2012

Chapter 5

Climate Change, Credit Risk and Financial Stability

Oluwaseun James Oguntuase

Abstract

Climate change is one of the greatest global challenges, posing an unprecedented challenge to the governance of global socioeconomic and financial systems. This chapter examines the climate change science and uncertainties associated with climate change, while identifying and explaining climate-related risks, the financial aspect of climate change, credit implications of climate change, integration of climate-related risks into credit risk assessment, and climate risk management. The chapter pays special attention to the triangular relationship between the three notions of climate-related risks, credit risk, and financial stability by enumerating the channels through which climate risks can cause credit risks and affect the stability of the financial system. Approaches to incorporate climate change into corporate risk management are also discussed.

Keywords: climate risk, risk management, financial stability

1. Introduction

Climate change is the disruption in the long-term seasonal weather patterns caused by global warming. How will long-term climate change affect businesses and the financial system, and how should impacts be managed over the course of the twenty-first century? These are some of the questions that have gained unprecedented attention in public discourse as global warming projections for the coming decades get worse.

Climate change exacerbates existing risks and creates new risks for natural and human systems [1]. The World Economic Forum's Global Risk Report specifies that three of the five topmost likely global risks are related to climate change. Specifically, it ranks failure of climate change mitigation and adaptation as the one most likely to impact on global risk [2]. *The adverse effects of climate change are pervasive and systemic, affecting* all asset classes, industries, and economies, and in turn, the financial system.

The bankruptcy of California's largest electric utility, Pacific Gas and Electric (PG and E), dubbed the first climate change bankruptcy [3], demonstrates the possible disruptions of production and consumption, and reduction in future asset values from impacts of climate change [4]. Notably, Mark Carney, the former governor of the Bank of England, has linked climate-related risks to financial stability. He noted that the combination of the weight of scientific evidence and the dynamics of the financial system suggest that in the fullness of time, climate change will threaten financial stability and longer-term prosperity [5].

From the foregoing that climate change has developed to one of the greatest global challenges, it is imperative to examine the climate change science and uncertainties associated with climate change, while identifying and explaining climate-related risks, the financial aspect of climate change, credit implications of climate change, integration of climate-related risks into credit risk assessment, and climate risk management.

The main aim of the chapter is to enumerate the channels through which climate change can cause credit risks and affect the stability of the financial system. Approaches to incorporate climate change into corporate risk management are also discussed. The chapter employs a systematic literature review approach to explore the relationship between the three notions of climate-related risks, credit risk, and financial stability toward achieving its objectives.

The rest of the chapter is divided into seven parts. Section 2 discusses the science and uncertainties involved in climate change. While various forms of climate-related risks are presented in Section 3, Section 4 enumerates their credit risk implications. How to integrate climate-related risks into credit risk assessment is the focus of Section 5. Sections 6 and 7 explore how climate change can negatively impact financial stability and how organizations could manage climate-related risks, respectively. Section 8 presents the findings and makes suggestions for further research.

2. Scientific uncertainty and climate change

Since Arrhenius [6] established and quantified the contribution of carbon dioxide (CO_2) to climate change, the consensus among publishing scientists, international agencies, and leading scientific societies in climate science is that the increase in the earth's temperature we are currently witnessing is anthropogenic, that is man-made [1, 7, 8] caused by the release of greenhouse gases (GHGs) into the atmosphere. The most prevalent of these GHGs is carbon dioxide (CO_2), associated with burning fossil fuels, industrial processes, forestry, and other land uses, but other gases—such as methane (CH_4) and nitrous oxide (N_2O)—are also contributing [9].

The decay rate of GHG in the atmosphere alters as the average temperature level increases. There has been a striking rise in temperatures over the last decade as the level of CO_2 in the atmosphere has skyrocketed. Global temperatures have been far higher in the past decade compared with their 100-year average, in tandem with an unprecedented rise in CO_2 in the atmosphere as shown in **Figure 1**.

Scientific advances that allow long-dated horizons suggest that irrevocable temperature increases have already been locked in (see **Figure 2**). Moreover, the current trends are on track to lead to systemic disruptions to ecosystems, societies, and economies [12] and may be catastrophic and irreversible for human populations, according to more than 11,000 scientists [13].

While the future is always unknown, we speak of risk if the probability distribution of possible future outcomes is known and of uncertainty if it is not. Human-induced climate change, its impacts, mitigation, and adaptation are fraught with uncertainty. The future pathways for GHG emissions and temperatures set out by climate scientists embody both risk and uncertainty.

The uncertainties involved in climate change preclude prediction of the precise nature, timing, frequency, intensity, and location of climate change impacts. These uncertainties also depend on a multitude of demographic and socioeconomic factors, such as technology, values and preferences, and policies, which are also deeply uncertain [14]. Added to these demographic and socioeconomic sources of uncertainty is scientific uncertainty which arises from our incomplete knowledge of the climate system [15].

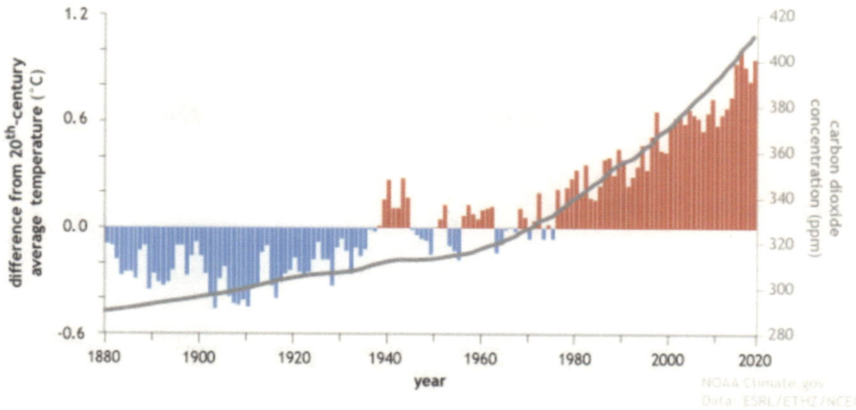

Figure 1.
Atmospheric carbon dioxide and Earth's surface temperature (1880–2019) [10]. Yearly temperature compared to the twentieth-century average (red and blue bars) from 1880 to 2019, based on the data from National Oceanic and Atmospheric Administration's National Centers for Environmental Information (NOAA NCEI), plus atmospheric carbon dioxide concentrations (gray line): 1880–1958 from Institute for Atmospheric and Climate Science (IAC), 1959–2019 from NOAA Earth System Research Laboratories. Original graph by Dr. Howard diamond NOAA Air Resources Laboratory, and adapted by NOAA Climate.gov.

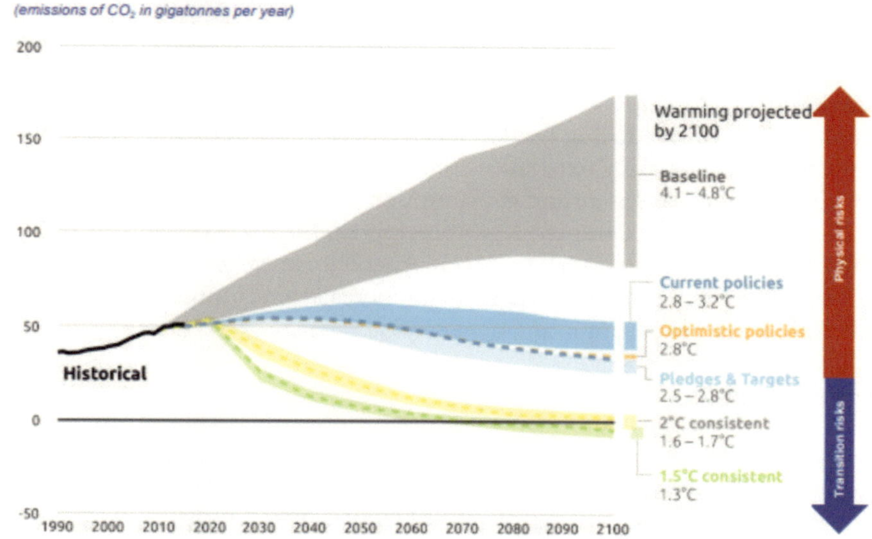

Figure 2.
Climate risk scenarios: Projections of carbon emissions and global warming (emissions of CO_2 in gigatons per year) [11].

Due to these interacting sources of uncertainty, studies of climate change and its impacts rarely yield consensus on the distribution of exposure, vulnerability, or possible outcomes. Thus, in contrast to risk situations where the probability distributions are known, there are no well-defined probability density functions (which are among the most common tools for characterizing uncertainty) for climate change [16].

Climate uncertainty leads to imprecision in estimating climate and economic outcomes. This implies not only imperfect understanding of the ability of mitigation pathways to deliver temperature outcomes but also suggests that there is a significant possibility that the tails of the distribution are considerably fatter than currently estimated. Fat-tailed climate events could not only significantly damage growth and welfare, but economic mechanisms may also be ineffective in responding appropriately. This could result in structural economic changes, and banks may find themselves facing abrupt adjustment which could be severely financially disruptive [17].

3. Climate-related risks

Climate-related risks are mainly divided into two basic sets: physical risks from more frequent and severe meteorological and hydrological events, and transition risks from the process of decarbonization that is aimed at mitigating global warming.

3.1 Physical risks

The physical climate-related risks represent the economic costs and financial losses due to increasing frequency and severity of climate-related weather events (e.g., storms, floods, or heat waves) and the effects of long-term changes in climate patterns (e.g., ocean acidification, rising sea levels, or changes in precipitation), resulting from continuously growing GHG emissions [18, 19].

Physical risks can affect both the supply and demand sides of the economy. On the supply side, natural disasters can disrupt business activity and trade and destroy infrastructure, diverting capital from technology and innovation to reconstruction and replacement [20]. It affects output levels and output growth by impacting labor productivity, speeding up the depreciation of capital stock, increasing cost of repair and replacement, and reducing funds allocated to research and innovation [21]. On the demand side, increasing expenditures for repair and replacement will, ceteris paribus, reduce investment on and consumption demand for other goods. Business investment could also be dampened by uncertainty about future demand and growth prospects and substantial price impacts [22]. Households confronted with more frequent extreme weather events might increase precautionary saving, which would depress private consumption in general [21].

3.2 Transition risks

Transition risks arise as a result of the shift to a low-carbon economy (such as changes in public regulation, technology, or in households' or investors' preferences) triggering changes in demand-related factors. This adjustment process is likely to have a significant impact on the economy and, in particular, on some financial asset values [11].

Transition risks are characterized by a radical uncertainty on the nature of the low-carbon pathway (i.e., the pathway for reducing greenhouse gas emissions, which restructures the economy) and a more usual uncertainty on the methods for implementing this pathway in economic and social terms [23].

Over the last few years, the topic of stranded assets, caused by risk factors like physical climate change impacts, as well as societal and regulatory responses to climate change, has loomed larger [24]. Stranded assets are defined as assets that have suffered from unanticipated or premature write-downs, devaluations, or conversion to liabilities [25]. With transition toward a lower-carbon economy, carbon assets are expected to suffer from unanticipated or premature write-offs, downward revaluations, or get converted to liabilities [26].

Estimation by McGlade and Ekins [27] shows that approximately one third of the current oil reserves, half the gas reserves, and almost 90% of the coal reserves would become stranded assets if global temperature target of the Paris Agreement is attained. While an early and smooth transition results in much fewer risks, too rapid an adjustment of asset prices due to a late transition might eventually bring about a climate Minsky moment—a sudden drop in assets prices [21].

3.3 Relationship between physical and transition risks

Physical risk and transition risks are correlated, because the more transition policies enter into force, the fewer physical risks are likely to materialize. On the other hand, the harder the economy is hit by physical risks, the stronger the demand will be for effective transition measures [21].

3.4 Liability risks

Materializing physical and potentially also transition risks will drive up liability risks [21]. Liability risks materialize when organizations are directly or indirectly adjudged legally responsible for climate-related losses and must financially compensate other parties [28, 29]. Organizations are also prone to increasing liability risk if they do not manage transition risks well as enshrined in the polluter pays principle. Organizations whose activities are negatively affected by unmitigated climate change could seek compensation from those who had caused or allowed the damage and thereby at least partially internalize the negative externalities [21].

4. Credit risks implications of climate change

Credit risk is the risk of a financial loss resulting from a borrower's failure to repay part of or all the interests and the principal of a loan. Climate-related risks affect all three dimensions of credit risk—a borrower's capacity to generate enough income to service and repay its debt as well as the capital and collateral that back the loan [30].

For financial institutions, credit risks can materialize directly, through their exposures to corporations, households, and countries that experience climate shocks, or indirectly, through the effects of climate change on the wider economy and feedback effects within the financial system. Exposures manifest themselves through increased default risk of loan portfolios or lower values of assets [31].

Corporate credit portfolios are also at risk, as highlighted by the PG&E's bankruptcy. Increase in extreme and severe weather events could have second-round effects on the price of corporate bonds, and the rise in debt defaults would induce climate-related financial instability which would adversely affect credit expansion and magnify the negative impact of climate change on financial activity [19].

Transition risks materialize on the asset side of financial institutions, which could incur losses on exposure to firms with business models not built around the economics of low-carbon emissions [31]. Climate change mitigation policies to reduce GHG emissions can create costs for carbon-intensive sectors and companies, thereby influencing the credit quality of GHG-intensive borrowers and also credit risks to banks [32]. Ongoing developments in the international climate policy arena show there will be more rigorous future global climate policy regime. Noncompliance with mitigation policies might become reputational risks and therefore credit risks. Hence, both compliance and noncompliance with the mitigation policies will have implications for loan providers, equity investors, and project financiers [32].

Literature establishing the link between climate change and credit risk is growing. Kleimeier and Viehs [33] show a significant and negative relation between CO_2 emission levels and the cost of bank loans. Delis, De Greif, and Ongena [34] observe that banks appeared to start pricing climate policy risk after the Paris Climate Agreement, while Ginglinger and Quentin [35] find that greater climate risk leads to lower leverage in the post-2015 period.

Capasso et al. [36] investigated the relationship between exposure to climate change and firm credit risk and found that the exposure to climate risks affects the creditworthiness of loans and bonds issued by corporates. Similarly, Delis et al. [34] demonstrated that climate policy risk is priced in syndicated loans, especially in sectors related to fossil fuel. Jung et al. [37] provided evidence of the existence of a positive association between the cost of debt and carbon-related risks for firms. Rajhi and Albuquerque [38] submitted that natural disasters are predictive of higher nonperforming loans and higher likelihood of default in developing countries. Battiston et al. [39] found that while direct exposures to the fossil fuel sector are small, the combined exposures to climate policy-relevant sectors are large, heterogeneous, and amplified by large indirect exposures via financial counterparties. Ilhan et al. [40] showed for a sample of S&P 500 companies that higher emissions increase downside risk—the potential losses that may occur if a particular investment position is taken. Monasterolo and De Angelis [41] indicated that investors require higher risk premia for carbon-intensive industries' equity.

5. Integrating climate-related risks into credit risk assessment

There are two approaches for integrating climate-related risks into credit risk assessments. On the one hand, there is a risk approach whose objective is to integrate a new source of risk in order to accurately measure credit risk and assumes that a risk differential between green and brown assets exists; on the other hand, there is an economic policy approach, aiming to foster the transition to a low-carbon economy by shifting credit from brown to green activities [42].

Under the risk approach, the risk-weight factor is recalibrated for all categories of assets to identify the differential due to climate-related risks. The differential should be taken into consideration when determining pricing and capital requirements. When the objective is to adjust capital requirements as an economic policy tool to allocate credit to specific sectors, the accurate level of climate-related risks is not a central concern anymore. This approach rather focuses on channeling credits to facilitate the transition toward a low-carbon economy. The objective is to foster transition by introducing a financial incentive through the capital adequacy regulation without following a risk reasoning [42].

Climate-related risks are expected to be included in all relevant stages of the credit-granting process and credit processing. Specifically, institutions are expected to form an opinion on how climate-related risks affect the borrower's default risk. The climate factors that are material to the borrower's default risk of the exposure are expected to be identified and assessed. As part of this assessment, institutions may take into consideration the quality of the clients' own management of climate-related risks. They are also to give appropriate consideration to changes in the risk profile of sectors and geographies driven by climate-related risks [28].

In quantifying, evaluating, and factoring climate-related risks into credit risk assessment, institutions require risk indicators or ratings for their counterparties that take into account climate-related and environmental risks. This is achieved by identifying borrowers that may be exposed, directly or indirectly, to increased climate-related risks. Critical exposures to such risks should be highlighted and, where applicable, considered under various scenarios with the aim of ensuring the ability to assess and introduce in a timely manner any appropriate risk mitigation measures including pricing [28].

Counterparty credit scoring requires detailed sectoral and geographic metrics to interpret climate-related risks as a view of financial vulnerability, taking into account mitigation measures. The resulting risk score can be used to inform credit decisions and to create a portfolio overview. The score can also be embedded in internal and external climate-related risk reporting (**Table 1**) [43].

1. Defining climate scenarios	**2. Estimating economic and financial impacts**	**3. Translating financial impacts into credit risk measures**
"The estimation of the impact of climate change and of the transition to a low-carbon economy on credit risk relies first on the definition of physical scenarios for climate change and for the transition. These scenarios define how climate change will impact the variables that are relevant for economic activities, how a transition will mitigate these impacts and which measures are taken to steer the transition."	"Once the impact of climate change on the variables relevant for economic activities has been estimated, its consequences must be translated into economic terms though macro and microeconomic simulations. This step basically assesses the direct and indirect repercussions of climate change and the transition to a low-carbon economy in economic terms and identifies which actors are affected by them and by how much. Once the economic effects on actors have been identified, the next step is to estimate the impact of these effects on both their cash flows and their balance sheets."	"Based on this assessment of financial impacts on firms and households, the next step is to compute how changes in cash flows and balance sheets will affect their credit worthiness in terms of probability of default and loss given default – and thus also in their credit ratings."

Table 1.
Steps for integrating physical climate risk into credit risk assessment processes [44].

For better integration of climate-related risks into credit risk assessment, Monnin [30] advocates addressing the limitations of historical data; expanding the horizon of credit risk models; finding the right level of data granularity; identifying the relevant climate-related risk exposure metrics; and translating economic impact into financial risk metrics.

6. Climate change and financial stability

Estimates of the aggregate economic impacts of climate change and the costs of mitigation both vary widely and are highly dependent on factors such as core assumptions, model design, sectoral coverage, and scenario selection [45]. On the one hand, available estimates suggest that physical damage from climate change could reach one tenth, or even one fifth, of global GDP by the end of this century, with considerable uncertainties around amplifying dynamics. In terms of current global output, this would amount to USD 8–17 trillion. On the other hand, some estimates suggest the transition to a low-carbon economy will require investment of between USD 1 trillion and USD 4 trillion in constant terms when considering the energy sector alone, or up to USD 20 trillion when looking at the economy more broadly [11].

Dietz et al. [46] employed standard integrated assessment model (IAM) and the climate value-at-risk (VAR) framework to quantitatively investigate the physical impact of climate change on the financial system. They found that without mitigation efforts, physical risks related to climate change could lead to a loss of USD

2.5–24.2 trillion of the value of global financial assets. For the transition risks, estimate by Mercure et al. [47] put the discounted global wealth losses from stranded fossil fuel assets may amount from USD 1–4 trillion.

Physical impacts of climate change as well as the transition toward a resilient low-carbon economy pose significant challenges for macro-financial management, as they can damage the balance sheets of governments, households, firms, and financial institutions due to the adverse and possibly abrupt impacts on investment and economic growth, fiscal revenue and expenditure, debt sustainability, and the valuation of financial assets. In turn, macro-financial risks translate into weakened resilience to physical climate risks and constrained capacity for climate adaptation and mitigation efforts. Transition risks are particularly high for countries that generate a significant share of public revenue from carbon-intensive industries. Lower-income and conflict-affected oil and gas exporters (mostly in Africa and the Middle East) are more vulnerable and less able to manage a low-carbon transition. They have not yet converted hydrocarbon rents into other sources of export revenues needed to grow and diversify [48].

For banks, climate-related risk factors manifest as increasing credit, market, and operational risks [49]. Climate-related financial risks may weaken financial sector balance sheets and induce or amplify macro-financial risks, particularly in the case of shocks. Such shocks could stem from disasters or sudden changes in policy, technology, or consumer preferences. The resulting financial sector losses and volatility in financial and commodity markets can adversely impact funding, liquidity, and lending conditions and weaken financial sector balance sheets, giving rise to negative feedback loops with macro-fiscal implications. Emerging markets and developing economies may be particularly affected, given that their financial markets are less resilient to such shocks [48]. By destroying the capital of firms and reducing their profitability and liquidity, climate change is likely to increase the rate of default of corporate loans that could harm the stability of the banking system [19]. A recent survey by the Bank of England on the preparedness of UK banks for climate change found their planning horizons averaged 4 years, likely too short even to account for likely physical and liability risks [50].

Climate change also has implications for insurance companies on both sides of the balance sheet: as investors and as underwriters. As institutional investors, insurance companies face largely similar transition and physical risks as other asset managers. They are disproportionally affected due to the long-term nature of their equity and infrastructure investments. As underwriters, pricing risks may arise from changing risk profiles to insured assets [48]. According to Lloyd's of London, damages from weather-related losses around the world have increased from an annual average of USD 50 billion in the 1980s to close to USD 200 billion in the past 10 years [51].

Institutional investors will be disproportionately affected by climate change, given their much longer-term investment horizons. In addition to the climate-related risks that affect financial stability, second-tier impacts from climate change (such as food security, social, and political unrest, and biodiversity loss) are likely to be nonlinear, characterized by tipping points, and material over the long term [48]. The Economist Intelligence Unit (EIU) [52] put the value of global stock of manageable assets at risk from climate change till the end of the century at USD 4.2–43 trillion (in 2015 value terms).

Climate change qualifies as a systemic event. A systemic event is defined in economics by three essential elements: a shock, which can be a broad shock simultaneously affecting a wide range of institutions, or a limited shock followed by an important domino effect; contagion effects through a web of interrelations; and the endogenous nature of this shock, meaning that it is caused by cumulated disequilibria over time [53].

Three fundamental reasons at least can justify this transposition of the financial concept of systemic risk to climate change. First, climate change impacts are systemic in nature. They affect the whole planet, in most of its dimensions. They have the ability to profoundly change the earth system as we currently know it. The second is the radical uncertainty. Historical data provide no useful guidance to future climate events or/and outcomes. Finally, the notion of a climate systemic risk at world scale provides a powerful new rationale in the debate on international monetary reform [53].

Climate and financial fragilities reinforce each other. They are intertwined into positive feedback loops so that climate systemic risks also incur financial systemic risks. Financial fragility to external risks may increase climate fragility through negative externality effects. Conversely, climate fragility incurs new risks that may reinforce financial fragility, as **Figure 3** illustrates. The realization of a climate systemic risk translates into potential financial turmoil and this in turn can increase around the provision of the ultimate liquidity [53].

Physical and transition risk drivers impact economic activities, which in turn impact the financial system. This impact can occur directly through, for example, lower corporate profitability or the devaluation of assets, or indirectly, through macro-financial changes [28]. Climate-related risks—in particular, transition risks—are actually closer to being in a state of uncertainty. Further uncertainty is created by the highly interconnected nature of the modern financial system. Interlinkages among financial institutions—both banks and nonbanks—can amplify both positive and negative shocks and significantly decrease the accuracy of default probabilities [54].

Physical risks can cause economic costs and financial losses across different financial portfolios (e.g., loans, equities, and bonds) and also affect the expectation of future losses, which can threaten the solvency of households, businesses, and governments and therefore financial institutions [18]. The exposure of financial institutions to physical risks can trigger contagion and asset devaluations propagating throughout the financial system [18]. Rapid and ambitious transition to low-carbon economy will lead to transition risks with large fractions of proven reserves of fossil fuel becoming stranded assets, with potentially systemic consequences for the financial system. Other fossil fuel-dependent sectors will probably be impacted indirectly as a consequence [55]. The size of the impact depends on the assumptions made about when and how the transition happens and which sectors it affects. The risk is that a sharp reassessment of climate change risks could

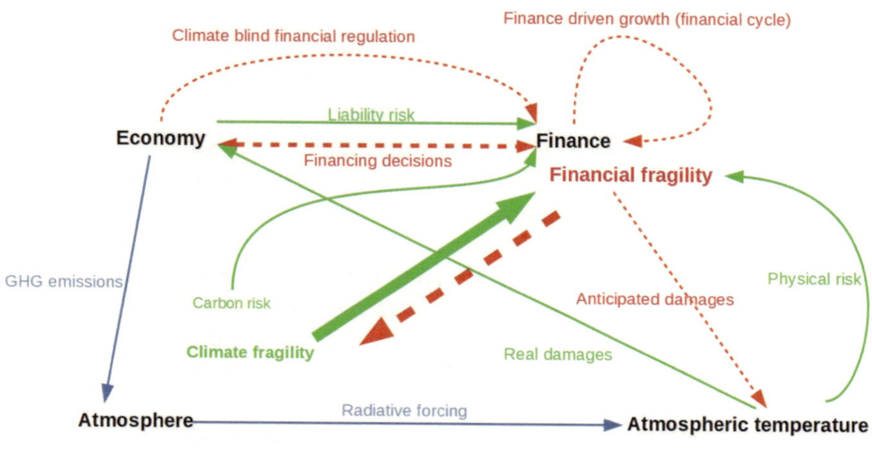

Figure 3.
Relationship between climate and financial fragilities [53].

lead to a financial market reassessment, leading to a spiral of persistent tightening of financial conditions as losses ensue [18].

A wholesale reassessment of prospects, as climate-related risks are reevaluated, could destabilize markets, spark a pro-cyclical crystallization of losses, and lead to a persistent tightening of financial conditions: a climate Minsky moment—involving a rapid, system-wide (downward) repricing of carbon assets which would threaten financial stability [56].

The economic effects of bank losses and asset price deflation can exacerbate climate-induced financial instability [57]. This calls for a collective prudential approach—monetary policies and banking regulations, which intend to act on eliminating possible future outcomes more than on internalizing externality, because of radical uncertainty [53].

7. Climate-related risk management

Risk management has increasingly become a well-established tool for climate change adaptation, given the significant uncertainty about future impacts and the inability to rely on historic data as a basis for current action [58, 59]. Risk management is part of a comprehensive suite of tools for climate change adaptation, with international and national standards being developed to assist governments, businesses, and communities [59].

ISO 14090:2019: Adaptation to climate change—Principles, requirements and guidelines specifies the principles, requirements, and guidelines for adaptation to climate change. These include the integration of adaptation within or across organizations, understanding impacts and uncertainties, and how these can be used to inform decisions. ISO 14091:2019 provides guidance for assessing the risks related to the potential impacts of climate change. It describes how to understand vulnerability and how to develop and implement a sound risk assessment in the context of climate change. It can be used for assessing both present and future climate change risks.

As part of their overall internal control framework, organizations should have an institution-wide risk management framework that extends across all business lines and internal units, including internal control functions [28]. The risk management framework should encompass financial and nonfinancial risks, on-balance-sheet risks, and off-balance-sheet risks, including risks that the institution is currently exposed to and for risks that the institution may be exposed to going forward [28].

Eceiza et al. [43] enumerate five principles of climate-related risk management to include formulation of climate-related risk governance, to ensure the board focuses on the risks and for climate-risk management, and to cascade throughout the organization; tailor strategic plans and business models toward embedding climate-related risks in risk frameworks and capital allocation processes; inject climate-related risk considerations into all risk-management processes to align climate-related risk exposure with risk appetite; periodic scenario analysis and stress tests to assess the organization's resilience; and focus on enablers and build capacity, including technology, data, and talent to manage climate-related risks.

A strategic approach to managing the financial risks from climate change developed by the Prudential Regulation Authority (PRA) (Bank of England) entails governance, risk management, scenario analysis, and disclosure. A firm's board should understand and assess the financial risks from climate change that affect the firm and should be able to address and oversee these risks within the firm's overall business strategy and risk appetite. Firms are expected to employ their existing business strategy and risk management frameworks to address financial risks from climate change, in line with their board-approved risk appetite. Firms should identify, measure, monitor, manage, and report on their exposure to these risks to their stakeholders. Material exposures should be included in their Internal Capital Adequacy Assessment Process (ICAAP) or Own Risk and Solvency Assessment (ORSA). Where appropriate, the PRA expects firms to consider a range of quantitative and qualitative tools and metrics to monitor their exposure to financial risks from climate change. Firms should provide evidence of how material risks will be mitigated and have credible plans or policies to manage these exposures. The management information should enable the board to discuss, challenge, and take decisions relating to the firm's management of the financial risks from climate change. Scenario analysis should also be used to explore the resilience and vulnerabilities of a firm's business model to a range of outcomes, based on different transition paths to a low-carbon economy, as well as a path where no transition occurs. Disclosures should be as insightful as possible, reflecting the firm's evolving understanding of the financial risks from climate change (**Figure 4**) [60].

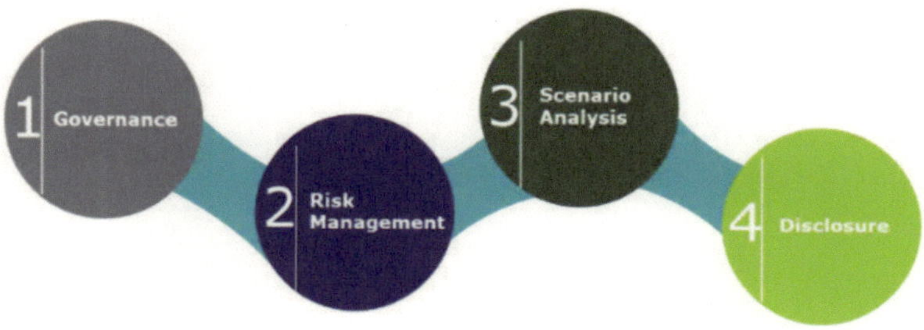

Figure 4.
Elements of climate-related risk management [60].

Similar good practices of governance and climate-related risk management recommended by the French Prudential Supervision and Resolution Authority (Banque de France) [61] include the following: integration of climate-related risks, including their implementation and monitoring, into the strategy of institutions; the internal organization of institutions, both in terms of the allocation of responsibility over all business lines, and in terms of the structuring of climate risk control, should align with the institutions' strategic orientations; full integration of the material risks induced by climate change into the risk appetite framework of the institution, and also mobilization of appropriate tools to allow for a thorough assessment of these risks; and disclosure of the institution's strategy and its risk management mechanisms with regard to climate change to ensure both a better understanding and a better integration of climate-related risks.

8. Conclusion

Climate change is rapidly proceeding, and climate-related risks are being exacerbated. While the mechanisms of physical climate change and the possible impacts are scientifically well understood, the specific estimates of these impacts are associated with uncertainty.

Climate change will affect all sectors of the economy, and it is relevant to investors and financial institutions, posing an unprecedented challenge to the governance of global socioeconomic and financial systems. Climate-related risks touch on the interests of a broad range of stakeholders across the private and public sectors, impact all the key dimensions of credit risk, and are the main channels through which climate change can affect financial stability.

This chapter establishes the need for organizations to have a holistic, well-documented, and institution-wide risk management framework that extends across all business lines and internal units to manage their climate-related risks.

In all, the chapter provides a preliminary view on how climate change can cause credit risk and financial instability. As such, the chapter does not comprehensively address the complex tasks of managing climate-related risks in organizations. A more comprehensive study is required on what strategies and approaches are needed to manage uncertainties and risks that are an integral part of climate change in organizations.

Author details

Oluwaseun James Oguntuase
Centre for Environmental Studies and Sustainable Development, Lagos State University, Lagos, Nigeria

*Address all correspondence to: oluwaseunoguntuase@gmail.com

References

[1] IPCC (Intergovernmental Panel on Climate Change). In: Core Writing Team, Pachauri RK, Meyer LA, editors. Climate Change 2014: Synthesis Report. Contribution of Working Groups I, II and III to the Fifth Assessment Report of the Intergovernmental Panel on Climate Change. Geneva, Switzerland: IPCC; 2014. p. 151. Available from: https://www.ipcc.ch/site/assets/uploads/2018/02/SYR_AR5_FINAL_full.pdf

[2] WEF (World Economic Forum). The Global Risks Report. 11th ed. Geneva; 2016

[3] Gold R. PG&E: The first climate-change bankruptcy, probably not the last. Wall Street Journal. 2019. Available from: https://www.wsj.com/articles/pg-e-wildfires-and-the-first-climate-change-bankruptcy-11547820006

[4] MacWilliams JJ, LaMonaca S, Kobus J. PG&E: Market and Policy Perspectives on the First Climate Change Bankruptcy. New York: SIPA Center on Global Energy Policy; 2019

[5] Carney M. Breaking the Tragedy of the Horizon – Climate Change and Financial Stability. Speech Given a Lloyd's of London by the Governor of the Bank of England; 2015. Available from: http://www.bankofengland.co.uk/publications/Pages/speeches/2015/544.aspx

[6] Arrhenius S. On the influence of carbonic acid in the air upon the temperature of the ground. Philosophical Magazine. 1896;**5**(7):237-276. DOI: 10.1080/14786449608620846

[7] Cook J, Oreskes N, Doran PT, Anderegg WRL, Verheggen B, Maibach EW, et al. Consensus on consensus: A synthesis of consensus estimates on human-caused global warming. Environmental Research Letters. 2016;**11**:048002. DOI: 10.1088/1748-9326/11/4/048002

[8] Powell J et al. Bulletin of Science Technology Society. 2017;**37**(4):183-184. DOI: 10.1177/0270467619886266

[9] Paisley J, Nelson M. Climate Risk Management at Financial Firms: Challenges and Opportunities. New York: GARP Risk Institute; 2019

[10] Lindsey R. If carbon dioxide hits a new high every year, why isn't every year hotter than the last? 2020. Available from: https://www.climate.gov/news-features/climate-qa/if-carbon-dioxide-hits-new-high-every-year-why-isn%E2%80%99t-every-year-hotter-last

[11] European Central Bank. Positively green: Measuring climate change risks to financial stability; 2020

[12] Steffen W, Rockström J, Richardson K, Lenton TM, Folke C, Liverman D, et al. Trajectories of the earth system in the anthropocene. PNAS. 2018;**115**(33):8252-8259. DOI: 10.1073/pnas.1810141115

[13] Ripple WJ, Wolf C, Newsome TM, Barnard P, Moomaw WR. World scientists' warning of a climate emergency. Bioscience. 2019;**70**(1):8-12. DOI: 10.1093/biosci/biz088

[14] Kalra H, Hallegate S, Lempert R, Brown C, Fozzard A, Gill S, et al. Agreeing on robust decisions: New processes for decision making under deep uncertainty. World Bank Research Working Paper 6906; 2014

[15] Heal G, Millner A. Uncertainty and decision in climate change economics. National Bureau of Economic Research Working Paper 18929; 2013

[16] Kunreuther H, Heal G, Allen M, Edenhofer O, Field CB, Yohe G. Risk

management and climate change. NBER Working Paper 18607; 2012. DOI: 10.3386/w18607

[17] Knight Z, Ganguly G. Managing Financial System Stability and Climate Change - a Preliminary Guide. London: HSBC Centre of Sustainable Finance; 2018

[18] Bolton P, Despres M, Pereira da Silva LA, Samama F, Svartzman R. The Green Swan: Central Banking and Financial Stability in the Age of Climate Change. Basel: Bank for International Settlements; 2020

[19] Dafermos Y, Nikolaidi M, Galanis G. Climate change, financial stability and monetary policy. Ecological Economics. 2018;**152**:219-234. DOI: 10.1016/j.ecolecon.2018.05.011

[20] Batten S. Climate change and the macro-economy: a critical review. Bank of England Staff Working Paper No 706; 2018

[21] Pointner W, Ritzberger-Grünwald D. Climate change as a risk to financial stability. Financial Stability Report. 2019;**38**:30-45

[22] Parker M. The impact of disasters on inflation. Economics of Disasters and Climate Change. 2018;**2**(1):21-48

[23] Nicol M, Hubert R, Cochran I, Leguet B. Managing Climate Risks for Financial Actors: From Theory to Practice. Paris: Institute for Climate Economics (I4CE); 2017

[24] Caldecott B, Harnett E, Cojoianu T, Kok I, Pfeiffer A. Stranded Assets: A Climate Risk Challenge. Washington DC: Inter-American Development Bank; 2016

[25] Caldecott B, Howarth N, McSharry P. Stranded assets in agriculture: Protecting value from environment-related risks. Smith School of Enterprise and the Environment Working Paper; 2013

[26] Ansar A, Caldecott B, Tilbury J. Stranded assets and the fossil fuel divestment campaign: What does divestment mean for the valuation of fossil fuel assets? University of Oxford's Smith School of Enterprise and the Environment Stranded Assets Programme Working Paper; 2013

[27] McGlade C, Ekins P. The geographical distribution of fossil fuels unused when limiting global warming to 2 °C. Nature. 2015;**517**(7533):187-190

[28] European Central Bank. Guide on climate-related and environmental risks: Supervisory expectations relating to risk management and disclosure. Frankfurt; 2020

[29] Monnin P. Central banks should reflect climate risks in monetary policy operations. SUERF Policy Note Issue No 41; 2018

[30] Monnin P. Integrating climate risks into credit risk assessment: Current methodologies and the case of central banks corporate bond purchases. Council on Economic Policies Discussion Note 2018/4; 2018

[31] Grippa P, Schmittmann J, Suntheim F. Climate change and financial risk. Finance & Development. 2019;**56**(4):26-29

[32] Allianz WWF. Climate Change and the Financial Sector: An Agenda for Action. London: WWF and Allianz; 2005

[33] Kleimeier S, Viehs PM. Carbon disclosure, emission levels, and the cost of debt. Maastricht University Graduate School of Business and Economics Research Memorandum 3; 2015

[34] Delis M, De Greif K, Ongena S. Being stranded on the carbon bubble? Climate policy risk and the pricing of bank loans. Swiss Finance Institute Research Paper 18-10; 2018

[35] Ginglinger E, Quentin M. Climate risk and capital structure. Université Paris-Dauphine Research Paper No. 3327185; 2019

[36] Capasso G, Gianfrate G, Spinelli M. Climate change and credit risk. EDHEC-Risk Institute Working Paper; 2020

[37] Jung J, Herbohn K, Clarkson P. Carbon risk, carbon risk awareness and the cost of debt financing. Journal of Business Ethics. 2018;**150**(4):1151-1171

[38] Rajhi W, Albuquerque P. Banking stability, natural disasters, and political conflicts: Time series evidence on causality in developing countries. Institute for the World Economy Economics Discussion Paper 2017-52; 2017

[39] Battiston S, Mandel A, Monasterolo I, Schütze F, Visentin G. A climate stress test of the financial system. Nature Climate Change. 2017;7(4):283-288

[40] Ilhan E, Sautner Z, Vilkov G. Carbon tail risk. 2019. Available from: https://ec.europa.eu/jrc/sites/jrcsh/files/presentation_emirhan_ilhan.pdf

[41] Monasterolo I, de Angelis, L. Blind to carbon risk? An analysis of stock market's reaction to the Paris Agreement. 2019. Available from SSRN: https://ssrn.com/abstract=3298298

[42] Berenguer M, Cardona M, Evain J. Integrating climate-related risks into banks' capital requirements. Institute for Climate Economics (I4CE). Paris; 2020

[43] Eceiza J, Harreis H, Härtl D, Viscardi S. Banking Imperatives for Managing Climate Risk. New York: McKinsey & Company; 2020

[44] Dépoues V, Bouchet V, Cardona M, Nicol M. Towards an Alternative Approach in Finance to Climate Risks: Taking Uncertainties Fully into Account. Paris: Institute for Climate Economics (I4CE); 2020

[45] Sullivan R. Climate change: Implications for investors and financial institutions. European Climate Foundation (ECF), the Institutional Investors Group on Climate Change (IIGCC), the United Nations Environment Programme Finance Initiatives (UNEP FI) and the University of Cambridge's Judge Business School (CJBS) and Institute for Sustainability Leadership (CISL). 2014. Available from: https://www.unepfi.org/fileadmin/documents/IPCC_AR5__Implications_for_Investors__Briefing__WEB_EN.pdf

[46] Dietz S, Bowen A, Dixon C, Gradwell P. Climate value at risk' of global financial assets. Nature Climate Change. 2016;**6**:676-679. DOI: 10.1038/nclimate2972

[47] Mercure J-F, Pollitt H, Vinuales JE, Edwards NR, Holden PB, Chewpreecha U, et al. Macroeconomic impact of stranded fossil fuel assets. Nature Climate Change. 2016;**8**:588-593

[48] Feyen E, Utz R, Huertas IZ, Bodgan O, Moon J. Macro-financial aspects of climate change. World Bank Policy Research working Paper 9109; 2020

[49] Bank of England. Transition in Thinking: The Impact of Climate Change on the UK Banking Sector. London: Bank of England; 2018

[50] (PRA) Prudential Regulation Authority. Transition in thinking: The impact of climate change on the UK

banking sector. 2018. Available from: https://www.bankofengland.co.uk/prudential-regulation/publication/2018/transition-in-thinking-the-impact-of-climate-change-on-the-uk-banking-sector

[51] Kollewe J. Lloyd's calls on insurers to take into account climate-change risk. 2014. Available from: https://www.theguardian.com/business/2014/may/08/lloyds-insurer-account-climate-change-extreme-weather-losses

[52] Economist Intelligence Unit. The cost of inaction: recognizing the value at risk from climate change. 2015. Available from: https://www.eiuperspectives.economist.com/.../The%20cost%20of%20inaction_0.pdf

[53] Aglietta M, Espagne E. Climate and finance systemic risks, more than an analogy? The climate fragility hypothesis. CEPII Working Paper No 2016-10; 2016

[54] Battiston S, Gatti DD, Gallegati M, Greenwald B, Stiglitz JE. Liaisons dangereuses: Increasing connectivity, risk sharing, and systemic risk. Journal of Economic Dynamics and Control. 2012;**36**(8):1121-1141

[55] Cahen-Fourot L, Campiglio E, Dawkins E, Godin A, Kemp-Benedict E. Looking for the inverted pyramid: An application using input-output networks. Ecological Economics. 2019;**169**:106554. DOI: 10.1016/j.ecolecon.2019.106554

[56] Carney M. Resolving the climate paradox. Text of the Arthur Burns Memorial Lecture, Berlin. 2016. Available from: https://www.bis.org/review/r160926h.pdf

[57] Batten S, Sowerbutts R, Tanaka M. Let's talk about the weather: The impact of climate change on central banks. Bank of England Staff Working Paper No. 603; 2016

[58] Godden L, Rochford F, Peel J, Caripis L, Carter R. Law, governance and risk: Deconstructing the public-private divide in climate change adaptation. UNSW Law Journal. 2013;**36**(1):224-255

[59] May B, Plummer R. Accommodating the challenges of climate change adaptation and governance in conventional risk management: Adaptive collaborative risk management (ACRM). Ecology and Society. 2011;**16**(1):47

[60] Prudential Regulation Authority. Enhancing banks' and insurers' approaches to managing the financial risks from climate change. Supervisory Statement | SS3/19; 2019

[61] French Prudential Supervision and Resolution Authority. Governance and management of climaterelated risks by French Banking Institutions: Some Good Practices. Paris; 2020

Chapter 6

Green Banking

Taslima Julia and Salina Kassim

Abstract

Green banking being a new trend deserves more attention. Understanding green banking, its nature, importance, impact on spreading green, its link to sustainable development goals (SDGs), and Maqasid Shariah is vital. Therefore, this chapter is going to cover the abovementioned essentials. Banks' financing that care about the environment is green banking. Banks can contribute enormously to restore environmental balance and to preserve a livable condition for future generation through green banking. Only binding regulation can ensure the involvement of banks in green practices, for example, Bangladesh. To face the reality, when leaders are committed to implement SDGs by 2030, involvement of banks in green practices could accelerate the process of implementation. Coincidently, green banking features and objectives are very close to Maqasid Shariah. Based on desk research and document analysis technique, this chapter is going to establish that green banking, SDGs, and Maqasid Shariah are complementary to each other.

Keywords: green banking, Islamic banking, Maqasid Shariah, green banking and Maqasid Shariah, SDGs and Maqasid Shariah

1. Introduction

Usually, the concept of financing covers many sources of financing, and banking is one of the sources. Green banking is a new trend of banks' financing. It is a product of green movement initiated by world leaders to maintain a livable condition for future generations [1]. The recent commitments of leaders to attain sustainable development goals (SDGs) by 2030 will be impossible without successful implementation of green banking. It is a new avenue for both conventional and Islamic banks to care for the environment while financing.

Green banking is an eco-friendly financing. Banks' concern about environmental well-being while financing to businesses is considered as green banking. To get a sustainable positive impact from business, green banking is essential. Businesses are the driver of the economy, and sustainable business can influence the sustainability of the economy; therefore, successful green business establishment is crucial. Central banks' role is imperative in introducing and implementing green banking.

Green banking has a positive connection with Maqasid Shariah as well as few of sustainable development goals such as goal no. 7, 9, 11, 12, and 13. On the other hand, green banking features and objectives are very close to Maqasid Shariah. The objective of Shariah (Islamic law) is known as Maqasid Shariah. The term Maqasid refers to purposes or goals in Arabic. Basically, the word Maqasid Shariah refers to the devotions of Islamic law. The purposes, rationales, as well as common good in the Islamic rulings are accentuated by the term Maqasid while basing itself on the Islamic scripts as well as observing the Islamic faith. In general, conservation, reduced dependency on paper, increased online banking, and environmental risk rating before granting financing to a borrower are few features of green banking which do not contradict with Maqasid Shariah rather meet the objectives of Shariah. This chapter is divided into various sections for easy representation of the detail of green banking: the second section is going to discuss about the methodology used to gather data, the third section explains what is green banking, the fourth section represents the importance of it, the fifth section elaborates the impact of it to introduce green business, the sixth section demonstrates the link among green banking, Islamic banking, Maqasid Shariah, and SDGs, and finally, the conclusion sums up the chapter.

2. Methodologies

This chapter has used secondary data. The data is gathered following desk research method, and the data is analyzed following document analysis technique. Document analysis is a methodical process of revising or appraising documents—both published and electronic (computer-based and Internet-transmitted) material. Like other systematic approaches in qualitative research, document analysis wants that data to be scrutinized and deduced to stimulate meaning, gain empathetic, and advance pragmatic knowledge [2]. Documents used for systematic evaluation may be a variety of forms. They include advertisements, agendas, attendance registers, and minutes of meetings, manuals, background papers, books and brochures, diaries and journals, event programs (i.e., printed outlines), letters and memoranda, maps and charts, newspapers (clippings/articles), press releases, program proposals, application forms, and summaries, radio and television program scripts, organizational or institutional reports, survey data, and various public records. The current chapter especially searched websites, articles related to green banking, Maqasid Shariah, SDGs, used published or working paper of various recognized institutions, green banking reports published by Bangladesh Bank, etc.

3. Definition of green financing, green banking, and green business

The green financing concept is an invention of green growth movement and green growth links to green economy; the origin of green economy is found in sustainable development concept. Until now there is no widely accepted definition of green financing; however, the definition given by the German Development Institute is considered as a recognized one—"Green finance comprise financing of (including preparatory cost and capital cost) green investments, financing of public green policies and green financial system." What Dr. Nannette's definition elucidates is the areas of green investments—climate change adaptation, energy efficiency, renewable energies, and other climate change mitigation, for example, reforestation. The components of financial system have made it clear that it should deal specifically with green investments, such as the Green Climate Fund or financial instruments for green investments (e.g., green bonds and structured green funds), as well as their detailed legal, economic, and institutional framework conditions [3]. According to the Deutsche Gesellschaft für Internationale Zusammenarbeit (GIZ), "Green Finance is a strategic approach to incorporate the financial sector in the transformation process towards low-carbon and resource-efficient economies, and in the context of adaptation to climate change" [4]. Green financing is an idea that is more comprehensive than green banking, and banks are one of the most important sources of financing; however, nonbank financial organizations are also a significant basis of funding for green projects.

Nevertheless, the concept of green banking had substituted banks' motive to "planet, people, and profit" from "profit, profit, and profit." Green banking is also known as environmental banking; in broad perception, green banking practices eco-friendly methods and encourages its patrons to reduce the carbon footprint by their banking procedures [5]. According to Bangladesh central bank—"Green banking is a component of the global initiatives by a group of stakeholders to save environment" [6]; the sustainable banking concept is the outcome of the society and environment-oriented banking practices. Recently, Bangladesh Bank has integrated "sustainability" into core banking practices through green banking, corporate social responsibility, and financial inclusion. Green banking is a category of banking practices considering all the social and ecological factors with an aim to defend the environment and preserve natural resources. It is also called as ethical banking or sustainable banking [7]. Saruti Garg stated that green banking is a shade that symbolizes practices and policies which help banks to be environmentally, economically, and socially responsible. Banks should conduct their operation in suitable manner and in suitable areas to reduce both external carbon emission and internal carbon footprint [8]. Consequently, business that took green financing from bank and other sources to involve in environmentally friendly business is considered as green business. According to Smith and Friend, "green businesses" are businesses and practices that are viewed as naturally detailed, used living and natural products to generate factories and supervision to protect against releases, and utilized eco-friendly materials [9, 10]. Earlier, Zsolnai explains in 2002 that business that ponders over the thought of ecology in undertaking numerous tasks of business is called green business [11]. Gilbert again classified that green businesses are those businesses which can interchange activity in a method so that either it ensures natural benefit or its activities limit negative ecological effect [12]. A business that uses lesser natural resources to accomplish the duties requires and utilizes sustainable methods and materials such as producing sustainable products as raw materials (recycled, plant-based or organically grown) and recycling (paper, plastic, electronics, glass, and aluminum) which is known by Morebusiness.com as green business.

4. Importance of green banking

Banks are very important financial intermediaries to collect money from surplus units to disburse money to deficit units. Banks by its financing activities help economy to move on. Therefore, to face the reality of achieving SDGs, banks should involve in green banking. The central banks' role here is imperative. Policy and guideline creation and enforcement of that can ensure the successful implementation of green financing by banks. Out of 17 SDGs, goal No. 7 affordable and clean energy; goal No. 9 industry, innovation, and infrastructure; goal No. 11 sustainable cities and communities; goal No. 12 responsible consumption and production; and goal No. 13 climate actions are goals with successful implementation of those are related to green banking.

5. Impacts of green banking to create green businesses

Since 1987 to achieve sustainable development, many new movements have been introduced; few of those were green economy, green growth, low-carbon development [13], millennium development goals, green financing, etc.; however, participation in those movements was nonbinding and voluntary in nature. Therefore, desired outcomes were difficult to attain; hence, in 2015, a binding agreement among world leaders has been signed, named as Paris climate agreements. After signing the agreement, introducing green banking became mandatory by all signing nations [14]. Binding regulation and strong enforcement of it really has a great impact on business as well as economy; the best example is Bangladesh. Atiur Rahman, known as a green governor, inaugurated green banking policy and guidelines in 2011 and strictly followed up that banks and nonbank financial institutions implemented the policy accordingly [15, 16]. Consequently all 60 banks and 34 nonbank financial institutions now have their own green banking units, in-house green activities, and publishing green reports [17]. Therefore, strict regulation, its enforcement, and regular follow-up can ensure proper implementation of green banking. The outcome of green banking is green businesses, and the spread of green businesses can move the economy to green economy. In a nutshell, the green banking policy and guideline currently known as sustainable banking policy introduced by Bangladesh Bank, the central bank of the country, are presented here.

Green banking policy introduced by Bangladesh central bank involves in a two-split approach: Firstly, green banking emphasizes on greening the internal operations of all banks. It means all the banks need to adopt to suitable ways of utilizing renewable energy, automation, and other procedures to lessen environmental degradation situations from banking activities. Secondly, banks should approve environmentally responsible financing; before making any financing decision, they should maintain environmental risk rating and support and foster growth of "green" initiatives and projects.

In-house green activities include reducing dependency on grid power by shifting to the use of solar power and other renewable energy sources to the maximum feasible extent; following green architecture while constructing bank offices; using energy-saving technologies such as light emitting diodes (LED), compact fluorescent lamp (CFL), etc.; using energy-efficient digital devices; reducing use of paper by adoption of online automated work practices; and conducting energy audit regularly to monitor carbon footprint.

Green activities in financing include carry out environmental risk assessment of projects, financing only those that meet environmental safeguards/sustainability guidelines; provide green loan to promote solar energy, biogas plants, effluent treatment plants, and other energy-saving output practices like Hybrid Hoffman kilns in brick fields; develop green banking products for clients; promote growth of mobile banking and online banking; and include environmental sustainability support initiatives in corporate social responsibility (CSR) programs, inter alia including financial support to climate risk fund.

Bangladesh Bank green policies and guidelines are divided into three phases. In phase-I, individual bank should develop their own green banking policies and display general commitment on the environment through in-house performance. Under phase-II, banks are responsible to create environmental policies and guidelines for different environmental-sensitive sectors. In phase-III, banks are likely to address environment-friendly initiatives and introduce innovative products by considering the whole ecosystem in their decision-making process and publish independent green annual report following standard formatting [16].

Green banking helps create green businesses; according to Bangladesh Bank green policy, there are 11 categories of green business such as renewable energy, energy efficiency, solid waste management, liquid waste management, alternative energy, fire burnt brick, non-fire block brick, recycling and recyclable product, green industry, safety and security of factories, and miscellaneous. Among these categories, there are 47 product lines, and these are projects financed having environmental treatment plant (ETP), biogas plant, solar home system and solar panel trades, and bio-fertilizer plant and projects financed having tunnel kiln, installation of zigzag kiln, waste and hazard disposal plants, waste paper recycling plant, waste battery recycling plants, financing of LED bulb production, PET bottle recycling plant, safe/clean water supply projects, improved cooking stove (Bondhu Chula), green finance at zero rate of interest, electricity generation from rice husk, rice bran oil production; etc. Both the conventional and Islamic banks are bound to finance these projects and plants as these are classified as green projects [18].

Green businesses adopt principles, policies, and practices that improve the quality of life for their customers, employees, communities, and the planet. Green businesses are socially and environmentally responsible and challenge themselves to bring the goals of social and economic justice, environmental sustainability, as well as community health and development, into all their activities—from production and supply chain management to employee relations and customer service. Green businesses improve their communities.

6. Islamic banking, Maqasid Shariah, and green banking

Principally, the idea of green banking that is originated from sustainable development concept aims to guarantee the highest utilization of natural resources as well as minimum dependency on artificial resources which is made by polluting atmosphere, ultimately impacting mankind as well as the environment. Islamic banking and green banking are not incompatible; in fact they are in line and supplementary to each other. The green banking concept originated from sustainable development concept that cares to nature and focuses on maintaining ecological balance, the Maqasid of Islamic banking is to guarantee divine principle in worldly transactions, and many of the divine principles are related to caring to nature and natural resources; hence, there is a connection between Islamic banking, Maqasid Shariah, and green banking.

6.1 Islamic banking

Islamic banking has significant synergies with the green economy concept and fits in well with the ethical requirements of green projects. As such, environmental protection and sustainability align strongly with the Islamic banking agenda that seeks to enhance the general welfare of society. Protection of the planet and the environment is clearly in conformity with Maqasid Shariah as well as with the goals of sustainable development. In this context, Islamic finance offers promising instruments that can provide solutions to financing climate change [19].

Islamic banking as a faith-based idea has come of age. Finance professionals view it largely as asset-based finance that is free from the elements of unjust and speculative gains. It involves use of a range of tools that create equities, participation, and ownership. Islamic bankers use them or combinations thereof for financing the needs of economic units, such as the government, the corporate, and the household sectors in the economy. Islamic finance has experienced steady growth over the past four decades as more and more countries and markets have come forward to experiment with this faith-based idea. The frenetic pace of growth has, however, raised concerns about a possible mission implication [20].

Theoretically, Islamic finance is resilient to shocks because of its risk sharing, limit on excessive risk taking, and strong link to real activities; however, empirically stability of Islamic banks is so far mixed. Islamic banks face similar risks as conventional banks do and expose to idiosyncratic risks, necessitating a tailoring of current risk management practices [21]. Islamic economists are particularly concerned that Islamic finance must contribute a lot more, towards addressing development-related issues and societal concerns.

Even though the principles of Islamic finance require the promotion of environmental and social goals, the industry has not contributed to these factors significantly. Moving forward, there is a need to incorporate the environmental social governance (ESG) factors in the broader concept of Shariah compliance and change the orientation of Islamic financial institutions to align them with the values and goals of Shariah [22]. Systematic efforts should also be directed to apply the concept in a more creative movement that would reflect Islamic values in financial dealings and would effectively deliver Islamic objectives in financial sphere. Islamic finance should be directed towards a bigger agenda of creating a new financial system [23].

In the West Asia-North African context, ethics, shared values, morality, and religion are interconnected and largely indistinguishable. Islam is a comprehensive way of life, "concerned with individual rights, practices and rules, but also with issues often associated with the state and governance" [24]. It comprises a wide range of rules, covering both the private and public spheres, ranging from hygiene and dietary norms and prayer and fasting to financial administration practices and civil and criminal law. Not surprisingly, in contrast to the West, in Islam there is no separation between religion and the state [25]. This gap might be filled by a development model that will be distinctly Islamic in nature, one that reflects the values, goals, priorities, and challenges shared by the people who are Muslim of the region [26].

6.2 Maqasid Shariah

Shariah is grounded on Islamic values and beliefs which include every section of life such as social, personal, economic, political, as well as intellectual life. Shariah refers to Islamic law that basically originates from the Shariah sources (Quran). The ultimate importance of the objectives and philosophies of Shariah is in line with the basic beliefs, values, as well as objectives of Islam [27]. Islam is a thorough as well as a comprehensive code of life, encompassing every aspect of individual or social life, life here or hereafter. So, Shariah imitates Islam's entire outlook. According to the philosophy of Islam, life is joined together, and it never separates between, for example, political or economic aspects, spiritual and moral aspects, and vice versa. Therefore, every facet of life, by the term Maslahah (public interest) which is a contemporary concept, is articulated or led by the Shariah to an academic comprehension of science, economics, technology, the environment, and politics. Likewise, misinterpretation of this primary concept might disintegrate progresses in all these areas. For apprehending Shariah, the purposes of Shariah need to be grasped correctly that permits liveliness, resistance, as well as originality in social policy. Maqasid Shariah can be explained as "The Ultimate Objectives of Shariah or Islam which consist of Protection of Religion, Protection of Life, Protection of Offspring, Protection of Intellect and Protection of Wealth or Property" [28].

In accordance with many scholars, Maqasid Shariah is serving human's well-being as well as protecting them from mischief. Nevertheless, various scholars explained Maqasid Shariah in various manners. According to Imam al-Ghazali, the objectives of Shariah can be in two categories, the deeni (related to religion) and the dunyawi (related to this material world). The dunyawi purposes are further grouped into four types which are all entirely meant to serve the single deeni purpose. The four dunyawi purposes are protection of nafs (life), nasl (lineage), aql (intellect), and mal (wealth). There are three broad divisions of Maqasid: the daruriyyat (essentials), the hajiyyat (supporting), and the tahseeniyyath (embellishments). The daruriyyat are those which are necessary, with no exception, for the benefits of deeni and dunyawi; thus according to al-Shatibi, the five essentials mentioned by al-Ghazali fall under daruriyyat [29].

There are four chief characteristics of Maqasid Shariah. First, Maqasid Shariah is the constituent of law and aims to guarantee the well-being of every human being, as well as protect them from harm. Second, Maqasid Shariah caters to the interests as well as needs of every human being since they are extensive. Third, Maqasid Shariah is comprehensive or complete, incorporating every human action regardless of whether they are related to the answerabilities to God (ibadah) or to the responsibilities of other human beings (muamalah). Fourth, Maqasid Shariah is decisive, as explained or accepted by numerous scholars from various item, texts, or sources of validations [30].

In accordance with Ibn Ashur and Kamil, Maqasid Shariah is to be perceived in its totality, not partly, as Islam includes both worldly life and life hereafter. The midpoint of Maqasid Shariah is Maslahah or public interest. Since our modern life is filled with different financial activities, finance plays a great role in our everyday lives; therefore, it is very simple as well as lucid to affirm that the society's harmonization is limited to regulating on financial matters only. Islam acknowledges this, categorizing the protection as well as safeguarding of wealth in the classification of essential matters (dharuriyyat), symbolizing finance's gratitude through the Maqasid Shariah is a treasured facet of life. As outlined in Maqasid, even Islamic rulings based on the five provisions acknowledge both the requirements of current and upcoming generations. So, the safety and well-being of upcoming generation is the Islamic values' foundation. Human safety as well as life on earth can be disturbed by climate change, probable risk, as well as extortions; therefore, it is commanded to demonstrate new rules, ethics, as well as public policies that enhance innovation (ijtihad) and leadership for saving people as well as nature. It is also important to distribute public goods in an unbiased manner for achieving public interest by fair trade as well as by maintaining Hima (protected areas) schemes as adapted in Islamic regime [31].

6.2.1 Green banking and Maqasid Shariah

The Shariah's greatest intentions rests within the concepts of thoughtfulness as well as administration, which aim to eliminate partiality, initiate fairness, as well as abate hardship through encouraging support as well as joint provision within the family and society in general. Shariah's objective as well as holistic value in accordance with Islamic scholars has commonly known to be Maslahah and Maqasid; both notions are entrenched by comprehending the public interest. Scholars make use of Maslahah and Maqasid nearly conversely as both the concepts often indicate the same meaning [30].

Muhammad bin Ibrahim, ex-governor of the Central Bank of Malaysia, shared his opinion by mentioning to support green technology towards a diverse as well as spirited financing ecosystem for green undertakings Islamic finance has great potential. Additionally, he articulated citing from the holy Quran (surah Al-Fajr: 11–14) that it is human's liability to maintain the atmosphere as well as natural possessions that Allah has made on this earth, counting the various forms of life. Every Muslim will be rewarded by Allah (swt) for contributing towards enlightening greenery. A hadith in Musnad Ahmad by Prophet Muhammad (pbuh), it is cited that the Almighty will recompense those who take care of the neighboring environment. Promoting preservation of natural resources and respecting every living being are the fundamental connection between the environment and mankind. In Surah

Al-Rum: 41, Allah (swt) the Almighty cautions human beings by announcing that unembellished destruction of the sea and land would come upon those who abuse the environment; therefore, not being able to treat the environment appropriately would be harmful. Hence, for ensuring ecological sustainability, it is crucial for everyone to count Islamic banks to resolutely play their roles. The governor debates that achieving environmentally friendly sustainability is the liability of everybody and the banking industry must do its part [32].

Islamic teaching is always compatible with the benefit of ummah. The concept of sustainable development, which is a greatly discussed matter in modern time, is looking for the way out to guarantee development in a sustained way which is only likely to be achieved by adhering to the divine law of ethics. To conclude, Islamic banks are focusing on achieving Maqasid Shariah so does the green banking. By analyzing green banking policy and guidelines of Bangladesh, it is ascertained that green banking aims to also protect life, family, and property [33, 34]. Moreover, green business activities also resemble to attaining Maqasid Shariah [35].

6.2.2 SDGs and Maqasid Shariah

The idea of a sustainable development model that is connected to religious values stands somewhat in opposition to the current model, which reflects a separation of religious ideology and public policy making. The sustainable development discourse has, however, acknowledged that the three pillars of sustainable development need to be completed by an ethical dimension at the level of popular values. The World Summit on Sustainable Development in Johannesburg (2002) added a short paragraph 6 to its Programme of Action: "We acknowledge the importance of ethics for sustainable development and, therefore, emphasize the need to consider ethics in the implementation of Agenda 21" [36]. Therefore, there is convergence of SDGs in general and the intention of climate management with the Maqasid Shariah. Maqasid Shariah should drive Islamic banking and finance is self-evident. Islamic economists invoke the framework of Maqasid Shariah to chart a new trajectory for Islamic finance. While many classical and contemporary Islamic scholars have discussed and elaborated upon the Maqasid Shariah framework, the Islamic Research and Training Institute (IRTI) has undertaken pioneering research that underlines the fact that many SDGs clearly align with Maqasid Shariah. The Maqasid Shariah-driven Islamic finance, therefore, would work towards achieving the SDGs. There is a growing realization that Islamic financial institutions should align their goals with the SDGs so that they would be able to protect and promote Maqasid Shariah. The SDGs are 17 in numbers. The next section will try to find the convergence SDGs and the MS framework prescribed by Imam al-Ghazali.

The UN Sustainable Development Summit was held in New York from September 25 to 27, 2015, for the adoption of an ambitious, bold, and universal sustainable development agenda that will end poverty and promote prosperity by 2030 while addressing the environment. The summit outcome document, entitled "Transforming our World: The 2030 Agenda for Sustainable Development," was agreed on by the 193 member states of the United Nations and includes 17 sustainable development goals and 169 targets. The 17 goals are No. 1 no poverty; No. 2 zero hunger; No. 3 good health and well-being; No. 4 quality education; No. 5 gender equality; No. 6 clean water and sanitation; No. 7 affordable and clean energy; No. 8 decent work and economic growth; No. 9 industry innovation and infrastructure; No. 10 reduced inequality; No. 11 sustainable cities and communities; No. 12 responsible consumption and production; No. 13 climate action; No. 14 life below water; No. 15 life on land; No. 16 peace, justice, and strong institutions; and No. 17 partnerships for the goals.

To appreciate the SDGs understanding, five Ps are vital; these are people, planet, prosperity, peace, and partnership. These five Ps are considered as elements of SDGs, and among them three are the pillars of SD—people, planet, and prosperity. The 2030 Agenda is indivisible; therefore, countries should avoid cherry picking goals and carefully assess the trade-offs across goals/targets. SDGs are very comprehensive, designed to achieve universal goals, agreed by world community in general, and have no direct conflicts with Islamic percepts. Maqasid Shariah is also very systematic and attempts to address human welfare and well-being in a comprehensive and organized way. The following paragraph is trying to map SDGs into Maqasid Shariah.

One of the first pillars of Imam al-Ghazali's Maqasid Shariah framework is protection of faith, and SDG goals 1, 2, 3, 6, and 10 focus on reducing vulnerability which in turn is believed to help strengthen their faith. The second pillar is protection of life (nafs), and goals 2, 3, 6, 8, and 11 in ensure healthy lives and promoting well-being for sustainable development. The third pillar is protection of progeny (nasl) and Zakat (one of the pillars of faith in Islam) that helps people escape the poverty trap, promoting peace and protecting the environment such as goals 3, 5, 7, 11, 12, 13, 14, 15, and 16, which is consistent with human progeny. The fourth pillar is protection of intellect (aqal), and it is in alignment with SDG 1, 2, and 9 which facilitates access to healthy nourishment and quality education and makes children more productive in the future. The last pillar is protection of wealth (mal), and Zakat has inbuilt wealth transfer SDG 10 which can help generate economic activity, SDG 8, and a social safety net, SDGs 1 and 3 [37].

7. Conclusion

This chapter is divided into several sections to describe essential ideas related to green banking. The first section is the introduction, and the second section covers the definition of green banking—banking activities that are concerned with the environment and provide financing to green business which is involved in environmental restoration. The third section represents the importance of green banking for successful implementation of the sustainable development goals. The fourth section discusses about the impact that green banking must create green business. The fifth section focuses on the relevance of Shariah in Islamic banking, SDGs, and green financing. Green banking being a new trend needs more attention from policymakers and regulators; specifically, the central banks can play a vital role to enhance green banking movement and to set up more and more green business. Beside banks, nonbanks financial institutions also should involve more in green financing to restore environmental balance and to preserve a livable condition for future generation. Bangladesh is a very good example of introducing and enforcing green banking policy and guidelines among the Southeast Asian countries. In fact, the reality of the country is that it is situated in an extremely risky zone based on a report published by a British consultancy firm [38]. Moreover, in terms of pollution, the country scored one of the top positions and vulnerable to climate change risk too [39]. Therefore, the country is serious about green banking and can be a very good example for others. To face the reality, when leaders are committed to implement SDGs by 2030, the involvement of financial sector in green banking is an essential condition to accelerate the process of implementation. Indeed, green financing would help attain few SDGs such as goal Nos. 7, 9, 11, 12, and 13. On the other hand, the features of green banking and objectives are very close to Maqasid Shariah. In general, conservation, reduce dependency on paper, increase online banking or financing, and environmental risk rating before granting financing to borrower are few features of green banking which do not contradict with Maqasid Shariah but rather meet the objectives of Shariah. Therefore, Islamic bank along with conventional banks have huge opportunities to focus on green financing and to attain the SDGs.

Author details

Taslima Julia* and Salina Kassim
IIUM Institute of Islamic Banking and Finance (IIiBF), IIUM, Kuala Lumpur, Malaysia

*Address all correspondence to: taslima.julia1602@gmail.com

References

[1] Brundtland Commission. The World Commission on Environment and Development. Oxford: Brundtland Commission; 1987

[2] Corbin S. Basics of Qualitative Research: Techniques and Procedures for Developing Grounded Theory. Thousand Oaks, CA: SAGE; 2008

[3] Lindenberg N. Definition of Green Banking [Internet]. 2014. Available from: file:///C:/Users/User/Desktop/New folder/Green folder/Green finance

[4] GIZ. Green Finance—An Innovative Approach to Fostering Sustainable Economic Development and Adaptation to Climate Change. Germany: Bonn and Eschborn; 2011

[5] Tara K, Singh S, Kumar R. Green banking for environmental management: A paradigm shift. Current World Environment: An International Research Journal of Environmental Sciences [Internet]. 2015;**10**(3):1029-1038. Available from: http://www.cwejournal.org/vol10no3/green-banking-for-environmental-management-a-paradigm-shift/

[6] Circular 2 GBPG. Green Banking Policy Guidelines. Bangladesh Bank. Dhaka: Green Banking and CSR Department; 2011

[7] BBSBD. Quarterly Review Report on Green Banking Activities of Banks and Financial Institutions [Internet]. Dhaka, Bangladesh: BBSBD; 2019. Available from: https://www.bb.org.bd/pub/quaterly/greenbanking/greenbanking_octdec2019.pdf

[8] Garg S. Green Banking: An Overview [Internet]. 2015. Available from: http://gjar.org/publishpaper/vol2issue8/d281r41.pdf

[9] Smith SE. What is green business? [Internet]. 2003. Available from: http://www.wisegeek.com/ what-is-green-business.htm [cited 13 May 2015]

[10] Friend G. The Truth about Green Business. 1st ed. New Jersey: Pearson Education; 2009

[11] Zsolnai L. Green business or community economy? International Journal of Social Economics. 2002;**29**(8):652-662

[12] Gilbert AJ. The Value of Green Marketing Education at the University of Wisconsin-La Crosse. St. La Crosse, USA; UW-L Journal of Undergraduate Research X. 2007

[13] Allen C, Clouth S. Green Economy, Green Growth, and Low-Carbon Development–History, Definitions, and a Guide to Recent Publications [Internet]. New York, United Nations: Division for Sustainable Development, Department of Economic and Social Affairs; 2012. pp. 1-63. Available from: https://sustainabledevelopment.un.org/index.php?page=view&type=400&nr=634&menu=1516

[14] UNEP. Towards a Theory of Sustainable Finance. UNEP Inquiry/CIGI Research Convening: Design of a Sustainable Financial System. Waterloo, Canada: UNEP; 2015

[15] UNCCC. Green Governor title is given to Dr. Atiur Rahmn. In: United Nation Climate Change Conference. Doha, Qatar: UNCCC; 2012

[16] Rahman A. Financial Services at People's Doorstep. Dhaka, Bangladesh: Governor, Bangladesh Bank; 2010

[17] Bank B. Bangladesh Bank: The Central Bank of Bangladesh [Internet]. 2020. Available from: https://www.bb.org.bd/fnansys/bankfi.php

[18] BBGBR. Quarterly Review Report on Green Banking Activities of Banks and Financial Institutions [Internet]. Dhaka, Bangladesh: BBGBR; 2014. Available from: https://www.bb.org.bd/pub/quaterly/greenbanking/greenbanking_octdec2014.pdf

[19] IRTI, IDBG. Climate Change Financing: Role of Islamic Finance. Manila, Philippines: IRTI, IDBG; 2016

[20] Abdulazeem A. Contemporary Islamic financing modes: Between contract technicalities and Shariah objectives. Islamic Economic Studies. 2010;**17**(2):19-20

[21] Hussain M, Shahmorhadi A, Turk R. IMF Working Paper: An Overview of Islamic Finance. Washington DC, USA: International Monetary Fund; June 2015

[22] Kasri R, Ahmed H. Assessing socio-economic development based on Maqāṣ id al-Sharīʿah principles: Normative frameworks, methods and implementation in Indonesia. Islamic Economic Studies. 2015;**23**(1):73-100

[23] Laldin MA. Shariah scholar, Shariah governance and Maqasid al Shariah application in Islamic finance. In: 4th International Conference on Islamic Business (ICIB). Islamabad, Pakistan: Riphah Centre of Islamic Business (RCIB); 2016

[24] Mohamad M. A black the West and Islam: Religion and Political Thought in World History. Oxford: Oxford University Press; 2008

[25] Rkiouak DL. Bridging the gap: An Islamic Sustainable Development Model for the WANA Region. Amman, Jordan: WANA Institute, Majlis El Hasan; 2016

[26] Holt P. The Cambridge History of Islam. Cambridge: Cambridge University Press; 1977. p. 18

[27] Dusuki AW, Abozaid A. A critical appraisal on the challenges of realizing Maqasid al-Shari'ah in Islamic banking and finance. IIUM J Econ Manag. 2007;**15**(4):143-165

[28] Othman S. Shariah and Maquasid al Shariah—A brief Overview [Internet]. SOIM Islamic Management; 2010. Available from: http://islamicstrategymanagement.blogspot.com/p/maqasid-al-shariah.htm [Cited: 12 October 2015]

[29] Dusuki AW, Bouheraoua S. The framework of Maqasid al-Shariah and its implication for Islamic finance. Islam Civilisational Renew Journal. 2011;**2**(2):316-336

[30] Dusuki AW, Bouheraoua S. The framework of Maqasid al-Shariah and it's implication for Islamic finance. Islam Civilisational Renew Journal. 2011;**2**(2):3

[31] Al-Jayyousi OR. Islam and Sustainable Development New Worldview. Surrey, England: Gower Publishing Limited; 2012

[32] Bin IM. Role of the Islamic financial system in supporting green technology. Kuala Lumpur, Malaysia: Deputy Governor of the Central Bank of Malaysia, at The Green Financing: Discover Green Technology Industry in Malaysia; 2013

[33] Julia T, Rahman MP, Kassim S. Shariah compliance of green banking policy in Bangladesh. Humanomics. 2016;**32**(4):15-16

[34] Julia T, Kassim S. Exploring green banking performance of Islamic banks vs conventional banks in Bangladesh based on Maqasid Shariah framework. Journal of Islamic Marketing. 2020;**11**(3)

[35] Julia T, Kassim S, Erae A. Are the green projects in line with the Maqasid

Shariah? An assessment of green firms in Bangladesh. In: The Global Conference on Islamic Economics and Finance 2018. Kuala Lumpur, Malaysia: Bank Negara Malaysia; 2018. pp. 317-335

[36] WSSD. The World Summit on Sustainable Development [Internet]. Johannesburg, South Africa: WSSD; 2002. Available from: http://www.cepal.org/rio20/

[37] Kasbani A. Sustainable Development Goals and Islamic Financing. KL, Ist Global Conference on Islamic Banking and Finance (GCIEF). Kuala Lumpur, Malaysia: Bank Negara Malaysia; 2018

[38] Maplecroft. Bangladesh Ranked World's Most Vulnerable Country to Climate Change [Internet]. Climate Home. 2013. Available from: http://www.climatechangenews.com/2013/10/30/bangladesh-rated-worlds-most-vulnerable-country-to-climate-change/

[39] WHO. Dirtiest Cities of the World. Dhaka, Bangladesh: The Daily Star; 9 May 2014-

Chapter 7

New Malaysia, Brexit and US-China Trade War: Credit Risk to Malaysian Banks

Wooi Keong Yong and Wooi Meng Yong

Abstract

A country's economic prosperity is intimately linked to the external and internal forces that exert influences on its economy. While some of these forces may not be under the overt control of the country's economic planners, any disruption to the economy by these forces may just tip the balance that causes financial hardship to millions of people. Certainly, national governments through fiscal and monetary policy measures may attempt to prevent such a catastrophe, but what happens if at such a critical time, the needed government leadership is suddenly not available? In such a situation, what will be the most appropriate reaction from the central bank and what is the likely effect to the country's banking industry? While this scenario might sound like an interesting thought experiment in a banking classroom, a similar situation is in fact unfolding in real life at this very moment in Malaysia.

Keywords: Malaysian banking, Malaysian economy, Bank Negara Malaysia, Brexit, trade wars, China, USA, New Malaysia, economic uncertainties, recession, credit risk, repayment risk, Corona virus, Malaysian politics

1. Introduction

2018 was a period of interesting change in Malaysia. The General Election held on May 9 resulted in the ruling Barisan Nasional (BN) coalition, which has held power in the country ever since Malaysia's independence in 1957, being voted out of power. In its place, the Pakatan Harapan (PH) coalition formed the new Malaysian government. It seemed that the unprecedented change of government also brought a new wave of hope for the Malaysian people. The Malaysian economy grew above market expectations in the fourth quarter of 2018, buoyed by strong domestic activities which grew 5.6% along with total external trade that grew at 6.9% [1].

This was excellent news for the people, as earlier in the year in March 2018, there appeared to be a looming threat of a full-on trade war between the United States and China. China is Malaysia's second largest trade partner at 13%, and 9% of Malaysian trade is with the United States, its third largest trade partner, respectively [2]. Worries about the trade war between these two countries had already caused Asian markets in general to trade lower—the KLCI (Kuala Lumpur Composite Index) dropped 0.6% to 1865.22 points, and Hong Kong's Hang Seng Index dropped 2.5% to 30, 309.29 points after US and China announced tariffs on each other on 26 March 2018 [3]. Despite the threat of a trade war, there were potential benefits for Malaysia. It was thought that China may scale back purchases of US Treasury bonds, and divert capital flows to Ringgit assets, which will be beneficial to Malaysian Government Securities' yields [2]. There is even the possibility that the price of oil, a key Malaysian export, will increase as a result of the trade war [2]. Indeed, by the fourth quarter of 2018, most Malaysians had a positive outlook on their personal finances and job prospects, with 70% of Malaysians believing that the state of personal finances in the next year would be excellent or good, and 71% had a positive view of their job prospects [4].

However, this positive mood had declined by the second quarter of 2019, with only 63% of Malaysians believing that the state of personal finances in the next year would be excellent or good, and 63% had a positive view of their job prospects [5]. In Ref., [5] also found that 70% of the Malaysian consumers already believed that the country was already in economic recession. In response, the central bank of Malaysia, Bank Negara Malaysia (BNM) signaled the banking industry that they should continue to give out more loans by reducing the Statutory Reserve Requirement (SRR) Ratio to 3% from 16 November 2019 [6]. This is the latest series of SRR ratio reduction by BNM, which started in 2016, when the central bank reduced the SRR from 4 to 3.5% [7]. This message was reinforced by BNM on 22 January 2020, when the Monetary Policy Committee of Bank Negara announced the reduction of the Overnight Policy Rate (OPR) to 2.75%, and considered the adjustment to the OPR as a pre-emptive measure to secure economic growth with price stability [8].

What had happened to Malaysia between 2018 and 2019 timeframe that had caused such a drastic change in its perceived economic fortunes is a point of conjecture at this time, but several external forces will be discussed here, which cumulatively, may explain the present situation that Malaysia has found herself in. Further, the recent shocking developments in the political scene in Malaysia on 24 February 2020 also add turmoil to the present situation of economic uncertainty. Through it all stands the Malaysian banker, duty bound to protect the interests of their respective employers, and at the same time fully aware that should they be too careful, they may just doom the country to another economic recession that they have tried so hard to avoid. Conversely, BNM is counting on the banking industry to continue to provide the necessary funds for economic activities despite the heightened risk of non-performing loans and the negative impacts this will have on the banking industry. It would almost seem that the BNM appears to be willing to expose the banking industry to more risks in order to protect the Malaysian economy.

2. Capital and lending

Giving loans has always been an integral part of banking operations [9]. In 2018, CIMB Group, Malaysia's second largest commercial bank by assets, recorded that its gross loans account for 63% of its total assets and Maybank, Malaysia's largest commercial bank with over 20 million customers, recorded that its gross loans in 2018 is 62.8% over its total assets [10]. This shows the importance of lending to banks, as it is the most important income generating activity to banks [11]. Banks would evaluate potential customers, and then decide the level of risk such a loan would impose, charge the appropriate interest and disburse the amount requested, while ensuring that the capital borrowed is returned over the agreed time-frame of the loan. The interest charged will then yield interest income to the banks. However, there are instances when the borrower defaults on paying back the loan, and this causes the lending bank to suffer financial loss, as their income will be affected and potentially there is a danger that the capital loaned may be lost as well.

This was the case in Malaysia during the Asian Financial Crisis of 1997–1998, when cases of Non-Performing Loans (NPLs)/Impared Loans (as expressed as the ratio of net impaired loans to net total loans in percentage) reached 8–9% [12]. Because of the Asian Financial Crisis of 1997, growth and innovation in Malaysia are constrained by banks whose capital has been eroded by accumulating non-performing loans [13]. This leads to the mergers of several banks that shaped the banking industry to the one that we see in Malaysia today [14].

Therefore, it is clear that anything that affects the banking sector's lending activity will adversely affect the income of the banks. The factors that may affect such activities may be divided into two types of factors, internal factors (bank specific factors), and external factors like the economic climate or political climate. By its nature, external factors may not be readily controlled by the bank [14]. This makes it harder for banks to maintain profitable lending. Malaysian banks loan growth remained low at 5% as of June 2018, due to the poor performance of working capital loans [15] and loan growth was projected to remain flat at 5–6% level in 2019 [16]. The external factors are discussed next.

2.1 Brexit and Malaysia

Brexit is a portmanteau for 'Britain' and 'Exit', following a referendum in the United Kingdom (UK) that resulted in London, Scotland and Northern Ireland electing to remain in the European Union (EU) while the rest of England and Wales deciding to leave the EU [17]. Following [18], there is little short-term impact of Brexit to Malaysia. The UK is not a large trading partner of Malaysia, and despite UK's status as the financial center of Europe, any impact of Brexit will not have a big effect to Malaysian financial markets [18]. In fact, the weakened British Pound (GBP) will even make the UK a favourable destination for Malaysian students, and well-to-do Malaysians may even find it a good time to holiday there or to buy properties in the UK. This view is echoed by [19], despite the UK contributing RM 1.9 billion worth of Foreign Direct Investment (FDI) while the EU invested RM 30.3 billion in the same period in 2016, and estimated that Brexit will not affect FDI to Malaysia.

However, Brexit's effect on the UK economy is expected to be not so benign. Following [20], a recession in the UK is a strong possibility. The Organization for Economic Cooperation and Development (OECD) has already predicted the UK economy to grow at only 1% in 2020. An impending economic recession in the UK will have a negative impact on the EU, since half of the UK's imports come from the EU. In addition, with a general slowdown in the global economy caused by instability in global trade due to trade spats, the OEDC concludes that it is likely to dampen the EU's growth rate to about 1% as well in 2020 [20].

Given that Malaysian trade with the EU is about 10%, a weaker EU economy will impact the Malaysian economy in general. Further, with the expected weakening of the GBP against the Ringgit, Malaysian exports to the UK, already at a tiny 0.2% of total exports, will increasingly become less competitive in the UK market [20]. These events do not bode well for the Malaysian economy.

2.2 US-China trade war

Malaysia has always been a trading nation, and international trade has consistently contributed to the Malaysian gross domestic product (GDP), and since 2017 its share of contribution to the GDP was higher than 130% [21]. Following [21], there is concern that the Malaysian economy will shift into lower gear on fears of a gloomier global economic outlook. The International Monetary Fund (IMF) had already reduced its 2019 forecast for the ASEAN region from 3.9 to 3.7%. Echoing a similar sentiment, the Asian Development Bank has put the region's growth rate expectation at 5.8%. The sole underlying cause that contributed to these downward revisions is the US-China trade war.

As discussed earlier, the US and China are two of Malaysia's largest trade partners. Therefore, any trade policies that harm trade between these countries could affect Malaysia's trade position, especially when Malaysia's intermediate goods exports to China are significant [21]. Further, the weakening global markets will impact demand for electronics, one of the key Malaysian exports. Palm oil demand is also expected to fall, as does the price of oil [21].

The slowdown in exports will result in the narrowing of the Malaysian current account surpluses [21] as well, giving the Malaysian government less money to spend on fiscal measures to stimulate the economy. Indeed, the 2020 Malaysian economic growth forecast had been continually downgraded, with Finch Solutions predicting only 3.7% expansion, down from an earlier projection of 4.7% [22]. To navigate the difficult economic situation, it is vital for the Malaysian government to establish forward-looking policies. Thus far, it appears to be contented to rely on BNM to apply monetary policies to shore up the economy. This may soon be insufficient.

2.3 New Malaysia

When the Pakatan Harapan (PH) party took over the reins of power after the 2018 General Election, Tun Dr. Mahathir Mohamad was made Prime Minister with an understanding that there will be a transition plan for Datuk Seri Anwar Ibrahim to succeed him mid-term [23]. However, the PH government collapsed on Monday 24 February 2020 by Tun Dr. Mahathir's shock resignation as Prime Minister. Tun Dr. Mahathir's resignation was speculated to be caused by a power struggle between the Prime Minister and his planned successor [22]. Economists quickly opined that the political uncertainty this has caused is harmful to the Malaysian economy [22].

The resignation by a country's Prime Minister at any time during the tenure of a government has the effect of causing the entire cabinet to be dissolved [24]. Effectively, Malaysia does not have a government anymore. Unfortunately, the dissolution of the Malaysian government cannot come at a worse time, as in the past few months, an additional threat to the Malaysian economy had emerged in the form of a novel corona virus, called Covid-19 [25]. While Covid-19 is currently under control, the disease has already caused a huge impact on the global economy, and Malaysia's economy has not been spared [25]. Accordingly, the Malaysian government was scheduled to announce an economic stimulus package to stimulate the economy on 27 February 2020. Unfortunately, the sudden resignation of the Prime Minister on 24 February 2020 has caused fears that the stimulus package has been put on hold [22, 25]. Indeed, this was stated by the former Finance Minister Lim Guan Eng on 25 February 2020 that Tun Dr. Mahathir will announce the economic stimulus at a later date [26].

Unease about the political uncertainty arising from a suddenly-defunct government and its possible effect on the Malaysian economy prompted BNM to announce on 25 February 2020 that it was closely monitoring the financial markets, and stated that there was sufficient liquidity in the financial markets [27]. The political situation had settled down somewhat by the 27th of February 2020, with Tun Dr. Mahathir appointed Interim Prime Minister. The irony of his actions now fully realized, Tun Dr. Mahathir had stated that he had intended to resign from his job, but now only he among his cabinet colleagues still had one.

As such, Tun Dr. Mahathir was able to announce the anxiously awaited economic stimulus on 27 February 2020. The economic stimulus package has three strategies—to manage the impact of Covid-19, spur a people-centric growth and encourage quality investment. With immediate effect, government employees who are in medical profession will receive an extra allowance of RM 400 a month, while Immigration and other civil servants involved with the fight against Covid-19 will receive RM 200 extra monthly, until the outbreak is over [25].

The effectiveness of the stimulus package to counter the effects of Covid-19 remains to be seen. Goldman Sachs warned that it does not expect US companies to generate earnings growth in 2020 due to the Covid-19 virus [28]. It also expected that a more severe pandemic would lead to a more prolonged disruption and even a US recession. Goldman Sachs also expected a severe decline in the Chinese economic activities as well [28]. Indeed, blue chip US companies like Microsoft, Apple, Booking Holdings and Anheuser-Busch InBev are already reporting that they no longer expect to meet revenue targets due to Covid-19 [28, 29].

With Malaysia's major trading partners expected to experience economic troubles, the Malaysian economy is expected to experience significant challenges going forward. Following [30], the Malaysian economic growth rate is expected to be 2.5% at the end of the first quarter of 2020. It is expected to slowly recover to 4.4% by the same time period next year [30]. How does this data on economic performance affect Malaysian bankers?

2.4 Malaysian banking

Following [11], economic and political factors have the potential to adversely affect the banking sector's lending activity and this will adversely affect the income of the banks. Consumer lending risks can be moderated by banks using computerized credit reporting as provided by CTOS Data Systems Sdn Bhd and BNM. CTOS produces the MyCTOS Basic Report and MyCTOS Score Report by using information sourced from various public sources such as the National Registration Department, Registrar of Societies, the Malaysian Insolvency Department, Companies Commission of Malaysia and publication of legal proceedings or litigation records [31]. BNM also provides credit reports and this is managed by the Credit Bureau of BNM, known as the Central Credit Reference Information System (CCRIS). CCRIS gathers credit related information from all borrowers of participating financial institutions in Malaysia, and this includes all licensed commercial banks, Islamic banks, investment banks, development financial institutions, insurance companies, payment instrument issuers, rehabilitation companies, building societies, credit leasing companies and government agencies. These financial institutions are required to report on a regular basis information like profiles of borrowers (name, business or personal identification number, date of birth/registration, and address, among others) credit application details (amount of borrowing applied, date of application, type of facility) and credit account details (type of credit facilities, credit limit, outstanding balance, instalment amount, conduct of account and legal action status, if any) [31].

Therefore, it is possible for financial institutions in Malaysia to access up-to-date financial records for any potential individual borrower and assess the suitability of lending risk by obtaining CCRIS or CTOS financial data. Even so, despite such a system in place, banks continue to suffer cases of Non-Performing Loans (NPLs)/ Impaired Loans. Data from BNM show the ratio of net impaired loans to net total loans in percentage [32] of a high of 9% in November 1998 to a low of 1.2% in January 2016, with this figure hovering around 1.2% throughout 2015. While the reduction of impaired loans since 1998 has been significant, the banking industry has seemingly been unable to completely eradicate impaired loans/NPLs. As a result of this inability, the collective impairment provisions that has to be made to account

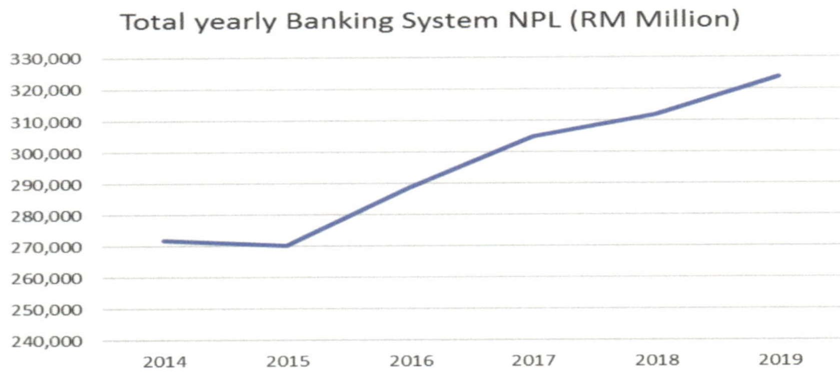

Figure 1.
Malaysian banking NPL. source: BNM.

for the impaired loans totaled in the region of RM 16,354 million in January 2016 alone, and this figure increased to RM 23, 914.4 million in February 2019, even though the ratio of net impaired loans to net total loans in percentage has been reduced to 0.93% by February 2019. Credit scoring methods are by nature quantitative methods of evaluating credit and are only as good as the scoring algorithms that predict consumer behavior. If it is implemented properly, then cases of impaired loans should not have happened at all.

More worryingly for bankers, such a system does not exist for another important consumer group of lending, small to medium sized Industries (SMEs). SMEs contribute one third of the country's Gross Domestic Product (GDP). This has increased to 37.1% in 2018 [11] and comprises 97% of all formal business establishments in Malaysia. SMEs employ 66% of the Malaysian workforce as of 2018 and BNM also believes that SMEs have the potential to contribute more to the Malaysian economy. It is expected that by the year 2020, SMEs contribution to the Malaysian GDP will increase to 41% [11]. Also, financial institutions like banks are the main source of financing for SMEs, and lending to SMEs constitute almost half of the total sum of the financial institutions lending to the business sector [11]. The financing approval rate from financial institutions has exceeded 80%, with the financing approval rate reaching 91% in 2019. As of February 2018, there was still RM 3.3 billion still available to SMEs to use for working capital and for buying machinery [11]. However, the higher loan approval rates to SMEs have also had some unintended consequences to financial institutions, which showed an increase in NPLs from the business sector in 2019 [11] (**Figure 1**).

Following [33], an increase in NPLs will affect the bank's profitability and liquidity which are the main components for the efficiency of the bank. There has been some research to find methods to mitigate this by using non-quantitative methods by analyzing the SME sales officers' psychological factors [11–14] as well as their past experiences [34]. Indeed, since there is no computerized credit analysis available for SMEs, banks have been forced to approach loan applications by SMEs using a case-by-case approach, where a personalized banking style is adopted. This makes the case for understanding how an individual bank sales officer approaches a lending case very relevant in order to minimize NPLs.

3. Conclusion

The global economic events of Brexit and the US-China Trade War in the last few years along with the unanticipated Covid-19 pandemic are still influencing the

Malaysian economy, and as a result, it poses great credit risks to Malaysian banks. One might even be tempted to call this a "perfect storm" for the banking industry. The surprise political events of 24 February 2020 had just magnified those risks. Faced with a lack of governmental fiscal policy, BNM must rely on the tools it has on hand to get on with the task of protecting the Malaysian economy. It is expected that BNM will soon be forced to further reduce the OPR yet again [35]. This will mean that Malaysian banks' interest income, already under strain, will be further reduced. Even so, the BNM is fast running out of options. As an analogy, if BNM was an archer, its two quivers of OPR and SRR is running out of arrows. It is clear that BNM cannot prevent an economic disaster on its own. However, for Malaysian bankers, a time of hardship is just beginning.

Acknowledgements

The authors acknowledge Dato' Sia Cheong Lin, Business Partner, Bangun Usaha Sukses Sejahtera (BUSS) Malaysia Sdn. Bhd. for his informative views on Entrepreneurship of the Malaysian insurance industry and the way forward; Yvonne De Souza, Customer Service and Operations Manager, Hong Leong Bank Malaysia Bhd. for her valuable insights into customer sentiments and front-line banking staff alike; and Nicholas Ho Keng Yeong, District Sales Executive, Expeditors (M) Sdn. Bhd. for his insights on the Malaysian logistics industry.

Thanks

The authors thank Aiden Yong Ern Liang, for his help in clarifying economic concepts and sorting research documents and classifying them accordingly. Dr. Maizaitulaidawati Md Husin, for her knowledge, continuous support, and encouragement.

Author details

Wooi Keong Yong[1,2*] and Wooi Meng Yong[3]

1 Centre for American Education, Sunway University, Subang Jaya, Malaysia

2 Azman Hashim International Business School, Universiti Teknologi Malaysia, Kuala Lumpur, Malaysia

3 Corporate Banking, United Overseas Bank Malaysia Bhd, Kuala Lumpur, Malaysia

*Address all correspondence to: wooikeongy@sunway.edu.my

References

[1] Ministry of Finance. Malaysian Economy Fourth Quarter 2018: An Update [Internet]. Available from: https://www.treasury.gov.my/pdf/ekonomi/Q4-2018/Q4-2018.pdf

[2] Macquarie Equities Research. How Will a Trade War Affect Malaysia? [Internet]. 2018. Available from: https://www.malaysiawarrants.com.my/marketnews/highlight?cat=todayhighlight&id=4089&gclid=Cj0KCQiAqNPyBRCjARIsAKAWFyE4Y7PDUkx5sT7SzyLeJEBaqB9SB5LvmvX1wO-CUrDhufrtaxn7aYaApwsEALw_wcB

[3] Macquarie Equities Research. Fears of Trump's Trade War Escalate [Internet]. 2018. Available from: https://www.malaysiawarrants.com.my/marketnews/highlight?cat=todayhighlight&id=4085

[4] Neilsen. Malaysia's Q4 2018 Consumer Confidence Dips [Internet]. 2019. Available from: https://www.nielsen.com/my/en/insights/article/2019/q4-2018-consumer-confidence-dips/

[5] Neilsen. Malaysians Remained Confident in Q2 2019, But Post Election Optimism Is Fading [Internet]. 2019. Available from: https://www.neilsen.com/my/en/insights/article/2019/malaysia-consumers-remained-confident-in-q2-2019-but-post-election-optimism-is-fading/

[6] Bank Negara Malaysia. Decrease in SRR Ratio [Internet]. 2019. Available from: https://www.bnm.gov.my/index.php?ch=en_press&pg=en_press&ac=4948

[7] Bank Negara Malaysia. Decrease in SRR Ratio [Internet]. 2016. Available from: https://www.bnm.gov.my/index.php?ch=en_press&pg=en_press&ac=2952&lang=en

[8] Bank Negara Malaysia. Monetary Policy Statement [Internet]. 2020. Available from: https://www.bnm.gov.my/index.php?ch=en_press&pg=en_press&ac=4980&lang=en

[9] Wei-Shong LP, Kuo-Chung MA. The internal performance measures of bank lending: A value-added approach. Benchmarking: An International Journal. 2002;**13**(3):273-289. DOI: 10.1108/14635770610668785

[10] Straits Times. Top Malaysian Lenders Maybank, CIMB Post Mixed Quarterly Results [Internet]. 2018. Available from: https://www.straitstimes.com/business/banking/top-malaysian-lenders-maybank-cimb-post-mixed-quarterly-results

[11] Yong WK. Factors influencing bank officers into recommending financial products to SME's: A literature review. International Journal of Innovation and Business Strategy. 2019;**12**(2):1-26. Available from: https://business.utm.my/ijibs/issue/vol12-no2

[12] Bank Negara Malaysia. Monthly Highlights and Statistics [Internet]. 2019. Available from: http://www.bnm.gov.my/index.php?ch=en_publication_catalogue&pg=en_msb&ac=258&lang=en

[13] Karim MZA, Chan SG, Hassan S. Bank efficiency and non-performing loans: Evidence from Malaysia and Singapore. Prague Economic Papers. 2010;**2**(1):118-132. Available from: http://www.vse.cz/pep/pdf/367.pdf

[14] Yong WK. Identifying key beliefs of bank officer's intention to minimize NPL's from small to medium sized industries, a preliminary study. Middle East Journal of Management.

[15] Asian Banking and Finance. Malaysian Bank Loan Growth Remains Dismal at 5% in June [Internet]. 2018.

Available from: http://www.asianbankingandfinance.net/retail-banking/news/malaysian-banks-loan-growth-remains-dismal-5-in-june

[16] Star Online. 5%–6% Growth Seen for 2019 [Internet]. 2018. Available from: https://www.thestar.com.my/business/business-news/2018/12/24/56-loan-growth-seen-for-2019/

[17] Ching Y. What you Need to Know about Brexit [Internet]. 2016. Available from: https://poskod.my/cheat-sheets/need-know-brexit/

[18] Nambiar S. Why Brexit Matter So Much to Malaysia [Internet]. 2016. Available from: https://www.theedgemarkets.com/article/my-say-why-brexit-matter-so-much-to-malausia

[19] Lee I. How Will Brexit Affect Malaysia? [Internet]. 2016. Available from: https://www.imoney.my/articles/brexit-uk-votes-to-leave-eu

[20] Xavier JA. The Brexit Deal: What's Next? [Internet]. 2019. Available from: https://www.nst.com.my/opinion/columnist/2019/10/534461/brexit-deal-whats-next

[21] Samirul A. US-China Trade War and its Impact on Malaysia [Internet]. 2019. Available from: https://www.theedgemarkets.com/article/my-say-uschina-trade-war-and-its-impact-malaysia

[22] The Star. Malaysia's Power Struggle Puts economy's Outlook at Risk [Internet]. 2020. Available from: https://www.thestar.com.my/business-news/2020/02/25/malaysias-power-struggle-puts-economys-outlook-at-risk#cxrecs_s

[23] Teoh S. Mahathir's Meeting with King Ends amid Speculation some PKR MP's Set to Return to PH [Internet]. 2020. Available from: https://www.straitstimes.com/asia/se-asia/malaysia-awaits-result-of-royal-search-for-pm

[24] Suriati SA. The Cabinet Automatically Dissolves when the Prime Minister Resigns, Said Legal Experts. [Internet]. 2020. Available from: https://www.bernama.com/en/general/news.php?id=1816227

[25] Mazwin NA, Kaos J. Govt Unveils RM20bil Stimulus Package over Covid-19 Impact [Internet]. 2020. Available from: https://www.thestar.com.my/news/nation/2020/02/27/govt-unveils-rm20bil-stimulus-package-over-covid-19-impact#cxrecs_s

[26] Zakiah K. Dr M to Announce Economic Stimulus Package at a Later Date, Says Guan Eng [Internet]. 2020. Available from: https://www.thestar.com.my/news/nation/2020/02/25/dr-m-to-announce-economic-stimulus-package-at-a-later-date=says=guan-eng#cxrecs_s

[27] The Star. Bank Negara on the Alert [Internet]. 2020. Available from: https://www.thestar.com.my/news/nation/2020/02/25/dr-m-to-announce-economic-stimulus-package-at-a-later-date=says=guan-eng#cxrecs_s

[28] La Monica PR. Goldman Sachs: American Companies Will Have Zero Profit Growth Growth this Year [Internet]. 2020. Available from: https://edition.cnn.com/2020/02/27/investing/earnings-coronavirus/index.html

[29] Liao S. Microsoft doesn't Expect to Meet Sales Guidance on Windows and Surface Computers Due to Coronavirus [Internet]. 2020. Available from: https://edition.cnn.com/2020/02/26/tech/microsoft-coronavirus-sales-windows/index.html

[30] Trading Economics. Malaysia GDP Annual Growth Rate [Internet]. 2020. Available from: https://tradingeconomics.com/malaysia/gdp-growth-annual

[31] CompareHero. Difference between CCRIS and CTOS Explained [Internet].

2019. Available from: https://www.comparehero.my/banking-finance/articles/difference-between-ccris-ctos

[32] Bank Negara Malaysia. Monthly Statistical Bulletin [Internet]. 2019. Available from: https://www.bnm.gov.my/index.php?ch=en_publication_catalogue&pg=en_msb&ac=258&lang=en

[33] Ismail N, Azlan NDA, Husin M, M, Ishak I, Hashim M, SL. Bank efficiencies and non-performing loan of commercial banks in Malaysia. Journal of Humanities, Language, Culture and Business. 2017;**1**(5):34-40. Available from: http://www.icohlcb.com/images/Articles/vol_1_No.5/Paper-077-.pdf

[34] Yong WK. Should past experience be ignored? An insight from the decomposed theory of planned behaviour. Global Business and Management Research: An International Journal. 2019;**11**(3):14-18. Available from: http://www.gbmrjournal.com/vol11no3.htm

[35] Shahirah SJ, Syafiqah S. RHB Expects Further OPR Cuts [Internet]. 2020. Available from: https://www.theedgemarkets.com/article/bnm-cut-malaysia-opr-further-rhb-predicts

Chapter 8

Organizational Culture and Knowledge Sharing in Banking Management

Naima Andleeb, Md Fauzi Ahmad and Shahab Aziz

Abstract

The objective of the chapter is to explore the importance of knowledge sharing in the banking management along with organizational culture. To meet the objective of the study, a framework is proposed with knowledge sharing (KS) that is expected to be influenced by organizational culture (OS). OS itself is contributed by uncertainty avoidance, performance orientation, and gender egalitarianism.

Keywords: knowledge sharing, banking management, organizational culture, uncertainty avoidance, performance orientation, gender egalitarianism

1. Introduction

Knowledge plays a vital role in the growth of an organization. Knowledge is represented as the most fundamental part for driving innovation and maintaining competitive advantage in the market [1]. Knowledge management is the backbone for the success of an organization [2]. While an organization focusing on knowledge management unfortunately neglect knowledge sharing, knowledge sharing is more effective by encouragement and stimulation-based activities than by force-based ones. Organizational culture is regarded as one of the approaches for encouraging and stimulating employees to display necessary behaviors that benefit organizations [3]. Knowledge sharing (KS) is undoubtedly a significant element for all organizations, especially for banking institutions that pursue knowledge as an intangible and sought-after asset. Knowledge sharing plays an important role in distinguishing the competitive and rapidly changing environment because it not only enables intellectual reuse, but also the renewal of knowledge held by bank employees. The innovations in products, processes, and Shariah of Islamic banking need are ever increasing due to Islamic concept. Therefore, implementation of knowledge management strategies like knowledge sharing is necessary to meet ever-increasing challenges.

Further than this, [4, 5] underline that these organizations must constantly encourage their employees to share valuable information so that their intellectual capital can be used. In recent years, many researchers and academics have emphasized the need to create an organizational culture conducive to knowledge sharing between organizations and to implement more knowledge-friendly business strategies.

Organizations around the world are trying to take initiatives in familiarizing effective knowledge management (KM) by implanting knowledge sharing practices in their organizations for the purpose of achieving organizational performance growth and sustainability in the ever-increasing competitive environment [6]. For centuries, numerous banking services have grown to include financial services directed at both businesses and individuals at large, indirectly influencing economic practices, particularly in the Pakistani banking arena. Hence, implementing KM initiatives with managing knowledge sharing is considered by the banking sector to be extremely important in leading the Pakistani economy.

This is why banks are taking the initiative to set up KM teams within their organizations [4]. With this in mind, banking institutions have realized that KS in KM should not be abandoned or neglected to improve their survival in this increasingly difficult competitive environment. This study aims to investigate KS strategies that help to increase the tendency of Islamic bank employees in Pakistan to continue KS practices.

Islamic banking has grown into a substantial and fastest growing industry in the past four decades. It followed the rules and principles of Islamic transactions (Sharia) to carry out its activities [5, 6]. According to the Sharia's principles, any payment or receipt of interest is strictly banned. However, Islamic banking now offers a good range of products and services but still more creative and innovative developments are required to meet the requirements of competitive market of current era. What sets Pakistan apart other Islamic countries is how the Pakistani government has managed to establish a parallel system where Islamic and conventional banking services can work side by side instead of full Islamization. It was the country's first step toward development of a dual system, whereby Islamic banking could operate alongside the conventional system [6, 7].

The fundamental role of knowledge management in Islamic banking organization is very important in providing updated information and knowledge-based services [8]. In other words, effective KM should contribute to organizational performance through the progress of organizational knowledge capacity [5–7]; empirical research shows that an organizational capacity to learn or acquire the necessary knowledge from other organizations is an important source for sharing successful knowledge. Increasing knowledge capacities as a basis for organizational development is therefore beneficial for the effectiveness of the organization.

2. Literature review

This section will discuss the previous literature of the studies of knowledge sharing and organizational culture.

2.1 Knowledge management

In a knowledge-based economy, a knowledge sharing culture forms an important condition for the realization of knowledge management [9]. It is contended that knowledge sharing behavior among the staff of an organization would have an impact on the organization in terms of how duties are executed, and in retaining its competitive advantage [9]. Cheng et al. [10] defined knowledge as information combined with experience, context, interpretation, and reflection. He et al. [11] suggests that knowledge and organizational culture are highly related: making a decision requires knowledge and the culture itself can become a piece of knowledge. Knowledge is considered the most significant asset of an organization [12]. Knowledge management has been introduced in business to help organizations effectively create, store, share, and use knowledge; [13] said that knowledge management is an area that covers the organizational perspective, the process and technology perspective, and the cognitive science perspective. Tett and Burnett [14] describes knowledge management as the process of organizing and disseminating the collective wisdom of organizations so that the right knowledge is imparted to the right person at the right time. Knowledge management defines [15] as accumulation, protection, create, store embody and leverage of new in the terms of introduction of new and product services and processes. Conversion of knowledge refers to the sharing of knowledge to transform personal knowledge into organizational knowledge [15].

In the modern economy, Islamic banking management is now paying more attention to knowledge management for the purpose of staying successful and meeting the expectations of their internal and external customers [2]. According to Aqib [16], the new developments and innovations in products and processes and Shariah laws are only possible when banking management implements different innovative strategies for knowledge management [17]. A perfect knowledge management strategy is necessary and it should be linked with the business objective. Literature supports that knowledge management strategies effectively work toward creativity and innovation and effectively motivate banking employees to reinstate their dull routine [17, 18].

2.2 Knowledge sharing

Knowledge sharing, an important element of KM, is the behavior of disseminating an individual's acquired knowledge to others within an organization [19]. It is describes that more knowledge is shared informally within organizations and that the sharing of knowledge mainly depends on the social relationships between employees and the culture of organization [17]. Previous knowledge management research has shown that information systems, such as KM, can be used as significant facilitator to share knowledge [20]. Knowledge sharing is often different from knowledge transfer and exchange. Knowledge transfer concerns the sharing of knowledge by the knowledge source and the acquisition of knowledge by the recipient [21, 22]. Knowledge transfer is generally used to describe the movement of knowledge among teams, divisions, or organizations, rather than individuals [23]. The exchange and sharing of knowledge have been used interchangeably; but, transfer of knowledge often refers to both sharing of knowledge and the pursuit of knowledge. In this study, I use the term "knowledge sharing" because this study concerns the transfer of knowledge from an experienced employee to other members of the Islamic bank.

Studies on knowledge sharing have documented that to gain a competitive advantage, organizations need to understand how to transfer expertise and knowledge from experienced employees who possess novices and who need it [24]. Knowledge sharing literature has also shown that knowledge sharing is positively related to reduction in production costs, firm innovation projects, faster completion of new product development, team performance, and firm performance, organizational culture, gender egalitarianism, humane orientation, future orientation, and organizational growth [25, 26].

Knowledge sharing literature has examined the difference between knowledge sharing via KM and face-to-face interactions [24]. The factors that influence the decision to share knowledge in personal interaction vs. KM are different. For example, employees with a high level of extroversion are more likely to share their knowledge in personal interactions than technology-supported interactions, because sharing of knowledge in a personal interaction is more about relationships [27]. Unlike knowledge sharing through personal interaction, when a person shares their knowledge with the company's KM, the KM will be able to capture, store, and disseminate knowledge with other members. More firm members can access and use this knowledge to enhance performance.

In other words, sharing knowledge with KM allows knowledge to be transferred within individuals at the organizational level. Siddiqui [28] suggests that sharing of knowledge cannot be imposed, it may only be encouraged. Thus, this study examines whether behavioral interventions may be used to stimulate employee sharing of knowledge behavior with KM. Literature shows that knowledge sharing via KM or face-to-face interactions only depends on the organizational culture. If Islamic banks possess a supportive organizational culture, then it allows knowledge sharing in the organizations; otherwise employees need to face hurdles [19, 29].

2.3 Organizational culture

Organizational culture varies from institution to institution. The description of organizational culture provided by Schein summarizes best how it will be defined for this study:

Organizational culture can contribute into the enhancement of employee creativity because it is the process that can break the status quo of traditional banking system and can bring new instrumental measures for banking organizations [30]. Organizational culture also can contribute in a way that people can understand and change new factors regarding banking industry [31]. While the existing systems need new upgradation in software to make knowledge sharing easy and accessible for all of the employees [32]. Internal marketing should be another factor that can contribute in enhancement of employee creativity, if employees are willing to share knowledge so, keeping in view all these concepts of organizational culture, internal marketing and knowledge sharing we suggested this conceptual model or the study.

Empirical data collected on this model will provide the evidence for this study that will contribute to enhance employee creativity in Islamic banking. There are so many other factors that can considered as a research gap or novelty of this model like the way of selecting sample and the mixed results in different variable connections [30, 33]. So, these variables have some inconsistent results; based on this gap supported by the literature different methodologies and techniques will be a part of this study later on.

Conceptual model of this study for organizational culture including its three dimensions, uncertainty avoidance, performance orientation, and gender egalitarianism toward knowledge sharing, finds that organizational culture has its vivid importance to support knowledge sharing in the Islamic banking management [23]. Organizational culture can mean different things to different individuals, industries, or organizations.

This chapter considered three of the dimensions of organizational culture with knowledge sharing to explore how these dimensions of organizational culture work to support knowledge sharing in Islamic banking of Pakistan. Uncertainty avoidance, performance orientation, and gender egalitarianism are three dimensions of GLOBE organizational culture that have been followed from the GLOBE study.

2.4 Hypothesis development

Studies by Nguyen [34] have shown that organizational culture affects all aspects of an organization and this effect is identifiable in individual behavior, organizational performance, motivation, job satisfaction, creativity, innovation, and sharing of knowledge. Organizations today are concerned about rapid changes in professional cultures, and competition between organizations has increased due to this problem; authorities say using existing knowledge in organizations and seeking successful management could help organizations.

Glosser's studies have shown that the discovery and dissemination of knowledge has positively impacted the speed and quality of performance in organizational culture [35]. Improving knowledge sharing can lead to faster performance and promoting the quality of an organization's performance has increased customer satisfaction. But the way in which organizational knowledge was managed was important and this issue required knowledge management. Studies by Delong and Fahey have shown that organizational culture can influence knowledge management in four ways:

Organizational culture is invisible but it plays a central role in knowledge sharing. The role that culture plays in creating a relationship between employees' intention to share knowledge from an organizational culture that has identified how to use knowledge in a particular situation. Create, legitimize and disseminate processes in an organization [36]. Mirzaee and Ghaffari [37] stated that 80% of knowledge management concerned employees in the organizational culture and 20% knowledge management technologies.

Consequently, the current culture in an organization has been significant to the success of knowledge management, and the important prerequisite for sharing knowledge between employees, in banking culture, was the interaction of people, the sharing of their knowledge and their ideas [13]. In this section it was necessary to examine two related issues: first, the scope in which organizational culture can influence people's attitudes to participate in knowledge innovation, and second, the scope in which management efforts could create a culture of positive and appropriate knowledge to create. Further, the findings of this study show that there is positive relationship between organizational culture and knowledge sharing [38]. The findings of this study have been found to be the same as those of the previous studies.

H1: There is a significant relationship between organizational culture and knowledge sharing.

Avoiding uncertainty refers to uncertainty about the future, resistance to change, and risk aversion [38, 39]. We anticipate that avoiding uncertainty will have a nonlinear moderating impact on the sharing of knowledge relationship. The high level of avoidance of uncertainty reflects cultures where standards are clearly expressed and unambiguous and where severe sanctions are imposed on those who deviate from these standards [39, 40]. In such organizations, rules and process limit improvisation and experimentation [29]. This makes knowledge sharing quite modest. That said, avoiding high uncertainty can be beneficial for intention to share ideas and knowledge because it imposes order, conformity, routine, and stability [40, 41]. Therefore, high uncertainty avoidance tends to enhance idea implementation and suppress idea generation, thereby impeding the conversion of creative ideas into innovations and resulting progress of an organization . It is said that organizational culture dimension uncertainty avoidance supports knowledge sharing in Islamic banking of Pakistan.

H1a: There is a significant relationship between uncertainty avoidance and knowledge sharing.

The cultural dimension called "performance orientation" emerged from the study as extremely important in cultural studies. It "reflects the degree to which a community boosts and rewards innovation, high standards, excellence and enhanced performance" [13]. The GLOBE researchers concluded that an organizational level of performance orientation strongly affects the degree to which knowledge sharing is viewed as effective. Excellent leaders and organizations from around the world are associated with a strong focus on performance orientation (this association was not well recognized before this study) [36]. More specifically, a high value attached to performance orientation was found to be strongly and positively linked with knowledge sharing (findings show that when employees get benefited from the organization and rewarded upon their performance, they tend to set their goals higher than before which motivates them to share knowledge [42]). Empirical findings of this study show that there is a positive relationship between performance orientation and knowledge sharing in Islamic banking of Pakistan. Finding the formulated hypothesis of this study found the support from the literature that there is a positive relationship between uncertainty avoidance and knowledge sharing.

H1b: There is a significant relationship between performance orientation and knowledge sharing.

Gender egalitarianism is an important part of our cultures to be considered while talking about societies or organizations. Egalitarianism (from French égal, meaning "equal") is a mindset within political philosophy that orders equality for all. Egalitarian doctrines are commonly characterized by the idea that all people are equal in fundamental value or in moral status.

The underlying causal assumption of most past research in this area is that an "acceleration of economic development is accompanied by inevitable improvement in other spheres of organizations" [43]. According to this modernization perspective [44], economic development creates new opportunities for women and other marginalized groups because it both increases available jobs and changes the social and cultural climate. Although theoretically and intuitively compelling, there is mixed evidence for the impact of economic development on women's roles and status in the organizations [45]. One 162-nation study, for example, examined the relationship between knowledge sharing and the integration of women into Islamic banking [13,]. Islamic banking, or the value of all products and services produced by an organization, served as the measure of organizational development, and participation rates of women served as a measure of their integration into Islamic banking [46].

From the preceding discussion, one gains a sense of the complex nature of gender egalitarianism and related constructs. Gender egalitarianism is complex in the sheer number and range of antecedents that drive cross-cultural differences in the division of roles between the sexes. It is complex, too, in that studies within a particular area sometimes yield contradictory findings. Even so, portraits begin to emerge of societies that seek to minimize gender-role differences as opposed to those that seek to maximize these differences. Islamic banking of Pakistan has been identified as an organization with a slight tendency toward high gender equality [47]. This defines an organization in which men and women are equally treated, both enjoy the same benefits and rights and both assume the same responsibilities and tend to share knowledge that is useful for others or whoever is in need of knowledge. This hypothesis has a positive relationship between gender egalitarianism and knowledge sharing [25, 43].

H1c: There is a significant relationship between gender egalitarianism and knowledge sharing.

2.5 Conceptual framework

Integrated conceptual framework is new in nature and based on the recommendations and findings of the previous literature. This framework is integrated by formulating five variables: whereas knowledge sharing is working as a dependent variable, organizational culture is an independent variable, and other three variables uncertainty avoidance, performance orientation, and gender egalitarianism are taken as dimensions of organizational culture. The integrated framework discussed in this chapter is the result of extensive literature review. The originality of this framework

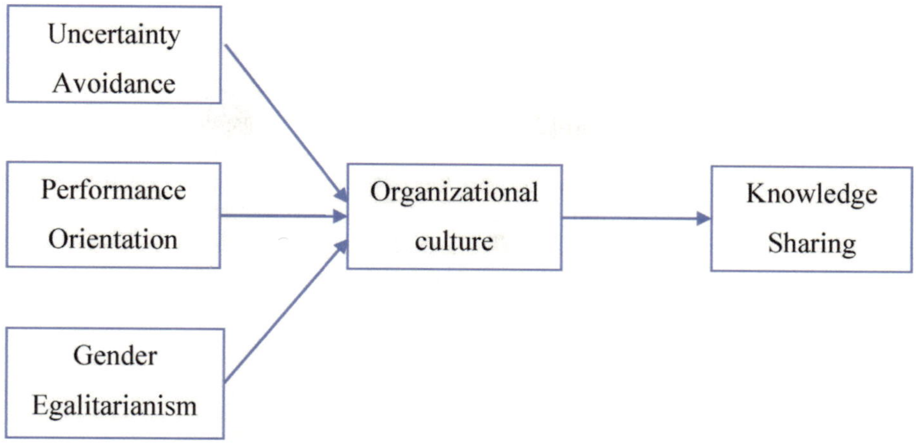

Figure 1.
Conceptual framework.

is considered new in its nature by formulation different variables from literature and this study prior to give the concept of implementation of this framework in Islamic banking. **Figure 1** contains the conceptual framework of this chapter.

2.6 Implications of the chapter

The designed framework of the current study in the coming future would be beneficial for both Islamic banking and its customers as this study demonstrates the combination and relationships of different variables for this chapter, researchers considered organizational culture with along its three dimensions named uncertainty avoidance, performance orientation, and gender egalitarianism toward knowledge sharing. Generally, these are the terms that grab the attention of researchers and academicians especially, where novelty and innovations are truly required for success. For that academician, this study will contribute in the body of knowledge. This study will also put the contribution in the enhancement of the literature regarding all variables of this proposed framework. Furthermore it will also contribute in the empirical result in future while providing empirical findings.

The banking industry will also be benefited from by this study as to develop strong OC and proper IM strategies, which can act as a platform to share knowledge, employee's interaction is a way of knowledge sharing that can enhance employee's creativity and innovation in an organization. This study will also play its very important rules and regulations government perspective to design policies, rules and regulations to formulate overall instruments and mechanisms for an organization and also offers some recommendations to improve product, services, and procedures in different states of the world. From the Islamic Shariah point of view, this study will also play a significant role as a guide in shaping and implementing economic and financial systems while having focus on employee creativity.

3. Conclusions

A framework for knowledge sharing has been proposed for this chapter conceptualizing the role of OC along with its three dimensions. A new concept for knowledge sharing is generated by this chapter by refining organizational culture with advancement of knowledge sharing considered as the dependent variable in Islamic banking of Pakistan; it would activate the critical role to lead banking organizations around the world and would increase the employment and can play active role to revitalize national economy. However, there is a lack of research found on all variables of selected framework for Islamic banking; after a rigorous examination of literature, this framework has been proposed for this study. Further, in coming future empirical studies will lead to determine the validity of given framework. Suggested implications will also make contributions to academicians and serve Islamic banking industry as a platform. This framework will assist the policymakers in formulation of rules and regulations and formulation of laws to advance the mechanism and will be helpful to Islamic Shariah to establish new systems.

Author details

Naima Andleeb[1*], Md Fauzi Ahmad[1] and Shahab Aziz[2]

1 Faculty of Technology Management, University Tun Hussein Onn Malaysia (UTHM), Johor, Malaysia

2 Business Studies Department, Bahria University, Islamabad, Pakistan

*Address all correspondence to: naima@uthm.edu.my

References

[1] Khalid S, Amjad S. Risk management practices in Islamic banks of Pakistan. The Journal of Risk Finance. 2012;**13**(2):148-159

[2] Lee C, Hidayat N. The influence of knowledge sharing and absorptive capacity on service innovation performance of Islamic banking in North Borneo Indonesia. Advances in Management and Applied Economics. 2018;**8**(4):17-28

[3] Al Shehri M, Mclaughlin P, Al-ashaab A. The impact of organizational culture on employee engagement in Saudi banks. Journal of Human Resource Management Research. 2017;**2017**:1-23

[4] Chang W, Liao S, Wu T. Relationships among organizational culture, knowledge sharing, and innovation capability: A case of the automobile industry in Taiwan. Knowledge Management Research and Practice. 2017;**15**(3):471-490

[5] Tang AD, Chang M, Cheng C. Enhancing knowledge sharing from self-initiated expatriates in Vietnam: The role of internal marketing and work-role adjustment in an emerging economy. Asia Pacific Business Review. August 2017;**2381**:1-20

[6] Panahi E, Khomeini BI. Exaining the Role of Knowledge Sharing on Employee Creativity of the Special Economic Zone of Bandar Imam Khomeni. Journal of Fundamental and Applied Sciences. 2016;**2016**(8(2S)):2877-2886

[7] Mittal S, Dhar RL. Transformational leadership and employee creativity: Mediating role of creative self-efficacy and moderating role of knowledge sharing. Management Decision. 2015;**53**(5):894-910

[8] Zhou L, Zhao S, Tian F, Zhang X, Chen S. Visionary leadership and employee creativity in China. International Journal of Manpower. 2016;**8**:28

[9] Islam MZ, Jasimuddin SM, Hasan I. Organizational culture, structure, technology infrastructure and knowledge sharing: Empirical evidence from MNCs based in Malaysia. Journal of Knowledge Management. 2015;**11**(2):22-42

[10] Cheng ECK, Wu SW, Hu J. Knowledge management implementation in the school context: Case studies on knowledge leadership, storytelling, and taxonomy. Educational Research for Policy and Practice. 2017;**16**(2):177-188

[11] He W et al. Linking knowledge sharing and employee creativity: decomposing knowledge mode and improving the measure of tacit knowledge sharing. In: Pacis. Vol. 219. 2013

[12] Andleeb N, Chan SW, Nazeer S. Triggering employee creativity through knowledge sharing, organizational culture and internal marketing. International Journal of Innovative Technology and Exploring Engineering. 2019:2-6

[13] Ashkanasy N, Wilderom C, Peterson M. Handbook of Organizational Culture and Climate. New Delhi, India: Sage Publications; 2004

[14] Tett RP, Burnett DD. A personality trait-based interactionist model of job performance a personality trait-based interactionist model of job performance. Journal of Applied Psychology. 2014;**83**(3):200-517

[15] Omerzel DG, Biloslavo R, Trnavcevic A. Knowledge management and organisational culture in higher

education institutions. Journal of East European Management Studies. 2011;**16**(2):111-139

[16] Aqib MA. Evolution & development of Islamic banking – The case of Pakistan. European Journal of Islamic Finance. 2014;**1**:1-7

[17] Ahmad N, Haron S. Perceptions of Malaysian corporate customers towards Islamic banking products & services. International Journal of Islamic Financial Services. 2000;**3**(4):2-16

[18] Awan AG, Azhar M. Consumer behaviour towards Islamic banking in Pakistan. European Journal of Accounting, Auditing and Finance Research. 2014;**2**(9):42-65

[19] Cohen JF, Olsen K. Knowledge management capabilities and firm performance: A test of universalistic, contingency and complementarity perspectives. Expert Systems with Applications. 2015;**42**(3):1178-1188

[20] Ali MA. The roots & development of Islamic banking in the world & in Pakistan. South East Asia Journal of Contemporary Business, Economics and Law. 2015;7(1):58-63

[21] Magd HAE, Mccoy MP. Islamic finance development in the Sultanate of Oman: Barriers and recommendations. Procedia Economics and Finance. 2014;**15**(14):1619-1631

[22] Hakimah W, Ibrahim W. Conventional bank and Islamic banking as institutions: Similarities and differences. Humanomics. 2015;**3**(3):272-298

[23] Najaf K, Najaf R. Arabian Journal of Business and Growth of Islamic Banking in Pakistan. Arabian Journal of Business and Management Review. 2016;**6**(4):2-6

[24] Sdahsiah N, Sepahvand R. Investigating the effect of knowledge sharing and market orientation in the development of organizational performance. Asian Journal of Information Technology. 2016;**15**(24):4964-4969

[25] Aboelmaged MG. Knowledge sharing through enterprise social network (ESN) systems: Motivational drivers and their impact on employees' productivity. Journal of Knowledge Management. 2018;**22**(2):362-383

[26] Yang J. Effect of internal marketing on knowledge sharing and organisational effectiveness in the hotel industry. Total Quality Management & Business Excellence. 2012:37-41

[27] Mursaleen M, Roberts KW, Asif M. Islamic work ethics as mediator between trust and knowledge sharing relationship. Pakistan Journal of Commerce and Social Sciences. 2015;**9**(2):614-640

[28] Ahmed R, Siddiqui K. Islamic banking in Pakistan – Problems and prospects introduction. Asian Journal of Research in Banking and Finance. 2013;**3**:42-72

[29] Malik A, Abumustafa NI, Shah H. Revisiting creative accounting in the context of Islamic economic and finance system. Asian Social Science. 2019;**15**(2):80-89

[30] Hahn MH, Lee KC, Lee DS. Computers in human behavior network structure, organizational learning culture, and employee creativity in system integration companies: The mediating effects of exploitation and exploration. Computers in Human Behavior. 2015;**42**:167-175

[31] Zaid A, Jaaron AAM. Green human resource management bundle practices and manufacturing organizations for performance optimization: A conceptual model. International

Journal of Engineering and Technology. 2018;7(3):87-91

[32] Bortolotti T, Boscari S, Danese P. Successful lean implimentation: Organizational culture and soft lean practice. International Journal of Production Economics. 2014;**2014**(4):1-65

[33] Baig J, Abusalah A, Mohammed E. The moderating effect of individual culture orientation on the relationship between leadership styles with perceived employees performance. European Journal of Scientific Research. 2015;**136**(4):432-445

[34] Nguyen P. The impact of coordination and competition on cross-functional knowledge sharing and organisational performance. Bachelors thesis submitted to University of Western Sydney; 2014

[35] Alhakimi W, Alhariry K. Internal marketing as a competitive advantage in banking industry. Academic Journal of Management Sciences. 2014;**3**(1):15-22

[36] Hussein ATT, Singh SK, Farouk S, Sohal AS. Knowledge sharing enablers, processes and firm innovation capability. Journal of Workplace Learning. 2016;**28**(8):484-495

[37] Mirzaee S, Ghaffari A. Investigating the impact of information systems on knowledge sharing. Journal of Knowledge Management. 2018:1-21

[38] Zhang Z. Organizational culture and knowledge sharing: Design of incentives and business processes. Business Process Management Journal. 2018:1-32

[39] Min J. Mergers in higher education: A case study of organizational culture, communication, and conflict management strategies in the university system of Georgia. PhD thesis submitted to University of Georgia; 2017

[40] Thomas AR, editors. Business Ethics and Leadership from an Eastern European, Transdisciplinary Context; 2017

[41] Gruver JB, Metcalf AL, Muth AB, Finley JC, Luloff AE. Making decisions about forestland succession: Perspectives from Pennsylvania's private forest landowners. Society and Natural Resources. 2017;**30**(1):47-62

[42] Robbins RN, Bryan A. Relationships between future orientation, impulsive sensation seeking, and risk behavior among adjudicated adolescents. Journal of Adolescent Research. July 2004;**19**(4):428-445

[43] Shao Z, Wang T, Feng Y. Impact of organizational culture and computer self-efficacy on knowledge sharing. Industrial Management & Data Systems. 2015;**115**(4):590-611

[44] Omojola AA. Culture, leadership, and organizations: The GLOBE study of 62 societies. Journal of Applied Christian Leadership. 2011;**7**(1):1-6

[45] Nadeem S, Sully de Luque MF. Developing an understanding of the human resource (HR) complexities in Pakistan with a GLOBE cultural lens. Journal of Management & Organization. 2018:1-19

[46] Chan SW, Ang SF, Andleeb N, Ahmad MF, Zaman I. The influence of transformational leadership on organization innovation in Malaysian manufacturing industry. International Journal of Supply Chain Management. 2019;**8**(2):971-976

[47] Khan MA, Alireza Nasiri JH, Shafique MN. The impact of market orientation on organizational performance: Empirical evidence from banking sector of Pakistan. Sarhad Journal of Management Sciences. 2017;**3**(2):232-249

Chapter 9

Bank Service Delivery in Nigeria

Akinbode James Olalekan

Abstract

Nigeria as a country has recorded significant efficiency in bank service delivery considering her history of banking services. This assertion reflects in the views of banking sector stakeholders in the country and foreign assessors. One milestone was the introduction and effective use of electronic banking system in the last two decades which eliminated hurdles overt with the conventional banking era. Today, banking activities in Nigeria are possible at any time of the day and anywhere without any stress. This is not to say that it has fully complied with global best practices as there are still pockets of complaints from stakeholders especially customers which have expressed dissatisfaction in the quality of banking services rendered to them. In spite of the level of customers' dissatisfaction, bank service delivery is better than what it was, and the Nigerian banking sector is presently at the front burner in terms of banking service delivery in Africa. Although challenges of employees' knowledge gaps, technology, inadequate legal framework, incompetent manpower and staff improper attitude remain contentious in the Nigerian banking system, efforts from stakeholders especially the regulator to eliminate these challenges would bring about improved banking service delivery in Nigeria and make it close to global best practices, if not achieve it.

Keywords: bank, banking sector, Nigeria, service delivery

1. Introduction

Nigeria is the most populous black nation with about 190 million people on an approximate area of 923,769 square kilometres situated between 40 and 140 north latitude and 30 and 140 east longitude in sub-Saharan Africa. It is currently the second biggest economy and the tenth oil producer in the world. In spite of this record, Nigeria Economic Outlook of 2019 described her economy not to be among the fastest growing economies in sub-Saharan Africa. The economic institution of the country, in which the banking sector plays the intermediation role between the surplus and deficit sectors of the economy, drives growth and development.

Historically, the country's banking sector like others is meant to allocate savings to improve productivity and promote economic growth. However, this has not been possible through economic changes of the country whether during the pre-independence epoch or post-independence epoch. During these epochs, the Nigerian economy has undergone a series of economic reforms and policies to address banking failures such as undercapitalisation, delays of transaction, congestion and long queues in and outside of the banking hall, among others. This made the Nigerian economy beclouded with many problems such as weak industrial base, and that is why the economic narrative of the country has been epileptic.

It is remarkable to note that in the last two decades, policies of government through the Central Bank of Nigeria have made bank services to have increased tremendously. For instance, the cashless policy of the Central Bank of Nigeria has eliminated some of the early challenges of banking services in Nigeria [1]. This brought about service availability, promoted service capacity in general and specific terms, and service delivery. But to observers, banking service delivery which is the extent to which the bank is able to meet with the banking service requests of customers (individuals or organisations) in the most efficient manner is below what is expected by customers. This chapter discuses salient issues to provide background knowledge on the subject before taking positions.

2. Structure of banks in Nigeria

The banking system in Nigeria is structured along six layers, namely, central bank, deposit money banks, merchant banks, development finance institutions, microfinance bank, and mortgage banks.

2.1 Central Bank of Nigeria

This is the apex monetary authority in Nigeria established by 1958 Act of CBN and started operations on July 1, 1959. At that time it was saddled with the responsibilities of enhancing the quality of banking operations in the country. To achieve this mandate, the bank has evolved different programmes such as industry remedial programmes, risk-based supervision, establishment of regulatory framework, customer protection and internal transformation of the bank activities. Among the functions of the bank are to serve as the banker to the government, act as a banker to all other types of banks, hold foreign reserve of the country, manage the national debt of the country, serve as a lender of last resort and control deposit money banks.

2.2 Deposit money banks

This is a financial institution that is registered to render financial services to the general public such as accepting deposit, providing loans, keeping valuables and serving as financial advisers to customers, among others. Banks in this category are older than the emergence of the Nigerian State. Foremost was the Bank of British West Africa which was founded in 1894. It is on record that indigenous banking started in 1929 with the establishment of the industrial and deposit money bank by a group of Nigerian and Ghanaian entrepreneurs. After independence in 1960, the Bank of British West Africa became the first Nigeria-based bank which is now known as First Bank of Nigeria. Presently, there are 25 deposit money banks in Nigeria as of October 2019 (www.cbn.gov.ng).

2.3 Merchant banks

A merchant bank is a specialist financial bank that provides wholesale banking, medium- and long-term finance, equipment leasing, debt factoring investments management and so on. This type of bank evolves in Nigeria back in the 1960 with the establishment of NAL Merchant Bank Plc. Over the years, a number of merchant banks have been registered by the government.

2.4 Development finance institutions

This is a government bank established to perform itemised developmental functions in the economy. These functions include but are not limited to infrastructural developments in industry, agriculture, and commerce. These development banks' names project their function. In Nigeria, there is the Nigerian Industrial Development Bank and Bank of Industry for industrial development and the Nigerian Agricultural and Cooperative Bank for agricultural issues, among others.

2.5 Microfinance bank

The Central Bank of Nigeria described microfinance bank as a financial institution at the grassroots level to perform basic banking services to the poor. This bank is different from conventional deposit money bank because of its ease of operations, absence of asset-based collateral and smallness of loans advanced and/or savings. The roles of microfinance bank are not limited to address banking shortfall at the grassroots and provide timely, reasonable, varied and reliable banking services to the poor. It is meant to provide financial service intervention for the low-income earners at lower echelon of the society.

2.6 Mortgage bank

This type of bank in Nigeria is floated to coordinate housing development in the country. To achieve this mandate, individuals and corporate bodies are granted loans for this purpose, while repayment of loans is in instalments over the years. Like deposit money banks or microfinance banks, mortgage banks receive deposit from individuals and corporate bodies at a rate of interest, while such fund is lent out at a higher rate of interest. In Nigeria, the Federal Mortgage Bank is saddled with this responsibility.

3. Bank services in Nigeria

Based on the structure of banks discussed above, bank service is centred on financial intermediaries, that is, deposit collection and lending. However, in the Nigerian banking industry, different types of services have emerged but can be categorised into three major arms, namely, general banking covers account opening, deposit management and cash handling, credit such as loan disbursement and loan management and foreign exchange such as foreign currency and remittance management [2].

An overview of these services in Nigeria by the banks is provided below:

The Central Bank of Nigeria coordinates with other banks, and this has been efficiently delivered over the years. For deposit money banks, some banking services such as account openings, deposit mobilisation, advancing of loans, agency services such as making payments and collecting receipts, among others, and general utility services such as issuing letters of credit and safe custody of valuables, among others, are offered. In the case of merchant banking, services offered include but are not limited to corporate finance services such as management of private and public equity shares to corporate debt securities and provide expertise on investment advisory services, finance of large-scale industrial projects, advice on portfolio management, company floatation, financial planning as well as mergers and acquisitions. Basic services rendered by the merchant bank in Nigeria are the provision of medium- and long-term credits, arrangement of syndicated loans, provision of acceptance of credit facilities to their clients, equipment leasing, issuing house function, acceptance of deposits, provision of foreign exchange services, management/advice on portfolio of investment and unit trust management.

4. Legal and institutional framework of banks in Nigeria

There are laws and institutional framework in Nigeria that govern the banking industry and services therein. First of such laws are the Central Bank of Nigeria Act 1958 and the Banking Act 1969 to guide the operations of the Central Bank of Nigeria. These laws stipulate paid up capital for indigenous banks as N250,000, while in the 1962 amendment, banks were allowed to buy real estate for expansion purposes, and the bank was empowered to regulate the interest rate structure of the commercial banks. In 1969, another amendment was effected on the 1962 Act as it broadens the sphere of monetary control to include other banks than commercial banks. A significant hallmark in the banking legal history in Nigeria was the enactment of the Banks and Other Financial Institutions Act (BOFIA) in 1991.

BOFIA granted limited autonomy to banks in some areas of operations. The Act gave operational autonomy to CBN to carry out its traditional functions as listed above to enhance its flexibility. In the Act, CBN Governor was mandated to chair the board of directors of the bank with other members of the board being the deputy governors, the permanent secretary, Ministry of Finance, and five part-time directors, from the Security and Exchange Commission, Commissioner for Insurance and Registrar General of Corporate Affairs Commission, and a representative of the Federal Ministry of Finance not below the rank of director.

Also, the regulatory power of the CBN was strengthened by the Banks and Other Financial Institutions (Amendment) Decree no. 4 of 1997. Through the amendments, CBN was empowered to vary or revoke any condition subject to which a licence was granted or may impose fresh or additional condition to the granting of a licence to transact banking business in the country. It was also stated that books of these banks and other financial institutions such as development banks, mortgage institutions and microfinance banks can be examined by the apex bank from time to time. With the decree, the bank has the power to withdraw licences of distressed banks and appointment of liquidators of these banks.

5. Efficiency of banking services in Nigeria

There has been poor and inconsistent bank service delivery in Nigerian banking sector over the years, and that was why a series of reforms had evolved in the sector [3, 4]. However, there are variations in the quality of these banks' service delivery over the years, and this varied with the categories of banks in the country and who the assessor is (local regulator such as the Central Bank of Nigeria, Customers, and International raters such as International Monetary Fund (IMF), and World Bank [5]. As reported by the International Monetary Fund in 2016, Nigeria has the lowest percentage (14%) in terms of the ratio of broad money supply to gross domestic product (GDP) among selected countries. Fitch ratings report of 2015 revealed a decline in the performance of Nigerian banks in terms of service delivery. Earlier studies conducted in the country by [6, 7] also suggest this.

Scenarios in the Nigerian banking industry portrayed divergent opinion. From the customers' perspective, customers of banks in Nigeria have also expressed great displeasure with the quality of services offered to them over the years in spite of the policies of the government through CBN. For instance, the study of [8] found extreme level of Nigerian bank customers' dissatisfaction. The study revealed long queues in the banking halls, ATM locations, needless delays in resolving complaints and interbank cheques issues as major problems of the sector. Seven years after, the study of [9] admitted poor service quality in the Nigerian banking sector. This means the trend of Nigerian bank customers' dissatisfaction remained unresolved. On the contrary, [10] study on customer service delivery and customer satisfaction in the banking industry found out that an increase in the number of working days and number of bank branches led to better levels of service delivery but can be improved upon as he subsequently recommends that the Nigeria banking industry should improve the quality of service delivery.

Electronic banking introduction in the last two decades brought in another twist to banking services in Nigeria. This has made banking services more convenient due to the associated benefits such as efficiency and accessibility. [11] in Nigeria revealed that customers enjoying electronic banking services are still not satisfied with the quality and efficiency of the services. This is expressed in the number of times customers physically visit banks and length of time spent before such services are received. Furthermore, [12] study on mobile banking and banks' service delivery reveals that it has improved transactional convenience and quick transaction alert. Similarly, [13] studied technological innovation and service delivery in Nigeria and found positive relationship between the variables.

However, like any other banking services around the world, cases of insecurity and hacking of accounts remain a problem [14, 15]. For instance, the study of [16] on customer service and banking business in Nigeria found that customers are dissatisfied with long waiting times. The study of [14] identified users' network failure as a major problem to service delivery in the country, while [17] study examined how adoption of information technology impacted the banking industry in Nigeria. The authors found that IT adoption fundamentally transformed the content and quality of banking services delivery, thereby strengthening the competitiveness of Nigerian banks.

In the study of other banks like microfinance bank, [18] identified diversion of funds, inadequate finance and frequent changes in government policies, heavy transaction costs, huge loan losses, low capacity and low technical skill in the industry as impediments to the growth of this subsector.

6. Challenges undermining bank service delivery in Nigeria

1. **Knowledge gaps of bank personnel:** As established in the work of [19], representatives of the bank which are "frontline employees" have not been adequately trained to provide and exceed service required by customers due to knowledge gap in the areas of banking services and regulatory rules that guide the provision of the services.

2. **Technological challenge:** In spite of the level at which electronic banking is presently adopted in the Nigerian banking industry, the ease and use of modern technological innovations is still not at its best. Developed world banking system is far beyond the use of ATM, mobile banking and other forms that Nigeria currently uses because of fraud and hackers. It is also on record that the technological infrastructure to support modern banking system in the country is still lacking. Aside from this, imbalance in the availability of ICT infrastructure remains a challenge.

3. **Inadequate legal framework:** Existing legal banking provisions in the country have loopholes. Criminals and fraudsters have taken this opportunity in the past to perpetrate cybercrimes on bank customers in the country.

4. The shortage of competent manpower attributable to high labour mobility is also a core challenge which has impaired the capabilities of these banks to execute their corporate objectives. In the Nigerian banking sector, employees with poor and inappropriate academic/professional backgrounds are common, while the engagement of contract staffing and employment of unqualified personnel into the sector have caused the sector a lot of harm.

5. **Staff attitude:** The emotional intelligence of personnel in the sector is another factor. Handling of difficult customers and reacting to requests of customers have generated a lot of dissatisfaction to customers. This is because most of the bank employees are not emotionally intelligent to deal with customers and their issues.

7. Conclusion

Historically, Nigerian banks' service delivery has no doubt improved when compared with that in the last two decades but can be improved when compared with what her contemporaries in the developed climes have achieved. Hiccups in the areas of employees' knowledge gap of banking services and regulatory rules, technology and weak legal framework are no doubt obvious. In spite of these, the Nigerian banking industry remains vibrant among her peers in Africa. Today, banking business in Nigeria is waxing stronger as customers can transact banking request at the comfort of their rooms and offices and in transit. This is not to say that all is well with the banking service delivery in Nigeria as much is still desired to achieve global best practices in service delivery.

Author details

Akinbode James Olalekan
Department of Business Administration, College of Social and Management Sciences, Bowen University, Iwo, Osun State, Nigeria

*Address all correspondence to: james.akinbode@bowen.edu.ng

References

[1] Oladejo M, Akanbi T. Banker's perception of electronic banking in Nigeria: A review of post consolidation experience. Research Journal of Finance and Accounting. 2012;**3**(2):1-11

[2] Masukujjaman M, Akhter A. Quality of categorised service and customer satisfaction in banking industry: An empirical study on private commercial bank in Bangladesh. Journal of Business and Technology. 2010;**5**(2):17-29

[3] Ekong UM, Udonwa UE. Banking sector reforms and the performance of commercial banks in Nigeria. Journal of World Economic Research. 2015;**4**(3):45-60

[4] Sanusi LS. Banking reform and its impact on the Nigerian economy. In; Paper Presented at the University of Warwick's Economic Summit, Warwick, 17 February 2012; 2012

[5] Andow HA. Impact of banking reforms on service delivery in the Nigerian banking sector. International Journal of Research in Business Studies and Management. 2015;**2**(11):67-77

[6] Adegbie FF, Asaolu TO, Enyi EP. Distress resolution in Nigerian banking sector: The role of assets and liabilities management. International Journal of Financial Research. 2013;**4**(3):70-82

[7] Ekpenyong DB, Acha IA. Banks and economic growth Nigeria. European Journal of Business and Management. 2011;**3**(4):155-166

[8] Woldie A. Nigerian banks quality of services. Journal of African Business. 2003;**4**(2):69-87

[9] Olaleke OO. Assessing the relationship between service quality and customer satisfaction: Evidence from Nigerian banking sector. The Global Journal of Management and Business. 2010;**10**(3):12-22

[10] Adesoji F. Service delivery and customer satisfaction in Nigerian banks. Munich Personal RePEc Archive, Paper No. 73612; 2016. pp. 1-15

[11] Adeoye B, Lawanson O. Customers satisfaction and its implications for Bank performance in Nigeria. British Journal of Arts and Social Sciences. 2012;**5**(1):13-29

[12] Adewoye JO. Impact of mobile banking on service delivery in the Nigerian commercial banks. International Review of Management and Business Research. 2013;**2**(2):333-344

[13] Ilo JVC, Ani WU, Chioke NS. Impact of technological innovation on delivery of banking services in Nigeria. In: International Conference on Economics, Education and Humanities; 2014. pp. 162-168. DOI: 10.15242/ICEHM.ED1214048

[14] Otokpa O, Okpe IJ. *E*-banking and service delivery in eco bank Nigeria: A comparative analysis. International Journal of Business, Humanities and Technology. 2018;**8**(4):30-42

[15] Onodugo IC. Overview of electronic banking in Nigeria. International Journal of Multidisciplinary Research and Development. 2015;**2**(7):336-342

[16] Sokefun AO. Customer service and its effect on the banking business in Nigeria. JORIND. 2011;**9**(2):359-365

[17] Oluwagbemi O, Abah J, Achimugu P. The impact of information and communication technology in banking industry. Journal of Computer Science and Engineering. 2011;**7**(2):63-67

[18] Nwanyanwu OJ. Microfinance in Nigeria: Problems and prospects. African Research Review. 2011;**5**(2):87-103

[19] Adeniji AA, Akinbode JO. Knowledge of banking services among frontline personnel and quality of service delivery in the Nigerian commercial bank. Journal of Business and Retail Management Research (JBRMR). 2018;**12**(3):160-167

Section 2

Finance

Chapter 10

Stock Markets of the Visegrad Countries after Their Accession to the European Union

Wojciech Grabowski

Abstract

In this chapter, interlinkages between stock markets in CEE-4 countries and capital markets in developed countries are analyzed. Changes of variance on stock markets in Poland, the Czech Republic, Slovakia, and Hungary are identified. Differences among countries are analyzed. Capital markets of these countries are compared in terms of market efficiency. Moreover, co-movements of stock markets in Visegrad countries with capital markets in developed countries are studied. Different specifications of multivariate GARCH models are studied. Asymmetric GARCH-BEKK model and Asymmetric Generalized Dynamic Conditional Correlation model are considered.

Keywords: stock markets, Visegrad countries, market efficiency, multivariate GARCH, shocks' transmission

1. Introduction

The Visegrad countries are the four Central European Countries (referred to as the CEE-4 henceforth)—Czech Republic, Poland, Slovakia, and Hungary. These countries joined the European Union (EU) in spring 2004, and three of them are still (January 2020) committed to adopting the euro at some point. At the early stages of transformation, their stock markets were relatively poorly integrated with the stock markets of the EU countries (the so-called old EU countries). This is due to the shorter history of the free-market economy in Poland, Hungary, and the Czech Republic. Low level of correlation between rates of return on stock market indexes in CEE-4 countries and rates of return on stock market indexes of industrialized economies resulted in considering assets from post-communist economies in investors' portfolios (e.g., see [1, 2]). The accession of Poland, Hungary, and the Czech Republic to the EU on May 1, 2004 attracted the interest of numerous investors who had not earlier invested in these countries due to political, corporate governance, and liquidity risks (see [3]). In particular, the Slovakian stock market was strongly integrated with capital markets of developed economies due to the country's participation in the Exchange Rate Mechanism 2 (ERM2 henceforth) and euro adoption in 2009 (see [4]). A significant increase in the level of integration resulted in a decrease in the benefits from using the portfolio diversification strategy.

During the US subprime crisis, a significant increase in correlations between stock markets in CEE-3 countries and capital markets in developed economies was observed (see [5]). In particular, correlation between shocks in the Slovakian stock market and shocks in industrialized countries was very large. The outbreak of the euro area sovereign debt crisis resulted in a slight decrease in the level of correlation between stock markets in CEE-4 countries and mature capital markets. However, rates of return in the German stock market still strongly affected the rates of return in the Polish, Hungarian, Czech, and Slovakian stock market. After the introduction of the Outright Monetary Transactions program (OMT henceforth), the sensitivity of the stock market returns in Poland, the Czech Republic, and Hungary to external shocks decreased significantly. This phenomenon was not observed in the case of Slovakia, which is a member of the euro area.

Nevertheless, we still think that we can contribute to this body of literature. Previous studies devoted to the analysis of the performance of stock markets in Poland, the Czech Republic, Slovakia, and Hungary compared sensitivity of these markets to external and internal shocks in a priori defined subperiods. In most cases, the Winkler's [6] periodization of the global financial crisis was used. In this research study, we identify days of statistically significant breakpoints on the basis of the method proposed by Inclan and Tiao [7]. Stock markets of Poland, the Czech Republic, Slovakia, and Hungary are compared with regard to timing of significant breakpoints. Moreover, efficiency of stock markets in CEE-4 countries is compared across subperiods and across markets. Sensitivity of stock markets to external shocks is compared in the context of the volatility transmission and linkages between rates of return. Differences between resistance to shocks from the United States and Germany (main economy of the European Union) are analyzed as well. The obtained differences between Slovakia and noneuro-area member states should provide recommendations for policy makers of Poland, the Czech Republic, and Hungary in the context of the future accession of these countries to the euro area.

This chapter has the following structure. In Section 2, the literature review is provided. In Section 3, the methodology is presented. In Section 4, findings from the empirical research are presented and discussed. The last section concludes the study.

2. Literature review

Poor integration of capital markets in Poland, the Czech Republic, Hungary, and Slovakia in the twentieth century resulted in low level of interest in sensitivity of these markets to external shocks in academic literature. These stock markets were previously analyzed in the context of portfolio diversification opportunity (see, e.g., [1, 2]). The very low degree of global integration of capital markets of Central and Eastern European countries in the pre-accession period was identified, among others, by Mateus [8], Maneschiold [9], and Nielsson [10]. An analysis of the sensitivity of the CEE-3 stock markets to global shocks during the dotcom crisis, which was conducted by Bein and Tuna [11], has indicated their calmness and excluded possibility of their significant reaction to negative news.

After announcement of the CEE-4 countries' EU membership, all stock markets in the region started to show similar level of volatility reactions to both negative and positive news that had the same magnitude. This finding has been interpreted as an increase in confidence for international investors after the announcement of the accession of countries of the Central and Eastern Europe to the European Union (see [12]). The accession of Poland, the Czech Republic, Hungary, and Slovakia to the EU on May 1, 2004, attracted the interest of many investors who had earlier refrained from buying assets of these countries due to corporate governance, political, and liquidity risks (see, e.g., [13–15]). An increase in the level of integration resulted in a significant decrease in the benefits from using the portfolio diversification strategy (see [16]).

The impact of the subprime crisis on the performance of stock markets in CEE-4 countries has been broadly discussed in the economic literature. Very significant transmission of shocks to CEECs' stock markets during the subprime crisis was identified in numerous research studies (see, e.g., [17–19]). As Syllignakis and Kouretas [13] suggested, the contagion transmission from the major stock markets to capital markets of the CEECs in the period of financial turmoil as well as during the subprime crisis was due to increased financial liberalization and increased participation of foreign investors in these markets.

In turn, studies devoted to the role of the sovereign debt crisis in shaping stock market prices in the Central and Eastern Europe seem to be rare. The analysis of dynamic correlation coefficients conducted by Bein and Tuna [11] indicates that during the euro-area sovereign debt crisis, stock markets in the analyzed region have been highly correlated with the finance-led markets of GIIPS (Greece, Italy, Ireland, Portugal, and Spain) as well as with stock markets of the EU3 (France, Germany, and the United Kingdom). Moreover, significant spillover effect from capital markets of Italy, Ireland, Portugal, and Spain to stock markets of the Central and Eastern European countries has been identified. Differences in the level of reaction of stock markets in CEE-4 countries during the euro area sovereign debt crisis have been noticed as well. Due to the fact that Slovakia was a member of the euro area in 2010–2011, stock market in this country reacted stronger to positive and negative shocks. Moreover, the Polish stock market has shown a significantly higher level of conditional correlation than the Czech Republic and Hungary. Some results in the literature devoted to the sensitivity of capital markets in Visegrad countries to external shocks have pointed out their asymmetric reaction (see, e.g., [18, 20]). This finding has been interpreted as a problem of information asymmetry and the presence of agents with superior knowledge [21].

As Grabowski [20] and Moagar-Poladian et al. [22] have noticed, in the period of financial stability (2013–2019) in the case of Poland, the Czech Republic, and Hungary, the sensitivity of the stock market returns to external shocks became meaningfully weaker. In the case of the Slovakian stock market, drop in the level of integration was smaller (see, e.g., [23]). Moreover, after 2012, the evolution of the stock market indices in the CEE-4 countries has followed different paths. As a result of the lower level of market uncertainty, volatility spillovers have weakened. A within-group integration of stock markets of the CEE-4 countries has decreased significantly. Opportunities for portfolio diversification have increased with discrepancies between market returns observed after 2012 (see. [20]).

3. Methodology

In order to identify different states of stock markets, the methodology proposed by Inclan and Tiao [7] and Inclan et al. [24] should be used. On the basis of the following statistics,

$$IT = D_{k*}\sqrt{T/2} \quad (1)$$

moments of significant changes in the unconditional variance were identified. In formula (1), the number of observations denoted by T and D_{k*} is defined as follows:

$$D_{k*} = \max_{k} |D_k|, \quad (2)$$

where

$$D_k = \frac{C_k}{C_T} - \frac{k}{T}, \quad (3)$$

C_k is the cumulative sum of squares.

Market efficiency belongs to the most important features describing financial markets in the area of information processing mechanisms. According to the concept introduced by Fama [25], on informationally efficient market prices always fully reflect the available information. As a result, it is not possible to achieve permanently superior returns on the basis of publicly available information, and the changes in financial asset prices are random. There are three main statistical methods of testing efficiency (autocorrelation test, runs test, and the test for the presence of unit root).

Testing the autocorrelation is based on the autocorrelation of the kth-order (ACF) coefficient, which is defined as follows:

$$\hat{\rho}_k = \frac{\sum_{t=k}^{T}(r_t - \bar{r})(r_{t-k} - \bar{r})}{\sum_{t=1}^{T}(r_t - \bar{r})^2}, \quad (4)$$

where r_t denotes a rate of return of a financial instrument. The lack of autocorrelation of the first order does not preclude the existence of autocorrelation of higher orders (see [26, 27]). Since the autocorrelation coefficients of higher order ignore the information provided by the observations between the first and last one in the period, analysis of capital market efficiency is conducted within the framework of the statistical analysis of the partial autocorrelation coefficients (PACFs).

The second method of testing efficiency is based on the run tests. The null hypothesis says that the changes of prices of securities are random. The test statistic is as follows:

$$U = \frac{K - E(\tilde{K})}{S(\tilde{K})}, \quad (5)$$

where K denotes count of empirical runs, $E(\tilde{K})$ denotes expected number of runs, while $S(\tilde{K})$ denotes standard deviation of the number of runs. If we consider two series (e.g., negative and non-negative), then the expectation and variance are calculated as follows:

$$E(\tilde{K}) = \frac{2n_1n_2 + n}{n}, \quad (6)$$

$$S^2(\tilde{K}) = \frac{2n_1n_2(2n_1n_2 - n)}{(n-1)n^2}, \quad (7)$$

where n_1 and n_2 denote the numbers of different types of series, and n is the total number of series. If we consider three series (e.g., negative, zero, and positive), then the expectation and variance are calculated as follows:

$$E(\tilde{K}) = n + 1 - \frac{\sum_{j=1}^{3} n_j^2}{n}, \quad (8)$$

$$S^2(\tilde{K}) = \frac{\sum_{j=1}^{3} n_j^2\left(\sum_{j=1}^{3} n_j^2 + n + n^2\right) - 2n\sum_{j=1}^{3} n_j^3 - n^3}{(n^2-1)n}, \quad (9)$$

where n_1 , n_2, and n_3 denote the numbers of different types of series, and n is the total number of series.

The statistic (2) is normally distributed with 0 mean and standard deviation 1.

In order to test whether the series if securities follow random walk, the variance ratio tests (see [28]) are used. This test is based on the assumption that the variance of increments in a random walk is linearly independent. Variance ratio statistics are calculated as follows:

$$VR(k) = \frac{S^2(r_t + r_{t-1} + \ldots + r_{t-k+1})}{k * S^2(r_t)}. \tag{10}$$

In order to verify, whether the RW1 (assumption that increments of analyzed process are independent and identically distributed) null hypothesis is valid, the following statistic is used:

$$M_1(k) = \frac{VR(k) - 1}{\sqrt{\phi(k)}}, \tag{11}$$

where

$$\phi(k) = \frac{2(2k-1)(k-1)}{3kT}. \tag{12}$$

In order to verify, whether the RW3 (it is assumed that the process has dependent but uncorrelated increments), the following statistic is used:

$$M_2(k) = \frac{VR(k) - 1}{\sqrt{\phi^*(k)}}, \tag{13}$$

where

$$\phi^*(k) = \sum_{j=1}^{k-1} \left[\frac{2(k-j)}{k}\right]^2 \delta_j \tag{14}$$

and

$$\delta_j = \frac{\sum_{t=j+1}^{T} (r_t - \overline{r})^2 (r_{t-j} - \overline{r})^2}{\left[\sum_{t=1}^{T} (r_t - \overline{r})^2\right]^2}. \tag{15}$$

Both statistics $M_1(k)$ and $M_2(k)$ follow standard normal distribution. If the null hypothesis is rejected, the analyzed time series is not random walk, and the capital market is not efficient (see, e.g., [29]).

In order to analyze sensitivity of stock markets to external shocks, the following bivariate VAR(p)-AGDCC-GARCH(1,1) models (see [30]) will be considered:

$$\boldsymbol{r}_t = \sum_{i=1}^{p} \boldsymbol{\Pi}_i \boldsymbol{r}_{t-i} + \boldsymbol{\varepsilon}_t, \tag{16}$$

$$E(\boldsymbol{\varepsilon}_t \boldsymbol{\varepsilon}_t^T) = \boldsymbol{H}_t, \tag{17}$$

where $\boldsymbol{r}_t$ is the following vector of rates of return on stock market indices:

$$\boldsymbol{r}_t = \left[r_t^{VIS} \; r_t^{DEV}\right]^T$$

r_t^{VIS} denotes the rate of return on stock market index in a Visegrad country (VIS=PL,CZ,HU,SK), and r_t^{DEV} denotes the rate of return on a mature stock market index (DEV = DE,US). The covariance matrix is decomposed as follows:

$$\boldsymbol{H}_t = \boldsymbol{D}_t\boldsymbol{R}_t\boldsymbol{D}_t, \tag{18}$$

where the matrix $\boldsymbol{D}_t$ consists of squared roots of variances of shocks:

$$\boldsymbol{D}_t = diag\left[\sqrt{h_t^{VIS,VIS}} \quad \sqrt{h_t^{DEV,DEV}}\right]. \tag{19}$$

These variances of shocks are modeled according to the following GARCH(1,1) model:

$$h_t^{n,n} = \alpha_{0,n} + \alpha_{1,n}\left(\varepsilon_{t-1}^n\right)^2 + \beta_{1,n}h_{t-1}^{n,n}, n = VIS, DEV. \tag{20}$$

Correlations between shocks change in time and depend on negative and positive shocks in the following way:

$$\boldsymbol{R}_t = (diag(\boldsymbol{Q}_t))^{-1/2}\boldsymbol{Q}_t(diag(\boldsymbol{Q}_t))^{-1/2}, \tag{21}$$

where

$$\boldsymbol{Q}_t = \left(1 - \tilde{\alpha}_1 - \tilde{\beta}_1\right)\overline{\boldsymbol{Q}} + \tilde{\gamma}_1\left(\overline{\boldsymbol{Q}} - \overline{\boldsymbol{Q}^-}\right) + \tilde{\alpha}_1\boldsymbol{u}_{t-1}\boldsymbol{u}_{t-1}^T + \tilde{\beta}_1\boldsymbol{Q}_t + \tilde{\gamma}_1\boldsymbol{u}_{t-1}^-\left(\boldsymbol{u}_{t-1}^-\right)^T. \tag{22}$$

The elements of vector $\boldsymbol{u}_t$ are defined as follows:

$$u_t^n = \frac{\varepsilon_t^n}{\sqrt{h_t^{n,n}}}, \tag{23}$$

where n = VIS,DEV and $\boldsymbol{u}_{t-1}^-$ consists of zero-threshold standardized errors, while the matrices $\overline{\boldsymbol{Q}}$ and $\overline{\boldsymbol{Q}^-}$ denote the unconditional covariance matrices of vectors $\boldsymbol{u}_{t-1}$ and $\boldsymbol{u}_{t-1}^-$, respectively.

As a robustness check, parameters of the asymmetric VAR(p)-GARCH-BEKK model (see [30]) will be estimated. In this model, the covariance matrix evolves according to the following formula:

$$\boldsymbol{H}_t = \boldsymbol{C}\boldsymbol{C}^T + \boldsymbol{A}\boldsymbol{\varepsilon}_{t-1}\boldsymbol{\varepsilon}_{t-1}^T\boldsymbol{A}^T + \boldsymbol{B}\boldsymbol{H}_{t-1}\boldsymbol{B}^T + \boldsymbol{D}\boldsymbol{\xi}_{t-1}\boldsymbol{\xi}_{t-1}^T\boldsymbol{D}^T, \tag{24}$$

4. Results and discussion

In the empirical research, we use daily data covering period from May 2004 to December 2019. Logarithmic rates of return on WIG (acronym of the Warsaw Stock Index in Polish), BUX (acronym of the Budapest Stock Index in Hungarian), PX (acronym of the Prague Stock Exchange in Czech), SAX (acronym of the Slovakian Stock Index in Slovakian), DAX (acronym of the German Stock Index in German language), and S&P500 (Standard and Poor's 500) are used.

In the first step, the methodology proposed by Inclan and Tiao [7] and Inclan et al. [24] is used in order to identify dates of significant changes in the unconditional variance for Poland, the Czech Republic, Hungary, and Slovakia (**Table 1**).

Results of the analysis indicate that significant changes in volatilities of the rates of return were observed in similar days in all markets. Significant breakpoint in variance during the financial turmoil and short before the Lehman Brothers bankruptcy is in line with expectations. The second breakpoint date is observed during the euro area sovereign debt crisis. However, in the case of Slovakia, a significant change was observed short before the announcement of the OMT program. Difference between Slovakia and noneuro-area members does not come as a surprise, since the performance of financial markets in Slovakia was strongly linked to the situation in the euro area. The announcement of the OMT program turned out to have the long-term impact on markets in the euro area, so the obtained result confirms findings of other studies (see [31, 32]). Moreover, short after the Brexit referendum, significant breakpoint in variance is observed. This result confirms findings obtained by Kurecic and Kokotovic [33], who have also noticed a significant increase in volatility on stock markets after this event. Results of the British referendum could provide information about a threat of an illiberal turn all over the world. As a result, level of trust in financial markets decreased significantly, which was reflected by the appearance of the home bias phenomenon. All in all, in the case of all four countries, four in terms of volatility four states can be distinguished.

In the next step, hypothesis concerning efficiency of stock markets is verified on the basis of three methods for all four subperiods and four countries. Results of verification for Poland are presented in **Table 2**. Results of verification for the Czech Republic are presented in **Table 3**. Results of verification for Hungary and Slovakia are presented in **Tables 4** and **5**.

Results from **Tables 2–5** indicate that stock markets in four analyzed countries were efficient in most of analyzed subperiods. However, in some cases, conclusions depend on the used methodology. The lowest level of efficiency was observed during the subprime crisis in the United States. This result is not surprising, since after the Lehman Brothers bankruptcy, very large panic on stock markets was observed. As a result of this panic, efficiency of financial markets decreased significantly. Some studies set hypothesis that the phenomenon of I(2)-ness of prices of financial instruments in crisis periods exists (see, e.g., [34]). Inefficiency of stock markets in the crisis period may confirm validity of this hypothesis. It turns out that stock markets of countries of the Central and Eastern Europe differ with regard to efficiency. For example, after the Lehman Brothers bankruptcy, stock markets in Hungary and Poland turned out to be inefficient, while the H0 hypothesis about efficiency was not rejected in the case of Slovakia and the Czech Republic. Differences across subperiods suggest that it is difficult to infer about efficiency in the

Country	Poland	Czech Republic	Hungary	Slovakia	Event
Dates of breakpoint in variances	2008-09-12	2008-09-04	2008-09-12	2008-09-12	The US subprime crisis
	2011-12-21	2011-12-23	2012-01-23	2012-07-23	The euro area sovereign debt crisis
	2016-06-27	2016-07-18	2016-06-29	2016-06-28	The Brexit referendum

Table 1.
Results of the analysis of breakpoints in variance.

Description of subperiod	Dates	Variance ratio test	Autocorrelation function	Run test
Before the subprime crisis	2004-05-03 to 2008-09-12	0.9833	0.362	0.44
Subprime crisis and the euro area sovereign debt crisis	2008-09-15 to 2011-12-21	0.0488	0.012	0.64
Calming down after crisis and before the Brexit referendum	2011-12-22 to 2016-07-27	0.9715	0.306	0.76
The last period after the Brexit referendum	2016-07-28 to 2019-12-30	0.7031	0.248	0.96

P *values of statistical tests are provided.*

Table 2.
Results of testing efficiency of the Polish stock market.

Description of subperiod	Dates	Variance ratio test	Autocorrelation function	Run test
Before the subprime crisis	2004-05-03 to 2008-09-04	0.9050	0.403	0.64
Subprime crisis and the euro area sovereign debt crisis	2008-09-05 to 2011-12-23	0.9785	0.717	0.31
Calming down after crisis and before the Brexit referendum	2011-12-24 to 2016-07-18	0.6140	0.071	0.64
The last period after the Brexit referendum	2016-07-19 to 2019-12-30	0.7835	0.367	0.45

P *values of statistical tests are provided.*

Table 3.
Results of testing efficiency of the Czech stock market.

Description of subperiod	Dates	Variance ratio test	Autocorrelation function	Run test
Before the subprime crisis	2004-05-03 to 2008-09-12	0.3055	0.079	0.24
Subprime crisis and the euro area sovereign debt crisis	2008-09-15 to 2012-01-23	0.0211	0.003	0.13
Calming down after crisis and before the Brexit referendum	2012-01-24 to 2016-06-29	0.8756	0.005	0.88
The last period after the Brexit referendum	2016-06-30 to 2019-12-30	0.4549	0.274	0.20

Table 4.
Results of testing efficiency of the Hungarian stock market. P *values of statistical tests are provided.*

whole period, and some financial markets may be efficient in one period and inefficient in the other one.

In the last step, financial markets of the four analyzed countries are compared with regard to sensitivity to shocks from Germany and the United States. Multivariate GARCH models take into account time-varying volatilities. Therefore, division into subperiods according to **Table 1** is not necessary. In turn, analysis will be conducted in three large subperiods:

Description of subperiod	Dates	Variance ratio test	Autocorrelation function	Run test
Before the subprime crisis	2004-05-03 to 2008-09-12	0.3055	0.079	0.24
Subprime crisis and the euro area sovereign debt crisis	2008-09-15 to 2012-01-23	0.0211	0.003	0.13
Calming down after crisis and before the Brexit referendum	2012-01-24 to 2016-06-29	0.8756	0.005	0.88
The last period after the Brexit referendum	2016-06-30 to 2019-12-30	0.4549	0.274	0.20

Table 5.
Results of testing efficiency of the Slovakian stock market. P *values of statistical tests are provided.*

- before the Lehman Brothers bankruptcy,
- between the Lehman Brothers bankruptcy and before the announcement of the OMT program, and
- after the announcement of the OMT program.

Table 6 presents estimates of parameters reflecting impact of rates of return for developed markets on the rates of return for Visegrad stock markets, while the table average values of correlations

Results of the analysis indicate the strength of the impact of developed stock markets on Visegrad stock markets differed across subperiods (**Table 7**). The strongest linkages were observed in the crisis period. Between 2008 and 2012, shocks generated by stock markets in Visegrad countries were strongly correlated with shocks generated by stock markets in Germany and the United States. A significant drop in comovements of stock markets in Poland, the Czech Republic, Hungary, and capital markets of Germany and the United States was observed after the announcement of the OMT program. In the stable period, investors got knowledge which classes of assets were riskier or safer. Moreover, the illiberal turn in the Central and Eastern Europe could have impact on sensitivity of stock markets in Poland, the Czech Republic, and Hungary on external shocks (see, e.g., [35]) In the case of the correlation between shocks associated with SAX and DAX, a decrease in correlation was not so large, which should be attributed with participation of

	WIG	BUX	PX	SAX
First subperiod				
DAX	0.549	0.705	0.237	0.187
S&P500	0.313	0.743	0.226	0.278
Second subperiod				
DAX	0.643	0.792	0.289	0.367
S&P500	0.421	0.851	0.113	0.389
Third subperiod				
DAX	0.439	0.266	0.125	0.191
S&P500	0.206	0.299	0.098	0.235

Table 6.
Impact of rates of return of developed markets on rates of return of Visegrad countries.

	WIG	BUX	PX	SAX
First subperiod				
DAX	0.378	0.316	0.104	0.156
S&P500	0.279	0.178	0.373	0.211
Second subperiod				
DAX	0.511	0.489	0.723	0.375
S&P500	0.194	0.347	0.851	0.413
Third subperiod				
DAX	0.208	0.278	0.176	0.364
S&P500	0.386	0.198	0.251	0.278

Table 7.
Correlations between shocks generated.

Slovakia in the euro area. However, rates of return on WIG and BUX turned out to be more sensitive to changes in rates of return on DAX in particular in years 2004–2012. This may be due to large interactions between Germany and two economies of the Central and Eastern Europe (Polish economy and Hungarian economy).

5. Conclusions

In this chapter, the performance of stock markets in Visegrad countries after their EU accession was studied. Results of the analysis indicate that there were differences between the performance of the Slovakian stock market and the performance of noneuro-area member states. In the case of all four markets, three significant breakpoints in variance were identified. These breakpoints reflect the beginning of the US subprime crisis, the end of the euro area sovereign debt crisis and, the results of the Brexit referendum.

Stock markets in the CEE-4 countries turned out to be informationally efficient in three of four subperiods. Hypothesis about informational efficiency was rejected only in the case of Poland and Hungary and in the crisis period. In the case of the Czech and Slovakian stock market, there were no grounds to reject hypothesis about their efficiency. Results of three statistical tests confirmed it.

Stock markets in Poland and Hungary were more sensitive to changes of rates of return on DAX. However, in the stable period after 2012, correlation between shocks generated by Poland, the Czech Republic, and Hungary and shocks generated by Germany was much weaker than in earlier years. Integration of the Slovakian stock market with capital markets of developed economies did not decrease in the post-crisis period.

Acknowledgements

The chapter was written with the financial support of National Science Centre, Poland, under Grant No. 2015/19/D/HS4/03354.

DOI: http://dx.doi.org/10.5772/intechopen.92102

Author details

Wojciech Grabowski
Department of Econometric Models and Forecasts, University of Lodz, Lodz, Poland

*Address all correspondence to: wojciech.grabowski@uni.lodz.pl

References

[1] Zanzoni A, Montecchi-Palazzi L, Quondam MX. A molecular interaction database. FEBS Letters. 2002;**513**: 135-140. DOI: 10.1016/s0014-5793(01) 03293-8

[2] Gilmore CG, McManus GM, Tezel A. Portfolio allocations and the emerging equity markets of Central Europe. Journal of Multinational Financial Management. 2005;**15**:287-300. DOI: 10.1016/j.mulfin.2004.12.001

[3] Syllignakis MN, Kouretas G. Dynamic correlation analysis of financial contagion: Evidence from the central and eastern European markets. International Review of Economics and Finance. 2011;**20**:717-732. DOI: 10.1016/ j.iref.2011.01.006

[4] Kenourgios D, Samitas A, Paltalidis N. Financial market dynamics in an enlarged European Union. Journal of Economic Integration. 2009;**24**: 197-221. DOI: www.jstor.org/stable/ 23000878

[5] Dajcman S. The dynamics of return comovement and spillovers between the Czech and European stock markets in the period 1997–2000. Czech Journal of Economics and Finance. 2012;**62**: 368-390. DOI: https://ideas.repec.org/a/ fau/fauart/v62y2012i4p368-390.html

[6] Winkler A. The ECB as lender of last resort: Bank versus governments. Journal of Economics and Statistics. 2015;**235**:329-341. DOI: 10.101515/jbnst-201500307

[7] Inclan C, Tiao GC. Use of cumulative sums of squares for retrospective detection of changes of variance. Journal of the American Statistical Association. 1994;**89**:913-923. DOI: 10.1080/ 01621459.1994.10476824

[8] Mateus T. The risk and predictability of equity returns of the EU accession countries. Emerging Markets Review. 2004;**5**:241-266. DOI: 10.1016/j. ememar.2004.03.003

[9] Maneschiold PO. Integration between the Baltic and international stock markets. Emerging Markets Finance and Trade. 2006;**42**:25-45. DOI: 10.2753/REE1540-496X420602

[10] Nielsson U. Interdependence of Nordic and Baltic stock markets. Baltic Journal of Economics. 2007;**6**:9-27. DOI: 10.1080/1406099X.2007.10840434

[11] Bein M, Tuna G. Volatility transmission and dynamic correlation analysis between developed and emerging European stock markets during sovereign debt crisis. Romanian Journal of Economic Forecasting. 2015; **18**:61-80. Available from: http://www.ipe .ro/rjef/rjef2_15/rjef2_2015p61-80.pdf

[12] Harkmann K. Stock market contagion from Western Europe to central and Eastern Europe during the crisis years 2008–2012. Eastern European Economics. 2014;**52**:55-65. DOI: 10.2753/EEE0012-8775520303

[13] Syllignakis M, Kouretas G. German, US and eastern European stock market integration. Open Economies Review. 2010;**21**:607-628. DOI: 10.1007/ s11079-009-9109-9

[14] Syriopoulos T. Dynamic linkages between emerging European and developed stock markets: Has the EMU any impact? International Review of Financial Analysis. 2007;**16**:41-60. DOI: 10.1016/j.irfa.2005.02.003

[15] Bieńkowski W, Gawrońska-Nowak B, Grabowski W. Comovements of stock markets in the CEE-3 countries during the global financial crisis. Eastern European Economics. 2014;**52**:32-55. DOI: 10.1080/00128775.2014.1004907

[16] Brzeszczyński J, Welfe A. Are there benefits from trading strategy based on the returns spillovers to the emerging stock markets? Evidence from Poland. Emerging Markets Finance and Trade. 2007;**43**:74-92. DOI: 10.2753/REE1540-496X430404

[17] Pietrzak M, Fałdziński M, Balcerzak A, Melzuin T, Zinecker M. Short-term shocks and long-term relationships of interdependencies among central European capital markets. Economics and Sociology. 2007;**43**:74-92. DOI: 10.14254/2071-789X.2017/10-1/5

[18] Gjika D, Horvath R. Stock market comovements in Central Europe: Evidence from the asymmetric DCC model. Economic Modelling. 2013;**33**: 54-64. DOI: 10.1016/j.econmod.2013.03.015

[19] Grabowski W. Comovements of stock markets in Visegrad countries in years 2004–2017. Research Papers of the Wrocław University of Economics. 2018;**519**:88-98. DOI: 10.15611/pm.2018.519.07

[20] Grabowski W. Givers or recipients? Co-movements between stock markets of CEE-3 and developed countries. Sustainability. 2019;**11**:6495. DOI: 10.3390/su11226495

[21] Albuquerque R, Vega C. Economic news and international stock market co-movement. Review of Finance. 2009;**13**: 401-465. DOI: 10.1093/rof/rfn020

[22] Moagar-Poladian S, Clichici D, Stanciu CV. The comovement of exchange rates and stock markets in Central and Eastern Europe. Sustainability. 2019;**11**:3985

[23] Vychytilova J. Stock market development beyond the GFC: The case of v4 couuntries. Journal of Competitiveness. 2018;**10**:149-163. DOI: 10.7441/joc.2018.02.10

[24] Inclan C, Aggarwal R, Leal R. Volatility in emerging stock markets. Journal of Financial Quantitative Analysis. 1999;**34**:33-55. DOI: 10.2307/2676245

[25] Fama EF. Efficient capital markets: A review of theory and empirical work. Journal of Finance. 1970;**25**:383-417. DOI: 10.2307/2325486

[26] Kilon J, Jamróz P. Informational (in) efficiency of the Polish stock exchange. Proceedia: Social and Behavioral Sciences. 2015;**213**:390-396. DOI: 10.1016/j.sbspro.2015.11.556

[27] Kompa K, Matuszewska-Janica A. Efficiency of the Warsaw stock exchange: Analysis of selected properties. International Advances in Economic Research. 2009;**15**:59-70. DOI: 10.1007/s11294-008-9180-9

[28] Lo AW, MacKinlay AC. Stock market prices do not follow random walks: Evidence from a simple specification test. Review of Financial Studies. 1988;**1**:41-66. DOI: 10.3386/w2168

[29] Wright JH. Alternative variance-ratio tests using ranks and signs. Journal of Business and Economic Statistics. 2000;**18**:1-9. DOI: 10.2307/1392131

[30] Kroner K, Ng V. Modelling asymmetric comovements of asset returns. 1998;**11**:817-844. DOI: 10.1093/rfs/11.4.817

[31] Grabowski W, Stawasz E. Sovereign bond spreads in the EMU peripheral countries: The role of the outright monetary transactions. Prague Economic Papers. 2017;**26**:360-373. DOI: 10.18267/j.pep.618

[32] Grabowski W, Stawasz-Grabowska E. News releases, credit rating announcements, and anti-crisis measures as determinants of sovereign bond spreads in the peripheral euro-area

countries. Czech Journal of Economics and Finance. 2019;**69**:149-173. Available from: https://ideas.repec.org/a/fau/fauart/v69y2019i2p149-173.html

[33] Kurecic P, Kokotovic F. Empirical analysis of the impact of Brexit referendum and post-referendum events on selected stock exchange indexes. South East European Journal of Economics and Business. 2018;**13**:7-16. DOI: 10.2478/jeb-2018-0001

[34] Homm U, Breitung J. Testing for speculative bubbles in stock markets: A comparison of alternative methods. Journal of Financial Economics. 2012;**10**: 198-231. DOI: 10.1093/jjfinec/nbr009

[35] Enyedi Z. Paternalist populism and illiberal elitism in Central Europe. Journal of Political Ideologies. 2016;**21**: 9-25. DOI: 10.1080/13569317.2016.1105402

Chapter 11

Has the Yield Curve Accurately Predicted the Malaysian Economy in the Previous Two Decades?

Maya Puspa Rahman

Abstract

Previous researchers have argued that yield curve contains information for future growth, and to a certain extent, was accurate in predicting recessions through the signal of yield curve inversion. This paper provides new evidence on the long- and short-run relationship between economic growth and yield spread in Malaysia, based on a 20-year span of data ranging from January 1996 to December 2016. By using the autoregressive distributed lag (ARDL) framework, the sample data are divided into three samples after taking into consideration the two major crises occurred in Malaysia over the last two decades. We find strong evidence of cointegration between the yield spread and growth, concurring on the long-run and short-run dynamics between them. Though significant, the instability of the yield spread to affect the movement of growth does not support the priori expectation on the predictive ability of the yield curve in Malaysia.

Keywords: yield curve, predictive power, ARDL, Malaysia

1. Introduction

Predictive power of the yield curve is certainly not a new topic in finance. It has been empirically shown that a positive slope of the yield curve is linked with a future increase in real economic activity in the United States of America (US) in the early works by Estrella and Hardouvelis [1] while Estrella and Mishkin [2, 3] showed that yield curve provides a relatively strong signal in predicting US recession, particularly the one that had occurred during 1990–1991. In addition to that, Karunaratne [4] also finds that yield curve is a better and near perfect tool for forecasting economic activities compared to other macroeconomic indicators in Australia, whereas Hamilton and Kim [5] reexamined the predictability of the yield curve with updated data and confirmed the usefulness of the yield curve in predicting gross domestic product (GDP) growth. Apart from the above, there are voluminous studies that have been covering on the predictive ability of the yield curve. A much recent study by Boukhatem and Sekouhi [6], for example, also highlights that the yield curve can be considered as an advanced indicator for growth or recession for the Tunisian economy. As such, the slope of the yield curve, which typically referred to the yield spread or term spread, is deemed to act as a valuable forecasting tool[1].

Even though the use of the yield curve in predicting the economy has been empirically proven, recent research came up with new evidence questioning whether it is still as powerful. Chinn and Kucko [7], for example, show the predictive power of the yield curve in the United States of America (US) and Japan to be declining over time. In addition to that, they also show that for all of the seven countries examined, yield spread is indeed important and has significant predictive power when forecasting industrial production growth over a 1-year horizon, but the result deteriorates when forecasting growth 2 years ahead.

In Malaysia, the Treasury bill spread have been empirically shown to be a significant predictor of future growth of annual output, see Ghazali and Low [8], while Elshareif and Tan [9] find a long-run cointegrated relationship between the short- and long-term rates, confirming the existence of pure expectation theory in the Malaysian bond market. The recent work of Zulkhibri and Abdul Rani [10] is one of the first to examine the role of yield spread[2] in inflation and growth in Malaysia. Based on the data span of 1992–2009, they used simple regression to establish the relationship between yield spread, output and inflation, and then used the probit model for forecasting. It was shown that the yield spread contains little information about future output and inflation at short horizons. They also argued that the use of yield spread in monetary analysis beyond conventional indicators is rather limited.

This study aims to discover the ability of the yield spread to predict economic growth over a longer time horizon. In consideration that the Malaysian economy as well as the sovereign bond market has grown rapidly over the past 20 years, it would be interesting to see whether there exists a long-run relationship between the yield spread and growth.

In addition to that, this study also aims to use the autoregressive distributed lag (ARDL) approach to cointegration and error correction models (ECMs) to determine whether there is evidence of relationship between yield spread and growth, in long run and short run within the span of the 20 years. In consideration of the prerequisites possessed by the conventional Granger [11] and, Engle and Granger [12] to have all the underlying variables to be in the same order of integration, ARDL stands out to be the most appropriate technique in order to test for cointegration among the variables.

This paper makes two contributions to the existing literature. First, it examines the relationship between slope of the yield curve (in other words, yield spread) and growth based on updated data and over a 20-year time period. Second, it is the first to employ the ARDL method in consideration of the mixture of order of integration among the variables tested. The empirical result shows the existence of a long-run relationship between the yield spread and growth in Malaysia. Though significant, the instability of the yield spread to affect the movement of growth does not support the priori expectation on the predictive power of the yield curve, making it less reliable to be used as forecasting tool on the general economic condition.

The remainder of this paper is organized as follows. Section 2 highlights the theoretical framework and related literature on the predictive power of the yield

---

1 Normally calculated as the difference between the yields of the 10-year government securities against 3-month Treasury bill. See among others, Estrella and Hardouvelis [1], Estrella and Mishkin [2], Karunaratne [4], Hamilton and Kim [5].

2 Zulkhibri and Abdul Rani [10] used 'term spread' in their study instead of yield spread, but the calculation is similar as highlighted earlier.

curve. Section 3 discusses the major crises faced by the Malaysian economy, within our data span while Section 4 describes the estimation model, data and method employed. The empirical results are presented in Section 5 while the concluding remarks and recommendation for future research are presented in Section 6.

2. Theoretical framework of yield curve analysis

According to the economic research department of the Federal Reserve Bank of New York, the analysis on the behavior of interest rates of different maturities over the business cycle goes back to the early work of Mitchell [13]. Many years later, Butler [14] made a connection between the yield curve as a predictor of short-term interest rates and the implications of declining short-term rates for contemporaneous economic activity, of which he correctly predicted that there would be no recession in 1979[3]. Subsequently, numerous studies have been conducted on the predictability of the yield curve in charting the future state of the economy.

Fundamentally, yield curve analysis is developed based on the term structure of interest rates, strongly associated with pure expectation theory. This theory essentially equalizes the long-term interest rates with short-term interest rates and market expectation of future interest rates plus a risk premium, which refers to the opportunity cost and compensation for holding long-term bonds as investors generally prefer short-term rather than long-term bonds. The linkage between the long-term and short-term rate together with the risk (or liquidity) premium is as presented in the equation[4] below;

$$i_{nt} = \frac{i_t + ie_{t+1} + ie_{t+2} + \ \dots \ + ie_{t+(n-1)}}{n} + l_{nt} \tag{1}$$

where i_{nt} is the long-term rate, it is the current short-term rate; $ie_{t+(n\text{-}1)}$ is the future short-term rate; and l_{nt} is the risk (liquidity) premium, which posits that the yield on a long-term bond is the average of the one period interest rates expected over the lifetime of the long bond. Hence, this theory puts forward that the expectations of market participants are to be formed rationally, based on the anticipated economic situation, leading to the expected level of future short rates that would in turn influence the yields on long-term bonds.

Therefore, the link between the yield curve and growth of the economy is rationalized through the monetary policy actions undertaken by the government. For example, suppose the government undertakes a contractionary monetary policy. During this time, financial market participants would expect the short-term interest rates to be temporarily raised. If the current short-term interest rate is higher than the expected future short-term rate, the long-term rate should rise less than the short-term rate according to the expectations theory. Thus, the yield spread will be flattened, or, in extreme cases, be negative. This will also reflect situations where the yield curve will be inverted as the short-term rate is higher than the long-term rate. Inverted (or negatively sloped) yield curves have been excellent predictors of recessions for many years, whereby every recession after the mid-1960s was predicted by a negative slope—an inverted yield curve—within six quarters of the impending recession. During those times, the monetary contraction would eventually reduce spending in interest-sensitive sectors of the economy,

---

3 Federal Reserve Bank of New York.

4 Incorporating the modification into the expectation theory, with the risk/liquidity premium, widely known as liquidity premium theory, see Mishkin and Eakins [11].

causing economic growth to slow. Alternatively speaking, it just makes no sense when short-term interest rates pay investors more than the long-term bonds, and so when it does, something unusual (usually economic downturn or recession) is expected to occur. On the other hand, expansionary monetary policy would result in a high yield spread, signaling for a possibility of a higher future real economic growth, see Hamilton, and Kim [5].

Putting it in a more comprehensible perspective, in general, the higher the yield on 10-year government securities relative to the yield on 3-month Treasury securities—that is, the more steeply sloped the yield curve—the higher the rate of future economic growth. Similarly, the less steeply sloped the yield curve, the lower the subsequent rate of growth. Hence, by looking in terms of the correlation between the two variables, it has been emphasized that the pattern of positive correlation between the current GDP growth and lagged yield spread and negative correlation between current GDP growth and future yield spread is consistent, see Wheelock and Wohar [15].

It is important to highlight that early studies on the predictability of recessions by the slope of the yield curve were primarily focused on the US economy (see Harvey [16], Stock and Watson [17], Chen [18], Estrella and Hardouvelis [1], while subsequent research tended to focus on whether the relationship between the yield spread and future economic growth still hold for other countries, apart from the US, see Harvey [19], Davis and Henry [20], Plosser and Rouwenhorst [21], Bonser-Neal and Morley [22], Kozicki [23], Estrella and Mishkin [3], Estrella et al. [24]). Some other studies have also empirically proven that the spread contains useful information about the future path of inflation (Jorion and Mishkin [25], Gerlach [26]).

With regard of the different views on the predictive power of the yield curve over time, particularly in Malaysia, the present study develops a model to examine the ability of the yield spread to predict economic growth over a longer time horizon, within two decades. An overview on the Malaysian economy and major crises over the last 20 years is also presented in the next section.

3. Malaysian economy, bond market development and major crises since 1996

With the celebration of her 60 years of independence, Malaysia has been globally recognized not only for the recent and dedicated effort in the Islamic banking and finance development, but is also known for the multicultural and diverse ethnics, apart from being among the top ranks in terms of GDP growth within the South-East Asian countries. With a population reaching up to 30 million people, Malaysia has recorded a stable economic growth over the last 20 years, with the highest recorded at 10% in 1996. GDP per capita has also increased by 98% from USD4797 to USD9502 in 1996 and 2016, respectively[5].

It is important to highlight that healthy growth of the local bond market is essential in order to support the mobility of funds in the financial system. During the past 20 years since 1996, the bond market[6] in Malaysia has grown remarkably, with bond outstanding value recorded at RM1.17 trillion in 2016. The sovereign bond has also increased many-fold over the last two decades, from RM75 billion in 1998 to RM628 billion last year. This rapid growth of the bond market is one of the

[5] FRED Economic Data, Federal Reserve Bank of St. Louis.

[6] Comprises of sovereign and private debt securities, including sukuk (Islamic bonds), sourced from Securities Commission Malaysia (www.sc.com.my).

motivating factors to undertake the research apart from the interest to establish the long-run relation of the spread with the growth.

Nonetheless, with an open economy structure, Malaysia is not exempted from economic crisis, with two of the major crises occurred within the past 20 years. One of the most significant ones was the 1997 Asian financial crisis triggered by the Thai Baht speculative trading leading to the domino effect on all Asian countries, causing the Malaysian Ringgit to be heavily sold and depreciated by almost 50% in value by January 1998, see Athukorala [27]. Coupled with the internally induced banking crisis, massive short-term and un-hedged capital inflows and sudden reversal of capital outflows have exacerbated the situation leading the massive downturn of the economy. GDP growth was recorded at negative 7.4% in 1998 from a positive growth of 7.3% recorded just a year earlier. Given the negative growth, Malaysian economy was officially down with recession, with the number of retrenchments increasing from 19,000 in 1997 to over 83,000 in 1998, while inflation rate peaked at 6.2% in 1998 surpassing the previous peak of 5.3% in 1991, see Athukorala [27].

Another notable crisis is the global financial crisis that was initiated from the credit subprime mortgage market in the US in 2007, being one of the horrendous events that has ever occurred in the world's history. The innovation acts of financial engineering to securitize and increase the liquidity of the US subprime residential mortgage-backed securities[7] and packaged them into collateralized debt obligations (CDOs), had turned out to be an unimaginable crisis affecting not only the US economy but the rest of the world. The downturn impact arising from this crisis for Malaysia was evident when the growth was reduced from 6.5% in 2007 to 4.7% in 2008 with subsequent negative growth of 1.7% in 2009.

Mapping the movements of the yield spread over the past two decades, it is visible that the spread turned negative prior to the two recessions in Malaysia, as shown in **Figure 1** below. Whether the inversion of the yield curve could really signal for future declining of economic output should be proven through the

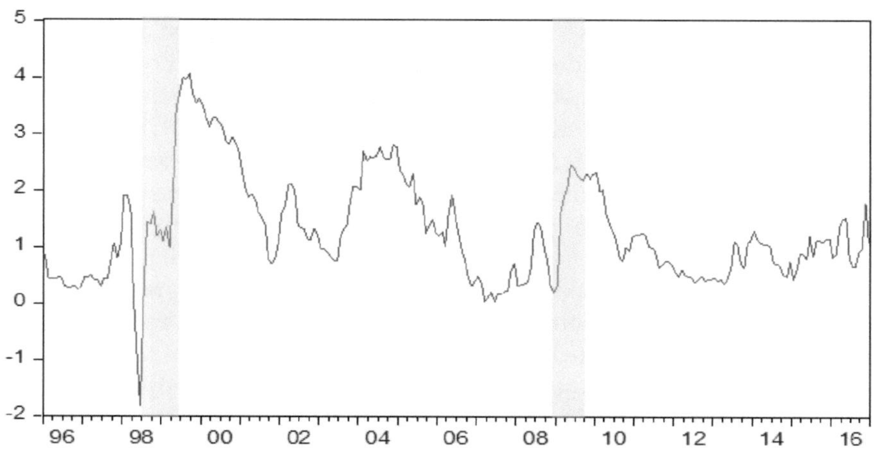

Figure 1.
Malaysian yield spread and major recessions over 20 years. Note: The yield spread is calculated as the difference between the yields on 10-year and 3-month Malaysian Treasury securities. The shaded areas denote major recessions.

---

[7] Subprime mortgages refer to mortagages made to borrowers who are less creditworthy than prime borrowers, see Dwyer and Tkac []. This study also presents an interesting series of events occurred during the crisis and how the tiny market of CDOs became the triggering factor.

empirical analysis undertaken to test the predictive ability of the yield curve in Malaysia, by establishing the long-run cointegration with economic growth. The following section will then discuss how the model is developed and how tests will be done on the collected data.

4. Data and methodology

All series examined in this study—industrial production index, yields of 10-year government bond and 3-month Treasury bill, FTSE-Kuala Lumpur Composite Index, broad money (M2) and exports—are collected from Thomson-Reuters Datastream. The data are monthly data and span the time period from January 1996 to December 2016. The industrial production index is used to signal economic growth, while the yield spread is calculated as the difference between the yields of 10-year government bond and 3-month Treasury bill.

In order to control for other leading variables that could be influencing economic growth, a single factor is constructed to extract the common signals from all the leading indicators. In this study, the leading indicators considered are FTSE-Kuala Lumpur Composite Index, broad money (M2), and exports value. It is also important to point out that the inclusion of all these leading indicators into the regression model could lead to multicollinearity issue, it is best to express them as a single controlled factor. Besides, the main objective of this study is to examine the cointegration of the yield spread and growth, without putting much emphasis on other leading economic variables. Hence, the principal component analysis technique is used to extract the single factor from the movements of these indicators.

In terms of methodology, the relationship between the yield spread and economic growth is established using the autoregressive distributed lag (ARDL) framework by Pesaran and Shin [28], Pesaran et al. [29], and Pesaran [30]. Given the characteristics of the cyclical components of the data, applying the conventional Granger [11] and, Engle and Granger [12] cointegration technique is not applicable in cases of variables that are integrated of different orders. This is because, a prerequisite for applying the abovementioned cointegration analysis is that all time-series are nonstationary and must be of the same order. The ARDL method stands out among other regression methods as it does not involve pre-testing variables, which means that testing on the existence relationship between variables that are integrated of different order of purely I(0), purely I(1), or mixture of both (Duasa [31], Nkoro and Uko [32]). Another superior feature of the ARDL method is that it avoids the larger number of specifications to be made into the regressions, particularly with regard to the decisions on the number of endogeneous and exogenous variables (if any) to be included, as well as the optimal number of lags to be specified. With ARDL, it is possible that different variables have different optimal lags, which is impossible on the application of the standard cointegration test. Most importantly, the model could be used with limited sample data (30–80 observations) since in our analysis, even though the total observations for the whole sample is 249, the sub-sample of the data will be much smaller in quantity. On top of that, the ARDL method will automatically run models with different lags to choose the best estimation model based on the specified selection criteria, in our case, using Akaike info criterion (AIC).

In order to establish the relationship between the yield spread and growth, a linear regression relating the future growth to the current values of the yield spread is considered. The model below is developed based on the model used by Stock and Watson [17] and Zulkhibri and Abdul Rani [10], which has been extended to incorporate the leading macroeconomics indicators and expressed based on the ARDL framework:

$$\Delta lnY_t = \alpha_0 + \sum_{i=0}^{p} \varphi_t \, \Delta lnY_{t-i} + \sum_{i=0}^{p} \theta_t \, \Delta_{\text{Spreadt}-\text{i}} + \sum_{i=0}^{p} \beta_t \, \Delta_{\text{Leadingt}-\text{i}} + \delta_1 \, lnY_{\text{t}-1} + \delta_2 \, \text{Spread}_{\text{t}-1} + \delta_3 \, \text{Leading}_{\text{t}-1} + \upsilon_t \quad (2)$$

where lnY_t is the economic growth indicated by industrial production index and expressed in natural logarithm, Spread_t is the yield spread between 10-year government bond and 3-month Treasury bill and Leading_t are the controlled variables for other macroeconomics leading indicators, Δ is first-difference operator, and p is the optimal lag length whereby the optimal lag length which represents the previous values, are being automatically selected based on Akaike info criterion (AIC). In consideration that the growth could be serially correlated, since previous growth might influence future growth, its past values are useful predictors themselves. This could also be the case for other independent variables, namely spread and leading.

The estimation model above will be applied onto three different samples, first on the whole sample (sample A) for the period of January 1996 to December 2016, while the second and third samples are based on the periods within the occurrences of the major crisis, from January 1996 to December 2000 (sample B) and from January 2007 to December 2009 (sample C), respectively. Our aim is to examine whether the long-run relationship among the variables, particularly the significance of the yield spread in explaining growth, still persists over different time periods.

The ARDL long-run form and bounds test is then undertaken for testing the existence of the long-run relationship, which is detected through the F-statistics (Wald test), and is said to be established if the F-statistics exceeds the critical value band, see Nkoro and Uko [32]. Specifically, the null hypothesis for no cointegration among variables in Eq. (2) is defined as H0: $\delta 1 = \delta 2 = \delta 3 = 0$ (where long-run relationship does not exist) against the alternative hypothesis of H1: $\delta 1 \neq \delta 2 \neq \delta 3 \neq 0$ (long-run relationship does exist). Upon running the ARDL long-run form and bound test in Eviews 9.5, two sets of critical values are generated of which one set refers to I(0) and the other one refers to I(1). Critical values for the I(1) series are referred to as upper bound critical values, while the critical values for I(0) series are referred to lower bound critical values (Duasa, [31]). This is the bound testing procedure generated through the ARDL model and widely used in the estimation of long-run relationships when the properties of the time-series data are a mixture of I(0) and I(1).

If there is evidence of long-run relationship (cointegration), the following model is estimated:

$$lnY_t = \alpha_1 + \sum_{i=0}^{p} \varphi_t \, lnY_{t-i} + \sum_{i=0}^{p} \theta_t \, \text{Spread}_{\text{t}-\text{i}} + \sum_{i=0}^{p} \beta_t \, \text{Leading}_{\text{t}-\text{i}} + \mu_t \quad (3)$$

Subsequently, the ARDL specification of the short-run dynamics is derived by constructing the error correction model (ECM) of the following form:

$$\Delta lnY_t = \alpha_2 + \sum_{i=0}^{p} \varphi_t \, \Delta lnY_{t-i} + \sum_{i=0}^{p} \theta_t \, \Delta_{\text{Spread}} + \sum_{i=0}^{p} \beta_t \, \Delta_{\text{Leading}} + \psi \text{ecm}_t + \varepsilon_t \quad (4)$$

where the ecm_t is the error correction term and is defined as.

$$ecm_t = lnY_t - \alpha_1 + \sum_{i=0}^{p} \varphi_t \, lnY_{t-i} + \sum_{i=0}^{p} \theta_t \text{ Spread}_{t-i} + \sum_{i=0}^{p} \beta_t \text{ Leading}_{t-i} \qquad (5)$$

with all coefficients of the above short-run equation are equations relating to the short run dynamics of the model's convergence to equilibrium with ψ represents the speed of adjustments. The ecm_t shows how much of the disequilibrium is being corrected, that is the extent to which any disequilibrium in the previous period is being adjusted in Y_t.

5. Estimation results and discussions

5.1 Unit root tests

Although ARDL cointegration technique does not require pre-testing for unit roots, this test is still carried out in order to avoid the ARDL model crash in the presence of integrated stochastic trend of I(2) (Nkoro and Uko [32]). In testing the nonstationarity of the series based on unit root test, there are two widely used tests by the econometricians, namely, the Augmented Dickey-Fuller (ADF) unit root test and Phillips-Perron (P-P) unit root test. Some important note on the presence or absence of unit roots, it helps to identify some features of the underlying data-generating process of a series. If a series has no unit roots, it is characterized as stationary, exhibiting mean reversion in that it fluctuates around a constant long-run mean. Alternatively, if the series feature a unit root, they are better characterized as nonstationary processes, which have no tendency to return to a long-run deterministic path, see Libanio [33].

The ADF test accounts for temporarily dependent and heterogeneously distributed errors by including lagged first differences of the dependent variable in the fitted regression. In contrast, the P-P test uses a nonparametric correction to take account for possible autocorrelation. The formula for the ADF test and the P-P test are not presented here, in consideration that it is a standard procedure in data inspection for stationarity. Nonetheless, a good explanation on the unit root stochastic process is covered by Nkoro and Uko [32]. In this study, the unit root test is testing based on ADF test. **Table 1** below presents the results from ADF indicating that there is a mixture of I(0) and I(1) with the absence of I(2) of the regressors, validating the use of ARDL in this analysis.

5.2 Estimation results

Subsequently, Eq. (2) is estimated on three samples of data, namely, sample A (January 1996 to December 2015), sample B (January 1996 to December 2000), and sample C (January 2007 to December 2009). This different estimation of the data

Variable	ADF test statistics		Order of integration
	Level	First difference	
Growth (*lnY*)	−2.3388	−4.9688*	I(1)
Spread	−3.6630*	−3.3490*	I(0)
Leading	−4.7416*	−6.0707*	I(0)

**Significant at 1% level.*

Table 1.
Unit root test.

period allows the testing on not only the significance of the yield spread on the growth, but on whether it is consistent throughout the periods, especially those during major crises. The optimal lag length is automatically selected by the ARDL method, based on the selection criteria of AIC as explained earlier. The calculated F-statistics for the cointegration test is displayed in **Table 2**. For sample A and B, the calculated F-statistics are above both the lower and upper bound critical values, leading to the rejection of the null hypothesis and to concur that there exists long-run relationship between the variables in the model. As for sample C, the calculated F-statistics is below the lower and upper bounds, which indicates that there is no cointegration, raising questions on the consistency of the relationship among the variables when the time period is altered.

The empirical results of the long-run relationship for sample A and B are presented in **Table 3**. It is interesting to note that during the longer time span of 20 years, the yield spread is not significant, as compared to a much shorter time span of 4 years and during the period of Asian financial crisis.

Next, the error correction model indicating the short-run dynamics is presented in **Table 4**, estimated for all of the samples A, B, and C. The lagged term of the yield spread appeared to be only significant during the crisis samples (B and C) but not for the whole 20-year period. A number of diagnostic tests for the error correction model are also applied where there is no evidence of serial correlation, heteroskedasticity, and ARCH (Autoregressive Conditional Heteroskedasticity) effect in the disturbances. All samples except for sample A passed the Jarque-Bera normality test, suggesting that the errors are normally distributed. Most importantly, the

Sample	Data span	Number of observations	F-statistics value	Lag (k)	Significance level	Lower bound critical values I(0)	Upper bound critical values I(1)
A	January 1996 to December 2015	236	**4.4619**	2	10% 5% 1%	2.63 3.10 4.13	3.35 3.87 5.00
B	January 1996 to December 2000	57	**5.2644**	2			
C	January 2007 to December 2009	36	0.8542	2			

Table 2.
F-statistics of cointegration relationship.

Sample	Dependent variable	Independent Variables	
		Spread	Leading
A	lnY_t	0.2179 (0.3282)	1.0540 (0.9671)
B		0.09514* (0.0207)	−0.0893* (0.0349)

*Significant at 1% level.

Table 3.
Long-run model.

Coefficients for the independent variables	Dependent variable ΔlnY_t		
	A	B	C
ΔlnY_{t-1}	−0.7082* (−12.2363)	−0.5669 (−5.4635)	−0.3976* (−2.8088)
ΔlnY_{t-2}	−0.3328* (−5.72900)	−0.2772* (−2.4433)	
ΔSpread	0.0187* (2.3919)	0.0504* (4.3587)	−0.0247 (−1.1328)
$\Delta Spread_{t-1}$	−0.0127 (−1.5925)	−0.0438* (−4.0941)	0.0474* (2.2004)
$\Delta Spread_{t-2}$			
ΔLeading	0.0001 (0.0619)	−0.0123* (−3.849)	
$\Delta Leading_{t-1}$	−0.0128* (−4.3831)		
$\Delta Leading_{t-2}$	−0.0091* (−4.4656)		
ecm_t	−0.0128* (−4.2378)	−0.2326* (−4.7301)	−0.1365* (−1.9418)
Diagnostic tests:			
Far	1.2449	0.4888	0.4381
Farch	2.0439	0.4346	1.6578
JBnormal	17.8131	0.0663	3.6493
R-square	**0.4238**	**0.5678**	**0.3701**

1. t-statistic in parentheses; 2. Far is the F-statistic of Breusch-Godfrey serial correlation LM test. Farch is the F-statistic of ARCH Test. JBnormal is the Jarque-Bera Statistic of Normality Test.
**Significant at 1% level.*
***Significant at 5% level.*
****Significant at 10% level.*

Table 4.
Error correction model for all samples.

significant of the error correction term (ecm_t) for all samples also provide evidence of causality in at least one direction, with the negative coefficient indicating high rate of convergence to equilibrium. Nonetheless, the mixed signs of the yield spread do not match with the theory previously discussed, rendering difficulty in making general inferences with regard to the relationship of the yield spread to growth.

Though significant, the instability of the yield spread to affect the movement of growth in this analysis does not support the priori expectation on the predictive power of the yield curve, in Malaysia. This is consistent with the finding of Zulkhibri and Abdul Rani [10] that yield spread contains little information on the direction of the overall economy. As such, despite the fact that the bond market (both conventional and Islamic) has grown rapidly over the past two decades, the market still needs to deepen more in terms of issuance and trading, so as to facilitate the efficiency of yield curve movement, which could possibly be tagged along with the growth in the future.

6. Conclusion

This study aims to discover the ability of the yield spread to predict economic growth over the last two decades, up until 2016. Based on the priori expectation on the predictive ability possessed by the yield spread on growth, this study uses ARDL approach to cointegration and error correction models to determine whether there is evidence of relationship between yield spread and growth, in long run and short run. This paper makes two contributions to the existing literature. First, it examines the relationship between slope of the yield curve (yield spread) and growth based on updated data and over a 20-year time period. Second, it is the first to employ the ARDL method on yield spread analysis, in consideration of the different order of integration among the variables tested.

The empirical result proves the existence of a long-run relationship between the yield spread and growth in Malaysia. Though significant, the instability of the yield spread to affect the movement of growth in this analysis does not support the priori expectation on the predictive power of the yield curve, making it less reliable to be used as forecasting tool in the general economic condition. Further expansion of the local bond market in terms of issuance and trading may be the one of the keys to establish a much stronger relationship and predictive power of the yield curve in assessing the direction of the Malaysian economy.

Acknowledgements

This study is funded by the Research Acculturation Grant Scheme RAGS15-061-0124, Ministry of Higher Education, Malaysia.

Author details

Maya Puspa Rahman
Department of Economics, Kulliyyah of Economics and Management Science, International Islamic University, Malaysia

*Address all correspondence to: mayapuspa@iium.edu.my

References

[1] Estrella A, Hardouvelis GA. The term structure as a predictor of real economic activity. The Journal of Finance. 1991; **46**(2):555-576

[2] Estrella A, Mishkin FS. The yield curve as a predictor of US recessions. Current Issues in Economics and Finance. Federal Reserve Bank of New York. 1996a;**1**(7)

[3] Estrella A, Mishkin FS. The yield curve as a predictor of recessions in the United States and Europe. The Determination of Long-Term Interest Rates and Exchange Rates and the Role of Expectations. Basel: Bank for International Settlements; 1996b

[4] Karunaratne ND. The yield curve as a predictor of growth and recession in Australia. Discussion Paper; 1999. p. 255

[5] Hamilton JD, Kim DH. A re-examination of the predictability of the yield spread for real economic activity. Journal of Money, Credit, and Banking. 2002;**34**(2):340-360

[6] Boukhatem J, Sekouhi H. What does the bond yield curve tell us about Tunisian economic activity? Research in International Business and Finance. 2017

[7] Chinn M, Kucko K. The predictive power of the yield curve across countries and time. International Finance. 2015;**18**(2):129-156

[8] Ghazali NA, Low SW. The expectation hypothesis in emerging financial markets: The case of Malaysia. Applied Economics. 2002;**34**(9): 1147-1156

[9] Elshareif EE, Tan HB. Interpreting term structure of interest rates in the Malaysian fix-income market. International Research Journal of Finance and Economics. 2010;**37**(1): 115-124

[10] Zulkhibri M, Abdul Rani MS. Term spread, inflation and economic growth in emerging markets: Evidence from Malaysia. Review of Accounting and Finance. 2016;**15**(3):372-392

[11] Granger CW. Some properties of time series data and their use in econometric model specification. Journal of Econometrics. 1981;**16**(1): 121-130

[12] Engle RF, Granger CW. Co-integration and error correction: Representation, estimation, and testing. Econometrica: Journal of the Econometric Society. 1987:251-276

[13] Mitchell WC. Business Cycles. Vol. 3. University of California Press; 1913

[14] Butler L. Recession? - A market view. Federal Reserve Bank of San Francisco Weekly Letter. 15 December; 1978

[15] Wheelock DC, Wohar ME. Can the term spread predict output growth and recessions? A survey of the literature. Federal Reserve Bank of St. Louis Review. 2009;**91**(5 Part 1):419-440

[16] Harvey CR. Forecasts of economic growth from the bond and stock markets. Financial Analysts Journal. 1989;**45**(5):38-45

[17] Stock JH, Watson MW. New indexes of coincident and leading economic indicators. NBER Macroeconomics Annual. 1989;**4**: 351-394

[18] Chen NF. Financial investment opportunities and the macroeconomy. The Journal of Finance. Jun 1991;**46**(2): 529-554

[19] Harvey CR. The Term Structure and World Economic Growth. Center for Research in Security Prices, Graduate School of Business, University of Chicago; 1991

[20] Davis EP, Henry SG. The use of financial spreads as indicator variables: Evidence for the United Kingdom and Germany. Staff Papers. 1994;**41**(3): 517-525

[21] Plosser CI, Rouwenhorst KG. International term structures and real economic growth. Journal of Monetary Economics. 1994;**33**(1):133-155

[22] Bonser-Neal C, Morley TR. Does the yield spread predict real economic activity? A multicountry analysis. Economic Review-Federal Reserve Bank of Kansas City. 1997;**82**(3):37

[23] Kozicki S, Sellon G. Longer-term perspectives on the yield curve and monetary policy. Economic Review-Federal Reserve Bank of Kansas City. 2005;**90**(4):5

[24] Estrella A, Rodrigues AP, Schich S. How stable is the predictive power of the yield curve? Evidence from Germany and the United States. The Review of Economics and Statistics. 2003;**85**(3):629-644

[25] Jorion P, Mishkin F. A multi-country comparison of term structure forecasts at long horizons. National Bureau of Economic Research; 1991

[26] Gerlach S, Bernard H. Does the term structure predict recessions? The international evidence. International Journal of Finance and Economics. 1998; **3**:195-215

[27] Athukorala P-C. Malaysian economy in three crises. Working Papers in Trade and Development, No. 2010/12. The Australian National University

[28] Pesaran MH, Shin Y, Smith RJ. Testing for the 'Existence of a long-run Relationship'. Vol. 9622. Faculty of Economics, University of Cambridge; 1996

[29] Pesaran H, Shin Y. An autoregressive distributed lag modeling approach to cointegration analysis. In: Strom S, Holly A, Diamond P, editors. Centennial Volume of Rangar Frisch. Cambridge: Cambridge University Press; 1999

[30] Pesaran MH. The role of economic theory in modelling the long run. The Economic Journal. 1997;**107**(440): 178-191

[31] Duasa J. Determinants of Malaysian trade balance: An ARDL bound testing approach. Global Economic Review. 2007;**36**(1):89-102

[32] Nkoro E, Uko AK. Autoregressive distributed lag (ARDL) cointegration technique: Application and interpretation. Journal of Statistical and Econometric Methods. 2016;**5**(4):63-91

[33] Libanio GA. Unit roots in macroeconomic time series: Theory, implications, and evidence. Nova Economia. 2005;**15**(3):145-176

Chapter 12

The Relationship between Economic Uncertainty and Firms' Balance Sheet Strength

Mehmet Selman Çolak, İbrahim Ethem Güney and Yavuz Selim Hacıhasanoğlu

Abstract

This chapter aims to elaborate on the relationship between economic uncertainty and balance sheet strength of nonfinancial firms in Turkish economy. In order to effectively measure the balance sheet strength, we make use of a multivariate indicator, namely, the Multivariate Firm Assessment Score (MFA Score), which is a composite index to gauge the credit risk of nonfinancial firms quoted in Borsa İstanbul. MFA scores are compared with some uncertainty indicators for the period of 2005–2019. Our results suggest that when the uncertainties in global or Turkish economy are high, we observe a significant causal relationship from uncertainty indicators to firms' balance sheet strength. More specifically, economic uncertainties negatively affect firms' balance sheet performance in such an environment. Moreover, different types of uncertainties such as trade policy uncertainty and consumer perceptions about the economy are found to have differential impacts on exporter and non-exporter firms.

Keywords: financial distress, MFA score, economic uncertainty, time-varying causality

1. Introduction

Economic uncertainty, in a broad sense, is defined as the situation where future outlook for the economy is unpredictable. In case of rising uncertainty, agents in the economy are negatively affected because their expectations are blurred and they are not able to foresee the consequences of their decisions. For instance, consumers having uncertain expectations about their future income stream would prefer to postpone their consumption today and save more in order to obtain smooth path of lifetime consumption. This behavior, named as precautionary saving motive [1, 2], may dampen economic activity and aggregate demand in the economy in the short run [3]. Governments' public policy decisions are also influenced, but in this case, they are generally in the role of alleviating the negative impact of diminishing economic activity due to rising uncertainty [4]. They enact countercyclical policies such as fiscal expansion, tax cuts, or social transfers when uncertainty rises [5].

Firms' investment decisions are also impacted by the economic uncertainty. If uncertainty rises in an economy, firms wishing to make investment today may need to delay their decision because they become unsure about whether the future cash

IntechOpen

flows of the firm will cover the cost of the investment [6, 7]. This situation will indirectly affect other decisions of the firms such as employment, credit usage, debt repayments, social insurance payments, and other factors. In addition to all these factors, it is inevitable that firms' balance sheet structure and ratios are also affected by uncertainty in an economy. In case of elevated uncertainty, since consumption is postponed, firms' net sales decline, and this negatively influences their profitability ratios. Furthermore, firms' indebtedness might decline because their investment is also postponed and they no longer need to borrow to finance their investment. Firms' cash holdings and liquidity ratios might improve, as they want to stay highly liquid against any negative shocks under rising uncertainty. Last but not least, firms' cost of finance and interest expenses may be negatively affected, as heightening uncertainty might lead to an increase in risk premium and depreciation in the currency where the firms' borrowing is denominated in. All these channels, and possibly more than these, explain the transmission between economic uncertainty and firm balance sheet performance. Motivating from these verities, the main objective of this chapter is to empirically analyze the impact of economic uncertainty on firms' balance sheet performance using the financial statements of real sector firms quoted in Borsa İstanbul.

There is a wide range of literature on the relationship between firm balance sheet performance and overall macroeconomic dynamics for different countries. For instance [8] analyzes the implications of macroeconomic instabilities and institutional factors on the financial distress of Chinese-listed companies. [9] assesses the influence of macroeconomic conditions on the debt currency composition of firms in Brazil and how exchange rate movements impact the balance sheets and investment decisions of firms. In a cross-country setting, [10] questions whether the use of macroeconomic and industrial indicators improves the performance measures of solvent and insolvent firms. Finally, [11] deals with the balance sheet impact of foreign currency debt and exchange rate depreciation on the investments of firms in Korea.

In addition, there is a huge literature dealing with the impact of uncertainty on overall economy as well as other dimensions of the economy. One strand of the literature investigates directly the possible influence of uncertainty shocks on economic activity and finds out that uncertainty negatively impacts the aggregate demand [12–16]. Another strand of the literature looks at the issue by empirically analyzing how uncertainty impacts the households' consumption [17–19]. There are also many studies analyzing the implications of uncertainty with firms' perspectives. Although the majority looks at the effect of uncertainty on firms' investment decisions [20–24], some studies focus on the impact of uncertainty on firms' balance sheets. Nguyen, Kim, and Papanastassiou [25] investigate the link between economic policy uncertainty and financial derivative usage of firms in East Asia and find that as uncertainty accelerates, firms use derivative instruments extensively to hedge their risks. Hankins et al. [26] document the relationship between political uncertainty and corporate cash holdings of the US firms and finds out that following an uncertainty shock, cash accounts increase and capital spending declines. A similar study by Feng, Lo, and Chan [27] on Chinese firms claims that firms with higher firm value increase their cash holdings more than other firms as economic policy uncertainty heightens. In their cross-country study with firm-level data set, Gungoraydınoğlu, Çolak, and Öztekin [28] report that firm leverage drops in the wake of rising political uncertainty. In their study on US public corporates, Tran and Phan [29] obtain that policy uncertainty is positively related to the cost of debt and negatively related to maturity of debt. Francis, Hasan, and Zhu [30] find that rising political uncertainty increases the borrowing costs of nonfinancial firms. Iqbal, Gan, and Nadeem [31] document that economic policy uncertainty adversely affects firms' performance proxied by return on equity, return on assets, net profit margin, and Tobin's Q.

The common point of the abovementioned firm-level studies is that they look at the impact of uncertainty on a univariate balance sheet indicator or a single aspect of firm performance. Nevertheless, so far no study deals with the link between uncertainty and overall firm performance measured by a multivariate indicator. In this respect, our study introduces a novel approach by analyzing the impact of uncertainty on a multivariate composite indicator produced from firms' balance sheets. There are several composite indicators suggested by the literature to measure the overall firm performance [32–35]. However, these indicators were mostly designed for the listed firms in developed countries and may not be appropriate for measuring the performance of Turkish firms. Hence, in this study, MFA score developed by Çolak [36] using the data of Borsa İstanbul firms is used as a more accurate indicator since it captures the distinctive characteristics of Turkish firms.

Additionally, in investigating the association between firm performance and uncertainty, another important issue is the type of uncertainty examined. In the literature, numbers of uncertainty measures are created, such as political, trade, fiscal policy, monetary policy, financial, news uncertainties, and many more [5, 37–40]. In our chapter, our main concern is the overall economic uncertainty, consumer, financial, and trade uncertainties since we believe these factors are directly related to firms' balance sheets.

The chapter is structured as follows: after introduction, we will explain the details of the data set we exploited and methodology used in our analyses. In the third section, we will explain our main results. And finally, we will provide concluding remarks.

2. Data and methodology

Our sample consists of the financial statements of 417 nonfinancial firms quoted in Borsa İstanbul between 2005Q1 and 2019Q1 at a quarterly frequency. This corresponds to, on average, 300 firm observations each quarter and 13,356 unique observations in total. Real sector firms are obtained by eliminating the financial sector firms, sport companies, and real estate investment funds from the population of BIST firms. Quarterly income statement items are annualized by aggregating the latest four quarters.

Initially, we measure balance sheet strength of the listed real sector firms in Borsa İstanbul (BIST) with a composite index called Multivariate Firm Assessment Score (MFA score) which combines different corporate finance ratios such as liquidity, leverage, and profitability. This index which have a 90 percent predictive power improves Altman Z-score [32] methodology for Turkish firms. Specifically, using the multivariate discriminant analysis (MDA) methodology for the seven financial ratios explained in **Table 1**, we obtain MFA score for each firm in the sample.

Later on, we removed the firms with MFA scores above the 95th percentile and below the 5th percentile in the entire sample, in order to eliminate the outlier observations. Finally, we take the average of MFA scores and obtain mean MFA scores for each quarter. The descriptive statistics of the ratios in the MFA score and MFA score itself is provided in **Table 2**.

In the analysis, we consider four uncertainty indices: economic uncertainty, financial uncertainty, and consumer uncertainty indices which are developed by Sahinoz and Cosar [5], and trade uncertainty index for the Turkish economy from Ahir, Bloom and Furceri [41]. Consumer uncertainty index is a survey indicator which shows the uncertainty perception of consumers in the economy, while

MFA score $= 0.24X_1 - 0.14X_2 - 0.03X_3 + 3.76X_4 - 0.72X_5 + 0.20X_6 + 1.14X_7$
$X1 = (CashEquivalents + Securities + ShortTermTradeRecievables) / (ShortTermLiabilities)$:
This indicator, also known as the acid-test ratio, shows how much the short-term debt of the firm can be met with cash and cash equivalents
$X_2 = ShortTermLiabilites / CurrentAssets$:
It measures the firm's ability to pay its short-term liabilities with short-term assets
$X_3 = TotalLiabilities / Equities$
It shows how much sufficient the firm's equities to pay its debt
$X4 = EBITDA / TotalAssets$
It is the profitability of the firm from its main activities by asset size
$X_5 = FinancialExpenses / NetSales$
Indicates the capacity of the company to pay the FX and interest expenses arising from its debts
$X_6 = NetProfit(Loss) / NetSales$
It is the net earnings (or loss) of the firm per sale at the end of the period
$X_7 = Retained\ Earnings / Total\ Assets$
It is the measure of cumulative profit or loss from the past periods. It also contains information about the age of the company

Table 1.
MFA score equation and variable definitions.

Variable	Obs.	Mean	Std. dev.	Min	Max
Acid-test ratio	13,356	1.43	1.59	0.00	28.68
ST liabilities/current assets	13,356	0.83	0.82	0.03	19.99
Total liabilities/equity	13,356	2.36	6.27	−1.52	134.45
EBITDA/assets	13,356	0.08	0.10	−0.80	0.86
Financial exp./sales	13,356	0.05	0.33	−14.84	6.46
Net profit/sales	13,356	0.02	0.93	−47.80	18.28
Retained earnings/assets	13,356	−0.01	0.43	−5.05	1.23
MFA score	13,356	0.42	1.02	−3.48	3.28

Table 2.
Descriptive statistics of MFA score variables.

financial uncertainty index mostly indicates market volatility through global financial conditions. On the other hand, economic uncertainty is a weighted index of consumers, producers, forecasters, and economic policy uncertainty indices in a dynamic factor model framework. Finally, trade uncertainty index measures uncertainty related to trade in the Economist Intelligence Unit country reports. The descriptive statistics of uncertainty indices are exhibited in **Table 3**.

The movement in the economic uncertainty index for Turkish economy over time is depicted in **Figure 1**. It is evident from the figure that there are two specific episodes, where uncertainty has risen sharply. The first one is the global financial crisis from 2008 till the last quarter of 2009 and the other one corresponds to the period after the 2018 foreign exchange market turbulence in Turkey. In this study, we will give particular attention to these episodes to investigate the causality from uncertainty to firm balance sheets.

Uncertainty indices	Obs.	Mean	Std. Dev.	Min	Max
Economic	57	0.07	0.83	−0.90	2.60
Financial	57	−0.05	0.93	−1.30	3.20
Consumer	57	0.02	1.13	−1.10	5.90
Trade	57	0.33	0.20	0.00	0.89

Table 3.
Descriptive statistics of uncertainty indices.

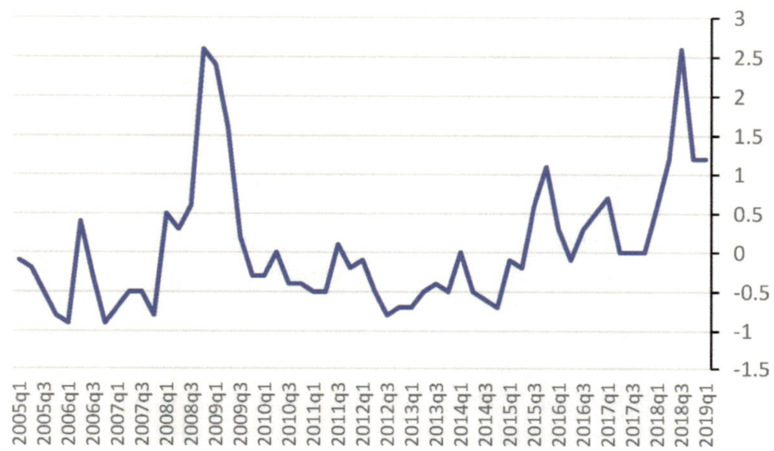

Figure 1.
Economic uncertainty index for Turkey. Source: Cosar and Sahinoz [5].

Our econometric analysis basically use time-varying Granger causality between an uncertainty index and MFA score based on Rossi and Wang [42] paper. This methodology is more powerful if the series have instabilities. In addition, classical Granger causality test does not allow to drive time-varying parameters. VAR-based reduced-form Granger causality test requires stationarity in the data, and its test statistics is not valid if the series have potential structural breaks. Because of the nonstationary nature and existence of structural breaks in **Figure 1**, Rossi and Wang's [42] is the best methodology to analyze time-varying Granger causality with this data.

Following Rossi and Wang [42], Eq. (2) shows a reduced-form time-varying parameter VAR:

$$A_t(L)y_t = u_t \tag{1}$$

$$A_t(L) = I - A_{1,t}L - A_{2,t}L^2 - \ldots - A_{m,t}L^m \tag{2}$$

$$u_t \overset{iid}{\sim} (0, \Sigma) \tag{3}$$

where $A_{j,t}, j = 1, \ldots m$ show time-varying coefficients, $[y_t, y_{t-1}, \ldots, y_{t-m}]'$ show variables in the model, and u_t shows error term.

The iteration of Eq. (2) and projection of yt onto the linear space created by $(y\,t-1, y\,t-2, \ldots, y\,t-m)'$ derive the following equation:

$$y_t = \beta_{1,t}y_{t-1} + \beta_{2,t}y_{t-2} + \ldots + \beta_{m,t}y_{t-m} + \varepsilon_t \quad (4)$$

where $\beta_{j,t}, j = 1, \ldots m$ show time-varying coefficients, $[y_t, y_{t-1}, \ldots, y_{t-m}]'$ show variables in the model, and ε_t shows heteroskedastic and serially correlated error term.

Finally, based on Eq. (4), robust Granger causality test figures out the validity of the null hypothesis in Eq. (5):

$$H_0{:}\beta_t = 0, \textit{for all } t = 1, \ldots, T \quad (5)$$

3. Empirical results

In the analysis we use two variables, an uncertainty index and a firm performance measure (MFA score). As these two variables are composite measures, although the methodology allow, we do not control other variables in the regressions. Based on Schwarz information criteria (SIC), we determine the number of lags included in the VAR model as two. In addition, following Rossi and Wang [39], we choose trimming parameter as 0.15 which is commonly used in structural break literature. After the estimation, we plot Wald test statistics through time which shows the strength of time-varying Granger causality from uncertainty measure to the firm performance measure.

We start our analysis by looking at the predictive ability of economic uncertainty on MFA score. Economic uncertainty index is constructed from five sub-uncertainty indices (forecasters' uncertainty index, financial uncertainty index, firms' uncertainty index, consumers' uncertainty index, and economic policy uncertainty index) via dynamic factor models explained by Cosar and Sahinoz [37].

Table 4 shows the results of classical Granger causality test for VAR (2) model which indicates that there is a causality only at 10% level for the whole sample. Moreover, traditional Granger causality test suffers from instabilities in the data and does not show time variability in causality which is the critical point that this chapter tries to address.

Figure 2 gives Wald statistics over time, which shows that the predictive power of economic uncertainty is increasing during 2008 global financial crisis. By choosing trimming parameter as 0.15, we are losing 16 observations from the beginning and end of the sample period. Hence, the latest observation is the 2016Q1 in this case, which leads us not to observe the recent financial distress period.

Figure 2 depicts that there is a significant Granger causality from economic uncertainty towards balance sheet performance of BIST firms in our sample. The global financial crisis is associated with significant contraction in economic activity, rise in unemployment, and fall in investment and consumption spending in Turkish economy. Year-on-year growth rate of GDP dropped as high as (−5) percent in 2009. These adverse developments in that era caused firms' financial health to worsen, as could be monitored through declining MFA scores. Following global crisis, Turkish economy did not experience substantial shrinkage in the economic activity till 2016, which would damage the firms' performance. Some temporary shocks such as European debt crisis or tapering tantrum have been alleviated by the effective fiscal and monetary policies. The statistically insignificant values of Wald

Zero hypothesis (H0)	Chi2	P-value	Decision
Econ uncertainty does not Granger-cause MFA score	5.8797	0.053	Do not reject

Table 4.
Granger causality test for the whole sample.

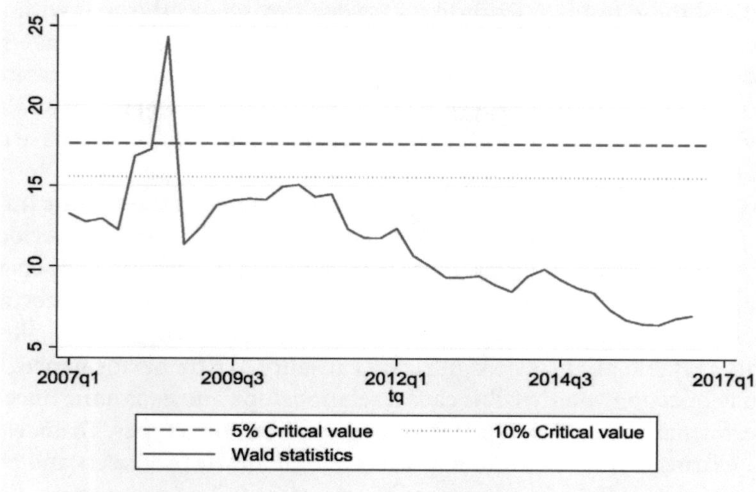

Figure 2.
Wald statistics of the test, Ho: economic uncertainty does not Granger-cause MFA score. Notes: VAR(2) under SIC, trimming 15%.

statistics after the global crisis indicate that, in normal times, there is no causality from economic uncertainty to firm performances.

In order to check the effect of Turkey-specific currency volatility observed in 2018 on firms' scores, we take trimming parameter as 0.03, which allows us not to lose any observation. With the coverage of data for the year 2018, **Figure 3** indicates that there is a jump in Wald statistics meaning that Granger causality occurs at this period as well. This local-sourced turbulent period in 2018 led Turkish lira to devaluate by nearly 35 percent against US dollar. Due to the rising volatility in exchange rate, inflation soared, interest rates climbed up, and economic activity contracted, which led to a mounting economic policy uncertainty.

Turkish firms accumulated large foreign currency debt after the global crisis since the expansionary monetary policies in advanced countries caused Turkish banks to reach foreign currency funding at low costs and with long maturities.

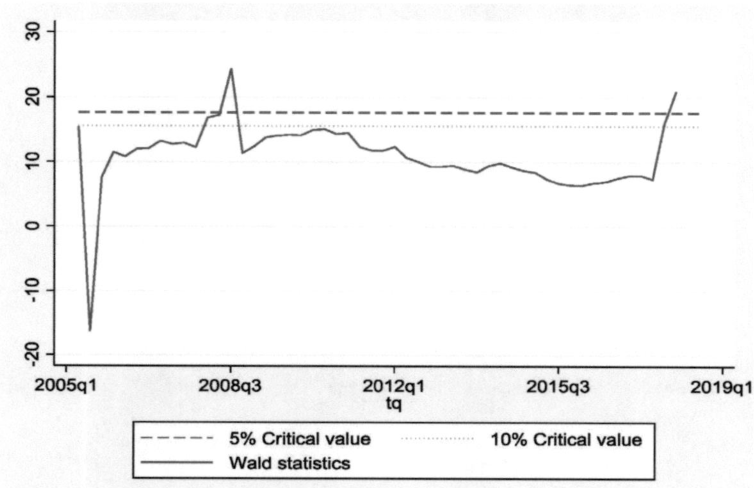

Figure 3.
Wald statistics of the test, Ho: economic uncertainty does not Granger-cause MFA score. Notes: VAR(2) under SIC, trimming 3%.

Banks utilized these funds as loans to real sector firms, even the ones without any FX income. Firms without FX income lived with considerable FX mismatches in their books. As a result, the sharp depreciation of Turkish lira in 2018 created a substantial deterioration in the balance sheets of real sector, and many firms defaulted since they could not repay their FX debts. In that period, MFA scores have dropped as high as the fall in global crisis.

The rising Wald statistics in that period is an evidence of the significant causality from economic uncertainty to MFA scores as observed during the period of global crisis. As **Figure 3** suggests, there is no significant causality in normal times. Our overall evaluation from **Figures 2** and **3** is that when economic uncertainty accelerates, it significantly Granger-causes MFA scores to drop; nevertheless, when uncertainty is stable, there is no significant causality to firm performance.

One may question whether this causal relationship from economic uncertainty to firm performance can differentiate among different firm types. To answer this, we split the firms in our sample as exporters and domestic producers and check which type of uncertainty is important for exporters and non-exporters. Firstly, we check the causality from financial uncertainty to MFA scores. Financial uncertainty is a measure of volatility in global financial conditions such as VIX, EMBI, CDS, and exchange rate uncertainty [5]. One would expect that exporters are affected more from global financial conditions measured by the financial uncertainty index. Although exchange rate volatility is crucial for all economic agents, its effect is even higher for exporters. **Figures 4** and **5** show the results for exporters and non-exporters, respectively. While financial uncertainty has a strong effect in exporters' score in 2008 and 2018 volatility periods, none of those periods have a significant effect on domestic producers.

The potential uncertainty that can affect domestic producers is the uncertainty measuring the perception of consumers in Turkish economy. Hence, we estimate VAR(2) model with consumer uncertainty for exporters and non-exporters (**Figures 6–8**). Because of the big jump in 2005 in **Figure 6**, the explanatory power of consumer uncertainty on exporters is not clear with a trimming parameter of 3 percent. By using a trimming parameter of 0.15, we eliminate this period and see the exact relationship in **Figure** 7. As it is clear in the figure, the relationship is far from 10% significance level in the whole sample period for exporter firms. This

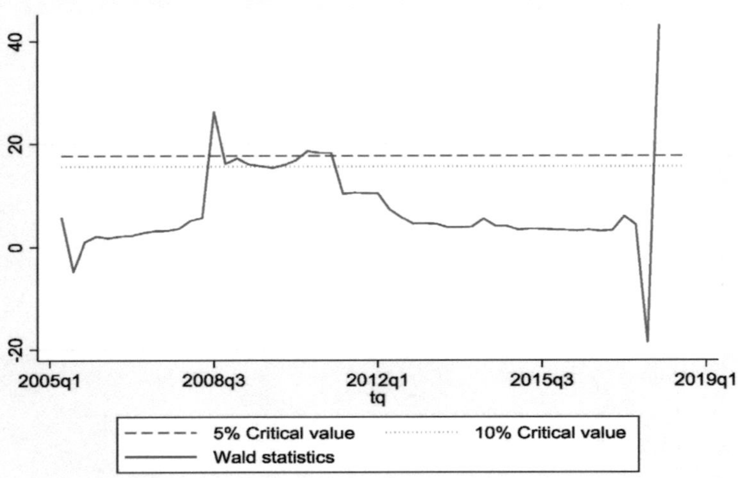

Figure 4.
Wald statistics values of the test, Ho: financial uncertainty does not Granger-cause MFA score for exporter.
Notes: VAR(2) under SIC, trimming 3%.

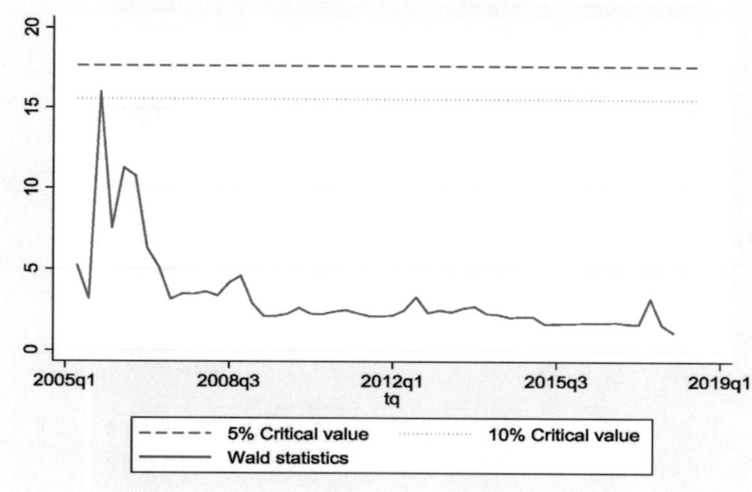

Figure 5.
Wald statistics values of the test, Ho: financial uncertainty does not Granger-cause MFA score for non-exporters. Notes: VAR(2) under SIC, trimming 3%.

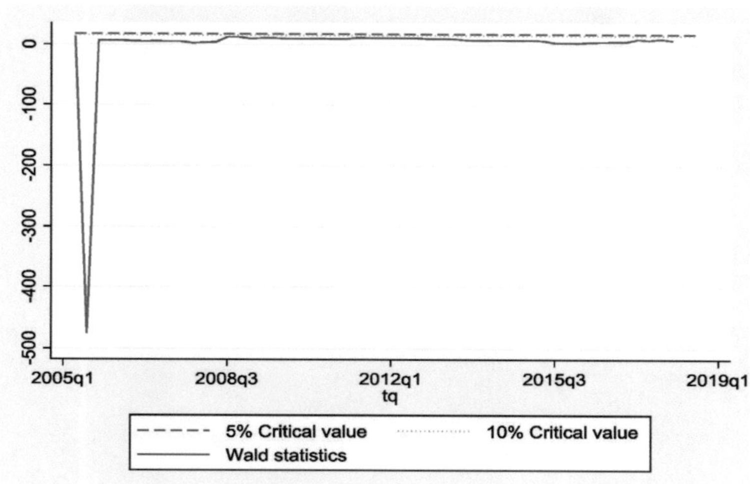

Figure 6.
Wald Statistics Values of the Test, Ho: consumer uncertainty does not Granger-cause MFA score for exporters. Notes: VAR(2) under SIC, trimming 15%.

might be an expected result since perception of domestic consumers should not have an impact on exporting firms selling abroad. Global financial conditions or global consumer uncertainties are anticipated to have a more impact on exporter firms' performance.

On the other hand, as seen in **Figure 8**, Wald statistics improved extensively after 2009 and exceeded 10% critical levels at some points till 2015 for non-exporter firms. The period between 2010 and 2015 is associated with a sound economic growth with a low-level of interest rates and stable exchange rate. In that period, households' perceptions and future expectations were robust, while their wealth was also improving. This led to soaring consumption expenditures, which increased the sales of non-exporter firms. As a result, the balance sheet performance of non-exporter firms significantly strengthened. We infer from those developments that, as consumers' perception worsens, this does not lead to a causality from consumer

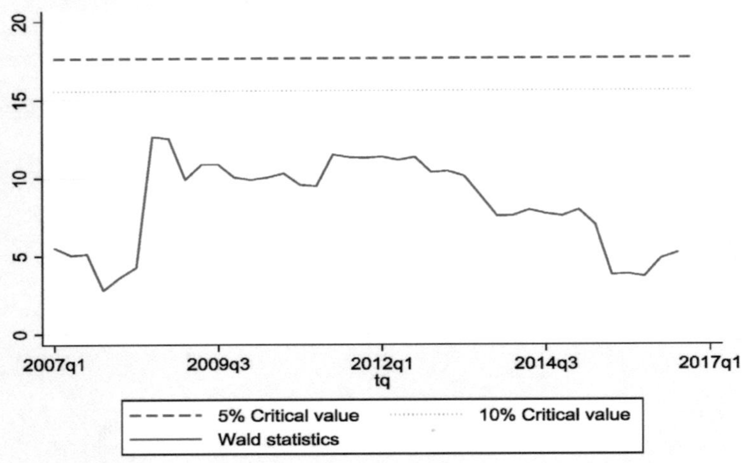

Figure 7.
Wald statistics values of the test, Ho: consumer uncertainty does not Granger-cause MFA score for exporters. Notes: VAR(2) under SIC, trimming 15%.

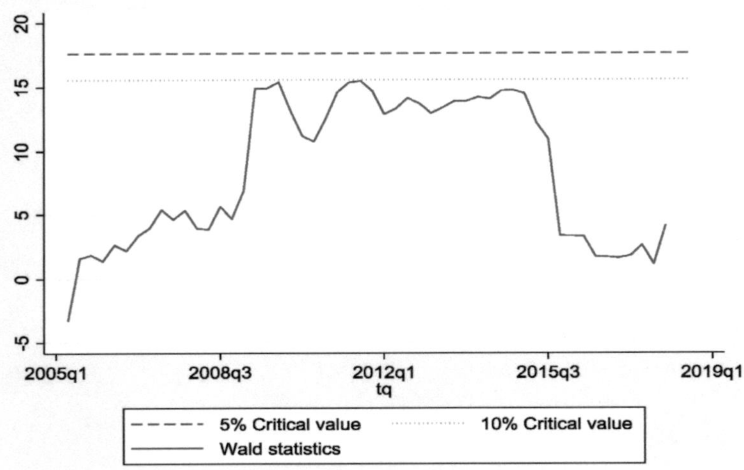

Figure 8.
Wald statistics values of the test, Ho: consumer uncertainty does not Granger-cause MFA score for non-exporters. Notes: VAR(2) under SIC, trimming 3%.

uncertainty to the performance of non-exporter firms; nevertheless, as consumer perceptions improve, significant causality from consumer uncertainty index towards MFA scores of non-exporter firms occurs. Besides, for exporter firms, we do not observe a causal relationship in the periods of both improving and worsening consumer perception.

Since the separation of firms depends on their exporting behavior in this analysis, it will be useful to check the effect of trade uncertainty for exporters and non-exporters. Trade uncertainty has increased since 2017 following of Trump's administration and the trade war between the USA and China. In **Figure 9**, trade uncertainty significantly impacts the performance of exporters, with the highest effect seen in 2017–2018. During that period, rising global trade uncertainty adversely influenced the global trade volume. Although high US dollar/Turkish lira exchange rate provided a competitive price advantage for Turkish firms, rising

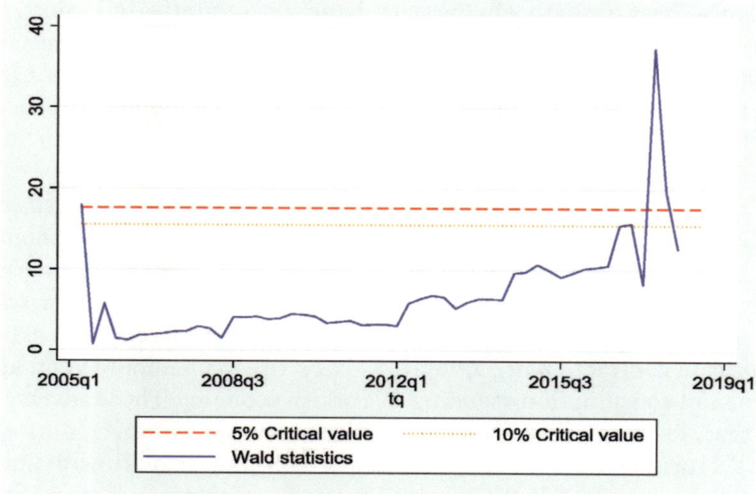

Figure 9.
Wald statistics values of the test, Ho: trade uncertainty does not Granger-cause MFA score for exporters. Notes: VAR(2) under SIC, trimming 3%.

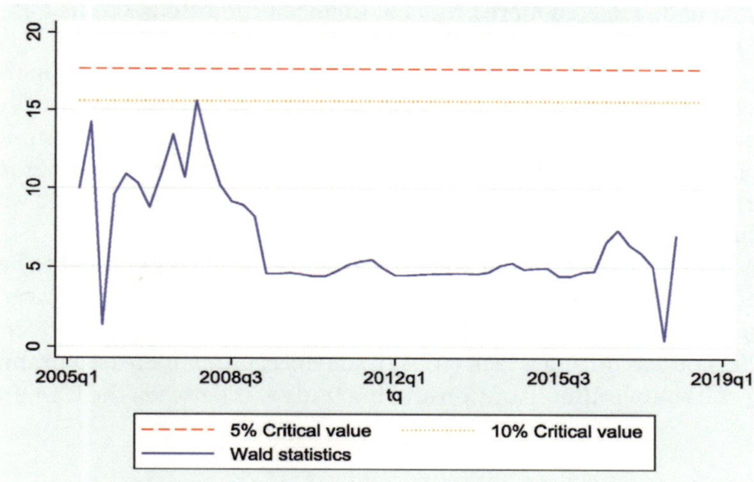

Figure 10.
Wald statistics values of the test, Ho: trade uncertainty does not Granger-cause MFA score for non-exporters. Notes: VAR(2) under SIC, trimming 3%.

global trade uncertainties significantly impacted the balance sheet performance of Turkish exporters. Nevertheless, since global trade was stable in earlier periods, it did not lead to a significant causal relationship. On the other hand, **Figure 10** illustrates that we do not observe such a significant effect on the non-exporters in our model since they do not interact with global trade conditions.

4. Conclusion

In this chapter, we use a time-varying vector auto-regressive model to analyze the relationship between economic uncertainty and firms' balance sheet strength in Turkish economy over the 2005–2019 period. For this purpose, we utilize Multivariate Firm Assessment Score developed by Çolak [36] to calculate Turkish firms' balance sheet strength. On the other hand, uncertainties in Turkish economy is measured by using four indices: economic uncertainty, financial uncertainty, consumer uncertainty indices which are developed by Cosar and Sahinoz [5], and trade uncertainty index introduced by Ahir et al. [41]. In our empirical analysis, based on Rossi and Wang [42], time-varying Granger causality between uncertainty indices and MFA score is evaluated.

Our first observation is that during heightened volatility periods such as the 2008 global financial crisis and 2018 Turkish domestic FX turmoil, economic uncertainties increased dramatically, and firms' balance sheet performances were negatively affected by those uncertainties. The transmission mechanism was different in those two turbulent periods. The global financial crisis was associated with significant contraction in economic activity, rise in unemployment, and fall in investment and consumption spending in Turkish economy. Those adverse developments in that era caused firms' financial health to worsen. However, during Turkish domestic FX turmoil in August 2018, the sharp depreciation of Turkish lira created a substantial deterioration in the balance sheets of real sector, and many firms were negatively affected since they have problems to repay their FX debts.

Second, while financial uncertainty is found to have a strong effect in exporter firms' performances, we do not observe a significant impact on non-exporter firms' in 2008 and 2018 stress periods. The intuition behind this result is that exporters are expected to be affected more by global financial conditions and heightened exchange rate volatility.

Third, since consumer perceptions about Turkish economy may be more effective on non-exporter (domestic producer) firms, we investigate to role of consumer uncertainty on the performance of Turkish firms. We show that as consumer perceptions improve, significant causality from consumer uncertainty index towards MFA scores of non-exporter firms occurs. However, we do not observe a causal relationship for exporter firms.

Finally, we check the effect of trade uncertainty, which is expected to be an important factor for exporter firms. Our analysis show that the trade uncertainty significantly impacts the performance of exporters, with the highest effect seen in 2017–2018 period during which global trade uncertainty increased dramatically following of Trump's administration and the trade war between the USA and China.

Author details

Mehmet Selman Çolak*, İbrahim Ethem Güney and Yavuz Selim Hacıhasanoğlu
Central Bank of Republic of Turkey, Ankara, Turkey

*Address all correspondence to: selman.colak@tcmb.gov.tr

References

[1] Skinner J. Risky income, life cycle consumption, and precautionary savings. Journal of Monetary Economics. 1988;**22**(2):237-255

[2] Carroll C. Buffer-stock saving and the life cycle/permanent income hypothesis. The Quarterly Journal of Economics. 1997;**112**(1):1-55

[3] Guiso L, Jappelli T, Terlizzese D. Earnings uncertainty and precautionary saving. Journal of Monetary Economics. 1992;**30**(2):307-337

[4] Auerbach A, Hassett K. Fiscal policy and uncertainty. International Finance. 2002;**5**(2):229-249

[5] Sahinoz S, Cosar EE. Quantifying uncertainty and identifying its impacts on the Turkish economy. Empirica. 2018. DOI: 10.1007/s10663-018-9424-8

[6] Ferderer J. The Impact of Uncertainty on Aggregate Investment Spending: An Empirical Analysis. Journal of Money, Credit and Banking. 1993;**25**(1):30

[7] Schwartz E, Dixit A, Pindyck R. Investment under uncertainty. The Journal of Finance. 1994;**49**(5):1924

[8] Bhattacharjee A, Han J. Financial distress of Chinese firms: Microeconomic, macroeconomic and institutional influences. China Economic Review. 2014;**30**:244-262. DOI: 10.1016/j.chieco.2014.07.007. ISSN 1043-951X

[9] Bonomo M, Martins B, Pinto R. Debt composition and exchange rate balance sheet effect in Brazil: A firm level analysis. Emerging Markets Review. 2003;**4**(4):368-396. DOI: 10.1016/S1566-0141(03)00061-X. ISSN 1566-0141

[10] Khoja L, Chipulu M, Jayasekera R. Analysis of financial distress cross countries: Using macroeconomic, industrial indicators and accounting data. International Review of Financial Analysis. 2019;**66**:101379. DOI: 10.1016/j.irfa.2019.101379. ISSN 1057-5219

[11] Kim YJ. Foreign currency exposure and balance sheet effects: A firm-level analysis for Korea. Emerging Markets Review. 2016;**26**:64-79. DOI: 10.1016/j.ememar.2016.02.001. ISSN 1566-0141

[12] Bachmann R, Elstner S, Sims E. Uncertainty and economic activity: Evidence from business survey data. American Economic Journal: Macroeconomics. 2013;**5**(2):217-249

[13] Bloom N. The impact of uncertainty shocks. Econometrica. 2009;**77**(3):623-685

[14] Carriero A, Clark T, Marcellino M. Measuring uncertainty and its impact on the economy. The Review of Economics and Statistics. 2018;**100**(5):799-815

[15] Gieseck A, Largent Y. The Impact of Macroeconomic Uncertainty on Activity in the Euro Area. Review of Economics. 2016;**67**(1):25-52

[16] Choi S. Variability in the effects of uncertainty shocks: New stylized facts from OECD countries. Journal of Macroeconomics. 2017;**53**:127-144

[17] Knotek II, Edward S, Khan S. How do households respond to uncertainty shocks? Federal Reserve Bank of Kansas City - Economic Review. 2011;**96**(2):05-34

[18] Gudmundsson J, Natvik GJ. That uncertain feeling—How consumption responds to economic uncertainty in Norway. Staff Memo-Norges Bank. 2012;**23**:1-26

[19] Zhang Y, Hua Wan G Liquidity constraint, uncertainty and household

consumption in China. Applied Economics 2004;36(19):2221-2229

[20] Jens C. Political uncertainty and investment: Causal evidence from U.S. gubernatorial elections. Journal of Financial Economics. 2017;**124**(3):563-579

[21] Gulen H, Ion M. Policy uncertainty and corporate investment. Review of Financial Studies. 2016;**29**(3):523-564

[22] An H, Chen Y, Luo D, Zhang T. Political uncertainty and corporate investment: Evidence from China. Journal of Corporate Finance. 2016;**36**:174-189

[23] Wang Y, Chen C, Huang Y. Economic policy uncertainty and corporate investment: Evidence from China. Pacific-Basin Finance Journal. 2014;**26**:227-243

[24] Kang W, Lee K, Ratti R. Economic policy uncertainty and firm-level investment. Journal of Macroeconomics. 2014;**39**:42-53

[25] Nguyen Q, Kim T, Papanastassiou M. Correction to: Policy uncertainty, derivatives use, and firm-level FDI. Journal of International Business Studies. 2017;**49**(2):248-248

[26] Hankins W, Stone A, Cheng C, Chiu C. Corporate decision making in the presence of political uncertainty: The case of corporate cash holdings. Financial Review. 2019 (Published online)

[27] Feng X, Lo Y, Chan K. Impact of economic policy uncertainty on cash holdings: Firm-level evidence from an emerging market. Asia-Pacific Journal of Accounting & Economics. 2019 (Published online)

[28] Gungoraydinoglu A, Çolak G, Öztekin Ö. Political environment, financial intermediation costs, and financing patterns. Journal of Corporate Finance. 2017;**44**:167-192

[29] Tran DT, Phan HV. Policy uncertainty and corporate debt maturity. 2017. Available at: http://www.fmaconferences.org/Boston/Policy_Uncertainty_and_Corporate_Debt_Maturity_Structure_01172017.pdf

[30] Francis B, Hasan I, Zhu Y. Political uncertainty and bank loan contracting. Journal of Empirical Finance. 2014;**29**:281-286

[31] Iqbal U, Gan C, Nadeem M. Economic policy uncertainty and firm performance. Applied Economics Letters. 2019 (Published online)

[32] Altman E. Financial ratios, discriminant analysis and the prediction of corporate bankruptcy. The Journal of Finance. 1968;**23**(4):589-609

[33] Ohlson J. Financial ratios and the probabilistic prediction of bankruptcy. Journal of Accounting Research. 1980;**18**(1):109

[34] Taffler R. Forecasting company failure in the UK using discriminant analysis and financial ratio data. Journal of the Royal Statistical Society Series A (General). 1982;**145**(3):342

[35] Zmijewski M. Methodological issues related to the estimation of financial distress prediction models. Journal of Accounting Research. 1984;**22**:59

[36] Çolak MS. A New Index Score for the Assessment of Firm Financial Risks. CBRT Working Paper Series No. 1904;2019

[37] Haddow A, Hare C, Hooley J, Tamarah S.Macroeconomic uncertainty: What is it, how can we measure it and why does it matter? Bank of England Quarterly Bulletin. 2013;**53**(2):100-109

[38] Scotti C. Surprise and uncertainty indexes: Real-time aggregation of real-activity macro-surprises. Journal of Monetary Economics. 2016;**82**:1-19

[39] Jurado K, Ludvigson S, Ng S. Measuring uncertainty. American Economic Review. 2015;**105**(3):1177-1216

[40] Rossi B, Sekhposyan T. Macroeconomic uncertainty indices based on nowcast and forecast error distributions. American Economic Review. 2015;**105**(5):650-655

[41] Ahir H, Bloom N, Furceri D. The World Uncertainty Index. 2018. Available at SSRN: https://ssrn.com/abstract=3275033

[42] Rossi B, Wang Y. Vector autoregressive-based granger causality test in the presence of instabilities. The Stata Journal: Promoting Communications on Statistics and Stata. 2019;**19**(4):883-899

Chapter 13

A New Approach for Assessing Credit Risks under Uncertainty

Teimuraz Tsabadze

Abstract

The purpose of this chapter is to introduce a new approach for an assessment of the credit risks. The initial part of the chapter is to briefly discuss the existing models of assessment of the credit risks and justify the need for a new approach. Since a new approach is created for conditions of uncertainty, we cannot do without fuzzy mathematics. The proposed approach is based on group decision-making, where experts' opinions are expressed by trapezoidal fuzzy numbers. The theoretical basis of the offered approach is laid out in the metric space of trapezoidal fuzzy numbers. The new approach is introduced and discussed, and two realization algorithms are given. The toy example of application of the introduced approach is offered as well.

Keywords: group decision-making, fuzzy set, linguistic variable, parameter, credit risk, assessment, trapezoidal fuzzy number, aggregation, algorithm

1. Introduction

A well-founded risk assessment is a mandatory stage in the effective implementation of almost any project. This chapter discusses credit risk assessments. Credit risk assessment includes determining whether or not to give a loan to a borrower and what is the probability of bankruptcy or inability to service a loan due to financial problems. Despite the fact that during this process the lender gets a lot of information from the borrower, there is no unambiguous rule for decision-making.

There are various models for assessing these risks. Before the 2008 financial crisis, emphasis was placed on developing models for assessing the financial stability of borrowers. But when, after this crisis, many companies faced a significant risk of bankruptcy, the vector of model developers took the direction to developing effective forecast models.

Existing forecasting models can be classified into two main groups: statistical and theoretical. A description of these models can be found in the literature (see, e.g., [1]). However, in a number of cases, these models are unacceptable. Basically, they are not suitable for assessing credit risks for corporations in developing countries, as well as for assessing the risks of lending to investment projects.

Let us dwell very briefly on the reasons for the unsuitability of these models for corporations in developing countries (a more detailed analysis can be found, e.g., in [2]). For statistical models:

- An insufficient defaulting history does not provide a relevant background for assessment of the credit risk.
- Problems arise with classification process too: a borrower may have so-called partial default status.

For theoretical models:

- A potential problem that could arise when applying this model is that majority of companies' stock is not traded on a stock exchange. In this case, a rapid evaluation of the market value of the assets is difficult.

It is very important to note that companies whose shares are not traded on the stock exchange are not so rare in developed countries.

Let us consider in more detail the credit risks when financing investment projects. It is known that an investment project involves planning over time of three main cash flows: investment, current (operating) expenses, and income.

When implementing an investment project, the investor never has a comprehensive risk assessment, since frequent changes in the dynamically developing world cannot be foreseen. Therefore, there is an unforeseen circumstance not taken into account by the project (e.g., a catastrophe), which nevertheless happened and disrupt the investment process. At the same time, the investor must be as informed as possible in order to assess the risk of his investment decisions both at the stage of project development and during the investment process itself. In addition, it is important to keep in mind that prices and volumes of products sold, as well as cash values for materials, raw materials, and other goods and services, in the future can radically differ from their expected values at the time of planning the investment project.

Thus, the incompleteness and uncertainty of the information significantly affects the effectiveness of the investment project and often poses insurmountable risks. Therefore, a project considered to be profitable, in fact, may be losing. This may occur due to the risk of deviation of the values of the design parameters from the actual values or due to the complete neglect of any factors.

Based on the foregoing and world practice, models for assessing any object of study, including risks, are suitable only if there is a sufficiently large statistical base (general population). Consequently, these methods do not result in cases under uncertainty. What to do in the absence of such statistics? The accumulated experience shows that the only way out in this case is to use expert estimates. Thus, we come to the process of group decision-making. Decision-making processes are used in quite a variety of applications. The inherent property of these processes is to represent the transformation of individual opinions of experts to the resulting one.

First you need to perform the parameterization process, i.e., identify parameters that experts should evaluate. Denote the set of selected parameters by $P = \{p_i\}, i = \overline{1,n}$. Next, you need to determine in what form and on what scale experts will evaluate the values of the selected parameters. Then generate risk criteria and aggregate expert assessments to make a decision according to the assigned criteria. A very important point is the determination of the form for expert evaluations. Here we propose to consider expert estimates in the form of fuzzy sets.

In 1965, a professor at California University (Berkeley) Lotfi A. Zadeh published a paper "Fuzzy Sets" that gave a birth to the modeling of human intellectual activity and allowed for new interpretations of some mathematical theories. According to classical mathematics, an object either belongs to some set or not, so the characteristic function of an ordinary set is defined as $\{0, 1\}$ (if an element does not belong to the set, then 0, and if it does, then 1).

Lotfi A. Zadeh was the first to propose a generalization of the range of values of the membership function {0, 1} to the closed interval [0; 1]. Thus, the value of the membership function can be any real number, starting from zero and ending with unity [3]. Such sets were called "fuzzy" sets. By gradually developing the proposed approach, Zadeh introduced the concept of a fuzzy linguistic variable, which was able to model mathematically linguistic variables [4]. For example, Zadeh made it possible to express mathematically the following linguistic notions: "childhood, young, middle-aged, old." Zadeh also introduced the concept of fuzzy relations and basic operations on them.

As noted above, in our study we cannot do without expert evaluations. Since subjectivity, vagueness, and imprecision influence the assessments of experts, the use of fuzzy set theory seems to be an effective tool for our research work (see, e.g., [5, 6]).

In [2], to assess credit risks, we used precisely fuzzy relations. In the present work, we propose to use trapezoidal fuzzy numbers as a form of presentation of experts' estimates. The rationale for this choice will be given in the third section.

The chapter consists of six sections. The second section includes all the necessary information to understand the material. The theoretical basis of the offered approach is laid out, and some theoretical results are given. In the third section, the approach to assessment of credit risk is introduced and discussed. In particular, the rationale for the choice of fuzzy trapezoidal numbers as a form for the presentation of experts' estimates is given. The fourth section looks at the algorithm for realization of the proposed approach. The fifth section contains toy example of the practical application of the introduced approach. The sixth and the final section summarize the chapter.

In conclusion, we note that when reading a chapter, the reader is not required to have knowledge of higher mathematics, but only elementary knowledge of arithmetic, algebra, and geometry. Nevertheless, we will try to explain meaningfully mathematical symbols and concepts that may be unfamiliar to the reader.

2. Essential notions and theoretical background

In the introduction, we gave a substantive description of a fuzzy set; now we give its mathematical description.

Definition 1. An ordered pair $\{x, \mu(x)\}$, where$x \in X, \mu : X \to [0, 1]$ is called a fuzzy set.

Here X is the universal set of real numbers (universe), $\mu(x)$ is the membership function of fuzzy set, and $\mu : X \to [0, 1]$ means that the membership function takes values from the interval [0; 1] for all x.

An important special case of fuzzy sets is fuzzy numbers. A *fuzzy number* is a fuzzy subset of the universal set of real numbers that has a normal and convex membership function, that is, such that: (a) there is an element of the universe in which the membership function is equal to one, and also (b) when deviating from its maximum left or right, membership function does not increase.

In this chapter we will deal with trapezoidal fuzzy numbers. Almost all the results given in this and third sections are, with minor modifications, taken from [7]; therefore we will refrain from further citation.

We denote trapezoidal fuzzy numbers in X by $\tilde{R} = (a, b, c, d),\ \ 0 < a \leq b \leq c \leq d$. The membership function's graph is a trapezoid with vertices $(a; 0)$, $(b; 1)$, $(c; 1)$, and $(d; 0)$.

We denote by $\Psi(X) = \{\tilde{R}_i = (a_i, b_i, c_i, d_i),\ \ i \in \mathbb{N}\}$ the set of all trapezoidal fuzzy numbers in the universe X.

The determinations of some operations on trapezoidal fuzzy numbers are given below.

$$\tilde{R}_1 = \tilde{R}_2 \Leftrightarrow a_1 = a_2, b_1 = b_2, c_1 = c_2, d_1 = d_2, \quad \tilde{R}_1, \tilde{R}_2 \in \Psi(X). \tag{1}$$

$$\tilde{R}_1 \oplus \tilde{R}_2 = (a_1 + a_2, b_1 + b_2, c_1 + c_2, d_1 + d_2), \quad \tilde{R}_1, \tilde{R}_2 \in \Psi(X). \tag{2}$$

$$\alpha \otimes \tilde{R} = (\alpha a, \alpha b, \alpha c, \alpha d) \ \alpha > 0, \ \tilde{R} \in \Psi(X). \tag{3}$$

Definition 2. Trapezoidal fuzzy number $\tilde{R}_1 = (a_i)$ is included in trapezoidal fuzzy number $\tilde{R}_2 = (b_i), \ i = \overline{1,4}$, i.e.$\tilde{R}_1 \preceq \tilde{R}_2$, if and only if

$$a_1 \le a_2, b_1 \le b_2, c_1 \le c_2, d_1 \le d_2 \tag{4}$$

It is known that fuzzy maximum and minimum of two trapezoidal fuzzy numbers is defined as follows [8]:

$$\begin{cases} \widetilde{\max}\{\tilde{R}_1, \tilde{R}_2\} = (\max\{a_1, b_1\}, \max\{a_2, b_2\}, \max\{a_3, b_3\}, \max\{a_4, b_4\}), \\ \widetilde{\min}\{\tilde{R}_1, \tilde{R}_2\} = (\min\{a_1, b_1\}, \min\{a_2, b_2\}, \min\{a_3, b_3\}, \min\{a_4, b_4\}). \end{cases} \tag{5}$$

Hence it follows that the above definition is equivalent to those given in the literature (see, e.g., [9, 10]):

$$\tilde{R}_1 \preceq \tilde{R}_2 \Leftrightarrow \begin{cases} \widetilde{\min}\{\tilde{R}_1, \tilde{R}_2\} = \tilde{R}_1, \\ \widetilde{\max}\{\tilde{R}_1, \tilde{R}_2\} = \tilde{R}_2, \end{cases} \quad \tilde{R}_1, \tilde{R}_2 \in \Psi(X). \tag{6}$$

Now we are going to introduce a metric on $\Psi(X)$, i.e., define a distance between trapezoidal fuzzy numbers.

We say that the function $v\colon \Psi(X) \to \mathfrak{R}^+$ is *isotone valuation on* $\Psi(X)$ if

$$v\left(\widetilde{\max}\{\tilde{R}_1, \tilde{R}_2\}\right) + v\left(\widetilde{\min}\{\tilde{R}_1, \tilde{R}_2\}\right) = v(\tilde{R}_1) + v(\tilde{R}_2) \tag{7}$$

and

$$\tilde{R}_1 \preceq \tilde{R}_2 \Rightarrow v(\tilde{R}_1) \le v(\tilde{R}_2). \tag{8}$$

The isotone valuation v determines *the metric* on $\Psi(X)$:

$$\rho(\tilde{R}_1, \tilde{R}_2) = v\left(\widetilde{\max}\{\tilde{R}_1, \tilde{R}_2\}\right) - v\left(\widetilde{\min}\{\tilde{R}_1, \tilde{R}_2\}\right) \tag{9}$$

$\Psi(X)$ with isotone valuation v and metric (Eq. (8)) is called a *metric space* of trapezoidal fuzzy numbers.

Definition 3. In the metric space, the trapezoidal fuzzy number $\tilde{R}^*$ is *the representative* of the finite collection of trapezoidal fuzzy numbers $\{\tilde{R}_j\}, \ j = \overline{1,m}, \ m = 2, 3, \ldots$ if

$$\sum_{j=1}^{m} \rho\left(\tilde{R}^*, \tilde{R}_j\right) \le \sum_{j=1}^{m} \rho(\tilde{S}, \tilde{R}_j), \quad \forall \tilde{S} \in \Psi(X) \tag{10}$$

Let us clarify the meaning of this definition. A representative of the given finite collection of trapezoidal fuzzy numbers is a trapezoidal fuzzy number such that the sum of the distances between it and all members of this collection is minimal.

For an accommodation of posterior theoretical constructions, we need to introduce a concept of *regulation* of finite collection of trapezoidal fuzzy numbers. We begin with an example.

Suppose we have the finite collection of trapezoidal fuzzy numbers:

	a_j	b_j	c_j	d_j
$\tilde{R}_1$	7	7.5	8	8.8
$\tilde{R}_2$	6	6.1	7.7	9
$\tilde{R}_3$	1	3	5	9.5
$\tilde{R}_4$	7.6	7.9	8.1	8.9

Compare with it the following finite collection of trapezoidal fuzzy numbers:

	a'_j	b'_j	c'_j	d'_j
$\tilde{R}_1'$	1	3	5	8.8
$\tilde{R}_2'$	6	6.1	7.7	8.9
$\tilde{R}_3'$	7	7.5	8	9
$\tilde{R}_4'$	7.6	7.9	8.1	9.5

We see that the matching columns in both tables consist of equal sets; at the same time the elements of the sets in the second table form nondecreasing sequences. By the regulation of the finite collection of trapezoidal fuzzy numbers $\{\tilde{R}_1,\tilde{R}_2,\tilde{R}_3,\tilde{R}_4\}$, we will mean the finite collection of trapezoidal fuzzy numbers $\left\{\tilde{R}'_1,\tilde{R}'_2,\tilde{R}'_3,\tilde{R}'_4\right\}$. The strict definition of regulation will be given below.

Definition 4. The finite collection of trapezoidal fuzzy numbers $\left\{\tilde{R}'_j\right\}$ is a regulation of the finite collection of trapezoidal fuzzy numbers $\{\tilde{R}_j\}$ if the finite sets $\{a_j\}$ and $\{a_j'\}$, $\{b_j\}$ and $\{b_j'\}$, $\{c_j\}$ and $\{c_j'\}$, and $\{d_j\}$ and $\{d_j'\}$ are pairwise equal and $a_1 \le a_2' \le \ldots \le a_m', b_1 \le b_2' \le \ldots \le b_m, c_1' \le c_2' \le \ldots \le c_m', d_1' \le d_2' \le \ldots \le d_m'$, and $j = \overline{1,m}, m = 2, 3, \ldots$.

Due to this definition and Eq. (9), it is obvious that the equality

$$\sum_{j=1}^{m} \rho(\tilde{S},\tilde{R}_j) = \sum_{j=1}^{m} \rho\left(\tilde{S},\tilde{R}'_j\right) \tag{11}$$

holds in the metric space for any $\tilde{S} \in \Psi(X)$ and the finite collection of trapezoidal fuzzy numbers $\{\tilde{R}_j\}$, $j = \overline{1,m}, m = 2, 3, \ldots$. From Eq. (11) it follows that representatives of finite collection of trapezoidal fuzzy numbers and its regulation coincide.

It is obvious that the regulation represents a finite collection of nested trapezoidal fuzzy numbers: $\tilde{R}'_1 \preceq \tilde{R}'_2 \preceq \ldots \preceq \tilde{R}'_m,\ m = 2, 3, \ldots$.

The following theorem yields a formal definition of a representative.

Theorem 1 [7]. *In the metric space of trapezoidal fuzzy numbers, the representative* $\tilde{R}^*$ *of the finite collection of trapezoidal fuzzy numbers,* $\{\tilde{R}_j\}$, $j = \overline{1,m},\ m = 2, 3, \ldots$, *is determined as follows:*

$$\tilde{R}'_{m/2} \preceq \tilde{R}^* \preceq \tilde{R}'_{m/2+1} \text{ if } m \text{ is even;} \tag{12}$$

$$\tilde{R}^* = \tilde{R}'_{(m+1)/2} \text{ if } m \text{ is odd.} \tag{13}$$

It follows from the theorem that when the number of members in a finite collection of trapezoidal fuzzy numbers is even, a representative can take on an infinite number of values. Now we introduce the specific aggregation operator that uniquely identifies the representative (here and further on, expression $[r]$, where r is a real number, denotes the integer part of this number):

$$\tilde{R}^* = \begin{cases} \left(a'_{[m/2],i} + a'_{[(m+3)/2],i}\right)/2 \text{ if } \sum_{j=1}^{[(m+1)/2]} \rho\left(\tilde{R}'_j, \tilde{R}'_{[m/2]}\right) = \sum_{j=[m/2]+1}^{m} \rho\left(\tilde{R}'_j, \tilde{R}'_{[(m+3)/2]}\right), \\ a'_{[m/2],i} + \left(\frac{\sum_{j=1}^{[(m+1)/2]} \rho\left(\tilde{R}'_j, \tilde{R}'_{[m/2]}\right)}{\sum_{j=1}^{[(m+1)/2]} \rho\left(\tilde{R}'_j, \tilde{R}'_{[m/2]}\right) + \sum_{j=[m/2]+1}^{m} \rho\left(\tilde{R}'_j, \tilde{R}'_{[(m+3)/2]}\right)} \left(a'_{[(m+3)/2],i} - a'_{[m/2],i}\right)\right) \text{ otherwise} \end{cases} \quad i = \overline{1,4} \tag{14}$$

Remark 1. It can be easily shown that the representative determined by Eq. (14) is a trapezoidal fuzzy number.

Summary. In this section, we presented the definitions of fuzzy sets and trapezoidal fuzzy numbers. Operations on trapezoidal fuzzy numbers are considered, and definitions of concepts that are necessary for constructing the proposed approach are given.

3. Credit risk assessment method

First of all, it is necessary to parameterize the risk assessment process, i.e., identify those parameters that to one degree or another affect credit risks. Such parameters may be credit history of the borrower, revenue, provision, market share, etc. The number and characteristics of risk assessment parameters are determined by an experienced lender manager.

As already mentioned in the introduction, there is always uncertainty in forecasting the values of the parameters for assessing credit risks, and, unfortunately, this fact cannot be completely avoided. An effective way out of this situation is to attract experts whose estimates are based on experience and intuition.

A very important point is the determination of a form for the submission of expert assessments. Here we present expert estimates in the form of trapezoidal fuzzy numbers. Let us justify our choice.

The expert has the opportunity to outline the following intervals (**Figure 1**):

- [a, b]—Where the parameter takes positive values, increasing from 0 to 1
- $[b, c]$—The confidence interval where the parameter takes values 1
- [c, d]—Where the parameter takes positive values, decreasing from 1 to 0

If, according to the expert's opinion, the parameter takes the maximum value at a single point, then $b = c$, and the estimate will take the form of a triangular fuzzy number (**Figure 2**).

If the expert is confident that the parameter reaches its maximum value in the interval $[b, c]$, and its eastern values are nonpositive, then $a = b$, $c = d$, and the estimate takes the form of a segment of straight line $y = 1$ (**Figure 3**).

If in an extreme case the expert considers that the maximum value of the parameter is reached at a single point, and at all other points the values are zero, then $a = b = c = d$, and the graph of the membership function degenerates into the point with coordinates $(a; 1)$.

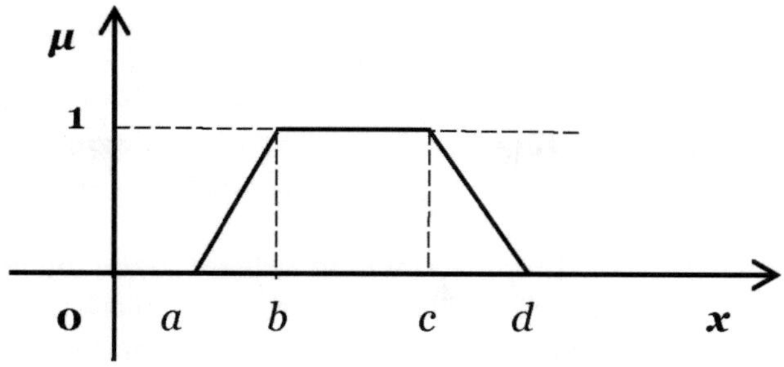

Figure 1.
General form of trapezoidal fuzzy number.

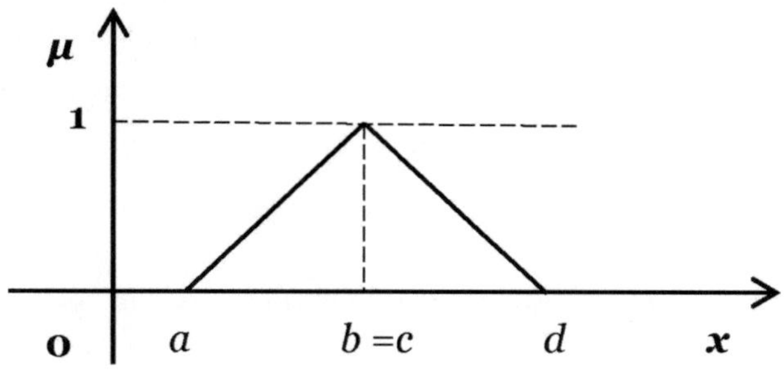

Figure 2.
General form of triangular fuzzy number.

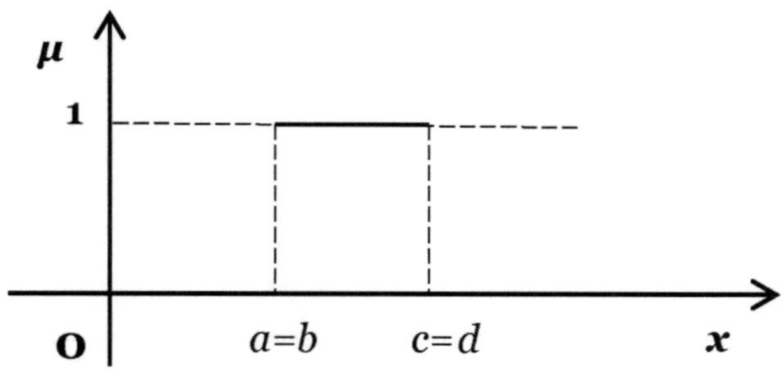

Figure 3.
Segment of straight line $y = 1$.

Thus, the membership function of a trapezoidal fuzzy number is common to the cases considered and can easily be reduced to particular cases.

Now we need to aggregate expert assessments for each parameter and obtain the result of group decision-making.

Suppose a group of experts estimates the rating of an alternative under some given criterion. Though the experts are professionals of the same level, their subjective estimates may be essentially different. The problem consists in processing these estimates so that a consensus could be found. In constructing any kind of aggregation method under group decision-making, the key task is to determine the well-justified weights of importance for each expert.

Let us consider the finite collection of trapezoidal fuzzy numbers formed by experts' estimates. To our mind, the representative of this collection, i.e., a trapezoidal fuzzy number such that the sum of distances between it and all other members of the given finite collection is minimal, is of particular interest.

A representative can be regarded as a kind of group consensus, but in that case the degrees of experts' importance are neglected. A representative is something like a standard for the members of the considered collection. As the weights of physical bodies are measured by comparing them with the Paris standard kilogram, it seems natural for us to determine experts' weights of importance depending on how close experts' estimates are to a representative.

Thus, the main idea of the proposed method reduces to the following. The weight of importance for each expert is determined by a function inversely proportional to the distance between his estimate and the representative of the finite collection of all experts' estimates, i.e., the smaller the distance between an expert's estimate and the representative, the larger the weight of his importance.

Let $\tilde{R}_j, j \in \{1, 2, \dots, m\}, m = 2, 3, \dots$ be a trapezoidal fuzzy number representing the jth expert's subjective estimate of the rating to an alternative under a given criterion. Estimates of all experts form the finite collection of trapezoidal fuzzy numbers $\{\tilde{R}_j\}$. By Definition 4 and formula (14), we find the regulation $\left\{\tilde{R}'_j\right\}$ and the representative $\tilde{R}^*$ of this collection. Denote the jth expert's aggregation weight (weight of importance) and the final result of aggregation by ω_j and $\tilde{R} = \left(\tilde{a}, \tilde{b}, \tilde{c}, \tilde{d}\right)$, respectively.

By the above reasoning, the weights and the final result of aggregation can be defined as follows:

$$\omega_j = \frac{\left(\rho\left(\tilde{R}^*, \tilde{R}_j\right)\right)^{-1}}{\sum_{j=1}^{m}\left(\rho\left(\tilde{R}^*, \tilde{R}_j\right)\right)^{-1}}, \quad m = 2, 3, \dots \tag{15}$$

and

$$\tilde{R} = \sum_{j=1}^{m}\left(\omega_j \otimes \tilde{R}_j\right) \tag{16}$$

It is obvious that $\sum_{j=1}^{m}\omega_j = 1$. In [7] it is proved that the function in expression (15) is always continuous (the denominator does not turn into 0 in any case).

In the following proposition and its corollaries, the properties and values of the aggregation result for special cases are established.

Proposition 1 [7]. *For any finite collection of trapezoidal fuzzy numbers* $\{\tilde{R}_j\}$, $j = \overline{1, m}, \ m = 2, 3, \dots$, *the following holds:*

a. $\tilde{R} = \sum_{j=1}^{m}\left(\omega_j \otimes \tilde{R}_j\right)$ *is always continuous* (*here* ω_j *is given by Eq.* (15)).

b. *If there exists at least one* $j \in \{1, 2, \dots, m\}$ *such that* $\rho\left(\tilde{R}^*, \tilde{R}_j\right) = 0$, *then* $\tilde{R} = \tilde{R}^*$.

Corollary 1. *If for all* $t, j \in \{1, 2, \dots, m\}$ $\tilde{R}_t = \tilde{R}_j \Rightarrow \tilde{R} = \tilde{R}^*$.

Corollary 2. *If the all estimates are identical then* $\omega_j = 1/m$.

Summary. The section introduces the approach to assessment of the credit risk. It also considers the rationale for the choice of fuzzy trapezoidal numbers as a form for the presentation of experts' estimates. The section contains important formalisms for determining the degrees of experts' importance and the result of aggregation of experts' estimates.

4. Realization of proposed approach

Let m experts evaluate the values of n parameters in the form of trapezoidal fuzzy numbers. As a result, we get a rectangular matrix of dimension $m \times n$:

$$\left(\tilde{R}_{ij}\right) = \begin{matrix} \tilde{R}_{11} & \tilde{R}_{12} & \cdots & \tilde{R}_{1n} \\ \tilde{R}_{21} & \tilde{R}_{22} & \cdots & \tilde{R}_{2n} \\ \cdots & \cdots & \cdots & \cdots \\ \tilde{R}_{m1} & \tilde{R}_{m2} & \cdots & \tilde{R}_{mn} \end{matrix}, \quad i = \overline{1,n}, j = \overline{1,n}. \tag{17}$$

The i-th column of the obtained matrix represents a collection of estimates of the jth parameter given by the expert number i.

To assess the values of the parameters according to the credit risk criterion, we find a representative of each column of the matrix. As a result, we obtain the following sequence: $\left\{\tilde{R}_j^*\right\} = \tilde{R}_1^*, \tilde{R}_2^*, \dots, \tilde{R}_n^*$.

Now we present an algorithm for finding a representative of finite collection of trapezoidal fuzzy numbers.

Algorithm 1.

Step 0: *Initialization: the finite collection of trapezoidal fuzzy numbers* $\{\tilde{R}_j\}$, *its regulation* $\left\{\tilde{R}_j'\right\}$, $j = \overline{1,m}$, $m = 2, 3, \dots$. *Denote the aggregation weight of the j-th expert by* ω_j *and the final result by* $\tilde{R}$.

Step 1: *Compute the representative* $\tilde{R}^*$ *of* $\left\{\tilde{R}_j'\right\}$, $j = \overline{1,m}$, $m = 2, 3, \dots$ *by Eq.* (14).

Step 2: *Do* Step 3 *for* $j = \overline{1,m}$.

Step 3: *Compute* $\Delta_j = \rho\left(\tilde{R}^*, \tilde{R}_j\right)$:

- If at least one $\Delta_j = 0$ then $\tilde{R} = \tilde{R}^*$;
- If $\Delta_j > 0$ for all j then compute ω_j by Eq. (15) and obtain the final result by Eq. (16).

For what follows, we need to determine a scale that can "measure" the opinions of experts regarding the risk of bankruptcy of the borrower. We use the general approach described in [11].

In almost any field, you can get a rating scale using the following principles:

a. Define a list of characteristics by which the concept (object) is evaluated.

b. Find polar characteristics in this list and form a polar scale.

c. At the poles, determine to what extent the concept possesses this characteristic (in the original, specific numerical closed intervals were used).

The collection of ratings on the scale was called the *profile* of the concept. Since the gradation values of the scale are approximate (expert opinions), with the exception of the assigned pole values, the profile represents a fuzzy set of the concept's characteristics list.

In the introduction, we mentioned the concept of a linguistic variable. This concept plays an important role in our study. Let us introduce the linguistic variable "degree of credit risk":

$$A = \{A_1, A_2, A_3, A_4, A_5\}, \tag{18}$$

where:
A_1 – the degree of risk is negligible.
A_2 – the degree of risk is low.
A_3 – the degree of risk is medium.
A_4 – the degree of risk is high.
A_5 – the degree of risk is extreme.

Therefore, by constructing the linguistic variable $\boldsymbol{A}$, we have satisfied condition (a). Condition (b) is also fulfilled: the polar characteristics are "the degree of risk is negligible" and "the degree of risk is extreme." To fulfill condition (c), it is necessary to build a profile, i.e., fuzzy set describing the linguistic variable $\boldsymbol{A}$.

We construct the membership function of profile $\boldsymbol{A}$ in several stages. Here we will give a description of the stages in a general form; the reader will clarify the specifics on a practical example in the next section.

Stage 1. Let us evaluate the confidence of risk degrees of the linguistic variable $\boldsymbol{A}$ on the percentage scale (0–100)% as follows: $A_1 \sim [0, k_1]$, $A_2 \sim [k_1, k_2]$, $A_3 \sim [k_2, k_3]$, $A_4 \sim [k_3, k_4]$, and $A_5 \sim [k_4,100]$. Here $0 < k_1 < k_2 < k_3 < k_4 < 100$.

Stage 2. Since expert estimates are given in the form of trapezoidal fuzzy numbers, first of all, it is necessary to determine the boundaries of the scale of expert estimates for each characteristic of the list from $\boldsymbol{A}$. Since m experts take part in the assessment process, we have m trapezoidal fuzzy numbers. It seems reasonable to take the following boundaries of the scale: the left one is the minimum, and the right maximum of the abscissas of all the vertices of m trapezoids, i.e.:

$$[\min\{a_i\};\ \max\{d_i\}],\ i = \overline{1,m}. \tag{19}$$

Stage 3. Now we will establish the conformity between the intervals of the percentage scale and the trapezoidal fuzzy numbers. Geometrically, the percentage scale that corresponds to five trapezoidal fuzzy numbers, may, for example, look like this (**Figure 4**):

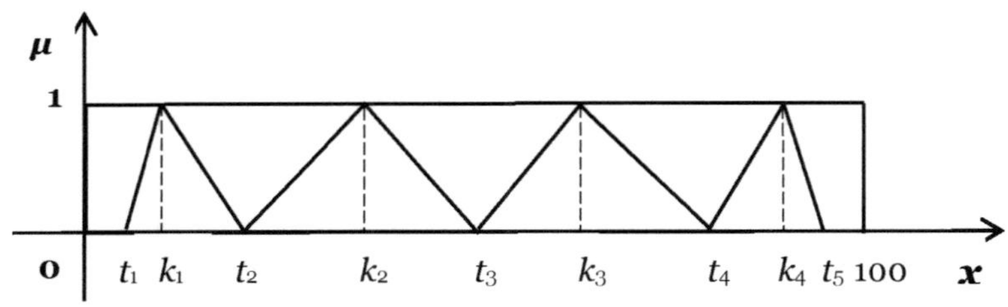

Figure 4.
Conformity between the percentage scale and the trapezoidal fuzzy numbers.

$$\tilde{A}_1 = (0, 0, k_1, t_2); \tilde{A}_{22} = (t_1, k_1, k_2, t_3); \tilde{A}_3 = (t_2, k_2, k_3, t_4); \tilde{A}_4 = (t_3, k_3, k_4, t_5);$$
$$\tilde{A}_5 = (t_4, k_4, 100, 100), \tag{20}$$

numbers *k, t* are appointed by experts.

To transform the coordinate system of the percentage scale to the coordinate system for expert estimates, the following mappings should be performed $[0, 100] \to [\min\{a_i\}, \max\{d_i\}]$. Thus, we moved the origin from point (0,0) to point $(\min\{a_i\}, 0)$ and point (100,0) to point $(\max\{d_i\}, 0)$. For more simplicity let us introduce the notation:

$$\nabla = \min\{a_i\}, \Delta = \max\{d_i\},\ i = \overline{1,n}. \tag{21}$$

It is easy to see that the coefficient of proportionality between the abscissas of the primary and the new coordinate system is

$$\lambda = 0.01(\Delta - \nabla). \tag{22}$$

Thereby, the coordinates of the original trapezoidal fuzzy numbers will change as follows:

$$\begin{aligned}&\tilde{A}_1 = (\nabla, \nabla, \lambda k_1 + \nabla, \lambda t_2 + \nabla); \tilde{A}_2 = (\lambda t_1 + \nabla, \lambda k_1 + \nabla, \lambda k_2 + \nabla, \lambda t_3 + \nabla);\\ &\tilde{A}_3 = (\lambda t_2 + \nabla, \lambda k_2 + \nabla, \lambda k_3 + \nabla, \lambda t_4 + \nabla); \tilde{A}_4 = (\lambda t_3 + \nabla, \lambda k_3 + \nabla, \lambda k_4 + \nabla, \lambda t_5 + \nabla);\\ &\tilde{A}_5 = (\lambda t_4 + \nabla, \lambda k_4 + \nabla, \Delta, \Delta).\end{aligned} \tag{23}$$

So, condition (c) is also satisfied.

We continue the description of the implementation of the proposed approach. Based on Algorithm 1, we find the value of the representative of the finite collection of the trapezoidal fuzzy numbers for each parameter. Consider a representative calculated for the i-th parameter. The risk assessment threshold value is assigned by the manager (group of managers) of the lender. It may be that different criteria thresholds will be set for different cases, for example, for one parameter, "no more than A_2—the degree of risk is low," and for the other "no more than A_3—the degree of risk is medium."

In general, if $A_j \in \boldsymbol{A}$ (see Eq. (18)) is taken as the threshold criteria value of the parameter, then credit risk is acceptable if the following addition condition is fulfilled:

$$\tilde{R}_i \preceq \tilde{A}_j, \ \ i = \overline{1, n}, \ \ j = \overline{1, 5}. \tag{24}$$

Here $\tilde{A}_j$ is the number corresponding to the characteristic A_j, while $\tilde{R}_i$ is the result of aggregation of the finite collection of expert estimates of the i-th parameter (see Algorithm 1).

Let us summarize the above as a generalized algorithm. So, we have the following input: m expert estimates of n parameters out of the set $P = \{p_i\}, \ \ i = \overline{1, n}$, the result of aggregation $\tilde{R}_i$ of the finite collection of expert estimates for this parameter, the threshold criteria value A_k, $k = \overline{1, 5}$ selected from Eq. (18), and coordinates k, t specified by the manager (group of managers) of the lender for use in Eq. (23).

Algorithm 2.

Step 0: *Initialization: fix* $p_i \in P, i = \overline{1, n}$, *the result of aggregation* $\tilde{R}_i$ *of the finite collection of expert estimates* $\{\tilde{R}_j\}, \ \ j = \overline{1, m}, \ \ m = 2, 3, \ldots$ *for this parameter, the threshold criteria value* $A_t, t = \overline{1, 5}$, *coordinates*: $k_1, \ldots, k_4; t_1, \ldots, t_5$.

Step 1: *Compute* ∇, Δ *by Eq.* (21) *and* λ *by Eq.* (22).

Step 2: *Compute* $\tilde{A}_t, t = \overline{1, 5}$ *by Eq*. (23).

Step 3: *Verification of the condition* $\tilde{R}_i \preceq \tilde{A}_j$:

- If the condition is met then the level of risk is acceptable;
- If the condition is not met then the level of risk is unacceptable.

Summary. The section looks at the realization of the proposed approach. The linguistic variable "degree of credit risk," polar percentage and coordinate scales are formed. The criterion for an assessment of the credit risks is generated. This section also presents two generalized algorithms for implementing the proposed approach.

5. Example

Here we give a toy example that will allow the reader to understand the essence of the proposed approach. To begin the practical implementation of our approach, it is necessary to determine the specific values of the isotone valuation v and the metric ρ (see Eq. (7)–(9)). For brevity, we denote trapezoidal fuzzy numbers by $\tilde{R} = (a_i)$. We will use the following isotone valuation $v(\tilde{R}) = \sum_{i=1}^{4} a_i$. It can be easily shown that this valuation satisfies the conditions of Eq. (7) and (8). From this it follows that distance between two trapezoidal fuzzy numbers $\tilde{R}_1, = (a_i)$ and $\tilde{R}_2 = (b_i)$ is determined as follows:

$$\rho(\tilde{R}_1, \tilde{R}_2) = \sum_{i=1}^{4} |a_i - b_i|. \tag{25}$$

Without loss of generality, we consider the process of determining the degree of risk for one parameter evaluated by three experts. For any other parameter, the procedure described below is similar. As noted above, the parameterization of the risk assessment process is carried out by the lender manager. Suppose that for evaluation the parameter "p_1 – revenue" has been selected.

We ask three experts to evaluate the parameter p_1 in the form of trapezoidal fuzzy number. As a result, we obtain

$$\{\tilde{R}_j\} = \{(1, 2, 3, 3.5), (1, 2.5, 2.8, 3), (1.5, 3, 4, 6)\} \tag{26}$$

We follow Algorithm 1, detailing it along the way.

Algorithm 3.

Step 0: *Initialization: the regulation of finite collection of trapezoidal fuzzy numbers* $\left\{\tilde{R}'_j\right\} = \{(1, 2, 2.8, 3), (1, 2.5, 3, 3.5), (1.5, 3, 4, 6)\}$. *Denote the aggregation weight of the j-th expert by* ω_j *and the final result by* $\tilde{R}$.

Step 1: *By Eq.* (14) *computes the representative* $\tilde{R}^* = (1.1053, 2.2105, 3.0526, 3.6315)$.

Step 2: *Do* Step 3 *for* $j = \overline{1, 3}$.

Step 3: *By Eq.* (15) *compute* $\Delta_j = \rho\left(\tilde{R}^*, \tilde{R}_j\right)$: $\Delta_1 = 0.499$, $\Delta_2 = 1.2789$, $\Delta_3 = 4.5$. *Since all* $\Delta_j > 0$ *then by Eq.* (15) $\omega_1 = 0.666$, $\omega_2 = 0.26$, $\omega_3 = 0.074$ *and by Eq.* (16) *we obtain the finite result*:

$$\tilde{R} = (1.037, 2.204, 3.028, 3.555) \tag{27}$$

Now we form the percentage scale of the linguistic variable $\boldsymbol{A}$ (see Eq. (18)). At stage 1 of the previous section, a graduation of this scale is given in general form (see **Figure 4**). Suppose lender managers have determined the lower and upper bases of trapezoidal fuzzy numbers corresponding to the components of the linguistic variable $\boldsymbol{A}$, i.e., definition and confidence areas as a percentage:

A_1—the degree of risk is negligible [0, 30], [0, 20].
A_2—the degree of risk is low [10, 50], [20, 40].
A_3—the degree of risk is medium [30, 70], [40, 60].
A_4—the degree of risk is high [50, 90], [60, 80].
A_5—the degree of risk is extreme [70, 100], [80, 100].

So, $t_1 = 10$, $t_2 = 30$, $t_3 = 50$, $t_4 = 70$, $t_5 = 90$, $k_1 = 20$, $k_2 = 40$, $k_3 = 60$, and $k_4 = 80$. Thus, **Figure 4** will be converted to the form shown in **Figure 5**:

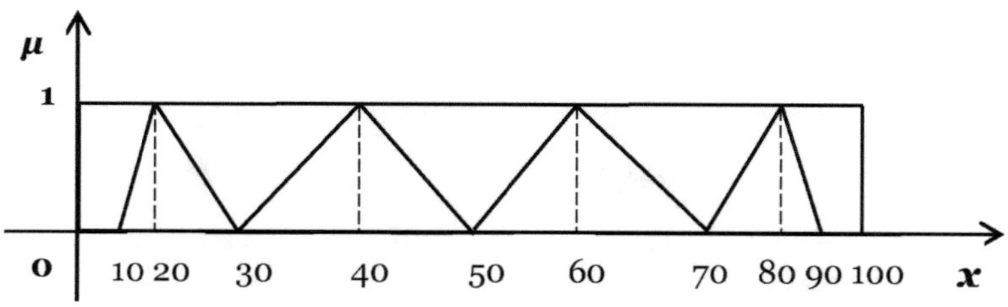

Figure 5.
Graphical expression of the degree of risk in percent.

So, we have the following input: three experts' estimates of the parameter out of the components of the linguistic variable $\boldsymbol{A}$ "revenue," the result of aggregation $\tilde{R}$ of the collection of three experts' estimates for this parameter, threshold criteria value A_3 selected from Eq. (18), and coordinates *k, t* specified by the manager (group of managers) of the lender for use in Eq. (23).

We follow Algorithm 2, detailing it along the way.

Algorithm 4.

Step 0: *Initialization: the result of aggregation of the collection of expert estimates for parameter "revenue"*– $\tilde{R} = (1.037, 2.204, 3.028, 3.555)$, *threshold criteria value lender's managers "not more than medium risk", coordinates*: 10, $t_2 = 30, t_4 = 70, k_2 = 40, k_3 = 60$.

Step 1: *Compute* ∇, Δ *by Eq.* (26), *Eq.* (21) *and* λ *by Eq.* (22), $\nabla = 1, \Delta = 6, \lambda = 0.05$.

Step 2: *Compute trapezoidal fuzzy number, corresponding to the component* A_3 - the degree of *risk is medium by Eq.* (23) $\tilde{A}_3 = (2.5, 3, 4, 4.5)$.

Step 3: *Verification of the condition* $\tilde{R} \preceq \tilde{A}_3$:

- the condition is satisfied and the level of risk is acceptable.

Summary. In this section a toy example of the practical application of the proposed approach is provided. The concrete isotone valuation and metric are considered. We calculate the risk level for one parameter based on the estimates of three experts. For other parameters and any number of experts, the process will be similar.

6. Conclusions

The presented work aims to propose a new approach for an assessment of the credit risks under uncertainty. The novelty of the proposed approach is the use of trapezoidal fuzzy numbers, which makes it possible to adequately form and process the experts' estimates. An important fact is that the proposed approach takes into account the degrees of experts' importance.

The main results of the work are as follows:

- A brief analysis of existing models is carried out, and the feasibility of creating a new approach is justified.
- The rationale for the presentation of experts' assessments of the credit risk in the form of trapezoidal fuzzy numbers is given.
- The linguistic variable "degree of credit risk" is formed.
- A polar percentage and coordinate scales of trapezoidal fuzzy numbers with a gradation of assigned levels are defined. The formalization of the mapping of the percentage scale to the coordinate scale is given.

- The criteria for an assessment of the credit risks are generated.
- Generalized algorithms for implementing the proposed approach are constructed.
- A toy example which illustrates the practical application of the proposed approach is provided.

Author details

Teimuraz Tsabadze
Georgian Technical University, Tbilisi, Georgia

*Address all correspondence to: teimuraz.tsabadze@yahoo.com

References

[1] Saunders A, Cornett MM. Credit risk: Individual loan risk. In: Financial Institutions Management: A Risk Management Approach. NY: McGraw-Hill/Irwin; 2010. pp. 295-338

[2] Tsabadze T. Assessment of credit risk based on fuzzy relations. AIP Conference Proceedings. 2017;**1836**(1):020-027

[3] Zadeh LA. Fuzzy sets. Information and Control. 1965;**8**:338-353

[4] Zadeh LA. The concept of a linguistic variable and its application to approximate reasoning. Information Sciences. 1975;**8**: 199-249. 301-357; Vol. 9, 43-80

[5] Karol T. Fuzzy Logic in Financial Management. In: Dadios PE, editor. Fuzzy Logic - Emerging Technologies and Applications. London: InTech; 2012. pp. 259-285

[6] Brkić S, Hodžić M, Džanić E. Soft data modeling via type 2 fuzzy distributions for corporate credit risk assessment in commercial banking. In: Proceedings of the International Symposium on Innovative and Interdisciplinary Applications of Advanced Technologies (IAT 2018), 21–24 June. Vol. 1. Jahorina, Bosnia and Herzegovina; 2018. pp. 457-469

[7] Tsabadze T. A method for aggregation of trapezoidal fuzzy estimates under group decision-making. International Journal of Fuzzy Systems. 2015;**266**:114-130

[8] Dubois D, Kerre E, Mesiar E. Fuzzy interval analysis. In: Dubois D, Prade H, editors. Fundamentals of Fuzzy Sets. Boston, MA: The Handbooks of Fuzzy Sets Series, Kluwer Academic Publishers; 2000. pp. 483-581

[9] Heilpern S. Representation and application of fuzzy numbers. Fuzzy Sets and Systems. 1997;**91**:259-268

[10] Chai Y, Zhang D. A representation of fuzzy numbers. Fuzzy Sets and Systems. 2016;**295**:1-18

[11] Ragade RK, Gupta MM. Fuzzy sets theory: Introduction. In: Gupta MM, Saridis G, Gaines B, editors. Fuzzy Automata and Decision Processes. Amsterdam: Elsevier North-Holland; 1977. pp. 105-131

Chapter 14

A Bipartite Graph-Based Recommender for Crowdfunding with Sparse Data

Hongwei Wang and Shiqin Chen

Abstract

It is a common problem facing recommender to sparse data dealing, especially for crowdfunding recommendations. The collaborative filtering (CF) tends to recommend a user those items only connecting to similar users directly but fails to recommend the items with indirect actions to similar users. Therefore, CF performs poorly in the case of sparse data like Kickstarter. We propose a method of enabling indirect crowdfunding campaign recommendation based on bipartite graph. PersonalRank is applicable to calculate global similarity; as opposed to local similarity, for any node of the network, we use PersonalRank in an iterative manner to produce recommendation list where CF is invalid. Furthermore, we propose a bipartite graph-based CF model by combining CF and PersonalRank. The new model classifies nodes into one of the following two types: user nodes and campaign nodes. For any two types of nodes, the global similarity between them is calculated by PersonalRank. Finally, a recommendation list is generated for any node through CF algorithm. Experimental results show that the bipartite graph-based CF achieves better performance in recommendation for the extremely sparse data from crowdfunding campaigns.

Keywords: crowdfunding, recommender, bipartite graph, network structure

1. Introduction

As the largest crowdfunding platform in the world, Kickstarter has attracted 8,604,863 users who participated in 230,850 campaigns with 22,525,091 investment behaviors (www.kickstarter.com). However, about 60% of the campaigns are unsuccessfully financed. The main reason is that many campaigns failed to find enough investors, rather than the ideas were not good enough [1]. Therefore, a recommender for crowdfunding is the key to solving this problem.

A survey has shown that the sparseness of user behaviors in Kickstarter is about 99.99%, leading to the commonly used recommendation algorithms inefficient. For example, collaborative filtering (CF) algorithm based on cosine similarity aims to find users who have the same preference, then calculates interest similarity, and produces recommendation list. However, it is difficult for the algorithm to find similar users on a sparse data, which is one of the main problems faced by recommender systems [2].

Faced with large-scale sparse data, network analysis algorithms are effective approaches to overcome the problem. For example, the PageRank algorithm is applicable to calculate the weight of web nodes. As a global iterative algorithm, PageRank does not distinguish the types of nodes, making it hard to improve the recommendation performance. However, an improved algorithm based on PageRank (i.e., bipartite graph model) provides ideas for us. Using bipartite graph model, we divide the network into an item-user structure, where there is no direct edge between items or between users. Then, the global similarity is calculated by bipartite graph analysis, as opposed to local similarity calculated by cosine function, and can better deal with the problem of sparse data.

Experiments show that bipartite graph model can effectively produce recommendation lists with sparse data. Furthermore, in the global iterative process of bipartite graph model, the similarity between items or between users is also calculated, in addition to the similarity between items and users. Compared with cosine function, which can only calculate adjacent users, this kind of similarity is extracted from the network, thus it is able to solve the computation problem caused by sparse data. Therefore, we propose a bipartite graph-based CF model by combining the similarity calculated by bipartite graph model with CF algorithm.

2. Literature review

2.1 Graph model

PageRank is a classic algorithm to calculate the node's weight [3, 4]. PageRank determines the importance of all web pages based on the assumption that web pages linked from high-quality pages are also high-quality. A page is given a higher weight if more high-ranking pages point to it. Prior studies have raised improved PageRank algorithms, e.g., topic-sensitive PageRank [5]; the algorithm where the linked pages are content relevant but nondirectly adjacent pages, instead of directly adjacent pages [6]. PageRank is a computing-consuming and time-consuming algorithm, and its computational efficiency can be improved by some improved algorithms [7, 8].

When the node's weight is calculated by PageRank, the link weight and the content weight are not distinguished [9]. HITS algorithm separates the quality of nodes into link authority (Hub) and content authority (Authority) [10]. Based on content authority of pages, link authority of pages is determined, and then overall evaluation of web pages is given. A good hub is a page that points to many good authorities; a good authority is a page that is pointed to by many good hubs. This kind of mutually reinforcing relationship between hubs and authorities is applicable for the discovery of authoritative pages and automatic identification of the web structure and resources. Since there are problems of topic drift and irrelevant links in HITS algorithm, some improved methods are proposed [11, 12].

A bipartite graph is an extension of network theory and has attracted lots of attention, such as social network analysis [13]. A bipartite graph divides network nodes into two types, which is different from PageRank that treats nodes as homogeneous. Only nodes in different types are directly connected, while nodes in the same type are indirectly connected [14, 15]. The crowdfunding network can be abstracted as a bipartite graph, where one group of nodes is investors and the other group is items. The bipartite graph model can calculate the distance between nodes, such as Laplacian distance [16], though appropriate algorithms. The Laplacian matrix can measure the reachability of nodes in graph models. Since the distance between nodes is calculated in bipartite graphs, they can be transformed into the similarity between nodes [17]. Typical algorithms include mean similarity [18], and subsequent research has shown the upper and lower bounds of bipartite approximations [19]. On this basis, combined with hierarchical subgraphs, Hausdorff edit distance is proposed that can improve calculation accuracy and reduce computational complexity [20]. Visualization methods are also suggested [21]. In practice, the bipartite graph is applied to image segmentation [22]. In terms of recommender system, researcher uses aggregated bipartite graph model to reduce computational complexity of graph models, while recommendation accuracy is decreased [23].

2.2 Collaborative filtering

Collaborative filtering (CF) techniques are widely used in recommender systems [24]. Relaying on historical behaviors of users, similarity between users is calculated, and then products purchased by similar users are recommended. CF techniques are classified into item-based CF and user-based CF. User-based CF algorithm firstly identifies the user preference profile [25], next calculates the similarity based on the user preference profile, and finally applies the distance of user similarity to recommendation algorithms [26]. Since most users only have purchase behaviors for a few products, sparse data problem hinders the efficiency of recommendation [27, 28]. One solution is data clustering, which solves the problem to some extent.

How to evaluate the performance of recommender systems is a complex topic. In general, recommender systems more tend to provide a narrow recommendation list. Inspired by the Gini index, directed weighted conduction (DWC) is proposed. DWC is an evaluation metric based on bipartite graph model, which can effectively avoid recommendation congestion and greatly improve the novelty and diversity of recommendation [29].

3. Research gaps and problem definitions

Take **Figure 1** as an example, where black nodes A, B, C, and D denote users and gray nodes e, f, g and h denote items. If using the user-based cosine similarity CF algorithm, user A has adjacent users C and B. Item f is impossibly recommended to user A, because the adjacent users of A have no direct link to f. Similarly, f is also impossibly recommended to A in the item-based CF algorithm. Cosine similarity algorithm is a local algorithm, which cannot calculate the similarities of global nodes in a sparse network structure. The recommendation accuracy should be guaranteed using local similarity with dense data, but it is hard to get ideal performance in the case of sparse data.

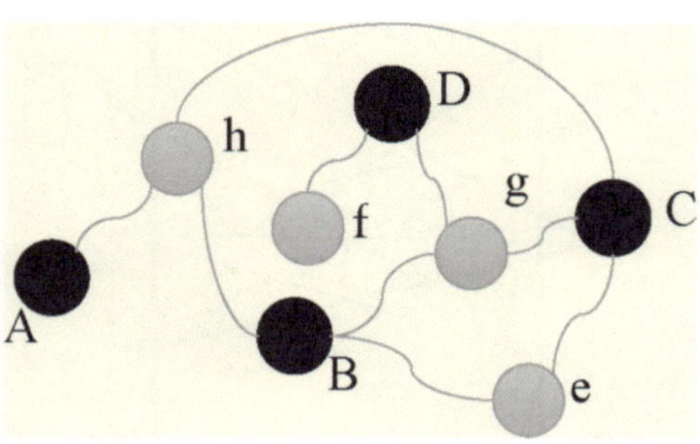

Figure 1.
The diagram of the application of CF algorithm in the network structure.

In bipartite graph algorithms, such as PersonalRank, the distance between items and users can be obtained directly. Therefore, the direct recommendation results can be obtained by transforming the distance into the similarity. For instance, the network in **Figure 1** is transformed into a bipartite graph as shown in **Figure 2**.

PersonalRank is used to calculate the bipartite graph in **Figure 2**. If a recommendation is provided to user A, iterative calculation starts at A. After 62 iterations, the calculation result converges, and the similarities between A and each item are obtained:

$$\begin{array}{ll} s(A,\mathrm{e}) = 0.07709, & s(A,f) = 0.01791 \\ s(A,g) = 0.09499, & s(A,h) = 0.26949 \end{array} \tag{1}$$

Except the node h with direct action to A, the recommended order of the remaining three items is g ranks firstly, e followed, and f lastly. In fact, in the calculation process, PersonalRank also repeatedly iterates to generate user similarities, but explicit output does not exist. In **Figure 2**, the implicit similarities between A and other users are:

$$s(A,B) = 0.13602, \quad s(A,C) = 0.13602, \quad s(A,D) = 0.04213 \tag{2}$$

The above similarities are different from the similarities based on cosine function or Pearson function. Local similarity between users is obtained by cosine or Pearson function (i.e., only the nodes directly adjacent to the user are calculated), while global similarity between users is obtained by bipartite graph algorithm. Taking **Figure 2** as an example, since A and D have no common actions, their similarity cannot be calculated by cosine or Pearson similarity function, or $s(A, D) = 0$. It is effective with dense data, since there are enough users with common actions and a neighborhood with a sufficient width is able to be obtained. However, in the case of sparse data, globally calculating user similarity is apparently more effective.

The research progress related to this paper is summarized in **Table 1**. For the personalized recommender for crowdfunding campaigns, although graph models have been used in present research, bipartite graph model is rarely used, especially focusing on solving the problem of sparse data in crowdfunding communities.

Crowdfunding platforms represented by Kickstarter use an *all-or-nothing* funding model, and the funding success rate is about 40%. Founders spend a lot in

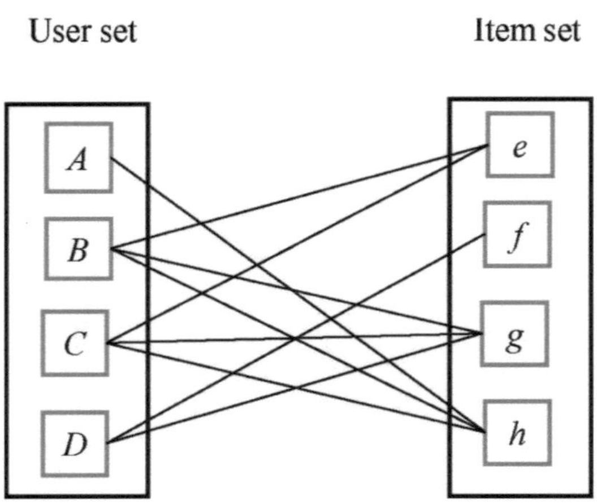

Figure 2.
The diagram of bipartite graph transformation.

Authors	Year	Conclusions	Comments
Rakesh and Choo [30]	2015	• Four research dimensions: temporal traits, personal traits, geo-location traits, and network traits • The backing habits of investors are influenced by their social circle	• Analysis is focused on project features, while recommender is just an application • Supervised machine learning lacks reporting on sparse data
An et al. [1]	2014	• Social networks can identify user preference more accurately • Different recommender strategies are adopted for different types of projects	• It is not aimed at the current situation of sparse data in crowdfunding communities • Information in social networks is needed, making operability reduced
Lu et al. [31]	2014	• Social networks can identify user preference	• There are similarities in research questions, but it is not aimed at sparse data • Identifying a large number text from social media has high cost
Stone et al. [32]	2013	• Traditional collaborative filtering algorithm is not suitable in the field of venture capital • The recommendation performance is improved by hierarchy information (group, segment, code)	• VC and crowdfunding have similarities and also many differences • There are differences between KNN and the method used in this paper
Zhou et al. [33]	2010	• Global recommendation algorithm overcomes some shortcomings of local recommendation algorithm • Nodes of "weak ties" have value in identifying user preference • Bipartite graph model can improve the diversity of recommendation	• The goal of the study is to achieve the balance between diversity and accuracy of recommendation, without considering the processing of sparse data

Table 1.
The main research progress related to this paper.

energy maintaining campaigns. A survey found that during the preparation period, it took an average of 30 minutes a day and 11 hours on weekends; during the fundraising period, it took 2–11 hours a day lasting 0.5–2 months [34]. Once the funding failed, the founder would get nothing. The reasons for failure might be the quality of the campaigns was poor or right investors had not been found. In the latter case, designing a reasonable personalized recommender system will increase the funding success rate. Therefore, taking advantages of PersonalRank in computing of bipartite graphs, combined with advantages of CF algorithms, the following research questions are proposed to investigate the recommender for crowdfunding campaigns:

1. In view of the extremely sparse data in crowdfunding communities, we extract user behaviors into the bipartite graph structure and calculate the global similarity between nodes in the graph model.

2. Depending on the node similarity matrix in bipartite graph model, we propose a bipartite graph-based CF model combined with CF algorithm to generate recommendation list for crowdfunding campaigns.

3. We conduct experiments on the dataset from Kickstarter to evaluate the effectiveness of the bipartite graph-based recommender algorithm, comparing differences between algorithms and suggesting feasible solutions.

4. Model overview

PageRank is an algorithm that measures the weight of a specific web page relative to other web pages, which is often used in page ranking. PageRank assumes that a user randomly selects a page to visit from all pages and then jumps to other pages through hyperlinks. After reaching each page, the user has two options: end here, or continue visiting by selecting a link randomly. Let d be the probability of continuing visiting. The user selects a hyperlink at random with the same probability from the current page to continue visiting, which is a random walk process. After many rounds of walks, the probability of visiting each page will converge to a stable value. This value is the weight of a web page. The algorithm is shown in Eq. (3):

$$PR(i) = \frac{1-d}{N} + d \sum_{j \in in(i)} \frac{PR(j)}{|out(j)|} \tag{3}$$

$PR(i)$ is the probability of visiting page i, d is the probability of continuing visiting pages (i.e., the damping coefficient), N is the total number of pages, *in (i)* is the page set pointing to page i (i.e., in-links), and *out (j)* is the page set pointed by page j (i.e., out-links).

PageRank is a global algorithm, which does not distinguish the types of nodes. However, the recommender system for crowdfunding campaigns is faced with both user nodes and campaign nodes. We can only obtain the weight of nodes themselves by PageRank, rather than the similarity between nodes. Based on PageRank, the improved algorithm PersonalRank is a bipartite graph algorithm [6], which can generate personalized item list for users, as shown in the Eq. (4):

$$PR(i) = (1-d)r_i + d \sum_{j \in in(i)} \frac{PR(j)}{|out(j)|}$$
$$r_i = \begin{cases} 1 & , \ if \ \ i = u \\ 0 & , \ if \ \ i \neq u \end{cases} \tag{4}$$

The difference between Eqs. (3) and (4) is that $1/N$ is replaced by r_i. In other words, initial probabilities vary in different nodes. In bipartite graph model, u is the target user, and Eq. (4) actually calculates the similarity of all nodes relative to node u.

Specifically, unlike PageRank randomly selecting a node to walk, PersonalRank starts from the special node u and can only walk to different types of nodes. Taking crowdfunding as an example, user nodes can only walk to campaign nodes, while campaign nodes can only walk to user nodes. After reaching a new node, the walk stops and restarts from u with a probability of 1-d or continues walking to a node in the other type with a probability of d. After many rounds of walk, the probabilities of visiting each node tend to be stable. Therefore, before running PersonalRank algorithm, an initial probability must be set for each node. In PageRank, if u is the user, let the initial probability of visiting node u be 1 and other nodes be 0. But in PageRank, initial probability of visiting each node is equal, and the initial probability is $1/N$.

A bipartite graph is a graph model composed of two groups of nodes with different properties, and the nodes in the same group are not connected. A bipartite graph can be defined as a network structure $G = <U, I, E>$, where U denotes the user set; I denotes the item set; and E denotes the edges of bipartite graph model.

Figure 2 is a typical bipartite graph structure, containing four users and four items. The actions between users and items are mapped as edges in the graph. For simplicity, the weights of edges are assumed the same. Take crowdfunding as an example, where U denotes investors; I denotes crowdfunding campaigns; and the edges denote users' investment behaviors in campaigns. G is actually a matrix structure, which can be calculated to obtain the global similarity by PersonalRank.

The core idea of CF is the calculation of similarity between users (user-based) or between items (item-based). The similarity algorithm commonly used is cosine function, as shown in Eq. (5):

$$similarity(A, B) = \cos(\theta) = \frac{A \cdot B}{\|A\|\|B\|} = \frac{\sum_{i=1}^{n} A_i \times B_i}{\sqrt{\sum_{i=1}^{n} (A_i)^2} \times \sqrt{\sum_{i=1}^{n} (B_i)^2}} \tag{5}$$

In bipartite graph model, the similarities between all nodes are calculated, which can be integrated with CF algorithm, and may achieve better performance than directly recommendation by bipartite graphs.

5. Experimental data and experimental settings

5.1 Experimental data

The research data was collected from Kickstarter, which contains 32,226 investment behaviors from 14,506 users which invest on 787 campaigns. This paper used an offline evaluation method to evaluate the recommender system, dividing the dataset into a training set and a test set. If a user has only one investment behavior, the recommendation list cannot be produced because if the behavior is classified into the training set, the accuracy of the recommendation list cannot be evaluated; if classified into the test set, preference similarity cannot be obtained through the user's behavior.

Data sparseness is defined as the probability of matrix elements without data, which is calculated by Eq. (6). The sparseness of the experimental data is 96–99%, that is, about 96–99% of the matrix elements in the users' behavior matrix lack values:

$$sparsity = 1 - \frac{|Behavior|}{|User| \times |Item|} \tag{6}$$

In the dataset, most users support less than five campaigns, also leading to the extremely sparseness of the dataset. Many campaigns have a small number of supporters, while popular campaigns have won a large number of supporters. Statistics show that campaigns in the dataset have one supporter at least, 9046 supporters at most, and 41 supporters on average.

5.2 Experimental settings

Firstly, the parameters are setting. PersonalRank has two parameters:

1. Convergence coefficient. According to the present research, it is set to 0.85.

2. Number of iterations. There is no fixed value, and it needs to be set depending on the data by following two methods: (a) specify the number of iterations

forcibly; and (2) judge whether the global computing result has converged, and stop iteration if converged. We integrate these two methods and use the following method for iteration setting.

Algorithm 1. Iteration setting of PersonalRank Algorithm

```
Input: network structure G
Output: computing results of PersonalRank
Define G; #Construct the network
Define max_iteration; # Define a maximum number of iterations
Define item; #Define the starting point of PersonalRank walking
Define previous_iteration = [Null]; # Predefine iteration result
For iteration in range(0,max_iteration)
        For I in G.nodes():
                Pr[i] = PersonalRank(G);
        End For
        If previous_iteration == Pr:
                Break; #Converged
        End If
        previous_iteration = Pr;
End For
Output Pr;
```

The time complexity of Algorithm 1 is $O(max\_iteration^{*}|item|)$, where *max_iteration* is the predefined number of iterations and $|item|$ is the number of nodes of items. The complexity of the algorithm means the complexity of the number of iterations, not the complexity of the complete algorithm. We tried to calculate the network, showing that the PersonalRank converges after 100 iterations.

All of the CF in experiments use item-based algorithm, for the following reasons: (1) The number of items is much smaller than the number of users so that the computing cost of the similarity between items is much lower than between users. (2) Item-based methods are used more often in practical applications due to computing convenience, such as Amazon recommender system.

The compared algorithms in this study are summarized in **Table 2**. The content-based recommender is based on the similarity of items. For instance, if a user has supported a "music" campaign, the content-based recommender algorithm assumes that the user has a greater preference for "music" campaigns. In the compared experiments, we chose six indicators to measure the similarity of campaigns: campaign category, social network of founders, funding status, number of pledge levels, minimum pledge money, and average funding amount.

Popularity-based recommender means the most popular items are directly recommended to users (user-based) or the most popular users are recommended to items (item-based). Popularity-based recommender is independent of neighbor nodes, which means the recommendation lists are the same for any users.

Two parameters need to be set in CF algorithms:

1. The number of neighbors K. K similar users (items) are selected as the source for producing recommendation lists, and the items which the users are interested in are recommended to target users.

2. The list length N. N items are recommended to target users (or N users are recommended to target items). Generally, N is set to 5 or 10, which is widely used in present studies.

	Compared algorithms	Description
1	Cosine-based CF	Collaborative filtering algorithm based on cosine similarity
2	PersonalRank	Recommendation directly using PersonalRank to calculate bipartite graphs
3	Bipartite graph-based CF	Using PersonalRank to calculate node similarity then using CF to recommend
4	Content-based recommender	Recommendation according to the content
5	Popularity-based recommender	The most popular items (users) are recommended to users (items)

Table 2.
Compared algorithms and description.

In addition to cosine similarity function, other similarity functions have also been tried. The results show that cosine similarity function performs best in the recommender for crowdfunding campaigns. Therefore, cosine-based CF is used as one of the benchmarks for comparing.

6. Experimental result

The sparseness of user behaviors is larger than 99%, and many users cannot find similar users. As a local similarity method, cosine function hardly produces recommendation lists in this situation. Thus, the similarity between any users without intersection is set to 0. **Tables 3** and **4** show the recommendation performance of CF algorithm based on cosine similarity.

From **Tables 3** and **4**, when K = 40 and K = 55, the best performances are achieved, respectively. However, on the whole, the accuracy is extremely low, which has large room for improvement. The reason is that on the extremely sparse dataset, users have few intersections, which makes it difficult to find users with similar interests, resulting in the low accuracy of recommendation.

Table 5 shows the performance of using PersonalRank to produce recommendation lists. Compared to cosine similarity CF algorithm, the accuracy of recommendation by PersonalRank has at least doubled, which indicates that on sparse data network, the global similarity algorithm can effectively solve the computing problem of node similarity and improve the recommendation accuracy.

Then we use bipartite graph-based CF algorithm. The recommendation result for N = 5 is shown in **Table 6**, where the algorithm achieves the best performance when K = 30. The recommendation result for N = 10 is shown in **Table 7**, where the algorithm achieves the best performance when K = 30. However, compared to the result of recommendation directly by bipartite graph model, bipartite graph-based CF algorithm does not perform better. It indicates that on this dataset, the accuracy of recommendation calculated by bipartite graph model is higher.

Comparing **Tables 5–7**, we can get the conclusion that the result of recommendation by bipartite graph model is superior to bipartite graph-based CF algorithm. The possible reasons are as follows. (1) Although bipartite graph-based CF algorithm can obtain the similarity between items (users) and generate neighbor items (users), which cannot be done by cosine similarity algorithm, the CF algorithm cannot extract enough items from the neighborhood for recommendation due to the extremely sparse data (e.g., A and B are very similar, but if B has few actions, the accuracy of the recommendation list is still quite low). Therefore, the recommender

K	Recall (%)	Precision (%)	Coverage (%)	Popularity
5	0.07	0.25	2.60	0.871
10	0.08	0.28	2.58	0.935
15	0.09	0.30	2.52	0.96
20	0.09	0.31	2.46	1.013
25	0.09	0.31	2.38	1.035
30	0.10	0.32	2.36	1.043
35	0.10	0.33	2.34	1.048
40	**0.10**	**0.35**	**2.33**	**1.052**
45	0.10	0.33	2.33	1.054
50	0.10	0.33	2.33	1.057
55	0.10	0.34	2.32	1.054
60	0.10	0.34	2.32	1.055
65	0.10	0.34	2.32	1.056
70	0.10	0.33	2.32	1.057
75	0.10	0.33	2.32	1.057
80	0.10	0.33	2.32	1.057
85	0.10	0.34	2.32	1.057
90	0.10	0.34	2.32	1.057
95	0.10	0.34	2.32	1.058
100	0.10	0.34	2.32	1.058

Table 3.
Performance of CF algorithm based on cosine similarity (N = 5).

K	Recall (%)	Precision (%)	Coverage (%)	Popularity
5	0.13	0.22	4.97	0.842
10	0.13	0.22	4.9	0.9
15	0.15	0.25	4.79	0.922
20	0.16	0.26	4.64	0.958
25	0.16	0.27	4.5	0.97
30	0.16	0.27	4.45	0.976
35	0.17	0.28	4.43	0.981
40	0.17	0.29	4.42	0.985
45	0.17	0.29	4.41	0.988
50	0.18	0.29	4.41	0.99
55	**0.18**	**0.3**	**4.4**	**0.99**
60	0.18	0.3	4.4	0.992
65	0.18	0.29	4.4	0.992
70	0.18	0.29	4.4	0.993
75	0.18	0.3	4.4	0.993
80	0.18	0.3	4.4	0.992

K	Recall (%)	Precision (%)	Coverage (%)	Popularity
85	0.18	0.3	4.4	0.993
90	0.18	0.3	4.4	0.993
95	0.18	0.3	4.4	0.993
100	0.18	0.29	4.4	0.993

Table 4.
Performance of CF algorithm based on cosine similarity (N = *10*).

N	Recall (%)	Precision (%)	Coverage (%)	Popularity
1	0.16	1.17	1.72	1.586
2	0.28	1.02	3.17	1.545
3	0.41	0.99	4.48	1.476
4	0.52	0.93	5.65	1.434
5	0.59	0.85	6.75	1.425
6	0.67	0.81	7.81	1.415
7	0.72	0.75	8.82	1.401
8	0.80	0.72	9.80	1.382
9	0.85	0.68	10.78	1.372
10	0.90	0.66	11.76	1.365

Table 5.
Result of recommendation by PersonalRank.

K	Recall (%)	Precision (%)	Coverage (%)	Popularity
5	0.39	0.56	7.72	1.298
10	0.38	0.55	6.22	1.468
15	0.39	0.57	5.62	1.572
20	0.39	0.56	5.40	1.607
25	0.40	0.58	5.27	1.627
30	**0.41**	**0.59**	**5.19**	**1.641**
35	0.41	0.59	5.16	1.653
40	0.40	0.59	5.10	1.654
45	0.41	0.59	5.09	1.663
50	0.40	0.59	5.08	1.655
55	0.39	0.57	5.07	1.638
60	0.40	0.58	5.04	1.643
65	0.40	0.58	5.03	1.645
70	0.40	0.58	5.02	1.647
75	0.40	0.58	5.01	1.649
80	0.40	0.58	5.00	1.65
85	0.40	0.58	5.00	1.652

K	Recall (%)	Precision (%)	Coverage (%)	Popularity
90	0.40	0.58	5.00	1.654
95	0.40	0.58	4.99	1.655
100	0.40	0.58	4.99	1.656

Table 6.
Result of bipartite graph-based CF algorithm (N = 5).

K	Recall (%)	Precision (%)	Coverage (%)	Popularity
5	0.56	0.41	14.11	1.235
10	0.58	0.42	11.51	1.406
15	0.59	0.43	10.32	1.466
20	0.60	0.43	9.91	1.495
25	0.62	0.45	9.67	1.521
30	**0.64**	**0.47**	**9.54**	**1.532**
35	0.64	0.47	9.49	1.532
40	0.64	0.47	9.41	1.536
45	0.63	0.45	9.39	1.544
50	0.62	0.45	9.41	1.541
55	0.62	0.45	9.39	1.536
60	0.61	0.44	9.34	1.539
65	0.60	0.44	9.29	1.541
70	0.60	0.44	9.26	1.543
75	0.60	0.44	9.24	1.546
80	0.60	0.44	9.23	1.547
85	0.60	0.44	9.23	1.548
90	0.60	0.44	9.22	1.55
95	0.60	0.44	9.21	1.551
100	0.61	0.44	9.20	1.552

Table 7.
Result of bipartite graph-based CF algorithm (N = 10).

performance of CF algorithm is poor. (2) Local algorithms only produce local optimal solutions, also resulting in the poor performance of bipartite graph-based CF algorithm, whereas recommendation directly by bipartite graph model is a global recommendation algorithm, which can overcome the shortage of sparse matrix.

The results of content-based recommender are shown in **Tables 8** and **9**, where the best performances are achieved when K = 90 and K = 100, respectively. The accuracy of content-based recommender is the lowest, which might be determined by the investment preference of investors on crowdfunding campaigns. For example, many investors have participated in multiple categories of campaigns, rather than focusing on one or several categories.

The comprehensive comparison result of various algorithms is summarized in **Table 10**. On this dataset, PersonalRank is the most effective in computing the node distance of bipartite graph model and converting it into similarity, followed by CF

K	Recall (%)	Precision (%)	Coverage (%)	Popularity
5	0.01	0.04	1.82	0.846
10	0.03	0.09	1.69	0.927
15	0.03	0.11	1.54	1.029
20	0.04	0.12	1.45	1.121
25	0.04	0.14	1.36	1.243
30	0.04	0.15	1.24	1.337
35	0.05	0.16	1.14	1.427
40	0.05	0.17	1.05	1.52
45	0.05	0.17	0.95	1.607
50	0.05	0.17	0.88	1.647
55	0.05	0.17	0.83	1.685
60	0.06	0.19	0.77	1.729
65	0.06	0.20	0.72	1.763
70	0.06	0.20	0.68	1.801
75	0.06	0.20	0.65	1.839
80	0.06	0.22	0.62	1.867
85	0.07	0.22	0.59	1.901
90	**0.08**	**0.25**	**0.55**	**1.933**
95	0.07	0.25	0.53	1.957
100	0.07	0.25	0.50	1.993

Table 8.
*Result of content-based recommender (*N = 5*).*

K	Recall (%)	Precision (%)	Coverage (%)	Popularity
5	0.02	0.03	3.45	0.819
10	0.04	0.06	3.25	0.876
15	0.05	0.08	3.02	0.936
20	0.05	0.09	2.91	0.999
25	0.06	0.10	2.76	1.082
30	0.07	0.11	2.56	1.152
35	0.07	0.11	2.38	1.232
40	0.07	0.11	2.20	1.316
45	0.07	0.12	2.03	1.393
50	0.07	0.12	1.85	1.452
55	0.08	0.13	1.71	1.507
60	0.08	0.14	1.56	1.549
65	0.09	0.15	1.45	1.581
70	0.09	0.15	1.36	1.608
75	0.10	0.16	1.29	1.645
80	0.10	0.17	1.23	1.673

K	Recall (%)	Precision (%)	Coverage (%)	Popularity
85	0.10	0.17	1.17	1.698
90	0.11	0.18	1.11	1.72
95	0.12	0.19	1.06	1.739
100	**0.12**	**0.20**	**1.01**	**1.76**

Table 9.
Result of content-based recommender (N = 10).

Recommender	List length *N*	Number of neighbors *K*	Recall (%)	Precision (%)	Coverage (%)	Popularity
Cosine-based CF	5	40	0.10	0.35	2.33	1.052
Cosine-based CF	10	55	0.18	0.3	4.4	0.99
PersonalRank	5	Global	0.59	0.85	6.75	1.425
PersonalRank	10	Global	0.90	0.66	11.76	1.365
Bipartite graph-based CF	5	30	0.41	0.59	5.19	1.641
Bipartite graph-based CF	10	30	0.64	0.47	9.54	1.532
Content-based	5	90	0.08	0.25	0.55	1.933
Content-based	10	100	0.12	0.20	1.01	1.76
Popularity-based	5	—	0.335	0.528	0.035	2.90
Popularity-based	10	—	0.509	0.400	0.069	2.729

Table 10.
Comprehensive comparison result of various algorithms.

algorithm using global similarity distance, while content-based recommender has the worst performance. Popularity-based recommender algorithm is superior to cosine-based CF and content-based recommender in precision, but its coverages are too low (0.035 and 0.069), since popularity-based algorithm always recommends those most popular users to the target campaign.

7. Conclusion and prospects

The sparseness in crowdfunding platform Kickstarter is more than 99% [35]. With such a high sparseness, cosine-based CF obtains poor recommendation performance. Therefore, we use the bipartite graph-based network structure to describe users' behaviors and use PersonalRank to calculate the distance between campaigns and users to directly produce recommendation lists. Next, we integrate bipartite graph model and CF algorithm, and the correlation among the items set (the users set) is obtained by PersonalRank as the measurement of interest similarity. Experimental results show that recommender based on bipartite graph model achieves better performance on a sparse dataset. This paper proposes a method to solve the problem of sparse data, providing a new idea for generating recommendation list in crowdfunding platforms.

Directions for future works are as follows. (1) In terms of bipartite graph model, PersonalRank is not the only algorithm, while other network algorithms are applicable to calculate the node similarity, such as SimRank [36]. Other graph models could be applied to recommendation for crowdfunding campaigns in the future. (2) Due to computing complexity, all of CF algorithms used in this paper are item-based, rather than user-based. However, we have to use user-based recommender in some cases. For example, when a new user enters the system, user-based method is more suitable in recommendation. Future research could make a comparison with user-based recommender algorithms. (3) The datasets are all from Kickstarter, but there are other crowdfunding platforms, such as Indiegogo [37]. Research could use other crowdfunding platforms to verify the applicability of bipartite graph model. (4) Based on the data from the crowdfunding platform, we have verified the usefulness of bipartite graph model. However, not all the information in crowdfunding communities is used. For example, some research found the home bias is a common phenomenon in investment [38], that is, offline relationships between founders and investors may have already been established, such as friends, classmates, acquaintances, colleagues, etc. Consequently, there is a psychological and cultural convergence between founders and investors, and the physical distance is relatively close. Therefore, in personalized recommender, the physical distance in graph model could be considered, and the physical distance between users could be modeled into binary graph model to improve the performance of recommender.

Acknowledgements

This work is partially supported by the NSFC Grant (71771177), the University Innovation Fund from the Science and Technology Development Center of the Ministry of Education (2019J01012), and Standardization of Trade in Service Fund (FMBZH-1947).

Conflict of interest

The authors declare no conflict of interest.

Author details

Hongwei Wang* and Shiqin Chen
School of Economics and Management, Tongji University, Shanghai, China

*Address all correspondence to: hwwang@tongji.edu.cn

References

[1] An J, Quercia D, Crowcroft J. Recommending investors for crowdfunding projects. In: Proceedings of the 23rd International Conference on World Wide Web (WWW '14). New York, US: ACM Press; 2014. pp. 261-270

[2] Chen L, Chen G, Wang F. Recommender systems based on user reviews: The state of the art. User Modeling and User-Adapted Interaction. 2015;**25**(2):99-154

[3] Brin S, Page L. The anatomy of a large-scale hypertextual Web search engine. In: Proceedings of the Seventh International Conference on World Wide Web (WWW '7). Amsterdam, NLD: Elsevier Science Publishers B. V.; 1998. pp. 107-117

[4] Page L, Brin S, Motwani R, et al. The PageRank citation ranking: Bringing order to the web. Technical Report 1999-66, Stanford InfoLab; Stanford, CA; 1999

[5] Richardson M, Domingos P. The intelligent surfer: Probabilistic combination of link and content information in PageRank. In: Neural Information Processing Systems 14. Cambridge, MA: MIT Press; 2001. pp. 1441-1448

[6] Haveliwala TH. Topic-sensitive PageRank. In: Proceedings of the 11th International Conference on World Wide Web (WWW '02). New York, US: ACM Press; 2002. pp. 517-526

[7] Kohlschutter C, Chirita P, Nejdl W. Efficient parallel computation of PageRank. In: Proceedings of the 28th European conference on Advances in Information Retrieval (ECIR '06). Berlin, Heidelberg: Springer-Verlag; 2006. pp. 241-252

[8] Arasu A, Novak J, Tomkins A, et al. PageRank computation and the structure of the web: Experiments and algorithms. In: Proceedings of the 11th International Conference on World Wide Web (WWW '02). New York, US: ACM Press; 2002. pp. 107-117

[9] Massucci FA, Docampo D. Measuring the academic reputation through citation networks via PageRank. Journal of Informetrics. 2019;**13**(1):185-201

[10] Kleinberg J. Authoritative sources in a hyperlinked environment. Journal of the ACM. 1999;**46**(5):604-632

[11] Bharat K, Henzinger M. Improved algorithms for topic distillation in a hyperlinked environment. In: Proceedings of the 21st Annual International ACM SIGIR Conference on Research and Development in Information Retrieval (SIGIR '98). New York, US: ACM Press; 1998. pp. 104-111

[12] Lempel R, Moran S. The stochastic approach for link-structure analysis (SALSA) and the TKC effect. Computer Network. 2000;**33**(1-6):387-401

[13] Tay DBH, Lin Z. Design of near orthogonal graph filter banks. IEEE Signal Processing Letters. 2015;**22**(6): 701-704

[14] Hammack RH, Puffenberger O. A prime factor theorem for bipartite graphs. European Journal of Combinatorics. 2015;**47**:123-140

[15] Kaya B. Hotel recommendation system by bipartite networks and link prediction. Journal of Information Science. 2020;**46**(1):53-63

[16] Niu A, Fan D, Wang G. On the distance Laplacian spectral radius of bipartite graphs. Discrete Applied Mathematics. 2015;**186**:207-213

[17] Gharibshah J, Jalili M. Connectedness of users-items networks

and recommender systems. Applied Mathematics and Computation. 2014; **243**:578-584

[18] Riesen K, Bunke H. Approximate graph edit distance computation by means of bipartite graph matching. Image and Vision Computing. 2009;**27** (7):950-959

[19] Riesen K, Fischer A, Bunke H. Estimating graph edit distance using lower and upper bounds of bipartite approximations. International Journal of Pattern Recognition and Artificial Intelligence. 2015;**29**(02):1550011

[20] Fischer A, Uchida S, Frinken V, et al. Improving hausdorff edit distance using structural node context. In: International Workshop on Graph-Based Representations in Pattern Recognition. Berlin, Heidelberg: Springer-Verlag; 2015. pp. 148-157

[21] Zhou H, Xu P, Qu H. Visualization of bipartite relations between graphs and sets. Journal of Visualization. 2015; **18**(2):159-172

[22] Wang X, Tang Y, Masnou S, et al. A global/local affinity graph for image segmentation. IEEE Transactions on Image Processing. 2015;**24**(4):1399-1411

[23] Lee S, Kahng M, Lee S. Constructing compact and effective graphs for recommender systems via node and edge aggregations. Expert Systems with Applications. 2015;**42**(7):3396-3409

[24] Billsus D, Pazzani MJ. Learning collaborative information filters. In: Proceedings of the 15th International Conference on Machine Learning (ICML '98). San Francisco, CA: Morgan Kaufmann Publishers; 1998. pp. 46-54

[25] Lin C-C, Tsai C-C. Applying social bookmarking to collective information searching (CIS): An analysis of behavioral pattern and peer interaction for co-exploring quality online resources. Computers in Human Behavior. 2011;**27**(3):1249-1257

[26] Dalcanale F, Fontane DG, Csapo J. A general framework for a collaborative water quality knowledge and information network. Environmental Management. 2011;**47**(3):443-455

[27] Liu H, He J, Wang T, et al. Combining user preferences and user opinions for accurate recommendation. Electronic Commerce Research and Applications. 2013;**12**(1):14-23

[28] Xu J, Zheng X, DingW. Personalized recommendation based on reviews and ratings alleviating the sparsity problem of collaborative filtering. In: Proceedings of the 2012 IEEE Ninth International Conference on e-Business Engineering (ICEBE '12). Piscataway, N.J: IEEE Press; 2012. pp. 9-16

[29] Ren X, Lu L, Liu R, et al. Avoiding congestion in recommender systems. New Journal of Physics. 2014;**16**(6): 063057

[30] Rakesh V, Choo J, Reddy CK. Project recommendation using heterogeneous traits in crowdfunding. In: Proceedings of the Ninth International AAAI Conference on Web and Social Media. Palo Alto, CA: AAAI Press; 2015. pp. 337-346

[31] Lu C-T, Shuai H-H, Yu PS. Identifying your customers in social networks. In: Proceedings of the 23rd ACM International Conference on Conference on Information and Knowledge Management (CIKM '14). New York, USA: ACM Press; 2014. pp. 391-400

[32] Stone T, Zhang W, Zhao X. An empirical study of top-n recommendation for venture finance. In: Proceedings of the 22nd ACM International Conference on Information & Knowledge

Management. New York, USA: ACM Press; 2013. pp. 1865-1868

[33] Zhou T, Kuscsik Z, Liu J-G, Medo M, Wakeling JR, Zhang Y-C. Solving the apparent diversity-accuracy dilemma of recommender systems. Proceedings of the National Academy of Sciences of the United States of America. 2010;**107**(10): 4511-4515

[34] Hui JS, Gerber E, Greenberg M. Easy Money? The Demands of Crowdfunding Work. Segal Design Institute, Northwestern University; Gerber, Greenberg; 2012. pp. 1-11

[35] Testa S, Nielsen KR, Bogers M, et al. The role of crowdfunding in moving towards a sustainable society. Technological Forecasting and Social Change. 2019;**141**:66-73

[36] Jeh G,Widom J. SimRank: A measure of structural-context similarity. In: Proceedings of the Eighth ACM SIGKDD International Conference on Knowledge Discovery and Data Mining (KDD '02). Association for Computing Machinery. New York, US: ACM Press; 2002. pp. 538-543

[37] Simons A, Kaiser LF, Vom Brocke J. Enterprise crowdfunding: Foundations, applications, and research findings. Business and Information Systems Engineering. 2019;**61**(1):113-121

[38] Lin M, Viswanathan S. Home bias in online investments: An empirical study of an online crowdfunding market. Management Science. 2016;**62**(5): 1393-1414

Chapter 15

Crowdfunding: The Case of Italy

Rosa Adamo, Domenica Federico, Mariantonietta Intonti, Simona Mele and Antonella Notte

Abstract

Crowdfunding is a fundraising process from a large audience to launch a new venture or entrepreneurial project. It is mostly based on the use of Web and represents a unique category of fundraising, with different vehicles, processes and goals. It is very diffused in the global economic landscape and in Italy where a specific discipline for crowdfunding was introduced for the first time in Europe. The chapter, after a summary of the peculiarities, spread and regulation of crowdfunding, intends to analyze the characteristics of a platform operating on the Italian market (Produzioni dal Basso), highlighting its characteristics, strengths and weaknesses. The work also intends to carry out a simulation for the realization of a crowdfunding project by an Italian Foundation operating in the social sector of child and adolescent distress, to be implemented through the use of the same platform.

Keywords: crowdfunding, Italy, regulation of crowdfunding, crowdfunding models, innovative start-up

1. Introduction

In recent years, with the development of Internet, a new and effective fundraising methodology, called crowdfunding, is diffused[1]. In particular, crowdfunding allows founders of for-profit ventures to fund their efforts by drawing on relatively small contributions from a large number of individuals, without traditional financial intermediaries, but using the web.

Crowdfunding is a growing sector also in Italy and it is characterized by the continuous novelty that affects both platforms and campaigns, which make innovation and sustainability some of the main strengths. In Italy, a specific discipline for crowdfunding was introduced for the first time in Europe.

The purpose of this chapter is to study the principal peculiarities of the crowdfunding in Italy and to analyze the characteristics of a platform operating on the Italian market (Produzioni dal Basso). The work also intends to carry out a simulation for the realization of a crowdfunding project by an Italian Foundation operating in the social sector of child and adolescent distress, to be implemented through the use of the same platform.

[1] Even if the study reflects a common view, Rosa Adamo mainly contributed to Sections 1, 2 and 7; Federico Domenica mainly contributed to Sections 4, 4.1 and 5; Mariantonietta Intonti mainly contributed to Sections 6, 6.3 and 6.4; Simona Mele mainly contributed to Sections 6.1, 6.2 and **Box 1**; Antonella Notte mainly contributed to Sections 3 and 4.2.

The chapter is divided into five sections. The first section analyzes the origin and the diffusion of the crowdfunding in Italy. The second section discusses the Italian regulation putting in evidence the principal problems and the prospect. The third section illustrates the modality of fundraising, in particular classic and new model are discussed. The fourth section analyzes benefits and risks of crowdfunding. Finally, in the fifth section, a study on characteristics of a platform operating on the Italian market and a simulation for the realization of a crowdfunding project by an Italian Foundation are realized.

2. Crowdfunding: origin and diffusion in Italy

The crowdfunding consists in the request to the public for financing, typically through an online platform, from subjects who need funds to develop projects or for personal purposes [1, 2].

The author of an entrepreneurial, cultural or social project can raise money by engaging the crowd directly to obtain the useful liquidity for the realization of the same project [3]. Unlike the classic request for a loan, crowdfunding guarantees to the borrower the possibility to contact, using online portal, a wide and heterogeneous audience, in which there are potential lenders. With the help of the lenders, in fact, it is possible to cover costs of various kinds, especially if the resources obtained from traditional funding sources are insufficient [4].

The phenomenon of crowdfunding has developed primarily in the Anglo-Saxon territory, and then it has spread in Europe and America. In particular, the first project funded by crowdfunding regards an Anglo-Saxon band in 1997 [5]. The musical group, known as Marillion, unable to bear the cost of their North American tour, turned to fans by launching a fundraiser online, with which they obtained 60,000 dollars. In 2001, the band used the same mechanism to record a new album. In 2008, former US President Barack Obama funded his election campaign through crowdfunding [6].

In Italy, crowdfunding started to spread very soon [7, 8]. However, the country did not take the typical advantages of the first mover due to the internal national peculiarities [9]. In fact, while in other economies the phenomenon was beginning to flourish, in Italy, crowdfunding has encountered more difficulties. The elements that have slowed the development of the phenomenon are the characteristics of the entrepreneurial system, the long bureaucratic chain, together with the high rate of digital illiteracy and the scarce diffusion of online payment systems [10].

In Italy, the first signs of crowdfunding took place in 2005 when Produzioni dal Basso launched an online service to finance projects on the web.

After that, some platforms of reward and donation crowdfunding have spread.

In 2013, there was a boom in the creation of crowdfunding platforms and do-it-yourself portals also began to emerge. This diffusion was supported by the issuing of the provision with which an ad hoc regulation for equity-based crowdfunding was introduced in the Italian legal system.

Next, in 2014, there have been two predominant tendencies, namely:

- the start-up of a process of proliferation of increasingly local portals, i.e., aimed at a specific Italian geographical area; and

- the application of crowdfunding also in other economic sectors, compared to those in previous years [11, 12].

These trends led to the emergence of platforms based on civic models, based on royalty and invoice trading.

Over the last few years, there has been a growth in the various types of crowdfunding portals. In particular, crowdfunding portals for real estate, financing through lending-based loans for the installment payment of purchases on e-commerce sites and the first industry index (Italian Equity Crowdfunding Index) for the equity-based market have also been launched [13].

Today, the crowdfunding sector in Italy shows substantial market specialization and segmentation. The main trends are as follows:

- Loyalty: a shift from the project to the organizers of the campaign has occurred.

- Decentralization: thanks to technological innovation, many platforms have lightened their interface, redistributing crowdfunding functions within more elastic infrastructures and also resorting to different forms of artificial intelligence.

- Internationalization: Italian portals would be able to compete with large multinational platforms.

- Complementarity: crowdfunding has begun to be used also by non-profit organizations, in fact the functioning of the third sector has developed an "integrated strategy with specific and complementary objectives with respect to traditional fundraising channels" [13].

In the coming years, crowdfunding growth is likely, thanks to its expansion to all Italian SMEs. At the same time, it is conceivable that bottom-up forms of financing are becoming part of the local economic fabric.

3. Italian regulation: problems and prospects

Italy was the first European country to have introduced a specific discipline for crowdfunding. In particular, the legislator has created legislation dedicated only to equity-based crowdfunding, while for other models—donation, invoice, pre-purchase, real estate, reward and royalty—the already existing regulation for similar financing methods is used [9, 14]. The only exception is social lending, which was recently, even if only minimally, regulated within the new provisions for the collection of savings from parties other than banks.

The interest in crowdfunding in Italy has grown above all because the companies are mainly of SME and encounter many difficulties in finding adequate financial resources for their development. This is even more evident for the start-up.

For this reason, a particular type of start-up, those c.d. "Innovative", was inserted into the Italian legal system by the Decree-Law no. 179 of 18 October 2012 (converted into Law no. 221 of 17 December 2012) (also known as "Decreto crescita bis") in the articles 25–32. The Decree has included in the Consolidated Law on Finance, i.e., Legislative Decree no. 58 of 24 February 1998, the article 50 quinquies "management of crowdfunding portals for the small- and medium-sized enterprises and for the social enterprises" and the article 100 ter "offers via crowdfunding portals". The Decree has also delegated to Consob the rules applicable to the management of portals and to offer for raising capital. In particular, the text is the "Regulation on "the collection of risk capital via on-line portals" (adopted by Consob with Resolution no. 18592 of 26 June 2013 and successively amended by resolutions no. 19520 of 24 February 2016, no. 20204 of 29 November 2017 and no. 20264 of 17 January 2018).

Over the last few years, the crowdfunding discipline has undergone numerous modifications, which have significantly changed its features. This evolution must be attributed mainly to two reasons: one of a political-economic nature and a second of a legal order.

From a political-economic point of view, it is important to support the development of entrepreneurial activities, offering alternative channels with respect to traditional lending for finding resources for growth, also through the promotion of forms of investment (and not real financing).

From a more strictly legal point of view, the modification interventions reflect a process of progressive refinement of the national discipline in light of the concrete application experience and the European regulatory framework. In fact, also due to the absence of a specific community framework, the regulation of equity crowdfunding has sometimes shown points of imperfect coordination with certain legal categories typical of financial market law, including in particular those of investment services and offers to the public.

The most significant change is represented by the extension of the audience of subjects who are allowed to offer shares of risk capital through portals.

Indeed, with the Decree Law no. 3 of 24 January 2015 (converted with Law no. 33 of 24 March 2015), also known as the "Investment Compact", the category of "innovative" SMEs was introduced, extending to them some of the facilitations envisaged for Innovative start-up.

In particular, together with innovative SMEs, UCITS and companies that invest mainly in innovative start-ups have been added. This extension has not achieved the objectives hoped for in terms of increasing the number of bidders, given the difficulty for companies to comply with the subjective requirements—related to the innovative nature—provided for by the Decree Law. Among these, for example, it includes the achievement of a volume of expenditure in research, development and innovation in an amount equal to or greater than 3% of the greater entity between cost and total value of the production of the innovative SME.

For this reason, with the Budget Law for 2017 (paragraph 70) the article 50 quinques of the Consolidated Law on Finance has been amended: the legislator has decided to allow, generally, to all SMEs, also constituted in forms of limited liability companies, to access financing channels different of banking channels, to thus more easily find the capital needed to carry out their projects. This is a very significant extension, as it greatly expands the number of companies which can use equity crowdfunding.

The objective of fostering SME development through the spread of the crowdfunding tool is the basis of other regulatory changes, such as the following:

- The enlargement of the list of so-called managers of rights to SGRs, SICAFs and SICAVs, limited to the offer on portals of UCITS shares, which mainly invest in SMEs

- The extension to all SMEs constituted in forms of limited liability companies of the simplified quota circulation mechanism provided by the paragraphs 2-bis. of the article 100-ter of the Consolidated Law on Finance

- The repeal of the obligation for intermediaries to register the shares held on behalf of the subscribers (or buyers) directly to them, after 2 years of the loss of innovative start-up qualification

The expansion of the crowdfunding subjects, on the other hand, required a strengthening of measures to protect investors. In this sense, the legislator has deemed it necessary to increase powers of the Consob of control over the activity of the portals. In particular, Consob calls the managers, directors, statutory auditors and personnel, requests the communication of data and of information and may request the communication of data and information and the transmission of deeds and documents, fixing the relative terms, and may also carry out inspections (article 50-quinquies, paragraph 6, of the Consolidated Law on Finance).

A further novelty in the discipline of equity crowdfunding concerns, directly or indirectly, the implementation in Italy of Markets in Financial Instruments Directive (MiFID II). In fact, although operating under the regime of exemption from the MiFID, the operation of the portals, precisely by virtue of the provisions of Directive 2014/65 (for "exempt" companies), was subjected to the application of more stringent conditions.

In particular, it regards the following profiles:

- The obligation for equity crowdfunding portals to adhere to system of indemnification to protect investors or taking out an insurance policy for professional responsibility that guarantees protection equivalent to clients according to the criteria established by Consob through its regulation (article 50-quinquies, paragraph 3, of the Consolidated Law on Finance)

- The obligation for portals to develop a more rigorous and detailed policy on conflicts of interest

- The delegation to Consob for the adoption of internal systems of reporting infringements (whistleblowing, i.e., specific procedures for reporting of the facts that could constitute violations of the regulations governing the activity done)

In particular, with reference to point (a), the article 3 of MiFID II states that: "member States shall require persons exempt from this Directive pursuant to paragraph 1 of this Article to be covered by an investor-compensation scheme recognised in accordance with Directive 97/9/EC. Member States may allow investment firms not to be covered by such a scheme provided they hold professional indemnity insurance where, taking into account the size, risk profile and legal nature of the persons exempt in accordance with paragraph 1 of this Article, equivalent protection to their clients is ensured".

With regard to management of the conflict of interest (point (b)), Consob strengthened the regulations already contained in Consob Regulation no. 18592 of 2013, requiring portals to communicate to customers the nature and sources of conflicts of interest, in the event that the measures adopted were not sufficient to exclude the risk of damaging interests of the same. In this perspective, the introduction of an ad hoc regime for the offer on the portal of quotas or shares issued by the same manager or by subsidiary/controlling companies (c.d. "autocollocamento") must be read, too.

With reference to the granting to Consob of the proxy to adopt the implementing provisions of the article 4-undecies of the Consolidated Law on Finance in the matter of whistleblowing (point (c)), it derives from the desire to extend the obligation to adopt internal reporting procedures for offenses, provided by article 71 of the Directive 2013/36/UE, also to those who provide investment services, even if exempt from the MiFID.

Finally, it is important to point out that, during the revision of the Crowdfunding Regulation, Consob has decided to reduce, only in specific cases, the threshold of financial instruments that must be signed, in relation to each offer, by qualified investors. Specifically, there is a lower threshold—equal to 3% (and not 5%)—for offers made by SMEs with financial statement certification, relative to the last 2 years prior to the offer, prepared by an auditor. This is a change made by Consob to the outcome of the consultation process, at the request of the market. In the consultation document, in fact, the 5% threshold had been confirmed, despite the difficulties (very) often encountered by the portals in meeting this requirement. Also driven by the sector operators, Consob has decided to introduce a reduced threshold at least for larger companies, for which a technical situation is available.

In conclusion, the frequent regulatory interventions have constituted an element of instability for the sector and, therefore, a brake on the development of crowdfunding operations.

4. Funds collection methods

Crowdfunding has had a great following in Italy and in the world as it manages to create a direct relationship between the author of the project and potential investors. The platform allows to give visibility to the borrower's project, thus facilitating the collection of funds.

Most platforms can operate according to two very specific collection models. These can have a decisive influence on the success of entering the project on the portal because they provide completely distinct features and modus operandi.

The first model is represented by "all-or-nothing." Its application starts from the assumption that the borrower inserts a target in his project, or indicates the sum of money to be obtained within a given period of time. During this period of time, the platform does not make any financial transactions vis-à-vis the author of the project, despite payments from investors. This is due to the fact that the transfer of the collected money is conditional on the achievement of the target: in fact, from the beginning it is established that, in the event that the objective is not achieved, all the sums of conferred money will be returned to the lenders.

On the contrary, the second collection model, called "keep-it-all" or "take-it-all" depending on the portals, provides the payment of the loans obtained regardless of whether or not the target is reached. Using this method, the proposer can periodically obtain payments from the platform or receive the credit at the end of the timing. Certainly the choice of "take-it-all" is preferred above all in cases where the sum of money determined upstream is very high or if the project is risky. To promote the use of this latter collection model, there is also the possibility of obtaining benefits if the target is exceeded; in this case, the model is called "all-and-more" or "everything and more." The incentives may consist, for example, in the exemption from the payment of the commissions withheld by the platform for the service offered or by the payment of the registration fee to the site [15].

There are different types of crowdfunding, both in terms of method and purpose.

In the literature, the "classic" models are: social lending (peer-to-peer lending), equity-based crowdfunding, reward-based crowdfunding, donation-based crowdfunding and royalty-based crowdfunding [9, 12, 16]. Four of these models (equity-based crowdfunding, reward-based crowdfunding, donation-based crowdfunding and social lending) have been codified—for the first time—in the 2012 Massolution Report [17].

In recent years, alongside these classic models, there have been new crowdfunding models that are civic, corporate and do-it-yourself. Invoice trading, real estate, recurring crowdfunding and energy crowdfunding have recently been added to them.

4.1 Classic models

In this section, the classic models are illustrated. In particular, they are social lending (peer-to-peer lending), equity-based crowdfunding, reward-based crowdfunding, donation-based crowdfunding and royalty-based crowdfunding.

4.1.1 Social lending

Social lending is one of the most widespread and articulated forms of crowdfunding. It is a money loan also known as peer-to-peer lending (P2P). Unlike other collection methods, social lending involves the direct or indirect signing of a real debt contract with the persons who request financial resources that is the promoter of the crowdfunding project. Essentially, it is an alternative to a bank loan, with the difference that investors have direct credit toward their financed subjects, contrary to savers who deposit their money in a bank that will provide credit, having so a credit toward the bank.

Generally, social lending is preferred by families, non-profit associations, SMEs, which, when registering on the platform, provide all the information needed to establish their creditworthiness. In the social lending to each subject that requests a loan, a rating is assigned, based on the data present in the central risk (as in the normal credit market). To supplement this information, social media opinions are also generally considered, such as reviews of companies that are already started and that offer services. Only if the creditworthiness is valuated adequate, the financial request will be included in the platform. The lower the rating, the higher the interest rate is required based on the risk-return ratio. Therefore, the critical success factor of the platform is the ability to correctly estimate creditworthiness in order to minimize the risk of insolvency. In this regard, some portals have created protection funds in the event of non-compliance; this on the one hand expands the protection of investors, and on the other hand, it increases the costs for the financed subjects.

It is possible to opt for one of the following hypotheses:

1. The borrower indicates upstream the reference interest rate for the calculation of the interest share to be paid. On the other hand, investors offer in a competitive auction the percentage of capital they are willing to cover and the relative interest rate. When the requested quota has been reached, the debtor will pay the interest by making an average of the rates offered, weighted on the basis of the different items.

2. The interest rate is chosen neither by the borrower nor by the investors, but it is determined in relation to the rating of the taxable person in the contractual relationship.

3. The lenders do not have the possibility to choose who to allocate their credit to because the platform automatically selects the borrowers, respecting always the duration of the loan and the risk-return profile indicated ex ante. Generally, to compensate the impossibility of choosing the recipient of the credit, the platforms provide the establishment of guarantee funds, managed by third companies, the amount of which is determined on the basis of expected losses.

4. Investors indirectly finance the project by buying investment funds, most often listed on the stock exchange.

In all the cases described therein, the typical risks of the active position of the obligatory report (credit, liquidity and interest rate risk) remain at the lender and this may compromise, in some occasions, the level of reliability of the platform. To remedy, for example, the hypothesis of an increase in liquidity risk, which would entail a significant loss of confidence by potential creditors, the possibility of transferring the contract in itinere is usually proposed, making use of secondary markets [7].

The investment on social lending platforms can take place—typically—in two ways. The first involves the subdivision of a single loan into shares (generally of the same value) that investors can purchase independently on the portals. The second mode, on the other hand, involves the presence of portals that create loan portfolios with the same risk-return ratio that can be purchased pro-rata. It is also possible that the money of the lenders is divided into several portfolios with the same risk-return ratio, so as to reduce—even more—the potential risk of insolvency. In addition to this, some platforms also offer the possibility of reselling their credits to third parties, so as to return more quickly than the investment, so creating a secondary market. It is customary to distinguish between two main business models for social lending: direct and widespread. The two types differ depending on the fact that investors decide, directly and independently, where to allocate their resources (direct model) or indirectly through the platform (common model).

Since the end of 2017, the use of social lending has begun to spread for the payment by installments on e-commerce sites. In Italy, aggregated data only for loans for natural persons are diffused and these loans vary from a minimum of € 250.00 to a maximum of € 40,000.00. A research by the Politecnico of Milan [18] found that access to this channel is generally more expensive than that in which credit institutions operate.

4.1.2 Equity-based crowdfunding

Equity-based crowdfunding is one of the tools most used by start-ups and SMEs, which, especially in the start-up phase of a business, find it difficult to access subsidized loans or government grants, although they have the required requirements. It assumes the role of equity-based when, as a consideration for the financing activity, the conferment of a participation title within a company is present. This type of crowdfunding guarantees the possibility of addressing to a more or less wide audience, thanks to which the initial feedback on their entrepreneurial activity can be seen from the initial phase. Furthermore, the only costs that the promoters will have to pay, using the platform, are mostly those linked to the commissions to be paid to the portal and to the cost of keeping the restricted current account. However, the start-up or the SME must operate in such a way as to create an intense flow of communication with the outside if it wants to reach a larger number of investors. It is possible, for example, by releasing interviews, publishing its objectives also on social media, participating or sponsoring some events of significant importance. This is still an extraordinary transaction concerning the collection of new risk capital, and therefore there are some repercussions on the level of patrimonial and administrative rights, because the company structure changes according to the number of interested investors.

As already highlighted, in Italy, Consob issued a regulation in 2013 in which the limits and obligations to be respected regarding the equity-based crowdfunding were indicated. In particular, Consob has set a maximum bid amount of 5,000,000 euros, which can only be collected through the use of the portals registered in the special section of the register of managers. Managers are obliged to provide all information regarding SMEs or start-ups registered in the portal, with a focus on individual offers, thus detailing the business plan, the curriculum vitae of the founding members and the risks associated with equity-based activities crowdfunding.

This is realized to reduce information asymmetries and to allow investors to make a rational and informed investment choice of their capital. Consob has also provided for a "conscious investment path" reserved for potential investors, thanks to which they can know the most difficult aspects linked to the activity of granting credit. Moreover, for non-professional lenders, the Regulation provides for the recognition of the right of withdrawal to be exercised even without the existence of a particular reason and without the payment of penalties. However, this right can only be exercised in the 7 days following the membership order.

4.1.3 Reward-based crowdfunding

With the term reward-based crowdfunding, a particular online fundraising method is outlined that envisages, on the one hand, the payment by the investor of a small amount of money, and on the other hand the payment by the taker of a reward. This reward can be various, but in general, it cannot include financial compensation. The borrower is therefore obliged to provide the service or to proceed with paying the reward, because, in the event of non-fulfillment of this promise, the project could lose credibility to the lenders; however, some platforms are used to frame the consideration of the subject as a real obligation to perform, from which the typical effects provided by the law arise. Over the years, reward-based crowdfunding has become widespread above all in the artistic field, in which the promoters of cultural and musical projects found the necessary funds for the realization of the projects, providing in exchange various benefits, such as free tickets, public mentions during the events, preemptive fees for the purchase of tickets.

Over time, it has become a perfect substitute of equity because it allows to obtain liquidity without altering the corporate structure. At the same time, it has also become an alternative way to get answers from consumers on new projects to carry out: in this case, the form is defined pre-placement, most often linked to a pre-order operation with the goal to get feedback from potential customers even before the product is launched. Even some large multinationals like Nike and Coca-Cola have decided to use this tool, lightening the workload traditionally entrusted to marketing companies. This method is particularly preferred by start-ups of young people and by SMEs in the constitution phase, which wish to obtain information on the outlet market [15].

In Italy, the reward-based crowdfunding model is associated to three legal categories. The first is the pre-order that is an operation that the Civil Code defines as e-commerce, which concerns a future sale that is perfected with the realization of the good. The second, again on the basis of the Civil Code, is a modal donation (art. 793 c.c.) with which the donor requires the donor to perform an obligation to his advantage or for the benefit of third parties. The third type is the royalty crowdfunding, which will be discussed below.

4.1.4 Donation-based crowdfunding

In the case of donation-based crowdfunding, those who decide to contribute financially to a campaign take on the role of real donors, due to the fact that the financing of the activity, regardless of the amount, is carried out in the form of good work. For this reason, most of the time no budget is foreseen and, in addition, there is often no return for the benefactor, who will find satisfaction only in having participated to the realization of a project whose main objective is a "good cause."

Within this model, it is possible to distinguish two different sub-typologies according to the end pursued: some projects in fact concern private or personal spheres, while others are aimed to third parties without the purpose of profit. At the base, therefore, there is the will to support through a kind of online collection the realization of an objective that brings advantage to a part of a community, which can include not only subjects with particular social or economic problems, but also the inhabitants of a circumscribed one territorial area (e.g., public events). An example of donation-based crowdfunding, even for no humanitarian purposes, was recorded in the political sphere and, in particular, during the election period in the United States of America: on this occasion, a targeted campaign was promoted to the re-election of President Barack Obama [15].

In Italy, the donation-based crowdfunding legislation generally refers to the donation regulation contained in the Civil Code.

4.1.5 Royalty-based crowdfunding

Royalty-based is a type of crowdfunding in which an initiative is financed, receiving part of the profits in return. Whoever launches the crowdfunding campaign offers quotas of future earnings of the project for which it requires funding. Royalty-based crowdfunding consists in the sale by the owner of the business and in the simultaneous purchase by the investor of a portion of the revenues that will be generated by future sales of the economic activity. Investors can therefore obtain a regular income guaranteed by sales and, at the same time, the owners of the business, remaining the only owners of the business, maintain full control over the performance of the business. However, royalties must be deducted from turnover and therefore they add costs to the business. For this reason, royalty-based crowdfunding is mainly recommended to all those activities that have high profit margins.

In Italy, the discipline, in general, is referable to the rules on the association in participation (articles 2549 ss. of the Civil Code), in which "those who finance participate in quote to the profits generated." In fact, the lender, in this particular crowdfunding model, receives the royalties based on the amount invested, which may concern, for example, copyright, intellectual property rights, patents, licenses, registered trademarks, etc.

Some authors believe that royalty-based crowdfunding is a sub-category of reward-based, already used in the music sector for the management of copyright on songs [19].

4.2 New models

In this section, new crowdfunding models are discussed. In particular, they are civic crowdfunding, corporate crowdfunding, do-it-yourself, energy crowdfunding, recurring crowdfunding, real estate crowdfunding and invoice trading.

4.2.1 Civic crowdfunding

The civic crowdfunding is a bottom-up financing method in which public works and projects are financed by the citizens themselves. This tool is able to favor the development of the territory and of the communities since both, individuals and social organizations, can give life to civic-based projects that benefit the entire community.

The civic crowdfunding increases the sense of belonging of citizens to their territory, favoring transparency through a more effective allocation of funds. In fact, citizens can follow and access all the information (both online and directly on the territory) relating to the projects they intend to support, starting from the first stages of development until their complete realization. Furthermore, with civic crowdfunding, public administrations and local authorities can create close relationships with citizens and SMEs test citizens' interest in each new project and invest their budget in those projects considered important by citizens themselves.

The civic crowdfunding can be of the type donation, reward or do-it-yourself, but it can be developed in the forms equity-based e-social lending, too.

In Italy, a bureaucracy that is too complex and sometimes difficult to overcome is a problem for this type of crowdfunding and this is making some civic crowdfunding projects impossible. There are also difficulties regarding payment systems: many of the potential donors are often in difficulty having to pay money through a crowdfunding campaign and they seem to prefer traditional channels, such as—for example—bank transfers.

Recently, the civic crowdfunding has become an increasingly useful tool for the implementation of match-funding projects, in which cooperation between bottom-up funding portals and public authorities is provided for the benefit of all local communities.

In 2018, in Italy, the civic-based and match-funding projects have raised a total of around 4 million euros [20]. The initiatives were mainly promoted by the public administrations themselves, also through partnerships with local entities, which increasingly play an important role for the administrations in the operational implementation of the projects. The combination between public administrations and civic crowdfunding is certainly an interesting phenomenon, given the commonality between the elements at the base of crowdfunding and the values to which the public administrations are called to respond: community involvement, transparency of funding, ease of access and dissemination, system innovation, issues of collective interest, bottom-up participation.

4.2.2 Corporate crowdfunding

The corporate crowdfunding is a type of financing of the crowd, which, starting from the concept of Corporate Social Responsibility, can help companies design products/services, directly involving customers in this phase.

In general, it can be of the type donation, do-it-yourself and reward. This is a typical Italian phenomenon. However, the mistake that the platforms often make is to orientate too much toward companies, while companies must be the result of work being done within the platform and not the opposite.

4.2.3 Do-it-yourself

The do-it-yourself is a form of crowdfunding that allows to create a campaign within the site of the organization, without switching to another specific crowdfunding platform. In essence, the do-it-yourself crowdfunding refers to customized campaigns developed on independent sites in line with the identity of the project. Generally, the do-it-yourself can be civic, corporate, donation, pre-purchase and reward.

4.2.4 Energy crowdfunding

Energy crowdfunding is a form of funding from below in the green and renewable energy sector. The purpose is the implementation of sustainable projects and energy transition, in order to reduce dependence on fossil-based fuels and contribute to the development of infrastructures and innovative technologies.

The interest toward this form of crowdfunding is demonstrated by the growth in Europe of energy cooperatives and participatory models for the development of investments in renewable energy. As in the context of energy cooperatives, crowdfunding platforms involve citizens and stakeholders allowing them to participate, invest and benefit economically from investments in the energy sector.

Over 90% of the active platforms are of financial type (crowdinvesting in equity and lending mode), that is, aimed at investing and raising capital. The rest of the platforms propose projects based on rewards in donation or reward mode.

The financial platforms propose projects defined, equity or community shares. By financing lending-based projects, investors lend their money in exchange for a future remuneration, which can sometimes be based on the sale of renewable energy produced through the project itself. The lending projects are differentiated according to the type of debt instrument offered (short- and long-term debt, mutual fund). In equity or community share projects, investors acquire shares in companies or cooperatives active in the production of clean energy, thus benefiting from dividends issued based on the economic performance of the underlying energy investment.

An Italian example of energy social lending is Edison Crowd, while an Italian equity-based company is Ecomill, which will soon be operational. There are examples of energy crowdfunding campaigns, too, such as some of those activated on WeAreStarting.

4.2.5 Recurring crowdfunding

Recurring crowdfunding is a type of fundraising that is donation-based or reward-based, which does not expire, unlike normal bottom-up funding campaigns.

In particular, in recurring crowdfunding, patrons contribute a recurring amount of money, either on a specific time period (like every month) or every time the creator makes something new (a new song, a new album, a new video, etc.). Therefore, it is a model adopted especially for editorial or artistic projects (ideal for managing subscriptions and for new content creators such as bloggers, freelancers, YouTubers, documentarians, journalists and artists who can generate a monthly financing for their work).

In Italy, this service was launched, for the first time, on 6 March 2018 by Produzioni dal Basso along the lines of the American platforms Patreon and Drip.

4.2.6 Real estate crowdfunding

The real estate crowdfunding is a type of collective loan for real estate investments. It allows investors, in exchange for a return on capital, to participate in the financing of a real estate project in a residential or commercial environment, such as the purchase of a property to be used for income, the restructuring of a property or the development of a greenfield project.

The real estate crowdfunding is a model attributable, on the basis of the currently operating portals, to equity crowdfunding or social lending. In the first case, the capital financed is divided into two components: equity and debt. Equity accounts for 65–70% of the investment and is divided as follows: 25–30% for the entrepreneur and 40% for the online 'crowd.' The remaining 30–35% of the amount is disbursed by a bank (debt) in the form of a loan, thus reducing the overall risk of the transaction. In the second case, that is, when the real estate crowdfunding uses social lending, the functioning mechanism is similar to that of this form of collective financing.

The real estate crowdfunding allows to solve some problems of the real estate investment, such as the following:

- The financing of a real estate project (even with low amounts of money) that allows to diversify the investment, allocating the capital in several real estate projects, in different geographical areas and on different types of properties

- The delegation of property management to the promoters

- The possible increase in the liquidity of investments, when the platforms of crowdfunding real estate allow to exchange their investment shares on a secondary market

In Italy, Walliance is the only Italian platform for equity crowdfunding specifically dedicated to real estate, while Housers is an online real estate crowdfunding platform, created and launched in Spain in 2015 and landed in Italy with an investment opportunity in Milan.

4.2.7 Invoice trading

The invoice trading allows businesses to sell individual invoices in order to free up cash, to an online community of investors. It replaces the traditional "invoice discounting" of the bank to support working capital. Investors advance the invoice amount, net of the required remuneration. The investors' remuneration is given by the difference between the liquidation value of the invoice and the relative purchase price [18].

The invoice trading takes place online through the platforms and the business model requires that the company interested to an invoice transfer submit the request to an invoice trading platform. The portal evaluates the proposals received on the basis of some indicators (such as creditworthiness) relating to all the operators involved and assigns a rating crossing the available data with those present in the databases of some providers such as Modefinance or Cerved Rating Agency. Once accepted, the invoice is published on the invoice trading platform.

There are three different buying mechanisms for investors, such as: upward bidding, competitive bidding or direct purchase by the platforms and securitization of the same through asset-backed securities.

In general, SMEs with difficulties in accessing the traditional banking channel resort to invoice trading. The SMEs use the advantages of the invoice trading, such as the speed with which the liquidity is paid to finance the working capital, without guarantees and without reporting to the Central Risk Office.

In Italy, the potential market of invoice trading exceeds 400 billion Euros.

5. Benefits and risks

The crowdfunding provides various indirect and non-financial benefits, too. First of all, it allows to understand if the entrepreneurial, social or cultural idea can be appreciated and shared by third parties. In fact, if the crowd is pushed to contribute in the first phase of the project, this means that the market will be well inclined to support it even later. Access to the crowd, which includes subjects with specific skills, is useful for obtaining professional feedback at low cost, too.

Furthermore, if it is evident that the project is supported on a large scale and the risk associated with the possible use of capital reduced, there will be greater chances that informal banks or investors (angel investors) will grant loans additional on better terms.

The crowdfunding can be used as a powerful marketing tool: it puts the attention of investors and potential customers on an innovative project even before it is implemented or concluded. Usually, the entrepreneur, or more generally the proposer, should start a campaign aimed to publicize the new service or product as best as possible, in order to reach a certain level of market interest in conjunction with the launch. In this way, it is possible to focus the attention of consumers in a completely innovative way, whose main purpose is to raise capital.

However, crowdfunding is not easy to implement, as it requires a long and thorough preparatory process in order to minimize the risks that may negatively affect the borrower and investors.

First of all, it is necessary to consider the hypothesis in which the objective is not fully achieved. In the case of the "all-or-nothing" model, failure to reach the set amount obliges the proposer to return the amount collected up to that point. For this reason, it is advisable to analyze the market and design an excellent strategy to ensure a high resonance of the project. If the platform allows it, the "keep-it-all" model is more secure.

Another widespread problem concerns the underestimation of costs, which could vary in itinere, as for example in the case of equity crowdfunding: following new share issues, in fact, there are additional administrative costs often not to be considered in the business plan.

A similar case concerns the information flow; before, during and after the fundraising phase, there must be a subject who carefully follows each step and, if the promoter does not have competence in the matter, the assignment to third parties could lead to costs not underestimate. The problem arises from the beginning when in the most complex forms of collection, such as social lending and equity crowdfunding, it is important to establish clauses that provide rights and obligations for both parties.

With regards to this, it is necessary to analyze thoroughly the concrete implications deriving from the recognition of significant rights to investors, and to avoid granting these rights with the sole purpose of making the proposal more attractive. Indeed, the failure to comply with the clauses would lead potential investors to lose confidence in the project. Therefore, it is important to consider also the complaints, which must be managed in the best possible way in order to prevent unpleasant situations from generating much more serious repercussions.

Furthermore, the fact that at the moment a national law on crowdfunding has not yet been enacted, which may be able to specifically regulate the various possible cases, raises the risk that the participants may inadvertently implement unlawful behavior. For this reason, it is advisable to carefully and meticulously refer to all the legislative texts issued to date both on the national and community territory.

The investors can lose interest in the project at any moment, without giving any notice, too. Specifically, in the case of donation or reward crowdfunding, the cessation of the interest manifests itself with the blocking of any future forms of financing; on the contrary, in the equity crowdfunding, the investors sell their share to other subjects interested. For this reason, it is important to be ready right away to up and down funding flows and to sudden changes in the social structure [19].

There are other types of risks on online projects, together with those of a financial and legal nature, for example, the possibility that the project is not successful. In this case, the promoter has a reputation damage because the promoter does not turn to a credit institution, but a heterogeneous plurality of people. For this reason, the failure to achieve the goals will be seen as a real public failure.

Moreover, even the possibility that the borrower fails to fulfill the promises made within the established terms, despite the successful collection of funds, is a risk. On the contrary, the timeliness and the perfect correspondence between when planned and when realized will allow the promoter to improve his reputation [2].

Finally, there is the risk of turning to fraudulent platforms or those unable to protect the rights of participants. In fact, the proponent exposes an innovative idea online, which becomes public knowledge. For this reason, the manager should develop a system of protection aimed at avoiding plagiarism [19].

6. Case study: crowdfunding on Produzioni dal Basso Italian platform

In Italy, there are several crowdfunding platforms currently active (**Table 1**).

Among these, Produzioni dal Basso is the oldest. Founded in 2005, it allows those who want and need to get funds for a business projects, to publish their idea

Platform name	Crowdfunding typology	Note
1 Caffè	Donation-based	It is a non-profit association that supports solidarity campaigns.
Actionworld	Equity-based	It is aimed at investors who are attentive to the new investment methods proposed by the markets.
BacktoWork24	Equity-based	It finances small businesses and start-ups.
Be Crowdy	Reward-based	It regards cultural and artistic projects.
Blender.loans	Lending-based	It aims to reduce the cost of debt.
BookaBook	Reward-based	It is dedicated to the publication of unpublished books.
BoomStarter	Reward-based	It gives the possibility to participate in the BoomContest, which gives an additional sum of money to the winner.
Borsa del Credito	Lending-based	It is a marketplace-lending that credits funds within 3 days of the request.
BuonaCausa	Ibrida	It promotes socially based ideas.
Clubdealonline.com	Equity-based	It allows SMEs and investors to find a controlled and secure counterpart.
Com-Unity	Reward&Donation-based	It aims to create synergies and collaborations for the development of new ideas.
Concrete	Equity-based	It is dedicated to real estate projects.
CrowdFundMe	Equity-based	It is based on connecting investors with start-ups and SMEs seeking funds. It is listed on the Italian Stock Exchange
Crowndarts	Reward-based	Events and shows are funded at national and European level.
De Rev	Reward-based	It is dedicated to innovative start-ups.
Distribuzioni Dal Basso	Reward-based	It supports the circulation of cultural works released under the Creative Commons License.
Donordonee	Reward&Donation-based	It elects 6 members a day, allowing them to realize their ideas.
Doorway	Equity-based	It is founded by four business angels, and it has set itself the goal of financing start-ups and creating an offline private market.
Ecomill	Equity-based	It is dedicated to high-level social sustainability campaigns.
Eppela	Reward-based	It is dedicated to any type of project (art, cinema, technology, etc.).
For Italy	Reward-based	It aims to preserve the Italian cultural heritage.
Fundera	Equity-based	It is dedicated to the cleantech sector.
Funditaly	Donation-based	It is based on the 'cooperative' crowdfunding, and it allows the investor to become a supporter of all the projects on the platform.
Giffoni Innovation Hub	Reward-based	It is dedicated to cultural-artistic start-ups.
Gigfarm	Reward-based	It finances artists and promoters, helping them to make concerts.
GoFundMe	Ibrida	It supports campaigns directed to support medical expenses and to help countries in a state of emergency.
Greenfunding	Reward&Donation-based	It finances green-economy projects.

Platform name	Crowdfunding typology	Note
Investi-Re	Equity-based	It is a platform dedicated to innovative start-ups/ SMEs
Kendoo	Reward-based	It is dedicated to digital projects (websites, social media, e-commerce, app, etc.).
Land2Land	Reward-based	It is dedicated to projects related to agriculture and gastronomy.
Let us donation	Donation-based	Its slogan is "Profit supports No-Profit."
Meridonare	Donation-based	It supports cultural and social projects for Southern Italy.
Microcreditartistique	Reward-based	It is specialized in contemporary art.
Motusquo.it	Lending-based	It offers lower interest rates for borrowers and higher returns for employers.
Muum Lab	Equity-based	It promotes fundraising for agro-industry, real estate and energy projects.
Prestiamoci	Lending-based	It offers personal loans online from private individuals.
Produzioni dal Basso	Ibrida	It promotes self-produced projects, without intermediation and without particular access requirements.
Schoolraising	Reward-based	It raises funds for school projects.
Sea-Crowd	Ibrida	It supports campaigns for the realization of ideas related to the nautical world (naval engineering, protection of the marine environment, fish, etc.).
ShinyNote	Donation-based	It is direct to promote solidarity campaigns.
Smartika	Lending-based	It is one of the first 10 platforms identified by Forbes for social lending in the EU.
Sport Supporter	Reward-based	It is dedicated to sports campaigns.
Starsup	Equity-based	It favors the collection of risk capital for start-ups with a high rate of innovation.
Starteed	Reward-based	It also offers the possibility of crowdcreation, improving ideas and projects.
Terzo Valore	Ibrida	It is part of the Intesa Sanpaolo group, and it allows the employers to assume the role of donor and/or creditor.
The Funding Spirit	Reward-based	It is dedicated to sportive and cultural projects.
Triboom	Reward-based	It is dedicated to sports projects, substantiated directly by the fans.
Ulule	Reward-based	It is born in France, and it is also very active in Italy. It has funded more than 24,000 projects.
Universitiamo	Donation-based	It collects funding for university scientific research.
Werealize	Reward-based	It finances projects related to the world of design.
WithYouWeDo	Reward-based	It is created by Italian company leader in telecommunications sector (TIM), and it raises funds for environmental, social and innovative projects.
WoopFood	Reward-based	It finances projects directed to enhance Italian food excellence.

Source: own processing.

Table 1.
Principal crowdfunding platforms currently active in Italy.

on the dedicated website. In accordance with the provisions of national and EU regulations, it is possible to include cultural and social projects, or relating to the launch of innovative products on the market.

Over the last decade, the platform has contributed to the creation of more than 2600 projects, allowing their promoters to raise over 6 million euros. The affirmation of the platform, especially on the Italian market was also supported by the partnership with several institutions and companies, including Banca Etica, a bank specialized in the field of ethical and sustainable finance, with the aim of facilitating access to credit and financial inclusion of people who are unbanked.

The collaboration between Banca Etica and Produzioni dal Basso platform consists mainly in the publication of periodic tenders, to which the holders of ideas conforming to the indications of the call (e.g., tenders for the financing of female entrepreneurial projects) can participate to obtain, together with the funds collected through the platform, funds provided by the bank to achieve specific collection targets.

Depending on the area of reference, it is possible to select other partners of significant importance such as Arci, Fastweb4School, Infinity, Telethon Foundation and ENPA, which give greater prestige to one's idea. In this way, it is possible to obtain a more effective sponsorship.

The Produzioni dal Basso portal provides four different ways to raise funds.

The first mode is called "collect all" and can be used for any type of project, regardless of nature and objectives. It reports the same characteristics of the "keep-it-all" combined with the methods provided by the reward-based crowdfunding. At the time of entering the project, the proposer will have to provide one or more types of reward to be sent to the lender when the funds are mobilized. In relation with the offered service, Produzioni dal Basso holds a 5% fee on the money collected, to which are added the costs related to the chosen payment method, indicated later. In order to access the "collect all" mode, information is needed regarding the timing, that is, the persistence of the project on the platform (max 365 days), and the indication of the budget necessary for the realization of the idea.

The second mode is the so-called "simple donation," comparable to the donation-based crowdfunding. This type is used particularly for altruistic projects and is directed toward lenders motivated by the desire to contribute to the realization of an idea that can improve collective well-being or of particular categories, without getting any kind of reward in return. In this case, Produzioni dal Basso provides a 3% deduction on the amount collected. In the "simple donation," the author is required to indicate only the timing.

In the "recurring donation," the third collection method, the lender undertakes to contribute periodically to the realization of the project, renewing the financing automatically, usually every 30 days. In this case, the fee is 3% and is calculated on each transaction, while the forecast of the reward is at the discretion of the borrower. In the "recurring donation," the indication of timing is not necessary.

"All or nothing" is the last expected mode, perfectly adherent to the "all- or- nothing" model described previously. The borrower receives the funding collected only if the target has been reached by term established (maximum 120 days). Also in this case, the sending of a reward and a simultaneous withholding of 5% by the site are planned.

Finally, fundraising on Produzioni dal Basso uses two payment methods: PayPal and LemonWay. In the case of PayPal, there is a 3.4% commission on the donated amount and a tax of 0.35 euro, which the payment system automatically holds for each transaction. In the case of the use of the payment institution LemonWay, for each transaction, there is a fee equal to 0.8% (increased by 0.15 euro in the case of bank transfer) or a deduction of 0.6% (increased by 0.15 euro if the loan is made by credit card) [21].

6.1 A simulation of crowdfunding project for an Italian Foundation

Crowdfunding, as analyzed in literature [2, 4, 7, 19, 22], is a tool used both by individuals (including informal groups) and by organizations of various kinds, such as companies, foundations and associations.

In this section, a simulation of crowdfunding project for an Italian Onlus Foundation is carried out.

It is hypothesized that the Onlus Foundation, that deals with the management of educational and housing services for children and single or underage mothers with children, uses the crowdfunding in order to obtain resources for the realization of a project aimed at diversifying activities and at supporting adolescents in conditions of social hardship. To this purpose, the study is aimed at evaluating the opportunity for the foundation to make use of the Produzioni dal Basso platform, carrying out a simulation of the steps necessary for inserting the project on the portal, based on the needs expressed by the non-profit organization.

After identifying the key points of the project and the objectives pursued by the foundation, the simulation starts with the hypothetical registration of the foundation on the portal and the indication of the personal data relating to the representative of the institution (name, surname, e-mail address, date of birth, country of origin and residence). Therefore, it is necessary to draw up a brief description of the activity carried out by the institution: the foundation manages three activities, namely an educational community for minors, a daytime socio-educational center for minors and a housing community for pregnant women and single or underage mothers with children, and it is born with the aim of offering contexts that can help the minors grow and be formed, following individual and group paths. In this way, by inserting the guests in contexts similar to domestic-family ones, with a constant presence of educators and other professionals appropriate to the case, the foundation contributes to overcoming the inconvenience that afflicts parents and children in difficulty, and helping to pursue social objectives of essential importance for the community and for the surrounding area, considering that the foundation is linked to the activities of the competent children's court. The registration ends with acceptance of the terms and conditions and subsequent validation of the account via e-mail.

After logging on to the platform, the simulation continues with the drafting of the project in the section of the platform called: "Start collecting funds," in which it is necessary to choose the collection method among the four available. In the specific case of the foundation, the most suitable are that of the "collect all" and the "simple donation." The first allows to set up a budget, which indicates the amount of funds necessary for the realization of the project, with the addition of an incentive for those who decide to contribute. The second mode involves lower commissions (3% compared to 5% of the "collect all"), and the possibility of saving costs related to the production and shipment of the reward.

As regards the choice of the payment system, the simulation aimed to compare the different rates is provided in **Table 2**.

	PayPal	LemonWay	
Transaction costs	1.8% + 0.35€	Bank transfer	0.6% + 0.15€
		Credit card	0.8% + 0.15€

Source: see [21].

Table 2.
Rates for the different payment systems.

Another aspect of particular importance, emerged from the simulation, concerns the availability of payments and the related cost: if the availability of funds associated with an account (e.g., PayPal) is immediate, the amounts of money are transferred to the beneficiary from time to time, financing for financing. This means that the transaction costs are multiplied by the number of supporters and this could be very disadvantageous from an economic point of view. The situation is different if it chooses to use a payment institution that allows to create an electronic wallet, in which the sums of money collected will be temporarily conveyed. Afterwards, it will be possible to make a single withdrawal, when it is wished, giving rise to a single transaction cost.

When the preliminary phase is completed, the simulation continues with the drafting of the project. In this regard, the Produzioni dal Basso platform leaves complete freedom to the author, both in terms of form and content. For this reason, the borrower will be able to choose, in complete autonomy, how much and what information to enter in the text box, preferring those that can give more value to his business, cultural or social idea.

In order to implement a high-quality project, the simulation is based on the guidelines of the National Commission of Chartered Accountants and Accounting Experts, in order to provide the project with completeness and greater chances of success. To identify the most correct way of creating the project, it is useful to consider the prospective lender, who chooses to approach a project rather than another according to a standardized procedure, called in the technical language "funnel" that can be represented using the shape of an inverted funnel (**Figure 1**).

The possible investor/donor approaches the project thanks to the traffic building action carried out by the platform. In this way, he obtains a generic view of all the proposals on which it is possible to invest, but in order to learn more about the individual projects, he will have to read the short presentation of each one.

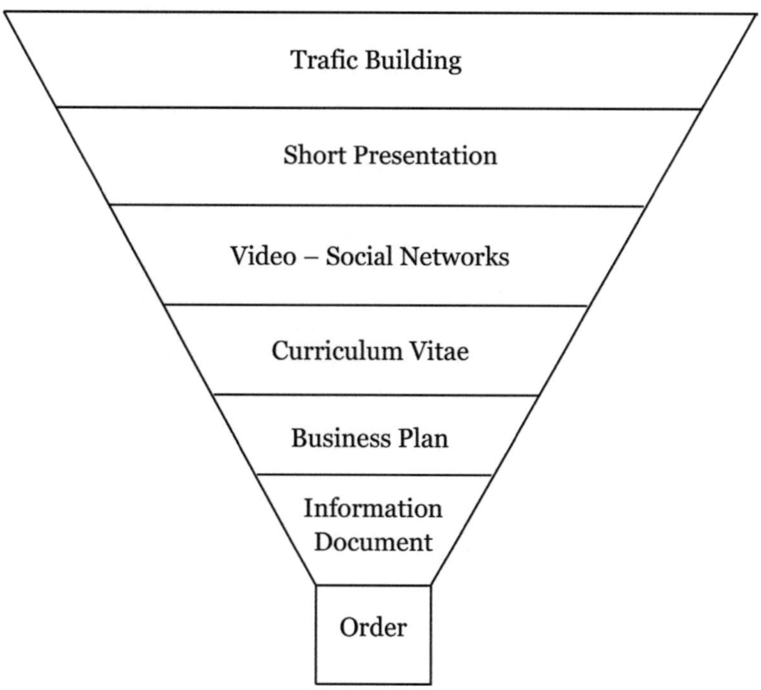

Figure 1.
Project selection process (funnel). Source: see [23].

The professional lender can therefore begin to build a summary idea of the project (requested funding, timing, progress, etc.), which will be completed later with the data obtained from the social networks linked to the project, from the multimedia files, from curriculum vitae of the promoters and from the business plan. In the specific hypothesis of equity crowdfunding, everything is summarized in an informative document, which can be consulted by the user before proceeding with the financing operation [15].

The inverted funnel shape is due to the fact that, in correspondence with each step, the number of possible lenders decreases; this screening is based on the interests and objectives indicated in the project. For this reason, it is necessary to pay particular attention to every single detail entered and published on the platform. Of great impact are the photos and videos, which represent one of the main communication tools on the web; they have a high synthetic power and allow to describe the "reason why" of the project in a few minutes. The promoter of the project therefore can insert in his landing page a "pitch," namely a presentation video of 2 or 3 minutes during which the advantages related to the realization of the project are highlighted.

6.2 A business plan hypothesis for the project

After general information, the simulation includes the preparation of the project business plan. In Italy, Consob has established that the business plan is mandatory only for equity-crowdfunding; however, the business plan, adapted to the collection method chosen by the foundation, can be an excellent cognitive tool for those who intend to support the project. The role of this document is in fact of fundamental importance especially because the project is sponsored at national, as well as local, level. For this reason, the supporters who are far from the territorial area in which the Onlus usually operates can use the business plan to know the scope of intervention, the strengths, the objectives achieved in the past and the reputation.

Therefore, within the business plan, the following questions must be answered: how is the foundation born? What are the objectives pursued? What activities will be carried out with the money raised? Are there any other sources of coverage for the project? Are the simulated economic-financial projections realistic and sustainable in the Long-term?

For the purposes of preparing the business plan, the self-assessment phase is of great importance. During this phase, the promoter must be able to determine the feasibility of the project and the necessary means for its realization, without resorting to optimistic visions. In addition, the business plan must contain information about the execution times and any costs that may arise later. Furthermore, three fundamental criteria must be met: consistency, since the statements must be faithful to the proposer's mission; reliability, since each data reported must to be demonstrated with appropriate documentation if requested; sustainability, that is, there must be a real connection between the budget included in the project and the expenses to be incurred. Furthermore, the language used must be simple and communicative, with the aim of retaining the investor/donor to the proposed idea.

The business plan for the project, carried out in accordance with the indications of the National Council of Chartered Accountants and Accounting Experts [23], is reported in **Box 1**.

6.3 A Canvas Model hypothesis for the project analyzed

The simulation was enriched subsequently with the preparation of a Canvas Model, that is, a useful tool to summarize immediately the information entered

Who we are: the mission of the Foundation is to face the discomfort of minors and their families, including them in a context in which they can find an environment appropriate to their age group and above all a point of reference for their personal growth.

The project: the goal of the Foundation is to redevelop and renovate a historic building, respecting the historical-artistic characteristics (such as the peculiar ceiling frescoes). Once the works will be completed, the building will have a new and important social function, as it will be used to build two apartments for adolescent minors, in compliance with the directives of Regional Regulation no. 4 of 18 January 2007. The goal is to provide a residential service for young people between the ages of 16 and 18, who have been temporarily or permanently removed from their family due to legal proceedings or interventions by the social workers. In addition, there will be the possibility of accommodating guests up to 25 years in the hypothesis that the educational and recovery path has not yet been completed. Two independent apartments will be built, one for boys and one for girls, each consisting of double bedrooms, bathrooms, a kitchen and a common living area where the minors can spend time together doing individual or group activities. The Foundation will also take care of facilitating relations with the family of origin, favoring the reintegration of minors. Moreover, the minors will follow a path aimed at the growth and coordination of typical activities of daily life, gradually assuming responsibility and autonomy, accompanied by the presence during the day and at night, of at least one qualified educator. The project aroused the interest of the entire community, which shares and supports the social work of the Foundation, and the project was supported by the Puglia Region, which decided to allocate 200,000 euros of funding for the redevelopment works of the building. The remaining 157,000 euros, equal to 44% of the entire budget (357,000 euros), will instead be provided by the Foundation and by those who decide to contribute.

Therefore, the call-to-action of the Foundation is aimed at acquiring donations outside the community and neighboring countries. Each contribution, even of a small amount, will help to pursue the social objective of giving to less fortunate children not only a daily life comparable to that of their peers, which can increase their confidence and their resilience, but also growth prospects, education and integration into the world of work.

The other projects carried out: the project represents the last link in the chain of support for adolescents in difficulty. In fact, the Foundation works in the social sphere for several years, assigning its organization to three important causes. In the vast structure in which it is located, there are:

a) a housing community for pregnant women and mothers with dependent children, with five bedrooms, a dining-living room and a kitchen. Guests are constantly supported by a coordinator and by educators.

b) an educational community for children from 3 to 18 years old, with comfortable and colorful bedrooms and a playroom for children to play. Here, 24-hour assistance is offered, thanks to the work of a coordinator and six educators with degrees in Education.

c) a day-time socio-educational center for children from 6 to 18 years, active during the whole school period in the afternoon, in daylight hours during the summer season. The space has been designed to accommodate up to 20 minors, which are followed by a coordinator, an animator and the staff required by the Regional Regulations. Outside the building, there are also 1800 square meters of garden and 500 square meters of outdoor gym.

Transparency: the Foundation strongly believes in transparency and, for this reason, provides any type of information regarding the project and its activities. To learn more about the budget items and the state of progress of the renovation work, it can consult the gallery, the official website or the Facebook page.

Economic and financial plan: the Foundation owns the property necessary to start the project (investment plan) and has identified the sources of funding (sources of coverage). With regard to returns, an income statement is prepared.

Box 1.
Draft of business plan for the foundation project.

in the business plan, highlighting the strengths. The model was created in accordance with the instructions provided by its creator, the scholar Alexander Osterwalder. In fact, the model has considered the evolution of the methods of exposure of entrepreneurial projects, which have become increasingly impactful and capable of quickly transmitting the key concepts underlying the business idea. Then, the project information is summarized in a single statement, divided into nine sections (**Figure 2**).

Although the Canvas Model can be reworked in its form at the discretion of the author, generally two macro-areas can be identified: the left one, concerning costs, and the right one, in which the modality of value creation is described. In each

Figure 2.
The canvas model. Source: see [23].

section, few and simple words are inserted, able in first to capture the attention of the user and then to transmit emotions.

Starting from the left, the first section concerns the "Key Partnerships": any successful project must rely on collaborations and alliances with external subjects, thanks to which it is possible to reduce costs. The "Key Activities" block summarizes the most important processes in such a way as to answer the question identified by Alexander Osterwalder: "What key activities are required for the value offered?". In the area of "Key Resources," all the factors in the absence of which the project could never get underway are indicated; for this reason, it is necessary to consider the strictly essential resources, including those of a non-financial nature. The left section concludes with the "Expenditure," in which the areas of intervention that envisage higher outgoing cash flows are indicated.

In the right area of the Canvas Model, there is a very important section, namely "Offered Value". This is the true heart of the prospectus: here, the lender/donor can discover the actual usefulness of the project. The information entered is both of a quantitative nature, expressing in terms of the volumes of the activity, and of a qualitative nature, concerning, in other words, the set of services offered.

Therefore, it is necessary to decide whether to approach through a so-called sartorial logic, building a more personal communication system, or whether to adopt the more detached and automated industrial logic. The information is entered in the "Relationship with customers" area. If in the previous section it is important to consider how the borrower intends to interact with third parties, in the "Channels" area, it is appropriate to provide all the elements useful to the user to understand how the project and the services will be brought to the knowledge of most people.

In the "Market Segment" area, the project creator will have to respond in a concise and immediate manner to the question: "What is the reference target?". Therefore, it is necessary to identify category of subjects to whom the main activity is aimed, thus selecting a precise slice of beneficiaries. The Canvas Model closes with a reference to "Revenue," considering the number of subjects who will use the products and/or services and the value of the services offered. Through this area, the lender can make a final and decisive assessment of the cost-effectiveness of the project by comparing it with the "Expenditure" section, which summarizes the costs associated with the services offered [23].

Following the guidelines of the National Council of Chartered Accountants and Accounting Experts on the Canvas Model, the simulation led to its realization. First the section on the "Key Partnerships" was compiled: in the particular case of the Foundation, the project received financial support from the Puglia Region, which contributed 56% of the total amount of the budget, that is, for an amount equal to 200,000 euros.

The project aims at the redevelopment of the historic building and, subsequently, at its preparation in such a way as to respect the provisions of the Regional Regulations for the two apartments: without this preliminary phase, the building would not be accessible and the value could never be created. For this reason, the words "Restructuring" and "Furnishing" have been included in the "Key Activities" section.

Considering that this is a humanitarian project, in the "Key Resources" area are indicated those human resources that predominantly interface with minors, such as educators and auxiliary personnel.

With regards the "Offered Value," the foundation focuses on welcoming minors, and then on a path that allows the guests of the structure to be able to grow and train. In the "Relationship with customers" section are inserted the two key concepts that are at the base of the project, namely "Support" and "Comprehension." The entire work of the Foundation, in fact, is aimed at guaranteeing help to all those who are welcomed inside the structure, with the right sensitivity that the situation requires.

Also the area dedicated to the "Channels" is important so that the project can be followed in its evolution. The Foundation will mainly use its official website, the Facebook page and the YouTube channel. The Canvas Model concludes with information regarding the main project beneficiaries. In this regard, in "Market Segment" adolescents aged 16 to 18 are identified as the target of reference. Article 51 of the Regional Regulation No. 4 of 18 January 2007 provides that the apartments are intended only for adolescents in this age group, except for those who have not been able to complete their training up to the age of majority. In the latter case, the stay is granted up to the 25th year.

Regarding the "Expenditure" section, the main cost centers are considered, above all relating to the realization of the project (for example, furniture, energy, heating and water system). Finally, in "Revenue," the main financial revenues are included, which, considering the typology of the proponent, are due to contributions made by public administrations, donations and especially the crowdfunding campaign [23].

In **Figure 3**, the Canvas Model is represented.

6.4 Some reflections

The simulation carried out shows the phases and steps necessary to start a crowdfunding activity and it allows to reflect on the advantages and criticalities of this instrument: in particular, it is useful to ask whether this instrument can replace the classic methods of finding funds or can only be used alongside them.

Although crowdfunding presents a less bureaucratic, more streamlined and innovative process, this form of finding financial resources shows in the same way some

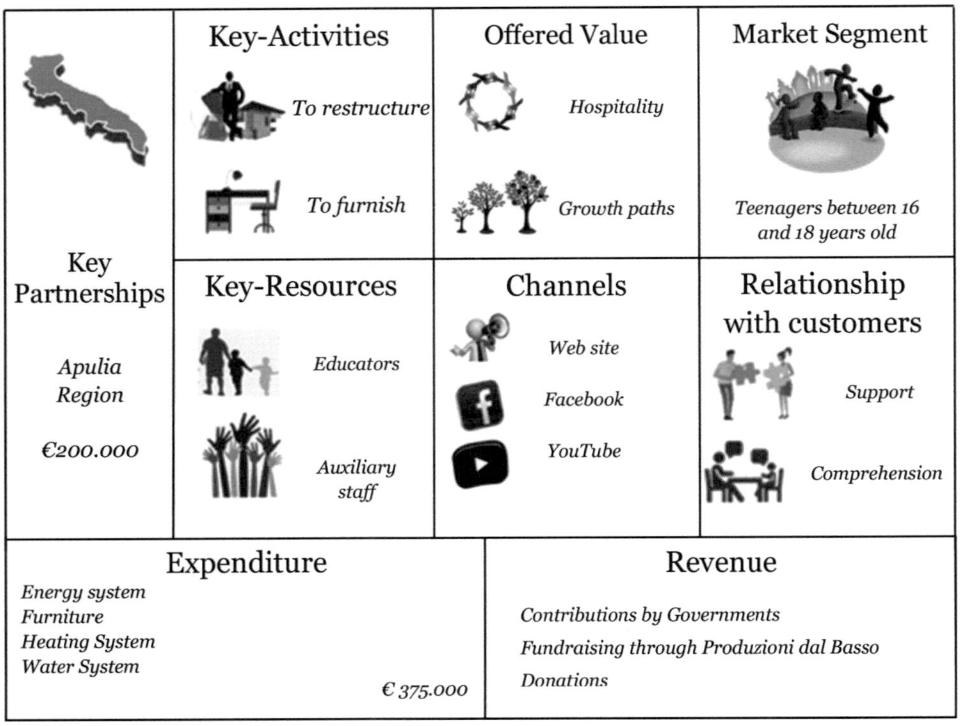

Figure 3.
The Canvas Model of the project. Source: own processing on [23] and CSVPadova.org.

critical points, first of all the uncertainty. The author of the project, in fact, at the time of publication cannot predict whether and to what extent he will find the crowd interest. In addition, it is not certain that the chosen network is willing to lend its support to the entrepreneurial, cultural or social idea in both financial and visibility terms. All these aspects, which manifest themselves in different ways depending on the chosen collection method, therefore designate crowdfunding as a supplementary and non-alternative channel, precisely because of its results that cannot be determined upstream.

In relation to the case study, if the inclusion of the project allows the Foundation to collect the funds necessary for its realization, it appears necessary, given the relevant amount to be collected, to operate with a different modality. In fact, to ensure that the structure receives the oblations useful for its sustenance, it is deemed necessary to resort to the "Recurring donation" method, thanks to which the institution will ensure for a certain period of time a flow of additional donations to those received previously or by other means.

Another relevant element for the choice of operating methods for the implementation of a crowdfunding project regards the aspect of the costs to be incurred. Beyond the possibility of creating a type of collection that does not provide for classic financial charges, in terms of interest to be paid, it is important to focus on the fees charged by operators that make it possible for financial resources to be transferred from the promoters to the lenders, as well as any costs associated with using the platform.

In a form of alternative financing to traditional channels, it is important that other types of costs do not grow in an excessive or disorderly manner, to the detriment of transparency and the social objective that this instrument pursues. In this context, the role of market supervisors, both nationally and internationally, is of crucial importance.

7. Conclusions

The crowdfunding has allowed the development of new fundraising methods and the support of new projects and business initiatives. The spread of crowdfunding in Italy depends on the fact that the Italian productive fabric is mostly made up of SMEs, which are starting to look with interest at alternative forms of financing.

In the European and international panorama, Italy is at the forefront of crowdfunding regulation: the legislator's goal was to encourage the exploitation of an alternative tool to encourage the financing of start-up companies, and consequently to support the economic growth and employment in Italy, where the use of traditional credit is often complicated, especially for young people.

In Italy, the most common types of crowdfunding are the social lending and the equity-based crowdfunding, which are diffused thanks to the improvement of the legislation. The largest number of platforms is donation/reward, that is, campaigns that collect funds through donations or in exchange for rewards.

Furthermore, the chapter illustrates a simulation of crowdfunding project for an Italian Foundation. The results of this simulation provide useful insights into reflections for policy makers and for potential entrepreneurs who intend to use crowdfunding to finance their business. The study can suggest further innovative analysis to strengthen the relationship between entrepreneurs and investors.

Acknowledgements

The authors would like to thank the Italian Onlus Foudation Saverio De Bellis and its president, law. Virginia Dibello, for providing useful data and information.

Conflict of interest

The authors declare no conflict of interest.

Author details

Rosa Adamo[1], Domenica Federico[2], Mariantonietta Intonti[3]*, Simona Mele[4] and Antonella Notte[2]

1 Department of Business and Law, University of Calabria, Arcavacata di Rende, Cosenza, Italy

2 Faculty of Economics, eCampus University, Novedrate, Como, Italy

3 Department of Economics and Finance, University of Bari "Aldo Moro", Largo Abbazia S. Scolastica, Bari, Italy

4 Ingegneria Starace, Bari, Italy

*Address all correspondence to: mariantonietta.intonti@uniba.it

References

[1] European Banking Authority. Opinion of the European Banking Authority on Lending-based. European Banking Authority. Crowdfunding. 2015

[2] Gagliardi G, Tonella A. Crowdfunding: Una nuova frontiera per la raccolta di capitali. Amministrazione e Finanza. 2013;**11**:51-60

[3] Schwienbacher A, Larralde B. Chapter 13: Crowdfunding of small entrepreneurial ventures. In: Cumming D, editor. The Oxford Handbook of Entrepreneurial Finance. Oxford: Oxford University Press; 2012

[4] Querci F. Il crowdfunding e l'innovazione nel finanziamento delle aziende. Bancaria. 2014;**10**:26-40

[5] Masters T. Marillion 'understood where the internet was going early on'. BBC. 01 September 2013

[6] Tremolda L. Crowdfunding, ma non per tutti. Il Sole 24 Ore. 16 September 2012

[7] Bofondi M. Il lending-based crowdfunding: Opportunità e rischi. Occasional Papers Bank of Italy. 2017;**375**:1-26

[8] Giudici G, Guerini M, Rossi-Lamastra C. Crowdfunding in Italy: State of the art and future prospects. Economia e Politica Industriale. 2013;**4**:173-188

[9] Piattelli U. Il crowdfunding in Italia. Una regolamentazione all'avanguardia o un'occasione mancata? Turin: Giappichelli Editor; 2013

[10] Castrataro D, Pais I, Analisi delle piattaforme italiane di crowdfunding. Italian Crowdfunding Network. 01 May 2014

[11] Guaccero A. La start-up innovativa in forma di società a responsabilità limitata: Raccolta del capitale di rischio ed equity crowdfunding. Banca Borsa e Titoli di credito. 2014;77:699-725

[12] Pais I, Peretti P, Spinelli C. Crowdfunding. La via Collaborativa All'imprenditorialità. Milan: Egea; 2014

[13] Starteed. Il Crowdfunding in Italia. Il report 2017. 2018. Available from: www.starteed.com

[14] Marabini F. L'intervento regolatorio in tema di crowdfunding. Per una teoria della regolazione. Diritto e Processo. 2015;**33**:5-52

[15] Iosio C, Valentinuz G. Fare Impresa Con Il Crowdfunding. IPSOA: Milan; 2016

[16] Quaranta G. Il crowdfunding. Diritto ed Economia dell'Impresa. 2017;**4**

[17] Crowdsourcing.org. Massolution Report. Crowdfunding Industry Report. Market Trends, Composition and Crowdfunding Platforms. 2012:31-36

[18] Politecnico of Milan. 2° Report italiano sul CrowdInvesting. Politecnico of Milan School of Management. 2017:40-45

[19] European Commission. Il Crowdfunding. Cosa è. Una guida per le piccole e medie imprese. European Union. 2015:9-11

[20] Starteed. Il Crowdfunding in Italia. Il Report 2018. 2019. Available from: www.starteed.com

[21] Produzioni dal Basso. Manuale d'uso. Creare, gestire, sostenere e comunicare una campagna di raccolta fondi. 2019. Available from: www.produzionidalbasso.com

[22] Visconti G. La disciplina del social lending dopo il codice del terzo

settore e la legge di bilancio per il 2018. Finanziamenti Su Misura—News. 2018;**04**:39-45

[23] National Council of Chartered Accountants and Accounting Experts. L'equity—Crowdfunding. Analisi sintetica della normativa e aspetti operativi. Position Papers. 2016;**08**:1-86

Chapter 16

Sales and Conformity of Goods: A Legal Discourse

Djieufack Roland

Abstract

This chapter is primarily concerned with the fact that the concept of conformity is dynamic and amorphous as it is recognised as an impetus to economic development and plays a major role in matters of sale of goods within an economy. In making an assessment of the seller's duty of conformity to a contract of sale of goods as governed by the OHADA Uniform Act on General Commercial Law, this study argues that the concept of conformity is limited rather than broad that should appropriately encapsulate the physical and non-physical things that could form the object of a contract of sale. It therefore explores other aspects that could be considered as part of the 'goods' for the purposes of the conformance duty in establishing the limits of the seller's liability. Thus, adopting an empirical and in-depth analysis of primary and secondary data, this study therefore holds that the question of conformity of goods can conveniently be addressed from a number of different angles: contract law, consumer patterns, local and international standards, and the principles of caveat venditor and caveat emptor.

Keywords: sales, goods, legal, discourse

1. Introduction

The preamble to the treaty of the Organisation for the Harmonisation of Business Laws in Africa (better known by its French acronym OHADA[1] points to the establishment of a new economic order based on the mutual economic benefit of cross border trade. The primary objective of this treaty was to provide a secure legal and judicial environment for business to operate in [1]. This was to be done through the elaboration and adoption of simple modern and common rules adapted to their economies, by setting up appropriate judicial procedures and by encouraging arbitration for the settlement of contractual disputes[2]. This suggests that uniform laws governing trans-national trade are essential to achieving these

[1] The Treaty creating OHADA was signed at Port-Louis, Mauritius Island on 17 October 1993, as revised at Quebec, Canada, on 17 October 2008. The revisions became effective on 21 March 2010. As of July 7, 2010, the West African members of OHADA are Benin, Burkina Faso, Cote d'Ivoire, Guinea, Guinea-Bissau, Mali, Niger, Senegal, and Togo, and the Central African members of OHADA are Central African Republic, Chad, Cameroon, Comoros, Congo, Equatorial Guinea, and Gabon. See http://<www.ohada.org > and http://<www.ohada.com>. On February 22, 2010, the Democratic Republic of Congo's president ratified the country's adoption of the OHADA treaty.

[2] The rules adopted are known as Uniform Acts.

goals. To effectively carry out the piece-meal harmonisation of the business laws of member states, specifically through the elaboration of uniform laws, nine Uniform Acts have been adopted till date[3]. Our interest being sale of goods contract, we shall examine the Uniform Act on General Commercial Law (UAGCL), with respect to its provisions governing sales contracts. Thus, the principal concern of this paper is to critically test the application of the UAGCL to barter-like transactions. The focus on the OHADA business law is to test its functionality in achieving its predictability of business transactions within its contracting states [2].

The rules on the conformity of goods are not only an integral part of sales law, but also an indispensable obligation by the seller by being inextricably linked to his obligation to deliver the goods. This may explain why 'goods' are the very subject matter of a sales contract, and the rules on conformity are what help define this subject matter. Forming part of the economic and legal rights of the buyer, the latter relies on and ascertains the seller's obligation to deliver the goods in conformity with the contract specifications. This right consists in the delivering of goods of right quality, quantity, description and packaging.

Consequently, any breach of this obligation would entitle the buyer to establish proof. In this regard, many buyers will base their complaints on defects of conformity of the goods, allege a breach, and invoke remedies. It is important therefore, that there be fairly clear legal rules, particularly those applied by default, that are capable of allocating risks, thereby producing legal certainty and possibly reducing litigation.

The burden of proof includes the burden of adducing the relevant evidence and the burden of persuasion. The reliance provision is, in other words, an exception to the buyer's entitlement to the goods fit for a particular purpose, and the burden of proof of the preconditions for that exception lies with the seller. Without these rules, it would often be impossible to say what it is that the seller has agreed to deliver. However, the inevitably broad nature of these rules, together with their considerable conceptual and practical significance, still makes them one of the most frequently litigated issues. All this leads to the conformity rules occupying a central place in any sales contract.

From the foregoing, the issue of the concept of conformity should be addressed with an open mind because it is dynamic and amorphous. This explains why this study will illustrate that the limits of conformity should not be guided by the distinction between physical and non-physical characteristics of the goods. Other conceptual tools for marking this boundary will be explored in consideration of other parameters irrespective of the intent of the parties as evident in their agreed contract.

With this in mind, this study seeks in the first place to take a critical look at the rules on conformity in Article 255 of the OHADA Uniform Act on General Commercial Law (UAGCL). The primary objective therefore is to make an expository study of the concept of "conformity" as the basis of the seller's duty by showing its limits in consideration to other components. It follows with a critical examination of the UAGCL's approach in allocating the burden of proof of lack of conformity of the goods to the contractual stipulations as agreed by the parties. The study also adopts a critical and analytical approach in interpreting the provisions of the Uniform Act and of foreign instruments regulating sale of goods contracts.

[3] The following Uniform Acts are already applicable in Member States: Commercial Companies and Economic Interest Groupings, Law of Securities, Simplified Recovery Procedures and Measures of Execution, Collective Proceedings for Wiping –off Debts, Arbitration Law, Accounting Law, and Law of Co-operatives Carriage of Goods by Road. Two other Uniform Acts have been enacted and adopted by the Council of Ministers but are still inapplicable, to wit; Consumer Law and Contract Law.

2. The legal conception of goods

2.1 Contract of sale of goods

'Goods' form the subject-matter of contracts of sale of goods between the seller and the buyer. The Uniform does not provide any definition to 'goods' as the case under the CISG[4]. Nor is it possible to deduce the meaning of the term by analysing different language versions of the statute. However, from a cursory reading of the Act, a restrictive meaning could be inferred as its provisions basically apply only to moveable tangible goods.

Reference can be made to the Uniform Act's Scope and General Provisions. In particular, Article 234 (a) provides that "the provisions of this shall apply to contracts of sale goods", whereas Articles 235 and 236 restrict the ambit of the Act and by implication, the ambit of 'goods'. By inference from the restrictions imposed by Article 236 UAGCL, it may be understood that the term 'goods' is fairly not extensive, indeed, virtually not all-embracing. It clearly excludes to a greater extent non-physical items, such as electricity, negotiable instruments, and company shares, which are technically 'things in action' or incorporeal movables and so are excluded by the plain words of Article 236. Similarly, items of 'intellectual property' such as copyrights, patents and trademarks are not corporeal movables and so fall outside the definition, although of course goods may exist, which embody these intellectual property rights

Even though under the Uniform Act, the notion of 'goods' serves to quantify the main obligation of the seller contained in Article 250, which requires that '... the seller must deliver the 'goods' ... as required by the contract and this Uniform Act', consideration must be given to the type or nature of goods.

The reason which may be advanced for dismissing intangible or immovable goods from the scope of the OHADA Uniform Act could be that even though these are assets available for trade, they can only be disposed by way of trade or security and not possibly to be transferred physically to another party. The absolute interest in such types of goods may be disposed of outright or may be made the subject of security. Since by virtue of Article 250 para. 1 UAGCL, the main duty of the seller under the contract of sale is to deliver the goods to the buyer, what matters here is the physical transferability of the goods and not necessarily the transfer of a legitimate interest in the goods. The peculiar consideration here does not lie on the identification of the type of goods but rather on the physical segregation and ownership of it. Only in this situation is segregation both possible and necessary to identify the subject of the transfer obligation of the seller under the Uniform Act.

3. Contracts consisting partially of services

The UAGCL does not apply to mixed contracts as the case under the CISG, under which the seller provides goods and services. Nevertheless, by inference, these can be treated as unitary contracts rather than separate sales and services contracts [3], and the UAGCL will apply to both parts. This provision further restricts the meaning of 'goods', excluding contracts 'in which the preponderant part of the obligations of the party who furnishes the goods consists in the supply of labour or other services'. The issue of whether software is a good is once again illustrative.

In modern commerce, an important point, not yet resolved by the OHADA Uniform Act on General Commercial Law, is whether computer software may

[4] Article 30 UAGCL.

constitute 'goods' within the meaning of Article 234 para. 1. Software is normally embedded in some physical form, such as disks or as part of a package in which it is sold along with computer hardware, that is, computers or computer parts. Therefore, it could be considered as a tangible object capable of it being possible to be transferable. This raises an argument in trying to understand why such an item cannot be considered as a 'good' under the Uniform Act. It could without any doubt be covered by the OHADA Uniform Act because such a good is being able to be transferred to another person in a contract of sale in its physical form. Again, there is probability that a disk be physically defective due to a virus for example. In this case, the seller should be liable as the seller of a physically defective car.

Under French law, goods are known as *marchandises*. This simply entails a collection of movable assets forming the subject-matter of a contract of sale. This is actually an element of *fond de commerce*. From this standpoint, there is one clear limit: this meaning will not include any form of immovable property in a contract of sale. Consequently, it can be inferred from the meaning of Article 235 para. 1 UAGCL that it limits the meaning of goods to movable property by its reference to *commerçants*. The meaning of 'sale of goods' limits the very meaning of 'goods'. Also, this would mean that no sale with a non-trader is of a 'good'. The general approach that is adopted under the Uniform Act is to apply the OHADA Uniform Act to the *commerçant* and not to *non-commerçant*.

4. The conception and nature of conformity in domestic sales law

In fact, conformity is a term with a variable content. In English language, conformity is a noun derived from the verb to conform, meaning "agree with" [4, 5]. From this, it becomes clear that the goods should agree with the terms of the contract for them to be in conformity. In other words, the concept of conformity concerns the difference between the object agreed in the contract and that delivered.

Some particularities of domestic law on the concept of 'conformity of goods' in a sale of goods deserves a careful interpretation and understanding [6]. For instance, rules on conformity under the Uniform Act differ considerably from those in common law and civil law. In fact, subtle distinctions can be between the different kinds of defects of conformity under the different laws. Under civil codes[5] as well as under the Uniform Act,[6] a hidden defect [*défaut caché*] is distinguished from an apparent defect [*vice apparent*]; the English Sale of Goods Act (SGA) [1893] distinguishes condition[7] from warranties[8]. Nevertheless, surely merchantability under common law is a similar concept to conformity as the case under UAGCL.

4.1 Conformity requirements under the Act: Material and functional conformity

The notion of conformity under the Uniform Act is almost identical to that under the CISG[9]. The Act views conformity from a dual perspective, that is,

5 Cameroon Civil Code, art 1641; Côte d'Ivoire Civil Code, art 1641.

6 Uniform Act, art 231.

7 SGA, sec 11(3) provides that a condition is a major term of a contract, breach of which is considered to go to the root of the contract so as to entitle the innocent party to treat the contract as discharged.

8 Id, secs 14–15.

9 CISG, art 35.

material and functional conformity. Whilst material conformity deals with the quality of goods, function conformity on its part focuses on the usefulness of the goods. A recent adoption by the Uniform Act is the condition that goods must conform both materially and functionally before they are judged acceptable by the Act. As such, sellers have to respect this prescription before delivering their goods[10] [7, 8].

The conditions of quantity, quality, description, packaging, particular purpose, and sample are encapsulated into the concept of conformity in the Uniform Act as contained in its Article 255 [9]. Article 255 thus states as follows:

"The seller shall deliver the goods according to the quantity, quality, specification, and packaging provided for in the contract. Where the contract is silent, the seller shall deliver goods in conformity with the purposes for which goods of that nature are generally used, and the goods must match the sample or model which was presented to the buyer by the seller. The seller also must deliver the goods that are packaged according to the usual method of packaging goods of the same nature or failing which, in a manner to ensure their conservation, and protection"[11].

These implied that conditions deserve careful treatment because of the protection that they now offer the buyer of goods, who is almost invariably in a weaker position than the seller. This can be explained by the fact that, most of the times, the seller seems to be the manufacturers of the goods. As a result, these terms protect buyers' interest since they ensure that the purchased goods are neither deficient nor defective. The Act thus makes it clear that any breach of the provisions by either parties shall be interpreted as non-respect of terms of contract. It is important to state that the terms of a contract, which include conditions and warranties, of sale of goods could be implied or expressly stated. It is now clear that the common law principle of *caveat emptor* which used to focus on the buyer now places emphasis on the seller's awareness (*caveat venditor)* [10]. Implied conditions and warranties are not stated by the parties during negotiations or included in a contractual document, but nevertheless form part of the contractual provisions.

Implied terms as implied by law are geared to ensuring a minimum of business efficacy[12], regardless of the parties' paramount intention to create a workable contractual agreement[13]. Some contracts of sale are very detailed; the parties deal with all or most eventualities. However, in others, the only element that the parties deal with is identifying the goods to be sold and the price to be paid.

The seller is obliged to be conversant with aspects of quality, quantity, specification, and the packaging of goods, which falls within material conformity as well as features linked to functional conformity such as the suitability, purpose, or purposes and specificities of the usefulness of goods of similar design.

Material conformity therefore consists of four elements derived from the contract: quantity, quality, description, and packaging.

---

[10] Under French law, the hidden defect element is dealt with under sales law. This is actually effectively the purport of the text: Pougoué et al Encyclopedie, above at note 11 at 55.

[11] This is the author's translation.

[12] The Moorcock (1889) 14 PD 64; Lister v Romford Ice Co Ltd [1957] AC 555.

[13] Compare with Lord Tomlin in Hillas & Co Ltd v Arcos [1932] ALL ER 494 at 499: "The problem for a court of construction must always be so to balance matters that, without violation of essential principle, the dealings of men may so far as possible be treated as effective, and that the law may not incur the reproach of being the destroyer of bargains."

4.2 An inquiry into the nature of lack of conformity

4.2.1 Apparent defects

Article 258 of the Uniform Act raises no difficulty as to defects which would have been apparent on a reasonable examination of the goods by the buyer immediately after delivery. In practical terms, examination by the buyer of any apparent defects to ascertain the seller's obligation operates from the moment delivery has been effected[14]. After this exercise, the buyer must give notice of a lack of conformity discovered within 1 month from the date of delivery. If he fails to observe these requirements, the buyer will be deprived of his right to claim redress for non-conformity.

4.2.2 Hidden defects

Moreover, it is advisable that the buyer declares any detected defect observed in a purchased item within a year to enable the seller to make up for any deficiency within his/her competence[15]. The period of 1 year is enough time for the buyer to notice hidden defect in a purchased good. The foregoing condition notwithstanding, it is necessary to state that the detecting of defect goes beyond according to a timeframe since some goods require immediate inspection and adjustment even before they are sold and bought. In this case, therefore, the buyer gets to understand any hidden defect before the commercial transaction.

However, the detecting of hidden defects is difficult, especially with frozen and canned/tinned goods that are always meticulously packaged. In such cases, there is little or no opportunity for instant or early detection of defects.

The problem raises two complex issues. The first is how to establish the liability of a seller or retailer who sells food products in tin or other sealed container because of the difficulty to identify any injury caused to his customers either from some foreign substance in the can or from unwholesomeness of the food and the second is how to establish the liability of a seller who sells goods with some defects in bulk. In this situation, the seller may not be faulted for such hidden defects owing to the difficulty involved in detecting such defects in bulk goods. These complex situations account for the emphasis of Uniform Act, in relation quality goods, that the seller shall be liable to deliver the goods "in the usual manner" that goods are packaged[16].

Examples of such nature regarding the determination of hidden defects in goods can never solve all the problems related to quality. Nevertheless, with the aid of Article 255(2) of the Uniform Act, the intent of the parties can be construed in their agreement. In striving to achieve this purpose, two questions could guide this exercise: The understanding of the contractual provisions defining quality goods as spelt out by Article 255(2) and the usefulness of the goods are two basic conditions that could guide the parties, as the strive to satisfy their intent. An understanding of these conditions would certainly curb misunderstanding with regard to fitness of 'ordinary' use of goods as stated in the contract.

It follows therefore that the nature of the kind of non-conformity that the buyer is expected to reveal are two, namely apparent and hidden defects. This type of test is likely to pose challenges involving goods of varying grades.

---

[14] Uniform Act, art 257.

[15] Id, art 259. Under CISG, art 39, the time frame is two years: J Huet, Contrats Civilset Commerciaux, Responsabilité du Vendeur et Garantie Contre les Vices Cachés [Civil and commercial contracts: Responsibility of the seller and guarantee against hidden defects] (1987, Litec) at 42.

[16] Uniform Act, art 255(2).

4.3 Different quality test: a matter of interpretation

A further inquiry into the notion of quality is necessary. This discussion points to the various quality tests the buyer may alleged non-conformity of goods. In fact, this raises a debate in trying to clear the confusion surrounding the basis of the seller's liability for the non-conformity of goods. This discussion, in turn, makes it necessary to choose between various quality tests.

Against this background, the Act's default rule in Article 255 para 2 appears narrow and limited in its content and scope. On its face, this provision does not rely on any notion of quality, with the only relevant question seemingly being whether the goods are fit for "the purposes for which goods of the same description would ordinarily be used". In other words, the Uniform Act only seems concerned with whether the goods are fit for their ordinary purposes and not with quality. Rather, quality is a broader notion that may include not only fitness for ordinary purposes, but a number of other aspects such as the goods' physical state and condition, intrinsic qualities and features, safety, durability, appearance, finish, and freedom from minor defects[17]. It is an undeniable fact that these other aspects of quality could be attributable to the dynamic decisions of individuals and group choices and satisfaction based on information gathering relating to a particular commodity [11]. Further exploration of the problem centres on the considerable evidence that quality variation is greater in group unanimity than in personal preferences over certain goods. Here, the commercial buyer may be inclined to conform and to choose goods required by group customers in the market.

As a general rule under the Uniform Act, conformity of the quality of the goods will be met if and only if the usage criterion is also satisfied[18]. In fact, the commercial utility of the goods seems to be the guiding rule to the commercial buyer under the Uniform Law in ascertaining the seller's responsibility. This can be best explained by the fact that the utmost preference to the commercial utility of the goods by the commercial is guided by several different ways in which interpersonal influences impact variety-seeking behaviour of consumers [12]. In fact, changing social habits may require merchants to select a variety of items appropriate to the demands of divergent contexts and audiences with the view of acting in conformity with consumers' preferences. Understandably, consumers' individual choices tend to conform to or diverge from the choice of another group of consumers [13]. It follows therefore that the material conformity of the goods to the commercial buyer is guided by individual and divergent preferences of its end users. The result of the non-respect of both material and functional quality or either of the qualities, often insinuates a breach of contract. In a case where the quality is deemed essential, the breach may result in a fundamental breach with *the consequence that the buyer may either ignore the contract or request the total substitution of the purchased good*[19].

Conversely, many domestic legal systems have used varied notions in ascertaining the ultimate default rule of conformity of the goods in order to safeguard the buyer's satisfaction. Notions of quality such as "average, "merchantable," "acceptable, or "satisfactory quality" have been the measuring yardsticks meanwhile "fitness for an ordinary or a common purpose" is merely one of the components

[17] Sale of Goods Act § 14(2)–(2)(B).

[18] As per the position in the civil codes of Cameroon (art 1641), Côte d'Ivoire (art 1641) and France (art 1641).

[19] Id, art 283.

referred to in some legal systems to make a sound judgement on the notion of quality or to know whether the goods meet the required standard of quality[20].

The above approach can be said to be associated with the merchantability test, which obtains with some common law systems. This test is viewed as comprising more than just the saleability of the goods as those terms in the parties' contract (with description, fitness for purpose, and acceptance being other relevant aspects of merchantability) [14].

4.3.1 Ethical values

Ethical value is an emerging applied subject. It is still currently debated as it is applied to all aspects of business conduct, the manufacturing of goods, and the quality standard of goods. In general, ethical values appear to contribute to the development of legal systems in which contracts are enforced fairly, and bribery and corruption are less prevalent, enabling business entities to have equal access to legal process and equal protection under the law.

At the international level for instance, private initiatives such as the principles laid down in the United Nations Global Compact covering issues such as human rights, labour, environment and anti-corruption aim to assist its member countries to comply with the international standards required on these issues. In Africa, ethical values are known and recognised in international and national sales contracts as one of the solutions to the defective goods as from the manufacturing process.

An ethical value contractual clause can be express or implied in the contract of sale. When implied, they may be inferred from trade and usages. Whether expressly or impliedly in a contract of sale, they become part of the contract and may be enforced, or their violation sanctioned, in the same way as with any other term. However, the parties agree on their express stipulation [15].

In Cameroon, for instance, most organised professions and some trade associations have codes of practice which set out ethical behaviour for members in their dealings with their clientele[21]. For instance, the company in charge of distributing energy makes available to the public an e-mail address for anyone who wants to make a complaint and report any violations of their Code of Business Conduct and Ethics. A clause ensuring ethical code and conduct is prior inserted in the contract signed by customers before they benefit from the services of the company. This is done in favour of its customers.

In line with the above example, it should be pointed out that in most, almost all contracts of sales of goods, including both domestic or international contracts, the quality of goods is not restricted to its physical appearance; it also has to comply with any other requirements which are prescribed by the law or subject to trade and usages[22]. Therefore, if the origin of the goods prescribes an ethical value standard at production, the standard will definitely constitute a quality of the goods. As a result, the requirement of quality will not be met if the goods produced do not meet with the ethical standard as required. It could therefore be agreed that people incorporate more variety into their consumption decisions when their behaviour is subject to public scrutiny [16].

---

[20] Sale of Goods Act, 1979, c. 54, § 14(2)–(2)(B) (Eng.), available at http://www.legislation.gov.uk/ukpga/1979/54; U.C.C.§ 2-314(2)(c) (1977).

[21] These would include the code of ethics of manufacturers' associations, association of advertising practitioners, etc.

[22] Uniform Act, arts 238–239.

It is not easy to determine the non-conformity based on the ethical value[23]. Such difficulty is due to the hidden character of its nature and also to the fact that it does not physically influence the physical feature of the goods. If the breaching party does not of good faith disclose or cure the defect, an expert may sometimes be required to determine the breach.

Unless the parties have agreed otherwise, failure from the seller to deliver the goods in conformity with the ethical standards amounts to a breach of contract. In particular, when the seller is required to deliver goods that are fit for the purpose for which goods of that nature are commonly used or when a special request on an ethic (such as health and environmental considerations) was made known to the seller[24]. The buyer remedy will be its rights of redress[25] and claim for damages[26].

4.3.2 Good manufacturing practice

GMP refers to the "Good Manufacturing Practice". This is a well-known regulation whose purpose is to ensure the appropriate manufacturing process that would impact on the quality of the products. Good Manufacturing Practice is a series of regulations that are binding on the contracting business parties, (is agreed upon) requiring food producers, manufacturers, pharmaceutical companies, and packagers of drugs to ensure that their products are safe, pure, and totally effective. These regulations are then meant to ensure a level of quality approach to manufacturers of goods in order to protect consumers from contracting for non-effective and dangerous goods. In summary, Good Manufacturing Practice plays a paramount role of quality assurance that ensures that products are consistently produced and controlled to the quality standards appropriate for their intended use and their legal requirements. In some cases, it is simply required by the marketing board or in some countries by the government department in charge of regulating trade and commerce[27].

Sometimes, GMP is referred to as Cgmp- meaning "Current Good Manufacturing Practice". This is a mere call to producers, packagers, or manufacturers to update their machineries, systems or equipment in order to comply with the new technology, capacity and /or legal requirement in their business. Generally, GMP's guidelines provide regulation on products such as foods, drugs, blood and medical devices. Accordingly, countries do update their cGMP regulations for local companies to act in accordance with the legislation. In Cameroon, for instance, the Medical Council is a statutory body that was established in terms of the medicines and related substances control to oversee the regulation of medicines. Nonetheless, the "Standard and Quality Agency (ANOR)" and the "Service of Norms" in the Ministry of Trade and Commerce have a wide mandate to ensure the quality of products in meeting the required standards[28].

Even though not prescribed by the UAGCL, such a business practice or measure is relevant in enhancing the warranty of quality of goods that flood the markets.

---

[23] Uniform Act, art 255 para. 1.0.

[24] Uniform Act, art 255 para. 2.

[25] Uniform Act, art 282-283.

[26] Uniform Act, arts 292-293.

[27] Definition of GMP by the World Health Organisation and as per GMP institute found at <http//www.gmp1st.com/index.htm>, Accessed on October 24th, 2009.

[28] It was created by Decree No.88/204 of 5 February 1988, re-organising the Ministry of Commerce. See Juridis Périodique no. 5 1991, p. 13. These structures were created with the objective of protecting consumers and ensuring the technical supervision of the quality and quantity of goods through inspection.

This goes a long way to improve on the quality of goods which the end users would obtain from commercial buyers. Respect of such a measure is left at the wishes of the parties in a contract of sale or could be implied from the trade and usages of specific goods in a given branch of business. This is the very meaning of Articles 237 and 239 of the UAGCL.

5. Conformity and other related concepts as characteristics of the 'goods'

Generally, goods have certain defined physical characteristics which in everyday business practice the parties have full knowledge of when contracting. In some cases, certain states of affairs may be so inextricably linked to the goods as to be 'non-physical characteristics' of the goods. In this regard, the parties may in concluding their sale insist on some features connected to the goods but are not physically part of the goods. These could concern the tangible and intangible things connected to the good. Nevertheless, the dichotomy between intrinsic and extrinsic characteristics of a 'good' is fundamental in determining the functionality of the goods. In effect, these characteristics are broad and can be described in various terms, for example, intrinsic/extrinsic; embodied/unembodied; tangible/intangible; corporeal/incorporeal; objective/subjective; real/intellectual and physical/non-physical.

A key example of non-physical characteristics that the parties may view as part of the goods emerges from the field of marketing. In that field, '[the idea of tangible and intangible attributes [of goods] is well established' [17]. Tangible characteristics are those that 'are physically present or can be seen, experienced or measured in some way'. Intangible characteristics, such as reputation, quality image, and country of origin, are 'understood using cognitive processes and also often contain an emotional dimension'[29]. It should be stressed that these intangible characteristics most impact the consumer behaviour in guiding their choices of goods they buy. It, therefore, ascertains the economic value of goods[30]. Hence, these non-physical attributes are conceived of as part of the goods.

5.1 Brand

A brand of a good is an exemplified example to be conceived as a non-physical attribute of the goods. By definition, a 'brand' is a commercial concept that describes' the impression of a product in the minds of potential users or consumers'. This explains the more reason why the wide sale of certain goods in some international markets is due to the strength of their brand and reputation publicised by mass advertisements and persistently demanded by a group of customers. That is why it is common today to find consumers in places across the world wearing, driving and drinking the same brands of certain goods [18]. This is considerable evidence that quality variation is greater in group unanimity than in personal preferences over certain goods [19]. This is another clear indication of the fact the commercial buyer of goods in her business will be seeking to conform to group norms.

Brand is conceived as an attribute of the goods, rather than something external to them[31]. Related to this is the notion of 'brand equity'. The brand equity in a

[29] Ibid, 438.

[30] Ibid, 438.

[31] Oxford English Dictionary (2nd edn, 1989), s.n. 'brand'.

good is measured by the difference between the inherent value of the good and the perceived value (or market value) of the good. Another justification for this is the public habits and beliefs in certain virtues of these goods, which have stood their test of time. Such a picture is typical in Cameroon where from socio-economic and psychological perspectives, the purchasing public still hold tight to the buying of some goods of old reputable trademark or taste. For example, certain brand of goods such as, shoes like "pierre cadin" from France, "clarks" from England are still believed to be durable even sold as used goods. The sale of used goods or second-hand goods is an everyday practice where is visible to find a line-up of stores in Cameroonian cities such as Douala and Yaoundé operating in this trade. Goods vary from cars, household equipment to consumer goods. Based on observations from field trips conducted by the researcher in the above mentioned cities, it was gathered that consumers prefer certain used goods irrespective of their diminished quality and safety but rather simply because of their cheap prices, accessibility and long standing brand [20].

The law recognises that reputation and customer awareness are worthy of protection by allowing the enforcement of intellectual property rights. Although it is not a legal concept, brand equity has been referred to as being '[a]t the core of a trademark's value and a manifestation of the legal concept of trademark good will' [21].

The branding and reputation of the goods are connected to intellectual property in the goods. The seller's duties in respect of conformance and intellectual property rights are interrelated rather than mutually exclusive. Certain characteristics of the goods may indeed be relevant to both duties. As will be demonstrated, the UAGCL's provisions relating to intellectual property are apt to deal only with the existence of certain non-physical characteristics of the goods. The content of those characteristics must be dealt with under the principle of conformity. The seller has express obligations in relation to trademarks and other intellectual.

property rights under Article 260(1) UAGCL: *the seller shall deliver the goods with the assurance that no third party has a right or claim to them, unless the buyer accepts to collect the goods under such conditions.*

From a reading of Article 275 UAGCL, it is clear that the main purpose and effect of the seller's duty to deliver is to require the seller to transfer the property or title to the goods to the buyer. This implies that the seller should not necessarily be the owner of the goods. The fundamental requirement here is to qualify the seller's right to sell and also the third party's right(s) over the goods. As concerns the seller's right to sell, the seller must not necessarily be in the possession of the goods and be able to transfer property to the buyer. To avoid any third party's claim, the seller must be the right holder of some patent, trademark or other proprietary interest over the goods. Any possibility for the third party to have access to the goods on such reasons will amount to a defect in title and the seller will be liable for this. The essence here is for the seller to be able to transfer to the buyer a title overriding that of the true owner.

6. Burden of proof for the non-conformity of the goods with the standard

As a general principle, the allocation of the burden of proof under the Act, seeks to know whether or not the goods are presently in conformity with the applicable standard as contained in Article 255. This mostly guided by the principle of proof proximity, which states that conformity or non-conformity of any good is determined by the individual who is in possession of the said good. This means that when a good is still with the seller, he/she is in the rightful position to establish and prove that the said good conforms or not. By the same token, once the buyer purchases the good, he/she assumes the responsibility of *establishing conformity or non-conformity of the good in the case of an incident.*

One relevant general principle under the UAGCL is that the assessment of the conformity of goods sold starts upon delivery[32]. In fact, it is understandable that it is the buyer's obligation to examine the goods in view to reveal any lack of conformity. Therefore, the law grants an opportunity to the buyer to inspect the goods and report to the seller whether or not the goods are in conformity with the contractual obligation as agreed upon with the seller [22]. The question that arises is whether the buyer's knowledge, usually derived from having an opportunity of pre-contractual examination of the goods, should be relevant to deciding what conformity obligations were imposed on the seller by the contract and, even if not, whether the facts of the buyer's inspection or assessment is hardly relevant to determine the content of the seller's obligation[33].

The philosophy behind the application of Article 255 UAGCL directs that a buyer ought to be able to rely on the agreed arrangements. Therefore, if there is any discrepancy between the contract and the goods inspected, the buyer has a right to cause the seller to redress the situation. This applies regardless of whether the buyer knows of a defect, or if it was agreed that the seller shall deliver the goods without defects [23]. At this point, the parties must be assumed to have expressed their wishes in their written agreement in relation to the requirements for the goods in question. This means that an analogous or expanded interpretation of the provision so as to apply it to Article 255 para. 1 of the Uniform Act seems in principle to be a restricted application of the *caveat emptor* principle.

When reference is made by the contracting parties, what is normally meant is inspection by the buyer. However, control of quality may also be effected by the seller, in which case its quality certificate is attached to other documents (which is significant in respect of certain goods since quality may be considerably affected during transport by reason of environmental and other circumstances). This method of inspection is provided by some governmental or international bodies. The certificate of inspection is the only proof of what it is bound to furnish under the contract. There is, however, another view to the effect that the other party is always entitled to a further inspection[34].

The answers to these preoccupations exert an influence on contract interpretation depending on the particular circumstances. Presumably, these points are too obvious for the drafters of the Uniform Act not to have been aware of them considering the fact that Article 255 para. 1 does not concern the terms implied by default but concerns what the contract itself provides. This clearly shows the limits of the application of the concept of conformity under the Act which presumably seems to be detrimental to the business climate. In actual fact, in addition to that standards contained in the contractual stipulations, other national and international norms of goods need to be considered. Rapid technological changes with a corresponding impact on consumer behaviour is taking place within an increasingly liberalised marketplace in which the global drive to compete brings new challenges to regulatory authorities in setting up conformity standards of goods.

From the above strand of reasoning, it is certain that irrespective of the contractual stipulations, it is also of prime importance to note that the commercial buyer

[32] Uniform Act, arts 256 & 258.

[33] Uniform Act, art 258.

[34] Uniform Act, art 256.

could dictate other requirements to the seller as driven by the desires of consumers. In addition, there is also necessity of the seller to have knowledge of surrounding facts requiring the goods to conform with certain local and international standards. Nevertheless, no matter the argument, the buyer's evidence as to any lack of conformity can only be validated through his duty to examine as well as supported by any information which was brought to him by the seller.

6.1 Burden of proof for the non-conformity of the goods at the time risk passes

In real commercial practice, there is usually the practical difficulty in ascertaining the allocation of the burden of proof with the purpose of establishing a defect of conformity of the goods which already existed at the time risk passed, or existed before that time. The situation under the Act is ambiguous in that there is no clarity with regard to the charge on the seller who deals in goods that do not conform or are observed to have hidden defects. Moreover, the Act does not clearly spell out the seller's responsibility when his/her goods are defective or *do not conform as a result of a particular kin*d. Arguably, the notion of conformity under the Act falls within the meaning of the subjective understanding of a "defect" [24].

As an evidence to the forgoing fact, the purport of Article 256 UAGCL which suggests the fact that a buyer can only make a case for any lack of conformity after the risk passes irrespective of the nature of the defect. In fact, the strong implication is that the burden of proof has shifted onto the buyer in order to establish the seller's liability when delivery has duly been effected. Most often when the buyer verifies a good to be purchased, the intension is hardly to establish its actual state; rather he/she tries to determine the good's non-conformity aspects in order to demand immediate reparation. The new Uniform Act has further empowered the buyer to notify the seller of any observable defect. Despite this responsibility given to the buyer, the nature or kind of defect the buyer is supposed to report to the seller is not clearly defined.

There remains, however, a serious problem about the kind of defects which the buyer is expected to report to the seller. Nevertheless, a clear right of action has been imposed unto the buyer to establish the seller's responsibility for apparent defects and for hidden defects[35] discovered by the commercial buyer particularly when delivery has taken place.

At this juncture, it would be necessary to make an inquiry into the type of risk that can be transferred or passed to the buyer after delivery before examining the kind of defects the buyer is expected to reveal.

6.1.1 Which risks are transferred to the buyer?

Risk of "loss" in a sales context refers to the allocation of financial responsibility for the injury or destruction of goods that occurs whilst the goods are changing hands from seller to buyer [25]. To identify the appropriate moment for passage of this risk is the task of the law governing risk of loss. That law is currently found in Article 277 *et seq*. of the Uniform Act. The Uniform Act contains no definition of the types of risks governed by the rules on transfer of risk, thus leaving uncertainty. First, one must look at the risks that fall within the scope of the Act[36].

[35] Under art 1641 of the French Civil Code, for the purpose of an implied or legal guarantee, the defects must be hidden defects (vices cachés), unknown to the buyer.

[36] For example, in complex agreements, a part concerning services may entail a certain risk in conjunction with a sale but not governed by the Uniform Act. (Art 235(b)).

6.1.1.1 Liability for loss or damage to the goods

The wording used in the Uniform Act is "loss or deterioration"[37] contained in the Article 277 para. 2. Physical risks to the goods including their destruction are covered by the concept of "loss". The Uniform Act's risk-of-loss rules clearly limit their ambit to loss or damage to "the goods" (that is, the goods sold) or "in respect of goods sold". By analogy, the causes of loss could be broad encompassing disappearance of the goods, including theft, misplacing the goods, their transfer to a wrong address or person, and mixing up the goods with other goods are included.

This situation was vivid during a field trip conducted by the researcher in markets of some big cities in Cameroon: Douala and Yaoundé[38]. Most big merchant-sellers of second- hand goods like shoes for example find in their bulk of goods damaged shoes and because the risk has already been transferred to them by their supplier in their country, such as Dubai and China, they are unable to return the goods. Therefore, because of financial interest, they are forced to sell them at relatively cheap prices.

Another concern is the documents pertaining to the goods. The risk-of-loss rules of the Uniform Act apply as easily to documents as to goods. This study rather holds strong to the fact that the risk -of- loss of a document connected to the goods, should simultaneously pass together with the risk for the goods. The time and place to hand documents may at times not reach the buyer concurrently. In a case where there exists no agreement to this effect, the delivery of documents may be expected just in time for their use, for taking delivery of the goods or for their import in accordance with the trade usage[39]. Thus, if the documents are lost before they are delivered; the risk would not be treated similarly as for goods. Consequently, the holding of relevant documents of the goods by the seller does not affect the passing of risk[40]. The buyer could rather be contended to claim remedies for non-conforming delivery of documents, by applying to the courts for avoidance of the contract, which would stop risk relating to those documents from passing[41].

7. Proof as matter regulated under the uniform Act

Considering that Article 255 of the Act neither states the liability attached to proof nor points out on whom the responsibility of determining the conformity and non-conformity standard of a good as well as the timeframe of declaring such information, UAGCL principle have to be applied to establish the seller's liability in a case where a purchased good does not conform with acceptable standards.

Nonetheless, one relevant general principle under the UAGCL is that a party who asserts a right must prove the necessary preconditions for the existence of that right. This is clearly evident under Articles 258 and 259 para. 1, which gives the burden to the buyer to notify the seller cases of lack of conformity. The buyer's right to do so is to ensure the seller's obligation in delivering goods in conformity with the express contract terms pursuant to Article 255 para. 1 of the UAGCL. It suggests that the burden of proof includes the burden of adducing the relevant evidence and

---

[37] This is the author's translation of the French version of the UAGCL, which uses the words: "la perte ou la deterioration".

[38] The Nkoulouloun and Mokolo markets respectively.

[39] Uniform Act, art 254.

[40] Uniform Act, art 278 para. 2.

[41] Uniform Act, art 281 & 296.

the burden of persuasion. This comes into play by the reliance of the buyer on the seller's conformity obligation. In other words, an exception to the buyer's expectation to the goods fit for a particular purpose, and the burden of proof of the preconditions for that exception lies with the seller. However, if the seller does not raise the issue of reliance, the goods' fitness under Article 255 para. 2 will be presumed.

The "rule and exception" principle of the allocation of burden of proof may not always be applied strictly in practice because the burden of adducing evidence is sometimes placed on a party who simply has better access to evidence but who would not otherwise bear this burden on strict principles of the allocation of burden of proof [42].

From the above, as well as in line with Articles258 and 259 para. 1, it can be deduced that the buyer has to prove the factual prerequisites of the provisions upon which he wants to rely for its claim or defence. It follows from the above that in absence of an explicit regulation in the UAGCL, the allocation of the burden of proof in relation to the various factual requirements in establishing the seller's liability for non-conforming goods has to be exercised primarily on the basis of the general principles underlying the UAGCL.

These general principles are to be found first of all in the few provisions which explicitly address the question of burden of proof, in particular Article 294(1). It states:

> *A party is excused from his duty to render performance if he can prove that it is made impracticable without his fault by the occurrence of an event, namely; due to a third party or the occurrence of a force majeure. A force majeure entails events which happen beyond the party's control and which could not be reasonably foreseeable. However, there is no exemption if the failure to perform has been caused by a third party appointed by the defaulting party to perform all or part of his contractual obligations*[43].

Inherent in these general statements of excuse are four elements: (1) performance has become impracticable; (2) the non-occurrence of the cause of impracticability was due to *force majeure*; (3) the party asserting the excuse is without fault; and (4) the party seeking excuse did not assume greater obligations in the contract.

On the strength of this, as well as in accordance with Articles 235 (a) and 282 UAGCL it can be deduced that each party is under the obligation to prove the factual prerequisites of the provisions as the basis of his/her complaint and justification. This situation originates from Roman practice expressed in Latin as *ei incumbit probatio, qui dicit non qui negator actori incumbit probatio*; translated in English as 'rule and exception-principle.' It is important to underline that the respect of equity is the driving force behind this rule, since both the UAGCL and the CISG do not expressly elaborate on the principle of proof proximity[44].

This rule is supplemented or modified by considerations of equity according to which each party has to prove those facts which originate from its sphere. The basis for this principle proof proximity in the UAGCL as in the CISG is less clear [26, 27]. Consequently, the courts will presumably generally limit themselves in

---

42 "If the buyer rejects the goods by invoking their non-conformity the seller must prove that the goods are in conformity with the contract; if the buyer already accepted the goods the buyer would have to prove their non-conformity."

43 The author's translation.

44 Sometimes this rule is broken down into two separate rules distinguishing between the burden for a party raising a claim and a party claiming an exception or raising a defence.

stating the existence of the principle without giving any further justification. The proof proximity pays attention to the ability of the party to gather evidence as well as the relevant facts and issues presented as proof. This implies that once a good is delivered to a buyer without a prior indication of deficiency from him/her (the purchaser), the responsibility to prove any claim based on lack of conformity of the delivered good becomes that of the buyer. This seems to be the spirit surrounding the provision of Article 256 of UAGCL. It states:

> *Conformity of the goods shall be appraised as of the day of delivery, even if defects appear only later*[45].

The rules on conformity under the UAGCL are by no means an exception in dealing with issues of proof as the case under the CISG. The point to be addressed here in the first place is the burden of proof. The burden of proof is not a legal obligation, but by its legal nature, a duty. The duty represents an obligation to oneself and not to the other party in a contract. The duty to proof is closely connected with the buyer's duty to examine the goods and to notify the seller. Namely, the seller will be liable for the non-conformity of delivered goods only if the buyer gives notice pursuant to Article of the UAGCL.

The main purpose of the examination is to determine whether or not the goods are in conformity with the contract, that is, to reveal defects in quality, quantity, description and packaging. In fact, it is only on the result of the examination that the buyer can make a claim for nonconformity. It follows therefore that, burden of proving non-conformity rests on the buyer.

8. Overview of the various allocation of burden of proof in practice

It is expressly clear from the provisions of the Uniform Act that the allocation of the burden of proof for the seller's liability for non-conformity of the goods at the time the risk passes is imposed on the buyer. It is however rare to find under the Act an apportion of the burden to proof to the seller. There is a lack of necessary specificity and distinction to attribute it clearly to the seller.

In light of that and other considerations, attention should also be given to the fact that the Act is completely silent on the procedure for establishing the burden of proof. This can be explained by the fact that such an issue which is beyond the OHADA's scope of application and consequently be governed by the non-harmonised national laws of member countries. Consequently, such a question must be left to the courts of member states as a matter of procedural law. In addition, it is inappropriate for the Act, which relates to the cross-border sale of goods, to deal with matters of evidence or procedure. In fact, they are still some hurdles that beset the uniform working of the OHADA Uniform Act on General Commercial, considering the glaring differences between the procedural and evidential laws operating in the member States on matters of proof. This is as a result of the prevailing differences in legal cultures, procedures in the area of criminal proceedings which is out of the scope of the Act. Therefore, a degree of non-uniformity can be expected in matters of taking evidence and more broadly in allocating burden of proof.

In fact, the allocation of the burden of proof under the Uniform Act rests primarily on the basis of the *actori incumbit probatio* principle. Thus, the burden of

[45] The author's translation.

proof is largely dependent on the position of the parties in the process, that is, who invokes Article 255 in its favour.

The common practice is that the responsibility of proof is often on the basis of proof proximity principle, whereby the responsibility to prove the non-conformity with standards of a good is transferred from the seller to the buyer once a purchased item is delivered to the buyer. The implication here is that the seller is responsible for proving the conformity or non-conformity of his/her good only a purchaser has not yet taken possession of or demanded the reservation of the particular good. *Therefore, the moment a buyer receives the delivered good raising the question of non-conformity, any further proof non-conformity would be his/her responsibility*.

It is suggested, however, that legal predictability should not be undermined any further by the introduction of the proof proximity principle into the UAGCL. As already alluded to, proof proximity can easily contravene the rule and exception principle, and its introduction necessitates a choice between the two, either as a matter of general principle or in the particular case. That, in turn, gives rise to an additional layer of complexity and unpredictability.

Reaching a substantial degree of international agreement on the rule and exception principle is a hard-earned achievement, which has potential to promote legal certainty in all areas falling within the Act's scope. From this standpoint, recognising proof proximity as the Act's general principle would be an unwelcome development.

9. Conclusion

The seller's duty in exercising his material duty of conformity under the UAGCL is fraught with some difficulties. One of such difficulty is to establish the seller's liability for the non-conformity of goods as to the specifications of a contract of sale of goods. There is still some confusion and uncertainty regarding the notion of conformity under the Act because the concept of conformity is dynamic and ambivalent. There is really a need to search for a quality standard, which can underpin the ultimate default of the fitness for ordinary purposes and engulf other aspects of conformity. This will greatly be in the interest of the commercial buyer in order to conform with the demands of his consumer buyers.

The seller is equally expected to deliver goods which will satisfactorily serve the purpose for which commercial buyers intend to use them. This suggests therefore that the seller's expected obligation to deliver the adequate requirements to the goods under the contract would hardly in practice be that. This therefore raises the confusion and uncertainty in determining the seller's liability for the non-conformity of goods as to the specifications of a contract of sale of goods under the UAGCL. The concept of conformity must be handled in consideration with a number of issues, irrespective of the contractual stipulations agreed by the contracting parties.

It has also been evident that the issues of proof of lack of conformity under the Act be useful to introduce an overarching quality standard. However, to what extent should a sales law instrument govern the matters of proof, such as burden and standard of proof, and the evaluation and admissibility of evidence? It has been argued that the UAGCL is not capable of dealing adequately with the admissibility of evidence. Consequently, this may have considerable impact in establishing the seller's liability and on substantive law rights. No consistency in the exercise of this right is available under the UAGCL. There are undeniably differences in legal cultures, procedural environments, and views of the purpose of judicial proceedings in the member states.

To conclude, there is little doubt that the UAGCL has proved to be capable of resolving the issue of conformity of the goods. Attention should be given in drafting new provisions on conformity. Finally, to what extent should the UAGCL govern the matters of proof, such as burden and standard of proof, and the evaluation and admissibility of evidence. This calls for a fundamental harmonisation of the adjectival laws on matters of proof in order to maintain a higher degree of the uniform character of the OHADA laws.

Author details

Djieufack Roland
Higher Technical Teacher Training College, Bambili, The University of Bamenda, Bamenda, Cameroon

*Address all correspondence to: orolly@yahoo.fr

References

[1] Pilkington N. The security of transactions and investment in Africa. In: Tumnde M, editor. Proceedings of the OHADA Seminar held at the University of Buea, Buea, Cameroon, 18-19 September 2003 on the Theme: The Applicability of the OHADA Treaty in Cameroon. Buea, Cameroon: University of Buea. pp. 28-41, pp. 28-30

[2] Ebi NJ. Reflecting on OHADA law reform mission: Its impact on certain aspects of company law in Anglophone Cameroon. In: Annales de la Faculté des Sciences Juridiques et Politiques. Vol. 6. Université de Dschang; 2002. pp. 97-119 at 102

[3] Schlechtriem P. Requirements of application and sphere of applicability of the CISG. Victoria University of Wellington Law Review. 2005;**35**:781-794, 787

[4] Collin PH. Dictionary of Law. 3rd ed. Peter Collin Publishing; 2000. p. 77

[5] Mba-Owono C. Non-conformité et Vices Caches dans la Vente Commerciale en Droit Uniform Africain [Non-conformity and hidden defects in commercial sales under the African Uniform Law]. Juridis Périodique. 2002;**41**:107, at 108

[6] Schwenzer I, editor. Commentary on the UN Convention on the International Sale of Goods (CISG). 3rd ed. Oxford University Press; 2010. p. 570

[7] Fourment F. Défauts de la chose vendue que reste-t-il de l'action en garantie des vices cachés? [Hidden defects of sold goods: What action to take for hidden defects?]. Revue Trimestrielle de Droit Commercial et de Droit Economique. 1997;**3**:416, at 419

[8] Awona SPL. Défaut de conformité et défaut cache dans la vente commercial OHADA: Retour à la case départ? [Defects of conformity and hidden defects in the OHADA commercial sale: Coming back to the starting point?]. Recueil d'Études sur l'OHADA et les Normes Juridiques Africaines. 2013;**VI**:317-320

[9] Pougoué PG, et al. Encyclopédie du Droit OHADA [Encyclopaedia of OHADA law] (2011, Lamy) at 55. See English Sale of Goods Act, secs 12-15 and CISG, arts 35-44

[10] Hamilton WH. The ancient maxim caveat emptor. Yale Law Journal. 1928;**40**:1133 at 1186

[11] Ariely D, Levav J. Sequential choice in group settings: Taking the road less traveled and less enjoyed. Journal of Consumer Research. 2000;**27**(3): 279-290 at 279

[12] Ratner RK, Kahn BE. The impact of private versus public consumption on variety-seeking behavior. Journal of Consumer Research. 2000;**29**(2):246-247

[13] Lee JC, Kim J, Kwak K. A multi-attribute examination of consumer conformity in group-level ordering. Australasian Marketing Journal. 2018;**26**(1):41-48, at 41-42

[14] Bridge M. The Sale of Goods. London: Oxford University Press. pp. 42-45

[15] Schlectreim PH. Non-material damages—Recovery under the CISG? Pace International Law Review. 2007;**19**:89-102, point III (3). Available from: http://www.cisg.law.pace.edu/cisg/biblio/schlechtriem15.html [Accessed: 07 April 2014]

[16] Ratner RK, Kahn BE. The Impact of Private versus Public Consumption on Variety-Seeking Behavior., cit op. p. 246

[17] Mudambi SMD, Doyle P, Wong V. An exploration of branding in industrial markets. Industrial Marketing Management. 1997;**26**(5):433-446, at 438

[18] Mitchiner J. Intellectual property in image—A mere inconvenience. Intellectual Property Quarterly. 2003;**2**:163-208, at 182

[19] Quester P, Steyer A. Revisiting individual choices in group settings: The long and winding (less traveled) road? Journal of Consumer Research. 2010;**36**(6):1050-1057, at 1050-1051

[20] Djieufack R, Mbifi R, Nyiawung M. Quality Control of Goods and the Pricing Policy in Cameroon: A Legal Discourse. Germany: Galda Verlag; 2019. pp. 42-44

[21] Hartman S. Brand equity impairment—The meaning of dilution. The Trademark Reporter. 1997;**87**: 418-354 at 418

[22] Santos AP, Toé JY. OHADA Droit Commercial Général, Bruylant, collection Droit Uniforme Africain, Bruxelles; 2002. p. 405

[23] Henschel RF. Conformity of goods in international sales governed by CISG article 35: Caveat Venditor, Caveat Emptor and Contract Law as background law and as a comparing set of rules. Nordic Journal of Commercial Law:10

[24] Santos AP, Toé JY. OHADA Droit Commercial, above at note 34 at 392-393; Schwenzer (ed) Commentary, above at note 4 at 569

[25] Stocks M. Risk of loss under the uniform commercial code and the convention on the international sale of goods: A comparative analysis and proposed revision of UCC sections 2-509 and 2-510. Northwestern University Law Review. 1993;**87**:1

[26] Saidov D. Article 35 of the CISG: Reflecting on the present and thinking about the future. Villanova Law Review;**58**

[27] Roberts T. Commercial impossibility and frustration of purpose: A critical analysis. Canadian Journal of Law & Jurisprudence. 2003;**16**:129, at 134